Visiting the Fallen:
Arras North

Visiting the Fallen: Arras North

Peter Hughes

Pen & Sword
MILITARY

First published in Great Britain in 2015 by
PEN & SWORD MILITARY
An imprint of
Pen & Sword Books Ltd
47 Church Street
Barnsley
South Yorkshire
S70 2AS

ISBN 978-1-47382-556-7

Typeset by Concept, Huddersfield, West Yorkshire, HD4 5JL.
Printed and bound in England by CPI Group (UK) Ltd, Croydon CR0 4YY.

Pen & Sword Books Ltd incorporates the imprints of Pen & Sword Archaeology,
Atlas, Aviation, Battleground, Discovery, Family History, History, Maritime,
Military, Naval, Politics, Railways, Select, Social History, Transport, True Crime,
and Claymore Press, Frontline Books, Leo Cooper, Praetorian Press,
Remember When, Seaforth Publishing and Wharncliffe.

For a complete list of Pen & Sword titles please contact
PEN & SWORD BOOKS LIMITED
47 Church Street, Barnsley, South Yorkshire, S70 2AS, England
E-mail: enquiries@pen-and-sword.co.uk
Website: www.pen-and-sword.co.uk

Dedication

To my wife, Lynn, whose love, patience, and support sustained me throughout the four years that it took to write these books and who shared with me the joys and frustrations of authorship; no words of gratitude can ever suffice.

Contents

List of Plates

Acknowledgements

I would like to express my sincere thanks to the following people for their help during various stages of this work.

To Ian Small at the CWGC office in Maidenhead, who had to contend with my frequent requests for photographic material despite having to prepare for the 70th anniversaries of D-Day and Arnhem, as well as the start of the 1914–1918 centenary commemorations. With each request, Ian trawled the CWGC archives producing whatever was available and was never less than helpful.

To Parveen Sodhi at the Imperial War Museum, London, for her courtesy and help regarding the licensing of several of the photographs used to illustrate these books.

To the team at Pen & Sword Books, but especially to Design Manager, Roni Wilkinson, for his support and guidance in the months prior to my submission of the work and for his help in procuring some of the photographs used to illustrate it. Also to Matt Jones who oversaw the production, to Jon Wilkinson who did an amazing job designing the book's cover, and to my editor, Irene Moore, for her guidance and encouragement throughout the final stages.

To Ronelda Peters, part of the team at the Canadian National Memorial, Vimy, for her help regarding matters pertaining to the memorial itself. To Nelly Poignonnec, Communication and Public Relations Officer at the CWGC in Beaurains, France, for putting aside the time to answer all my questions regarding the work of the Commission and for introducing me to many of the staff and craftsmen at Beaurains who somehow manage to cope with the extraordinary demands placed on the organization from around the world. To Isabelle Pilarowski at the Office de Tourisme, Arras, who shares my own desire to raise the profile of Arras and its battlefields as a key destination on the Western Front – we may yet succeed.

To Barrie Duncan, Assistant Museums Officer, Leisure & Culture, South Lanarkshire Council, who was ever ready to delve into long-forgotten editions of *The Covenanter* and provide information from all corners of the regimental archive. Similarly, thanks go to Sandy Leishman at the Highland Fusiliers HQ, Sauchiehall Street, Glasgow, who was extremely helpful on matters relating to the Highland Light Infantry and the Royal Scots Fusiliers in the Great War. He and Barrie were not the only keepers of regimental archives who gave up their time to answer questions, but both were especially helpful.

To the staff at the reading rooms of the British Library, the National Archives at Kew, the Guildhall Library in the City, and the Imperial War Museum, London, for their courtesy and service during the research phase of this project.

To author David Kent-Lemon, for his kind advice and support as I took my first steps towards having the work published and who was responsible for introducing me to Pen & Sword.

For many entirely different reasons, I should also like to extend recognition and thanks to the following: Hugh Harvey, friend and colleague for many years, who helped iron out some of the last remaining pieces of research required to complete this book. He has toured the Western Front with me since 1993, as have the following: Dave Beck, Jim Wilcox, Sam Oliver, Alan Oliver, Andy Cook, Douglas Mackenzie, Gareth Berry, not forgetting Dennis Harvey and Frank Wilcox, whose company we dearly miss. To Garry Reilly, Phil Hughes, Iain Petrie, Darren Bone, and countless other ex-colleagues from Camden who have been particularly supportive since I retired in July 2010, and who throughout the four years it took to complete this project provided encouragement along the way. A special mention goes to Danielle Louise Mackinnon, another friend and former colleague from Camden, who always believed in my ability to write and who encouraged me to do so, as did Jane Chiarello and Simon Turner. To all those other wonderful friends, whose kind invitations to lunch, etc. I sometimes had to decline and who never once complained. Finally, to Peter Gilhooley, who first introduced me to the Western Front Association in 1981. I made my first trip to the battlefields of France and Belgium with Peter in September that year and continued to tour with him for many years after that. His extensive knowledge and infectious enthusiasm fuelled my early interest in the Great War, an interest that has ultimately led to my writing these three books. If it were it not for that initial spark, I might never have been inspired to write them.

This work is also dedicated to the memory of Dave Pilling who one night went out beyond the wire never to return.

Peter Hughes

Introduction

Like Ypres, Arras was briefly occupied by the Germans in the very early days of the war, but the French soon drove them out. For the remainder of 1914 and throughout 1915, French soldiers held a line just east of the town. In March 1916 the sector was handed over to the British who extended their line southwards from La Bassée. Thereafter, Arras remained in British hands. It was only in the final two months of the war, when the fighting drifted eastwards away from the town, that Arras could finally breathe a sigh of relief. It never quite suffered the destruction that Ypres did, though it was frequently subjected to heavy shelling, and in many places its streets and buildings were very badly damaged. It was a town battered and bruised, but essentially still intact. Like Ypres, it had always been a front line town, and for two and a half years it served as 'home' to countless British and Commonwealth soldiers. Both towns shared, and still share, a great deal in common.

Today Arras receives far fewer visitors to its battlefields than either Ypres or the Somme. I would venture even further and say that, in comparison with the other two, it has been seriously neglected, the one notable exception being the Memorial Park at Vimy Ridge. Here, the tunnels, shell holes, craters, concrete trench reconstructions, and the crowning magnificence that is the Canadian National Memorial, provide sufficient visual stimulus to attract large visitor numbers. Sadly, for many, this is where their visit to the Arras battlefield begins and ends. I sincerely hope that the three books in this series help to change all that.

Prior to the publication of *Cheerful Sacrifice* by Jon Nicholls in 1990 it was difficult to find any account of the series of military operations, fought between April and May 1917, known collectively as the Battle of Arras. More recently, and assisted by Jeremy Banning and the Imperial War Museum, Peter Barton produced another fine publication, one of a series of books based on panoramas, 'then' and 'now', in many ways similar in style to the ones written by John Giles in his *Then and Now* series where original photographs were juxtaposed with their modern day equivalents. For several years, before either of these titles appeared, *Prelude to Victory* by Brigadier General Edward Louis Spears was on my bookshelf, along with the indispensable first volume of the Official History for 1917, but sadly, that was about it; Arras was truly neglected as a subject.

As for accounts of the 1918 fighting around Arras, these were, and still are, virtually non-existent; similarly with 1916. Leaving aside Norm Christie's short history, *The Canadians at Arras, August-September 1918*, which forms part of his

For King and Empire series, the only published sources, and not always readily to hand, were individual unit histories, the five volumes of the Official History for 1918, together with a handful of Canadian memoirs. With all this in mind, I would like to think that my three books on Arras manage to fill in some of the gaps regarding this neglected part of the Western Front, notwithstanding my slightly unusual approach to the subject. Hopefully, they will complement what little already exists, at least from a British and Commonwealth perspective, and I really hope that people find them a useful addition. Incidentally, any of the above-mentioned works are well worth reading before considering a visit to Arras and its battlefields.

However, unlike these other books, my trilogy is not an account of any particular battle that took place around Arras, nor is it a chronological narrative of any of the events that took place there; there is no conventional storyline. So, what exactly is it then?

Perhaps the best way is to describe it as a kind of 'Who's Who', though, strictly speaking, that should read: 'Who was Who', since all the 'protagonists' are dead, buried now in one of the many CWGC cemeteries that dot the landscape in and around Arras, or else commemorated nearby on one of the four memorials to the missing. The books are principally concerned with the men who fought and fell around Arras, including, in many cases, the circumstances in which they died; they are, I suppose, simply an expression of remembrance.

The 'stage' for this pageant of remembrance is the better part of the map that forms the end paper at the beginning of *Military Operations, France & Belgium, 1917, Volume One*. It stretches from Aix-Noulette and Liévin in the north to Morchies and Lagnicourt in the south; from Dury and Éterpigny in the east to Barly and Saulty in the west. Though it was conceived, researched, and originally written as a single project lasting four years, in one continuous 'flow of the pen', as it were, the work is now divided into three parts: *Arras – North, Arras – South*, and *Arras – The Memorials*.

The work is not really a guidebook in any conventional sense of the term. Although I have given a brief indication as to where each cemetery is located, I have deliberately steered away from the idea of anything approaching what might be referred to as an itinerary, though the cemeteries within each chapter are all grouped by reasonable proximity to each other. I would much prefer to let the visitor decide which cemeteries to visit and the order in which to visit them.

In the first two books I have tried to outline briefly the nature of each cemetery in terms of size, character, and composition, before taking the visitor through the various plots and rows of graves, halting at many of the headstones where I then talk about the individuals buried there. Similarly, the third volume covering the memorials highlights many of the individuals commemorated at each of the four sites. The books only become 'guidebooks' once the visitor is inside the cemetery itself or standing in front of the memorial.

In an age of satellite navigation and the internet, reaching any of the cemeteries or memorials should be an easy enough task. The list of CWGC cemeteries and memorials can now be downloaded onto a satellite navigation system and the organization's website now includes the GPS co-ordinates for each site. For anyone not relying on modern technology, I would suggest the 1:100,000 maps produced by the *Institut Géographique National* (IGN). Unfortunately, two of these maps are required; No. 101: Lille – Bologne-sur-Mer, and No. 103: Amiens – Arras. Investing in both will also come in very handy when visiting other parts of the Western Front. Personally, I would be inclined to run with both systems whenever possible. The 'Michelin' 1:200,000 series, with the CWGC cemeteries and memorials overlaid and indexed, provide a useful pointer, but again two maps, No. 51 and No. 52, are required, and the scale is just a little too small for my liking.

With regard to maps, I know that many people will wonder why I have not included any within the body of my work. This would have been difficult to achieve with any clarity, not least because the actions described are extremely diverse, both in terms of time-line and location. I had to consult well over 200 maps during the course of my research. To condense all the topographical information into a handful of maps would have been virtually impossible, as well as potentially confusing. My own IGN maps, the Blue 1:25,000 series, are entirely overwritten in pencil showing redoubts, trenches, etc. Such detail and scale is essential when walking and describing the battlefields, but perhaps less important in a work whose subject happens to be mainly people. For the really committed visitor, the 1:25,000 series are the ones to go for, though several of them will be required on account of the larger scale.

Each of my three books has been written with the curious reader in mind. At times the detail may amount to more than the average visitor requires, but I would much rather leave it to the reader to decide which bits are relevant and which are not. Every headstone and every name on a memorial represents a unique human life, and therefore a unique story. Not all of these stories can be told, but many can, and that is really what these books are about. Although none of the three books provides a chronological narrative to the fighting, I do think that, collectively, they serve to illustrate quite well many aspects of life, and indeed death, on the Western Front. That, at least, was the intention when I wrote them, and partly the inspiration behind them.

When I mentioned earlier that the books were a kind of 'Who's Who', they may, at times, also bear a slight resemblance to the popular BBC television series *QI*. The reason for that is that my own curiosity often has a tendency to take me off at a tangent. Whenever something struck me as 'Quite Interesting' I found it very hard to leave it out; after all, a good story is a good story. This confession should suffice to explain away the inclusion of a mammoth, a magician, and 'Mr Ramshaw', a golden eagle, as well as one or two passing references to decent drams. (I was once fortunate enough to spend several years on the London tasting panel of the Scotch Malt Whisky Society – a tough assignment, I know, but someone had to do it.) Hopefully, and occasionally, the reader will find time to smile.

On a more personal note, I have been visiting the battlefields of the Western Front for over thirty years and have been a member of the Western Front Association since 1981. From the very first visit I have always carried a notebook with me. Anything of interest ends up in the notebook; sometimes a note regarding an individual soldier, or maybe a particular group of headstones; sometimes recurring dates, or perhaps the predominance of a particular regiment in a cemetery; in fact, just about anything unusual or interesting that might be worth pursuing once back home in England with time to research. Very often curiosity pays off, sometimes spectacularly. This has always been my way when visiting the cemeteries and memorials on the Western Front and, at least in part, this is how these three books came to be written. I hope they encourage people to delve a little deeper and to be even more curious when next visiting the battlefields.

Finally, the original title for this work was *Withered Leaves on the Plains of France*. The words are taken from four lines of a poem by Edward Richard Buxton Shanks. While he and others from the Artists' Rifles were drilling in London's Russell Square, in the heart of Bloomsbury, he noticed the autumn leaves swirling on the ground, conscious of the fact that they would soon begin to moulder before turning to mud, and eventually dust. Within that image he saw a clear reflection of his own mortality and that of his comrades, soon to leave for France and the trenches.

During my former working life I came to know Russell Square very well. Its lawns, flower beds, and the same trees that once stirred Shanks's imagination, formed a pleasant and familiar backdrop; not a place of quiet, but still a place where one could think. Over a period of time, seated outside the café there, I first conceived the idea of writing this work, though only as a single book, never imagining it would emerge as a three volume text. It was there too that I decided to use Shanks's metaphor in the title of the book. For the next four years, as the work took shape, it existed only under its original title until it was eventually changed to *Visiting the Fallen* at the suggestion of my publisher. So much for good intentions and poetic licence! However, let me say at this point that I very quickly warmed to the new title, liking it not least for its simplicity and direct appeal. I still, however, think of the 'Fallen', referred to in the title, as all those 'Withered Leaves'. A hundred years on, it remains a powerful and compelling image.

Arras North

Broadly speaking, this first volume covers the area north of the town. This will be the more familiar part of the battlefield to many visitors. As for Arras itself, its cemeteries are covered in the second volume – *Arras South*. The one exception to that is the communal cemetery of Saint-Laurent-Blangy, which many people would now consider to be part of the suburban landscape of Arras. The reasoning behind this decision rests solely on the fact that I have taken the River Scarpe as the dividing line east of the town. West of the town, the dividing line is the D939, the road heading out to Saint-Pol-sur-Ternoise and Hesdin. However, Duisans British Cemetery, which technically sits a few hundred yards south of that dividing line, is also included within this volume.

This volume also contains some of the larger cemeteries in and around Arras. In the case of some of these I have adopted a slightly different approach by examining casualties according to the year of death rather than my more usual method of working through the cemetery plot by plot. This was the method by which I originally sifted the information contained within those cemetery registers when researching the casualties. Having done that, it seemed to make sense to retain that format in the final draft. Anyone visiting Cabaret Rouge British Cemetery in search of 1914 casualties, for example, will still have to go from plot to plot, but will, at least, find them grouped neatly together for the sake of convenience in the text.

Many of the cemeteries covered in this volume revolve around the Canadian Expeditionary Force and its exploits during 1917, and not just at the Battle of Arras. Although some of the actions described took place closer to Lens than Arras, including the capture of Hill 70 in August 1917, many casualties from these actions happen to be buried very close to Arras or are commemorated on the Canadian National Memorial on Vimy Ridge, hence the reason for their inclusion here. I very much hope that the visitor to this area will find the time to visit cemeteries such as Liévin Communal Cemetery Extension, Villers Station Cemetery, Sucrerie Cemetery, as well as those around Aix-Noulette. Bon Voyage!

Chapter One

Four Trenches – A Last Supper – A Sunken Road

Saint-Laurent-Blangy Communal Cemetery

There are just four burials here, three of whom are identified. All three are casualties from the 4th East Yorkshire Regiment who fell within a three-day period in May 1940. Two of the men identified are privates, but the third is Warrant Officer Class II James WARNER, who died on the 22 May (Grave 2). The cemetery is tucked away on the north side of Saint-Laurent-Blangy, just south of the D.950, and lies just behind what would have been the German front line in 1917.

Mindel Trench British Cemetery, Saint-Laurent-Blangy

On the opening day of the Battle of Arras Mindel Trench was a German communication trench that connected the village of Athies to the rear of the front line. It was captured on 9 April by troops of the 9th (Scottish) Division, after which time it pretty much served the same purpose, but in reverse. Begun in April at the side of the trench, the cemetery was used intermittently thereafter.

The area around the cemetery became busier as time went on, becoming known as Stirling Camp, and is often referred to in memoirs and battalion war diaries as troops moved back and forth between the front line and rear sectors. The cemetery has 182 identified burials and lies on the D.42, the main road leading out of Saint-Laurent-Blangy to Athies, on the north side of the road, near the fork with the D.42E. It is set back about 150 yards from the road and is reached via a path.

Around two thirds of the total casualties buried here are from 1917, while the remainder are from the following year. Casualties from the 4th Division, 9th (Scottish) Division and Royal Garrison Artillery make up a good part of the cemetery, but there are also men from the 17th, 34th, and 51st Divisions buried here.

Casualties from the first two days of the Battle of Arras include many from Scottish regiments of the 9th Division killed between Saint-Laurent-Blangy and Athies. Second Lieutenant George Duncan ROSS, 3rd Gordon Highlanders, attached 8th Black Watch, was killed on the opening day, 9 April (A.1). Ten other ranks killed during the advance towards the Blue Line, north of Saint-Laurent-Blangy, lie buried here with him. One other rank died the next day, very likely from the previous day's wounds.

Lieutenant Arthur Stanley MACK (B.2) and Second Lieutenant George Rowland Paget HOWSON (B.3), 1st King's Own (Royal Lancaster Regiment), were killed in action on 9 April 1917 by a shell as they were leading the last two platoons of their battalion through the former German positions near Saint-Laurent-Blangy. The same shell also caused a further forty casualties among the ranks, twenty-two of whom are also buried in this cemetery, including Company Quartermaster Sergeant Frederick UNDERWOOD (B.12). The cemetery register shows the death of another man from the battalion the following day: Lance Serjeant Arthur EMMETT probably died of wounds from the same shell (B.22).

Subsequent burials in April are few, but casualties from heavy artillery units begin to appear from the 15th and account for eleven of the eighteen burials during the latter half of April. The difficulty in moving heavy batteries across a shattered battlefield and re-establishing them in captured positions can readily be appreciated. The harsh weather, bombardments, shortage of road repair material, as well as heavy traffic, all contributed towards delays in moving guns and shells into forward positions after the opening day, hence the appearance of artillerymen in this cemetery six days into the battle.

Second Lieutenant Henry Erskine TYSER, 8th Black Watch, was killed on 9 April 1917, aged 43. He was an only son, educated at Eton and Trinity College, Oxford, and worked in his father's law firm. He had been elected an underwriting member of Lloyds in 1898. On the outbreak of war he chose to retire from what was clearly a promising career in the legal profession in order to enlist and was gazetted early in 1915. He was a keen cricketer and a member of the MCC. His death occurred while advancing from the first objective, the Black Line, to the Blue Line. (B.1)

Another casualty killed on 9 April was Private Lawrence James STURROCK, 7th Seaforth Highlanders. He had studied at St. Andrew's University, where he gained his MA, and came from nearby Dundee. He died, aged 23, and had previously served with the Black Watch (B.36). His brother, Private Arthur John Sturrock, was killed in action a couple of weeks later on 23 April 1917, aged 20, while serving with the 1/6th Black Watch. He is buried nearby at Brown's Copse Cemetery, Roeux.

The burials in May consist largely of casualties from Royal Garrison Artillery units, but there are also men attached to the Labour Corps whose work was vital to convert former German positions for our own use. Re-construction work, such as building dug-outs, burying telephone cables, laying water pipes, maintaining and improving roads, were just some of the many tasks necessary to support the battle that was still in progress a couple of miles away. Two casualties from the 51st Field Ambulance signal the presence of the 17th (Northern) Division, which also used this cemetery during May. The majority of artillery casualties here are from the Royal Garrison Artillery, rather than the Royal Field Artillery, roughly two thirds of them killed between April and June 1917.

Major William McGILDOWNY DSO, 124th Siege Battery, Royal Garrison Artillery, died of wounds on 26 May 1917, aged 47, though *Officers Died in the Great War* shows his date of death as 27 May. He began his military career in July 1889 when he was commissioned in the Royal Artillery and retired from the Special Reserve in September 1906 as a major. His DSO was awarded for distinguished service in the field and was gazetted on 4 June 1917 in the King's Birthday Honours List. He and his family came from Co. Antrim. (G.1)

Another significant group of casualties here can be found in Row D, Graves 1 to 22. The twenty-two men are all privates or NCOs of the 21st West Yorkshire Regiment, pioneers to the 4th Division, which spent much of 1917 and 1918 on the Arras front. All these men were killed on or around 27 and 28 March 1918 when the Germans tried to extend their gains northward from Bapaume and the old Somme battlefields during their March offensive. Their work, maintaining and strengthening defences, often placed them in or near the front line.

Even after the Battle of Arras had closed in May 1917, the 4th Division remained in the Arras sector. There are a handful of casualties from the summer of 1917 belonging to that division, one of whom is Second Lieutenant Nigel Hugh WALLINGTON, 1st Somerset Light Infantry, killed in action on 21 June 1917, aged 19. This was a relatively quiet time during which the 3/4th Queen's (Royal West Surrey Regiment) was attached to the 4th Division for instruction in trench warfare. The 1st Somerset Light Infantry had been relieved on 19 June and had then moved into reserve trenches located around the nearby railway embankment. The battalion then returned to the front line on 25 June. It is likely therefore, that WALLINGTON was killed by shell fire. (D.42)

Occasionally, casualties occurred in unusual circumstances; for example, Corporal Alexander MUTCH died from drowning on 9 August 1917 near Fampoux. Units holding the line often used the River Scarpe and the small lakes alongside it for swimming and bathing. This is likely to have been the case with Corporal MUTCH, but evidently something went tragically wrong. (D.40)

Private John GENTLEMAN DCM, 1/5th Gordon Highlanders, was killed in action on 8 July 1918, aged 34. His DCM was gazetted on 14 November 1916 and was awarded for conspicuous gallantry when, on three successive occasions, he carried urgent messages to the firing line, passing through two heavy enemy barrages in circumstances where several runners had been killed or wounded and others had failed. He had also come to notice frequently on previous occasions for great bravery and devotion to duty in similar circumstances. (E.4)

Finally, there are two holders of the MM buried here; Private Joseph COOK MM, 1/5th Gordon Highlanders, killed in action on 8 July 1918 (E.5) and

Gunner John WILSON MM, C Battery, 256 Brigade, Royal Field Artillery, killed in action on 27 August 1918 (E.8).

Hervin Farm British Cemetery, Saint-Laurent-Blangy

Nearly all the burials are from April 1917, with six relating to 9 April, the opening day of the Battle of Arras, including one officer, Second Lieutenant Victor Ayling BOLITHO of the Household Battalion, who died of wounds (C.5). The farm was captured by the 9th Scottish Division in the opening hours of the offensive and 4th Division troops then passed through this location en route to Fampoux. The 34th Division has three burials here dating to 9 April, even though it attacked well to the north of this point.

Anyone visiting this cemetery, before continuing on to Brown's Copse Cemetery and Roeux, might care to reflect that the ruins of the farm that once stood on the other side of the embankment to the cemetery was the last brief halt for the 7th Black Watch before they moved up to their assembly trenches with the rest of the 51st (Highland) Division ready for the attack on Roeux the next morning, 23 April 1917. It was here at Hervin Farm that the men of the 7th Black Watch received a hot meal which, for many, was to be their last. The cemetery at Brown's Copse lies adjacent to their assembly trenches and is where many of them are now buried. It is easy to imagine the Highlanders, cold and hungry, huddling around the embankment, and anxiously eating their meal before moving up for battle.

Once captured on the opening day, British units used the sheltered nature of the position to their advantage. The railway embankment offered quite a lot of protection against shell fire, hence why the farm was used as a feeding point with relative safety on the night of 22 April. Once on the far side of the embankment, the 7th Black Watch had to split and follow tracks either side of the main road to Fampoux in artillery formation in order to minimise the risk of casualties from shell fire on the way up to their trenches at the foot of Greenland Hill.

This is a very small, very intimate cemetery that takes little time to visit, but it is worth pausing here to reflect and to take in what is a good example of a battle-field cemetery. I find it a very moving place to visit. It lies on the south side of the D42, roughly half way between Saint-Laurent-Blangy and Athies, on the east side of the railway embankment.

There were two significant officer casualties on 12 April: Brigadier General (General Staff) Charles GOSLING CMG, King's Royal Rifle Corps, command-ing 10 Brigade of the 4th Division (C.6) and Lieutenant Colonel Sidney Goss MULLOCK, 2nd Essex Regiment (C.8). GOSLING was killed by a shell and had served on the Western Front since 1914. He had been wounded twice; in February 1915 near Saint-Éloi in Belgium, and again near Vimy Ridge in May 1916.

Between GOSLING and MULLOCK is the only casualty here from May 1917, Captain Hedworth George Ailwyn FELLOWES MC, whose parent regi-ment was an Indian cavalry unit, the 11th King Edward's Own Lancers (Probyn's

Horse), though at the time of his death he was serving as brigade major with 10 Infantry Brigade. He was killed by a sniper on 12 May 1917, aged 25. His MC was gazetted on 4 November 1915 and was awarded in recognition of his conspicuous resource and ability on 7 October 1915 when the had gone out with an NCO in broad daylight to locate the position of an enemy trench mortar near Beaumont Hamel. Once the pair had reached the enemy's wire and located the trench mortar they remained there for three hours, observing its activity, before returning with valuable information. He and another NCO had also been out on patrol on the night of 11 August that year and had attacked a German patrol, capturing its leader, and again bringing back valuable information. (Plot C.7)

Hedworth's father was 1st Baron Ailwyn, but he was equally well connected via his mother's side of the family to the Earls of Stafford. He was one of four children and both his brothers served throughout the war. Ronald Townshend Fellowes was awarded the DSO in 1918, and in 1915 had won the MC. Ronald's distinguished career included service as a staff captain with 22 Brigade between 1914 and 1915, and as deputy assistant adjutant and quartermaster general, III Corps, between 1915 and 1916. He spent the last two years commanding the 1st Rifle Brigade, but was only promoted to lieutenant colonel after the war. He had also been mentioned in despatches on no fewer than five occasions. He eventually succeeded his father, but died in 1936 as a result of complications from wounds received during the war. Eric William Edward Fellowes served with the Royal Navy.

Serjeant John WALKER DCM, 7th Seaforth Highlanders, was killed in action on 15 April 1917, aged 29, and had previously served with the 5th Reserve Cavalry Regiment. His DCM, gazetted on 16 November 1915, was awarded for conspicuous bravery at the Hohenzollern Redoubt on 25 September 1915. After the first line had crossed the enemy's trench, a group of Germans, who had remained hidden in a dug-out, opened fire from behind. WALKER, sending for bombs, returned fire until they arrived and then successfully bombed the party of Germans single-handed. (C.9)

The area around the farm was also used by Royal Engineer companies, as well as Royal Artillery units, which is evident from many of the headstones dated around the middle of April. Protection from incoming shells also made the west side of the embankment ideal for medical units, which used it to house dressing stations and as dug-out accommodation for staff and stretcher-bearers.

There are also eleven burials relating to 23 April 1917, mainly men of the 37th Division, and just two burials from 1918, both dating to late March and early April, and both from units of the 4th Division. Lieutenant William SLINGER, 1st East Lancashire Regiment, was killed by a shell while supervising a working party on 23 July 1917 (A.15). His brother, Lieutenant George Nicholas Slinger, is buried not too far away in Point du Jour Military Cemetery.

Athies Communal Cemetery

The extension followed on from the communal one, which now contains just one burial, that of Private S.C. PHILIP, Royal Army Medical Corps, attached to the South African Medical Corps. He was killed on 12 April 1917, aged 32 (Grave 1 – NE side).

The communal cemetery sits on the D42, on the north side of the road by the roundabout in the centre of the village. The communal cemetery extension is situated next to it along the side road that leads north off the roundabout towards Point du Jour. This side road was known to the troops as Highland Road.

Athies Communal Cemetery Extension

The extension is interesting in its variety. Early burials, in the first half of April 1917, are almost exclusively from infantry units, but this soon expands to include a significant number of supporting units; for example, Royal Field and Garrison Artillery, Signalling and Field Companies from the Royal Engineers and a handful of Field Ambulance personnel, all of which had moved forward by 14 April as the battle progressed. The nature of the fighting also became more attritional. This was equally as true for artillery units as it was for the infantry; between 14 and 22 April the majority of casualties in this cemetery are from the Royal Field Artillery and approximately one fifth of all burials here are from artillery units.

Corporal William Michael HEALY DCM, 1st South African Regiment, was killed in action on 12 April 1917, aged 22. Ian Uys's book *Delville Wood* shows him as having been killed in action on 17 April 1917; this seems very unlikely, as the South African Brigade had been relieved on 15 April and had then moved out of the line to the area around Hermaville, which is about six miles behind Arras. On 16 July 1916 at Delville Wood, HEALY and a handful of others found themselves pinned down by machine-gun fire from the front and flanks. Managing to take refuge behind a small bank of earth, HEALY and Lieutenant Leonard Isaacs chose to stay there while Private Emile Mathis, a 17-year-old, brought up more ammunition for HEALY's Lewis gun. On one occasion HEALY's gun jammed, but being a trained Lewis gunner, he repaired it under heavy fire and continued operating it throughout the day, eventually bringing it back with him though still under heavy machine-gun and sniper fire. HEALY and Isaacs managed to get back safely later that night, while Privates Mathis, Grimes and Neilson had managed to get back earlier in the day. Another man, Private Lange, was killed while attempting to return with the others. HEALY's DCM was awarded in October 1916 in connection with the above action. (A.7)

Captain Tom WELSH MC, 1st Field Ambulance, attached 2nd South African Regiment, was mortally wounded on 12 April 1917, aged 33. He and his team had been working constantly since 9 April with little or no rest. Welsh came from Edinburgh and had previously served in German South-West Africa. In civilian life he had been a doctor working for a mining company. His MC was gazetted on

12 January 1917 and was awarded for conspicuous gallantry and devotion to duty in organizing and leading stretcher parties under heavy fire, almost certainly during the later stages of the Somme fighting near Warlencourt. He had also been mentioned in despatches. (A.17)

In total there are eighteen South Africans buried here who were killed in action on 12 April and one who died the following day, probably from wounds received on the 12th when the South African Brigade made its ill-fated attack towards Greenland Hill. Among them are several veterans: Private Leo LEVINSON MM (A.3), Private SINCLAIR (A.9), Private POULTNEY (A.14), and Private LAING (J.29), who had all taken part in the intense fighting at Delville Wood the previous July, where LAING and LEVINSON had also been wounded.

Major William Hammond SMITH, A Battery, 52 Brigade, Royal Field Artillery, was killed whilst moving forward to locate infantry positions in front of his battery on 12 April 1917. His father, Charles Smith, was Master of Sidney Sussex College, Cambridge, from which William had also graduated. He was a promising painter who had studied at the Royal Academy in London and who also had connections to the Slade School of Art. He had enlisted in August 1914 and was then given a temporary commission in the Royal Field Artillery. In 1915 he had seen action at Festubert, La Bassée, then at Hill 60 near Ypres. He had also served on the Somme in 1916 where he received the first of two mentions in despatches. He was mentioned for a third time in 1917. (B.9)

The 36th Australian Heavy Artillery, with its 9.2-inch guns, had served on the Somme in 1916. However, it was frequently detached on loan to other sectors. In 1917, it supported the Canadian Corps at Vimy Ridge, then moved north to support the attack at Messines Ridge, before finally re-joining its fellow countrymen at the Third Battle of Ypres. One member of this unit is buried here, Gunner Ernest Edwin WOODLAND. He fell in action on 30 April 1917, aged 20. (E.26)

Pioneer battalions rarely get the recognition they deserve. The 9th North Staffordshire Regiment and the 21st West Yorkshire Regiment were pioneers to the 37th Division and the 4th Division, respectively. There are two men from the former unit and two from the latter buried here. One of the men, Private Henry WAUGH MM, 21st West Yorkshire Regiment, was killed in action on 1 May 1917. (F.8)

Private James MUNRO, 6th Seaforth Highlanders, was killed in action on 25 April 1917 when he was hit by shell fragments and suffered a fatal head wound (Plot F.34). His brother, Private John Munro, had also served in the same battalion and was killed earlier in the war on 15 June 1915, but he has no known grave. He is commemorated on the memorial at Le Touret. A third brother, George Munro, 6th Cameron Highlanders, also has no known grave and he is commemorated on the Soissons Memorial. He was killed on 24 July 1918.

The cemetery was also used to bury thirty-one men from battalions of the 51st (Highland) Division after the attack on Roeux and Greenland Hill on 23 April 1917, including one officer, Second Lieutenant Arthur Hamilton COLLYER, 5th Gordon Highlanders (G.3). Half of them are from the 6th Gordon Highlanders, while another four are from the 4th and 5th Battalions.

Second Lieutenant John Herbert POPE, 1st Royal Irish Fusiliers, had been with the battalion almost a year. He died of wounds, aged 22, on 11 April 1917 following the failed attack at noon that day from the sunken road at Fampoux (G.17). His father was a major with the East Surrey Regiment.

There are seven more Royal Irish Fusiliers from that unsuccessful attack buried in Rows G and H, one of whom is Lance Corporal James FRASER MM. He had been awarded the MM for gallantry during 1915 and was one of fourteen men from his battalion presented with gallantry awards by Major General Lambton, his divisional commander, on 26 November while the battalion was out of line at Ercourt (G.24). His brother Archibald, who served as a private with the 4th Black Watch, was killed on the opening day of the Battle of Loos in 1915. He is commemorated on the Loos Memorial. The family hailed from Dundee.

Buried next to Lance Corporal FRASER is one of two cavalrymen here; Private Ernest DALE, 2nd Dragoon Guards (Queen's Bays), was killed in action on 11 April 1917 (G.25). Private Harold HENWOOD, 5th Dragoon Guards (Princess Charlotte of Wales's), was also killed in action a day earlier (G.13).

Captain Russell Alexander COLVIN, 10th Argyll & Sutherland Highlanders, was killed in action on 1 May 1917, aged 36. He was the battalion's Intelligence Officer (G.37). Several members of his family, including his father, had distinguished careers in the Indian Civil Service.

The Household Battalion fought as an infantry battalion, but it had originally been formed back in England at Knightsbridge Barracks in September 1916 from men of the reserve units of the Household Cavalry. It went to the Western Front in November that year and served there with distinction until it was disbanded in February 1918. Though it served as an infantry battalion, it retained its character as a cavalry unit in its rank structure. There are four men buried here from the battalion, three of whom held the rank of trooper, while the fourth, Charles Theophilus RUDGE, held the rank of Corporal of Horse (H.3). All four men were killed on 11 April 1917.

Regimental Serjeant Major James Proctor ELLIS, 1st Royal Irish Fusiliers, is another of the casualties from 11 April 1917. He had formerly served with the Grenadier Guards (H.6). Corporal Christopher HAYDEN MM, 1st Royal Irish Fusiliers, was also killed in action that day and had been awarded the Medal of St. George, 4th Class (Russia) (H.21).

The other battalion involved in the disastrous attack from the sunken lane at Fampoux on 11 April 1917 was the 2nd Seaforth Highlanders, whose memorial now stands on the site of the trench where their attack towards Greenland Hill and Roeux began. Eight Seaforth Highlanders from that attack are buried in this cemetery, including Company Serjeant Major Donald MacDONALD of 'C' Company (J.33).

Corporal Thomas Edwin McNALLY DCM, 9th Divisional Signal Company, Royal Engineers died of wounds on 12 April 1917, aged 29. His DCM was gazetted on 21 June 1916 and was awarded for conspicuous gallantry and devotion to duty. He had continually repaired telephone wires under trying circumstances and very heavy fire. The citation continues by stating that his clothing was torn in several places by shrapnel splinters, creating a very vivid impression of the intensity of fire under which he had worked and of the man's bravery. (K.1)

Provision of supplies to the front line, and often the removal of casualties down the line, depended heavily on light railway systems. Such a system existed on this side of the river valley and ran through the villages of Athies and Fampoux. Staff Serjeant John Walter WILKINSON, whose date of death is shown as 22 December 1917, was killed in action and belonged to No. 2 Army Tramway Company, Royal Engineers. (M.2)

There are some 1918 burials in the cemetery, mainly from battalions of the 4th Division which spent much of 1917 in this sector. The division was also here during the German offensive in March 1918 and the Allied advance later that summer.

Three holders of the MM have already been referenced. The remaining four holders are:

Lance Corporal John HANNA MM, 7th Argyll & Sutherland Highlanders, killed in action on 17 April 1917, aged 20 (D.6).

Bombardier Frank MONTAGUE MM, C Battery, 50 Brigade, Royal Field Artillery, killed in action on 2 May 1917 (G.36).

Sergeant C.V. MOORE MM, 2nd South African Regiment, killed in action on 12 April 1917, aged 22. He had served in the German South-West African campaign and throughout the rebellion in 1914–1915 (H.24).

Bombardier Dennis COLLINS MM, 126th Battery, Royal Field Artillery, was killed in action on 14 May 1917, aged 26 (K.8).

A visitor to this cemetery may also notice the presence of twenty-three graves of the 4th Green Howards. All of them are casualties from May 1940 and are to be found in Plot 2, which now contains thirty-one identified burials from the Second World War. The most notable is Captain the Honourable Anthony Francis PHILLIMORE, 9th Queen's Royal Lancers, Royal Armoured Corps, who was killed in action on 23 May 1940 (Plot 2, Row A, Grave 17). He was the son of Walter Godfrey Phillimore MC, 2nd Baron Phillimore, whose first wife, Lady Phillimore, née Dorothy Barbara Haig, was the daughter of Lieutenant Colonel Arthur Balfour Haig CVO CMG, of Bemersyde, cousin of Sir Douglas Haig. Captain Phillimore was married to Anne Julia Pereira, second daughter of

Major General Cecil Edward Pereira KCB CMG, who had commanded the 2nd Coldstream Guards in August 1914 and who, by the end of the war, commanded the 2nd Division on the Western Front.

Point Du Jour Military Cemetery, Athies

The high ground that forms the Point du Jour ridge was captured on the opening day of the Battle of Arras by the 9th (Scottish) Division, which also took the village of Athies. There were two original cemeteries on this site, one of which became the present day cemetery after the Armistice. At the end of the war the original graves, mainly from April to November 1917, and a few from May the following year, formed part of what is now Plot I. However, the cemetery was considerably enlarged by bringing in isolated graves and closing small cemeteries to the north, south and east of this location.

The cemetery today has almost 800 burials, around half of which are unidentified. Given its size, it has very few holders of gallantry awards, but it is a cemetery rich in other aspects. The 9th (Scottish) Division's memorial cairn has recently been moved because of road improvements to a site close to the cemetery's entrance. The cemetery lies adjacent to the D950 and is best reached by retracing one's steps from Athies Communal Cemetery along the D42 towards Saint-Laurent-Blangy. After about 100 yards a road running north, the Rue du Chauffeur, leads straight to the cemetery.

The 9th (Scottish) Division consisted of the South African Brigade and two other brigades made up entirely of battalions from Scottish regiments. Despite that fact, there are relatively few burials here from Scottish units, and those that are to be found here come not only from the 9th (Scottish) Division, but also from the 4th, 34th and 51st Divisions, which all fought here in April 1917. Today, there are forty-one identified graves from Scottish regiments. By contrast, there are sixty-six men from the South African Brigade, including eight who were brought here after the war from Quarry Cemetery, Fampoux, along with twenty-five United Kingdom casualties.

Second Lieutenant George Nicholas SLINGER, 159 Brigade, Royal Field Artillery, was killed in action on 28 November 1916 (Plot I.A.5). He had enlisted in the 158 (Accrington & Burnley) Howitzer Brigade, Royal Field Artillery, in early February 1915, but after receiving his commission he was transferred to 159 Brigade. Given his date of death, it may seem somewhat unusual that an officer of the Royal Field Artillery should be buried here when, at that time, our artillery was much further back and when this area was well behind the German front line. We know, however, that SLINGER was buried by the Germans because his grave was found after Pont du Jour Ridge had been taken in 1917. His grave, which they had marked, indicated that he had been killed by a sniper on 28 November while out examining German wire. His elder brother, William Slinger, 1st East Lancashire Regiment, was killed by shell fire on 23 July 1917 while supervising a working party and is buried nearby at Hervin Farm Cemetery. The youngest of the three brothers, Tempest Slinger, who survived the war, served with the Royal Army Medical Corps. On the outbreak of war, their father, who had served as a major with the East Lancashire Regiment, was appointed adjutant and second-in-command of the 11th Battalion (Accrington Pals) East Lancashire Regiment. However, he was passed over for overseas service and he remained in the United Kingdom, where he was involved with the Training Reserve.

Lieutenant William Macliesh DURANT, New Zealand Engineers, was killed in action on the night of 14 September 1916. He, with a sergeant and eight sappers, had gone out with a raiding party from the Cheshire Regiment in order to blow a gap in the German wire using a Bangalore torpedo. The raid was not successful and only Lieutenant DURANT and two other men reached the German wire. Throughout the night DURANT's men went out trying to find him and his party, or recover their bodies. However, it was only in April the following year, after the capture of Saint-Laurent-Blangy, that his grave was found. It carried an inscription left by the Germans indicating that it contained four men, two of whom were NCOs, and one other rank. It did, however, confirm that the fourth body was that of Lieutenant DURANT. His body was re-interred here after the Armistice. (Plot I.A.6)

Second Lieutenant Victor Arthur HUNT, 4th South African Regiment, was killed in action on 9 April 1917, aged 25. He had served as a sergeant with that unit at Delville Wood in July 1916. (Plot I.H.17) Also killed that day in the same attack was Second Lieutenant Martin BURROWS, 3rd South African Regiment, aged 38. He is buried a few graves further back (Plot I.H.9). The CWGC register tells us that it is likely these two men, with another thirty South African dead, were brought here from one of the cemeteries that closed after the war. That cemetery was known as Brown Line Cemetery, so-called after the third line objective on the opening day of the Battle of Arras.

Private Thomas Potter McKINLAY, 9th Cameronians, was killed in action on 12 April 1917. He is one of two soldiers buried here aged 17 (Special Memorial B.1). The other man is Private Clarence Myvern McGREW, 'D' Company, 3rd Battalion, Canadian Infantry, killed in action on 14 October 1918 (Plot I.J.6).

Second Lieutenant Cecil Henry COXE, 6 Squadron, Royal Flying Corps, died of wounds on 1 July 1916, aged 18, the youngest son of the family. He had attended Balliol College, Oxford. However, in December 1915, having attained the age of 18, he applied for and was given a commission in the Royal Flying Corps. He gained his 'wings' in May the following year and then went to the front. On 1 July his squadron was involved in an attack on part of the railway system near Cambrai. However, while returning from the mission his aircraft was shot down and he died the same day in a German field hospital. (Plot II.A.13)

The cemetery has a liberal sprinkling of 1918 casualties, fifty-six, in fact, mostly from the 4th Division, 12th (Eastern) Division and the 15th (Scottish) Division.

The CWGC register points out that thirteen men belonging to the 12th Division were removed from Hénin-Liétard Communal Cemetery to this one after the Armistice. Six men of the 1st Cambridgeshire Regiment may have been part of this relocation, though only five are buried here consecutively in Plot II, Row B, the other being in Plot III.

Private George THOMPSON, 1st Cambridgeshire Regiment, was killed in action on 14 October 1918 (Plot II.B.1), as were Privates Charles LAWES (Plot II.B.2), Matthew SHAWLL (Plot II.B.3), Edward HOWARD, aged 19 (Plot II.B.4) and John Albert TINGLEY (Plot II.B.5). The sixth, Private Frederick William HUDSON (Plot III.E.12), died of wounds the same day, aged 19, and this may account for his separation from the others. Most of these men had formerly served with other regiments and only THOMPSON had served throughout with the Cambridgeshire Regiment. Private Albert Thomas HEP-DEN, 1st Worcestershire Regiment (Plot II.B.6), is buried among the group for reasons that will become apparent in the following narrative.

The men lost their lives in the attack on Auby, a small village just north of Douai. The artillery providing the creeping barrage had warned that its guns may well fire short owing to worn barrels, and, to complicate matters further, most of the barrage had to be fired from the flank. The 1st Cambridgeshire Regiment attacked the northern end of the village, clearing it; the 1st Worcestershire Regiment, part of the 8th Division, attacked the southern part. Each battalion, however, belonged to a different division, each operating under an entirely different line of command. Shells did fall short, and some casualties among the leading companies of the 1st Cambridgeshire Regiment were undoubtedly caused by friendly fire, but the German counter-barrage also took its toll. The 1st Worcestershire Regiment was delayed by shell and machine-gun fire, suffering heavy casualties, including a hit on the battalion's forward headquarters. The 1st Cambridgeshire Regiment sent two patrols into the village to try to establish contact with the Worcestershire battalion, but met opposition and retired to form a defensive right flank until difficulties could be overcome.

Meanwhile, the Germans on the north bank of the Haute Deûle Canal had already blown a small wooden bridge and their machine guns put down heavy fire, halting further progress. The battle then became an inconclusive fire-fight as the Lewis gunners of the 1st Cambridgeshire Regiment returned fire. However, shells intended to fall on the German positions north of the canal now fell on some houses on the southern bank causing further casualties. The 1st Worcestershire Regiment eventually cleared its part of the village and the Germans withdrew overnight from the canal.

The fluid conditions created by semi-open warfare often made communication and command and control even more difficult, but this was an action in which difficulties were resolved, not at brigade or divisional level, but by company and platoon commanders. Notwithstanding some very elementary mistakes in this battle, the account of it reads more like an infantry encounter in the Second World War rather than the First and illustrates perfectly the degree to which many battalion officers had become competent and confident in their own ability and that of their men. Total casualties for the 1st Cambridgeshire Regiment came to nine officers, one of whom was killed, and 107 other ranks.

Second Lieutenant Robert Arthur PATTERSON, 6th Rifle Brigade, attached 1st Battalion, was killed in action on 12 April 1917 when his battalion was involved in an attack alongside the 9th (Scottish) Division. The objective was to secure the road connecting the key villages of Roeux and Gavrelle, which was the very same ground over which 10 and 12 Brigades had attacked the day before, but without success. 'A' and 'B' Companies, 1st Rifle Brigade, assembled just north of Hyderabad Redoubt in preparation for the attack with 'C' Company in support. Just prior to the attack, which was scheduled for 5.30pm, the assembly position came under heavy bombardment and was also swept by intense machine-gun fire from the north and east. Within a few minutes of scrambling out of their trenches 'A' and 'B' companies had lost two officers and fifty-one casualties. It was wet and very muddy and PATTERSON died standing on the parapet helping his men out of the trench (Plot II.C.5). A fellow officer, Second Lieutenant Arthur Max Spencer, who is buried at Highland Cemetery, Roclincourt, was killed in exactly the same manner.

Company Serjeant Major Daniel A. FARRINGTON MC, 11th Royal Warwick-shire Regiment, was killed in action on 23 April 1917, aged 36. His MC was gazetted on 3 March 1917 and was awarded for conspicuous gallantry in action after he had rallied his men and led them forward under heavy fire. The citation concludes that he had set a splendid example of courage and coolness throughout. (Plot II.C.16)

Captain Thomas James PRICHARD MC, 1st King's Own (Royal Lancaster Regiment), was killed in action on 28 March 1918, aged 23. His MC was gazetted on 16 August 1917 and was awarded for conspicuous gallantry and devotion to duty as a temporary second lieutenant while in command of a raiding party, when he had shown great promptitude and coolness in attacking and dispersing a hostile patrol that would otherwise have interfered with the success of the raid. The citation adds that his work in patrolling had on all occasions been excellent. (Plot II.D.21)

Second Lieutenant Hubert John DICKINSON, 2nd Lincolnshire Regiment, was killed in action on 20 September 1916, aged 25. The CWGC register shows that his father served as a Territorial Army captain with the Royal Army Medical Corps. Hubert's death occurred not on this particular battlefield, but on the old Loos battlefield near the Hohenzollern Redoubt. He was part of a patrol that went out on the night of 19/20 September and never returned. It seems likely that he was either killed, or died soon after being wounded, and was probably then buried by the Germans. His remains were brought here after the war when isolated plots were cleared. (Plot II.E.1)

Lieutenant Colonel Francis Savage Nesbitt SAVAGE-ARMSTRONG DSO, 1st South Staffordshire Regiment, was killed in action on 23 April 1917, aged 36 (Plot II.E.12). He had served in the South African War where, as a lieutenant in the mounted infantry company of the South Staffordshire Regiment, he took part in one of the last actions of the conflict.

On 20 April 1902, an attack was planned against a party of Boers at a place called Moolman's Spruit. The Boers were tipped off and sent a native guide in their pay to offer to lead the attacking force to a location known as Olivier's Farm where the Boers prepared to ambush it. His company commander, Captain Blackwood, was severely wounded in the ambush, but was rescued by SAVAGE-ARMSTRONG and another man, Colour Serjeant Hazelwood, who dashed from their position on the edge of a wood and dragged Blackwood back to the meagre cover provided by the thicket. The Boer fire was intense and Hazelwood was also badly wounded in the rescue. Lieutenant Colonel Percival, commanding the 1st Battalion, Imperial Yeomanry, decided that the attack could no longer succeed and ordered a withdrawal. Unfortunately, Blackwood died of his wounds, but SAVAGE-ARMSTRONG later left a detailed account of the incident.

Lieutenant Colonel SAVAGE-ARMSTRONG was educated at Shrewsbury School and went to France on 1 November 1914 where he joined what remained of the 1st South Staffordshire Regiment during the First Battle of Ypres, briefly commanding it there. At Neuve Chapelle and Fromelles he was the battalion's machine-gun officer, and at Festubert he was seriously wounded in the right hand and had to spend several months recovering. His DSO was gazetted in June 1915 and he received it the following month. He returned to the front in May 1916 and was given command of a service battalion of the Rifle Brigade, before subsequently going on to command the 11th Royal Warwickshire Regiment. It was while commanding this battalion that he was killed. He had been also mentioned in despatches on four occasions.

His father, a Doctor of Literature, was also a published poet and Professor of English and History at Queen's College, Cork. He died in 1906, but a collection of his poetry was put together after the war as a dedication to '*the memory of his son and Major H.K. Redmond MP, and other brave Irishmen, in admiration of their faithful devotion to a great ideal, and in gratitude for their noble self-sacrifice in the cause of universal freedom*'. Profits from its sale went to the Irish Counties War Hospital.

The Reverend James Thomas LEESON, Chaplain 4th Class, Army Chaplains' Department, was killed in action on 23 April 1917. At the time of his death he was attached to the 13th Royal Fusiliers. In his memoir *A Passionate Prodigality*, Guy Patterson Chapman OBE MC, refers to an occasion, shortly after the fighting on 23 April, when he and fellow officers were dining in the village of Izel-lès-Hameau. One of the officers, commenting on LEESON's death, states: '*Poor old Leeson's gone ... Too old y'know. He ought never to have gone up, but you know what these Catholic padres are ... Hand blown off and he died of shock.*' (Plot II.G.14)

Lieutenant Colonel Charles James BURKE DSO, 2nd Royal Irish Regiment, was killed in action by a shell on 9 April 1917, aged 35. His orderly was also killed by the same shell. He was an outstandingly colourful character. (Plot III.C.2)

BURKE became one of the leading figures in early aviation, but had begun his long military career in the South African War. In September 1903 he was commissioned from the militia into the Royal Irish Regiment and then, between July 1905 and the end of 1909, he went on to serve with the West African Frontier Force. In 1910 he went to France and it was there that he learned to fly. He then returned to England where he worked for a time as part of the Army Balloon School. However, he continued to fly aircraft and had the honour of flying the first aircraft ever purchased by the British Government; but in January 1911 he was injured in a crash.

By this time he was probably the most experienced military aviator in the British Army and wrote a piece on flying for the Royal United Services Institute. He very much believed in the potential for aircraft to carry out reconnaissance on behalf of the army in the way that cavalry had previously done.

In May 1912 he joined the Royal Flying Corps, and soon became commanding officer of 2 Squadron. Later that year, he took a number of aircraft on army manoeuvres and on 1 August was again injured while flying. In February 1913 he flew to Montrose in several stages, establishing an airbase there.

On 14 August 1914 he took 2 Squadron to France. By rights, he ought to have been the first combatant of the British Expeditionary Force to land in France, but that honour was denied him by one of his squadron, the even more colourful and wildly eccentric fellow Irishman, Captain Hubert Dunsterville Harvey-Kelly. When the squadron reached the French coast, Harvey-Kelly took a shortcut across northern France instead of following the coast and landed just as BURKE and the rest of the squadron were approaching the airfield.

BURKE was mentioned in despatches in October 1914 by Sir John French, and the following month he was appointed commanding officer of No. 2 Wing, based at Saint-Omer. He was involved in the recruitment drive for pilots in Canada and his experience of military aviation led to his appointment in 1916 as Commandant of the Central Flying School back in England. However, he became hungry for action and believed that his place was now with his old regiment, the Royal Irish Regiment, or at least back with the infantry. He returned to France and was killed on the opening day of the Battle of Arras commanding the 1st East Lancashire Regiment.

His DSO had been gazetted on 18 February 1915 and was awarded for services to the Royal Flying Corps in connection with operations in the field. He was a member of the Meteorological Society and the Royal United Services Institute, and also an Associate Fellow of the Aeronautical Society. He was affectionately known as 'Pregnant Percy' on account of his pigeon-like, barrel-shaped chest.

Second Lieutenant Percival Edgar ARGYLE, 1st East Lancashire Regiment, was also killed in action on 9 April 1917, almost certainly by a shell, while commanding 'B' Company on the left of the battalion front near the ruins of Point du Jour House (Plot III.C.3). The battalion suffered fifty-nine casualties, including two officers killed and two wounded, which in context was considered fairly light. Those killed that day are buried here or in Highland Cemetery, Roclincourt, otherwise they are commemorated on the memorial at Arras. The CWGC register notes that twenty-two men of the 1st East Lancashire Regiment and the Royal Field Artillery were brought here for re-burial when Effie Trench Cemetery was closed sometime after the Armistice.

Corporal William BARRY DCM, C Battery, 79 Brigade, Royal Field Artillery, was killed in action on 5 July 1917 serving as part of the 17th Division's artillery. His DCM was won while serving as a bombardier with 81 Brigade HQ and was gazetted on 16 March 1916. It was awarded for conspicuous gallantry in mending telephone wires while under heavy shell fire. There is no reference to his having been awarded the DCM in *Soldiers Died in the Great War*. (Plot III.C.24)

This is not a cemetery where one expects to find graves of cavalrymen, but there are two buried here. Both were killed in action on 11 April 1917 with the 2nd Dragoon Guards (Queen's Bays). Private William Herbert CRACKNELL is buried here and the location is confirmed (Plot III.D.2), but Private Harry GODDARD's grave has since been lost, though he is known to be buried here (Special Memorial A.4).

Second Lieutenant Harold E. PORTEOUS, 3rd South African Regiment, was killed in action on 12 April 1917. His battalion was in reserve that day, so he may have been attached to 1st Regiment on the left of the South African line, but this remains uncertain. The previous year, PORTEOUS had been a private attached to a trench mortar battery at Delville Wood and had been among the last South Africans to be relieved from the wood on 20 July. (Plot III.D.7)

Together the Royal Naval Volunteer Reserve and the Royal Marine Light Infantry make up a significant number of casualties in this cemetery; the former has thirty and the latter twenty-two. Writer 1st Class G. MAJOR, Hood Battalion, Royal Naval Volunteer Reserve, died on 31 August 1917, aged 24 (Plot III.E.24). He has the distinction of being the only casualty of that rank from the Great War buried overseas. The associated job was an administrative one.

Major Charles Alan Smith MORRIS, 3rd Bedfordshire Regiment, attached 1st Battalion, died while a prisoner in German hands on 7 May 1917 at the age of 21 (Plot IV.D.16). By his death his parents lost their only son. Fifteen other majors were killed or died, aged 21, during the Great War; these being the youngest in that rank to lose their lives during the conflict. Casualties of this rank show a huge disparity in age.

Second Lieutenant Oliver Cyril GODFREY, 27 Squadron, Royal Flying Corps, was killed in action on 23 September 1916, aged 28, flying a Martinsyde G100 (Elephant) fighter-bomber (Plot IV.F.12). GODFREY had already made his name as a motorcycle racer and in 1911 he won the Isle of Man TT Race; in 1914 he came second. A natural choice for the Royal Flying Corps, he went to France in March 1916. He and five other aircraft were engaged in an operation to bomb railway yards at Cambrai when they were attacked by enemy scouts. One of those scouts was Manfred von Richthofen, but GODFREY and his operator, Second Lieutenant Eric James Roberts, were shot down by Erwin Boehme and Hans Reimann. Reimann was then killed when his aircraft was rammed in mid-air by Lieutenant L.F. Forbes. Richthofen scored his second victory in the fight by shooting down Serjeant Bellerby. Bellerby and Roberts have no known grave and are commemorated on the Royal Flying Services Memorial at Arras.

There are ten identified casualties from the Royal Guernsey Light Infantry buried here. Plot IV, Rows G, H and J, is the final resting place for nine of them; the other is in Plot III, Row D. The CWGC records indicate that 359 casualties from this regiment lost their lives during the First World War, of which 173 are buried or commemorated in France. In the cemeteries covered in this book, the only other two casualties from the regiment are buried at Cabaret Rouge British Cemetery.

In 1914 the Guernsey Militia consisted of two battalions. Although an infantry company from the regiment joined the 6th Royal Irish Regiment in March 1915, the 1st (Service) Battalion of the regiment only went to France in early October 1917, joining 86 Brigade of the 29th Division.

The men buried here fell in action on 1 December 1917 as part of this latter unit in a fierce encounter at Les Rues Vertes during the German counter-offensive at the Battle of Cambrai. Its casualties amounted to just over 500 for all ranks and today many of them are remembered on the memorial at Louverval.

Private Nico SARRE, 1st Royal Guernsey Light Infantry, was one of eight brothers who served during the war, two of whom were also killed in action on the same day as their brother (Plot IV. H.8). Privates Peter and Edmund Sarre were initially reported to have been taken prisoner, but Wilfred was known to have been killed. Sadly, both Peter and Edmund died from wounds. Peter died on 1 December 1917, while Edmund died in German captivity on 24 April 1918 and is buried at Lille Southern Cemetery. Peter and Wilfred have no known graves and are now commemorated on the memorial to the missing at Louverval. A final twist in this tragic family tale is that a brother-in-law, Private Ernest Martel, was also captured in the fighting at Rues Vertes and survived the war, only to die a few months after the Armistice on 30 March 1919. He is buried at Vale (Domaille) Churchyard on Guernsey.

Private Bertie DE LA MARE (Plot IV.J.1) and his brother, Private Walter De La Mare, also fell in action on 1 December. Walter is commemorated on the memorial at Louverval. The boys had been adopted, but it would also appear from CWGC records that another brother, or step-brother, was also killed during the war; Private Alfred De La Mare is shown as living at St. Peter-in-the-

Wood on Guernsey, as is Bertie. Alfred was killed in action on 13 April 1918 and is commemorated on the Ploegsteert Memorial.

Finally, there are three holders of the MM buried in this cemetery:
Private Hanson FARRAR MM, 7th Norfolk Regiment, killed in action on 18 October 1918. (Plot II.A.12)
Corporal Alexander James DON MM, D Battery, 52 Brigade, Royal Field Artillery, killed in action on 16 May 1917. (Plot III.C.10)
Lance Corporal Theodore HOOK MM, 2nd South African Regiment, killed in action on 9 April 1917. (Plot III.H.17)

Fampoux British Cemetery

Fampoux British Cemetery can be found along the lane running north from the village's western edge. This track was known as York Lane, and on the opening day of battle in April 1917 it lay within the path of 12 Brigade, 4th Division, in particular that of the 2nd Essex Regiment and 2nd Lancashire Fusiliers.

Further along this track the 1st Somerset Light Infantry, 1st Hampshire Regiment and 1st East Lancashire Regiment carried the trenches south of the Point du Jour ridge, which lies at the end of the track. The CWGC register tells us that this cemetery was once known as Helena Trench cemetery and that it was made by the 34th and 4th Divisions between April and June 1917. Ten graves that projected into the roadway had to be re-located to the far end of the cemetery after the Armistice (now Row E), which gives Rows A–D their irregularity. Only eight of the 118 graves are unidentified.

It will come as no surprise to find casualties from 9 April, notably from the 2nd Essex Regiment with sixteen burials and the 1st Somerset Light Infantry with eight. The 1st Rifle Brigade, 2nd Lancashire Fusiliers and 1st Hampshire Regiment are also represented.

Private William SWAN, 2nd Essex Regiment, was killed in action on 9 April 1917, aged 24 (Plot A.2). His younger brother, Herbert Swan, who served with the 9th Essex Regiment, was also killed in action on the same day, aged 19, when his battalion successfully captured Feuchy Chapel Redoubt, about 3 miles south of here on the other side of the River Scarpe. He is buried in Feuchy Chapel British Cemetery.

Lieutenant Arthur Leslie George HIDER, 'A' Company, 8th South Staffordshire Regiment, was killed in action on 27 May 1917, aged 23. He was a former pupil of Westminster City School. His battalion was part of the 17th (Northern) Division, which has a small number of burials here from May 1917. (A.46)

Private William SMITH, 1st Royal Irish Fusiliers, was killed in action on 11 April 1917 and had previously been wounded in July 1916. Given the movements of his battalion on the Somme that month, this must have occurred in trenches somewhere between Auchonvillers and Serre on or within a few days of 1 July. He was killed in the failed attack on Roeux, a short distance to the east of this cemetery. (B.4)

Twelve men of the 2nd South African Regiment and five of the 4th South African Regiment who fell during their attack on 12 April lie buried here; this latter battalion also has one further burial from September 1917. A number of these men were veterans of the epic fighting at Delville Wood in July the previous year. Private Louis Gay VICE (B.26) and Private Charles Samuel FARMAN (B.13), both from the 2nd South African Regiment, were wounded there on 17 July. Lance Corporal Anthony Reginald TIDBURY (B.18), also from the 2nd South African Regiment, was wounded there the following day, and Private Edwin William GIBSON, 4th South African Regiment, was also wounded in the wood (B.21). Private Gordon SPIVEY, 2nd South African Regiment, who was killed in action on 12 April 1917, aged 22, was born in Hampstead and had joined up while studying at Edinburgh University (B.17). With the exception of two, all eighteen South Africans are buried in Row B.

As with several cemeteries in this area, burials here from 1918 are dominated by headstones from the Guards Division, all from the first three months of the year. The Guards Division moved to the Arras sector on 1 January 1918 following its heavy involvement in the fighting at Cambrai in late November and the first few days of December 1917. The division's battalions all comment on how quiet the sector was at the start of 1918 and the few casualties sustained, usually as a consequence of occasional shelling, were considered little more than unfortunate accidents.

Private George Shearlaw YOUNG, 'B' Company 1st Scots Guards, was killed in action on 27 February 1918, aged 21. The 1st Coldstream Guards carried out a raid on the night of 26/27 February and although the 1st Scots Guards were not directly involved in this, the battalion had carried out much of the preliminary patrolling and reconnaissance work for it. YOUNG may have been killed while patrolling, but could equally have been the victim of shelling or trench-mortar fire that day. He came from Corstorphine, Edinburgh, where he had been a gardener for the Earl of Rosebery at Dalmeny House, which is now a stylish country house hotel. (C.4)

By March 1918, however, things were about to change. During its tour of trench duty between 8 and 12 March, the 1st Scots Guards reported that the German trench mortars had been more active, especially against the forward posts held by 'C' Company. It was here that the battalion lost two men who were buried alive and who died before they could be dug out. The incident happened on 10 March and the bodies were eventually recovered on the 11th. The two men, Private James HENDERSON and Private James HAIR, were buried side by side where they remain to this day. (C.6 and C.7)

Captain Alexander Murray CRAIGMILE MC, 6th Rifle Brigade, attached 1st Battalion, was killed organizing a counter-attack on 29 March 1918 during the German March offensive, which in this sector began the previous day. CRAIGMILE was at the 1st Rifle Brigade's HQ when he took a telephone call from Lieutenant Cecil Norbert ETHERIDGE warning him that the Germans were closing in. ETHERIDGE was in a ruined dug-out some 50 yards away and reported that a German machine gun had just set up in the trench above his dug-out. He was just able to add that a German officer was calling down to him to surrender when the line went dead. CRAIGMILE was ordered to counter-attack and re-take the front trench which, as ETHERIDGE had reported, was now occupied by Germans.

An account of this incident was left by the adjutant of the 1st Rifle Brigade, Captain J.A. Dawson MC, who recalled: *'With a cheerful smile, old CRAIGMILE, got up and went off …'* CRAIGMILE was assisted by Captain Ernest William Marshall MC, 1st Somerset Light Infantry. Marshall survived this encounter, but was killed by shell fire on 22 April. He is now buried at Choques Military Cemetery. However, the efforts of both men were not in vain and the German advance was eventually halted. CRAIGMILE, who was 23 years old when he died, had been awarded his MC on 21 November 1916, but I can find no citation for it. (D.3) ETHERIDGE, who was also killed, presumably soon after making the telephone call, is now buried in the next row. (E.2)

Second Lieutenant Edward Jasper GRAY, 6th Rifle Brigade, was also killed in action, but on 31 March 1918, aged 20. He was shot through the head by a sniper. (E.1)

Small numbers of dead from the 51st (Highland) Division and the 34th Division, dating from the attack on Roeux on 23 April 1917, can also be found here. The latter division also has a few burials from June of that year.

Fampoux Communal Cemetery

There are just ten graves here from the Second World War; only four are identi-fied. Three of them are men of the 4th Yorkshire Regiment (Green Howards), including an officer, Second Lieutenant Hubert George Henry WINTERS-LADEN, who was killed in action on 24 May 1940, aged 21 (Grave 8). The fourth man is a private from the 2nd Wiltshire Regiment (Grave 10). The cemetery is located near the village church.

Sunken Road Cemetery, Fampoux

Sunken Road Cemetery is situated north of Fampoux on the rising ground above the village. As one travels east through Fampoux there are three lanes running north. The third soon splits into two. The left fork is the sunken road from which the cemetery gets its name and along which the 1st Royal Irish Fusiliers and 2nd Seaforth Highlanders set out to reach their jumping off positions for the ill-fated noon attack on 11 April 1917. After about 500 yards the lane again forks as it emerges into the open. The right fork was known to the British as North-umberland Lane, the left fork as Lincoln Lane; take the right fork and the cemetery lies just ahead of the memorial to the 2nd Seaforth Highlanders. It contains 196 burials, of which 171 are identified, though, strangely enough, none are men of the 1st Royal Irish Fusiliers or the 2nd Seaforth Highlanders. Its location is half way between the third objective, the Brown Line, and the final objective for 9 April, the Green Line, which lay about 1,000 yards to the east of the sunken lane.

East of the cemetery, about 350 yards away in the fields, and straddling the D42E, is the location of the German defensive position known as the Hyderabad Redoubt, captured on the first day by the 1st Rifle Brigade. Again, there are no casualties from this battalion buried in the cemetery from the first day's action, though five of its ranks who fell later that month are buried here. The D42E, which links Fampoux with Gavrelle, became known subsequently to the troops as Staffordshire Lane.

Burials from April, May and June 1917 come from a number of different divisions that fought in and around the Scarpe Valley during those months; the 4th Division, the 9th (Scottish) Division, the 34th Division, the 37th Division, and the 51st (Highland) Division are all represented, while July, August and September casualties come mainly from 17th (Northern) Division.

The last burials from 1917 are all from the 15th (Scottish) Division. The Guards Division makes up the small contingent of 1918 graves here, all of which are dated January. The men are from the 1st Grenadier Guards, 4th Grenadier Guards and the 2nd Scots Guards.

Second Lieutenant William Rawlinson Garside HOLLAND MC, 10th West Yorkshire Regiment, attached 50th Trench Mortar Battery, was killed in action on 18 September 1917, aged 24. His MC was gazetted on 16 August 1917 and was awarded for conspicuous gallantry and devotion to duty in handling his trench-mortar battery with great coolness and skill at a critical time when the enemy was threatening to rush our position. His mortars in the front line were under heavy fire at the time, but they still succeeded in inflicting great losses on the enemy. (Plot I.A.32)

Corporal Fred MARSDEN DCM MM, 7th Yorkshire Regiment, was killed in action on 18 September 1917, aged 24. His DCM was won as a lance corporal for conspicuous gallantry in action by rendering most valuable service as part of the battalion bombers and materially assisting in the consolidation of an exposed flank. The award was gazetted on 26 March 1917. He had previously served with the King's Own Yorkshire Light Infantry. (Plot I.A.34)

Private Thomas ORMEROD, Tank Corps, was killed in action on 5 October 1917 and had formerly served with the artillery (Plot I.C.25). His presence here is unusual, particularly as all significant operations, and certainly any involving tanks, were taking place at Ypres. The only other Tank Corps casualty from October 1917 buried anywhere near Arras is at Bucquoy Road Cemetery, Ficheux.

Corporal Frederick John WOOLF, 24th Battalion, London Regiment, was killed in action on 4 November 1917 (Plot I.D.26). His battalion was part of the 47th (London) Division. This division did not spend very long in this part of the line, but it was here during the late autumn of 1917 before the Battle of Cambrai. WOOLF was not killed by random circumstances, but in a large raid carried out on the afternoon of 4 November. He is the only casualty from that raid buried here and seems sadly isolated from the rest of his comrades, one of whom is buried in similar circumstances at Point du Jour Military Cemetery. A few more casualties from that day can be found in Naval Trench Cemetery a short distance away, though they are mainly from the 21st Battalion. Eleven men were killed in the actual raid; most are on the memorial at Arras.

Lieutenant Angus John Charles DODGSHON, 5th Gloucestershire Regiment, was killed in action on 10 November 1917 by shell fire, aged 22 (Plot I.D.27). He was the great-great grandson of Viscount Duncan of Camperdown and was an only son. He was born in Pembrokeshire and was educated at Wellington College. He was set to go to Trinity College, Cambridge, but the outbreak of war interrupted his studies, as it did in the case of many of his generation. He joined the Inns of Court OTC and was gazetted as a second lieutenant in the 2/5th Gloucestershire Regiment in October 1914. However, he did not accompany the battalion when it crossed to France as part of the 61st (2nd South Midland) Division in May 1916. After serving at home with the King's Own (Royal Lancaster Regiment), he eventually rejoined the 2/5th Gloucestershire Regiment in August 1917 near Ypres.

In November, the 61st Division moved south to the area around the River Scarpe and it was while his battalion was in this sector that he was killed by shell fire. In a letter to his parents, a fellow officer wrote that he had soon become popular with his peers and had often amused them by performing magic tricks; something at which he was obviously well accomplished, having been admitted as a member of the 'Magic Circle' in 1913. He is one of six men of the Gloucestershire Regiment buried here from three of its 2nd line Territorial battalions: the 2/4th, 2/5th and 2/6th Battalions.

This is perhaps a good point at which to highlight some of the other unusual casualties to be found in this cemetery. There are eight men of the Queen's Own (Royal West Kent Regiment) listed in the CWGC register as men of the 3/4th and the 2/4th Battalions. The one casualty shown as belonging to the 2/4th Battalion, Private W.L. GRIFFITHS, was serving with the 3/4th Battalion at the time of his death. This is certain because the 2/4th Battalion never served on the Western Front, though it did serve in Gallipoli and Egypt with the 53rd Division. The 3/4th Battalion, however, landed at Le Havre on 1 June 1917. Once in France it was attached for a few weeks to the 9th (Scottish) Division and the 34th Division before serving for a short time with the 17th (Northern) Division as its pioneer unit. It then became part of the division's 52 Brigade until disbanded in February the following year. These eight casualties fell between July and September 1917 and are therefore scattered across four different rows.

Second Lieutenant Henry Rodham COOK, 12th Manchester Regiment, was killed in action on 7 September 1917, aged 34, and was serving as the battalion's intelligence officer at the time of his death. (Plot I.E.17)

Corporal Daniel DOVER MM, 7/8th King's Own Scottish Borderers, was killed in action on 27 December 1917. He came from Burnley in Lancashire. *Soldiers Died in the Great War* does not show the award of the MM next to his name. He had fought on the Somme in 1916, at Arras in 1917, where he won his Military Medal, and at Ypres later the same year. He was killed in action while his battalion was holding trenches north of the River Scarpe. (Plot II.A.10)

Two of the five holders of the MM have already been referred to. The remaining three in this cemetery are:

Serjeant Sam MARTIN MM, 7th Lincolnshire Regiment; killed in action on 29 August 1917. He came from Ilkeston, Derbyshire, and was aged 22 when he died serving with 'B' Company. (Special Memorial A.5)

Private James McGARRY MM, 2/7th Royal Warwickshire Regiment, killed in action on 8 November 1917. He had formerly served with the Highland Cyclist Battalion and came from Dunfermline. (Plot I.D.21) The 182nd Brigade, which was part of the 61st (2nd South Midland) Division, was composed entirely of men from the 2/5th, 2/6th, 2/7th and 2/8th Royal Warwickshire Regiment and there are twenty of them buried here, including Private McGARRY, mainly in Plot I, Rows C and D and a few in Plot II. A few men of the 2/7th, 2/8th Worcestershire Regiment, the 2/4th Royal Berkshire Regiment and the 2/4th Oxfordshire & Buckinghamshire Light Infantry are buried here and were from the same division.

Lance Corporal William Frank LONG MM, 4th Grenadier Guards, killed in action on 6 January 1918 (Plot II.A.15). He and the two men buried next to him, Company Serjeant Major William Henry STRETEN (Plot II.A.13) and Serjeant C.G. HATTON (Plot II.A.14), were killed by an aerial torpedo. *Soldiers Died in the Great War* makes no reference to LONG's MM. The same publication lists neither STRETEN nor HATTON as serving with the Grenadier Guards.

Chili Trench Cemetery, Gavrelle

The cemetery lies about 1,500 yards north of Fampoux on the road out to Gavrelle. The road was known to troops as Staffordshire Lane and the German strongpoint, the Hyderabad Redoubt, lay across it about 500 yards south of the cemetery.

The village of Gavrelle was captured on 23 April 1917 by the 63rd (Royal Naval) Division, but was lost the following year, on 28 March, when the German offensive edged its way across much of the old 1917 battlefield. It was, however, recaptured by the 51st (Highland) Division on 27 August. The cemetery, also known at the time as Gavrelle Road, or Fampoux Cemetery, was begun in April and May 1917 and was mainly used by the 37th Division. A number of burials were destroyed by shell fire and eighty-six are now represented by special memorials. There are now 181 identified graves in total. The earliest casualties are from the opening days of the Battle of Arras, and are from either the 4th Division or the 9th (Scottish) Division, though they are few in number and half are in the form of special memorials.

Second Lieutenant Joseph Plumptre GILBERT, 4th Hampshire Regiment, was killed in action on 11 April 1917, aged 31. The 4th Battalion never served on the Western Front, but saw much active service in Mesopotamia, where one of its companies was present at the siege of Kut-al-Amara, and later in Northern Persia. GILBERT was almost certainly attached to the 1st Battalion, which was part of the 4th Division, and which saw action on 11 April immediately north of the River Scarpe. The 2nd Battalion was also in action that day, but south of the river near Monchy-le-Preux, supporting the 4th Worcestershire Regiment. Given the location of this cemetery, it is far more likely that he fell in action with the 1st rather than the 2nd Battalion. (Plot C.9)

Though the village of Gavrelle was captured by the 63rd (Royal Naval) Division, there is not a single member of that division buried here, though the date of its capture is prominent among the headstones of the 37th Division, which has fifty-eight burials here from 23 April. Most of these are from the 10th Royal Fusiliers with thirty-seven, followed equally by the 10th York & Lancaster Regiment and the 13th Royal Fusiliers, each with six. The latter has a further twelve men who fell here in the two days that followed.

The 28th April was another day of heavy fighting and yet again the 37th Division was committed to battle. A further fifty-nine headstones bear this date, mainly men of the 10th York & Lancaster Regiment with twenty-six, and the 8th Lincolnshire Regiment with twenty-one. The remainder come from the 6th Bedfordshire Regiment, the 13th Royal Fusiliers and the 10th West Yorkshire Regiment.

There are only a handful of burials from May 1917 and only two from 1918. Lieutenant Thomas Handing BROADLEY, 62 Squadron, Royal Air Force, was killed in action flying a Bristol F2B on 15 September 1918. (E.20) Next to him is his observer, Second Lieutenant Reginald Herbert DILLOWAY, aged 19. (E.19)

Lieutenant Harold George HUGHES MC, 197th Company, Machine Gun Corps, was killed in action on 4 May 1917. His MC was gazetted on 26 July 1917 and was awarded for conspicuous gallantry and devotion to duty during an advance under heavy fire in which he handled his four guns with great skill and courage. In doing so, he provided valuable assistance, leading to the capture of nineteen prisoners. (Special Memorial A.1)

Captain Douglas Alexander HALL, 10th York & Lancaster Regiment, was the son of Major Douglas Hall, 1st Life Guards. Born at Colchester cavalry barracks, he was educated at Oakham School, and when war broke out he joined the 5th Leicestershire Regiment. He was killed in action on 23 April 1917, aged 22, though *Officers Died in the Great War* shows his date of death as 25 April. (Special Memorial B.3)

Second Lieutenant Frederick William OSBORNE, 5th King's Royal Rifle Corps, attached 13th Battalion, was killed in action on 23 April 1917 (Special Memorial E.16). He was one of three officers from his battalion killed that day, and although the 13th King's Royal Rifle Corps reached the Gavrelle–Plouvain road, which was its final objective, its flanks were temporarily exposed until the 63rd (Royal Naval) Division on its left managed to capture Gavrelle. The battalion then remained there for several days, often under bombardment, during which several counter-attacks were made across its front as the Germans tried to recapture Gavrelle.

There are just two other gallantry award holders buried in this cemetery. They are:

Private Joseph TAYLOR MM, 8th Lincolnshire Regiment, killed 28 April 1917, aged 21. (A.1)

Corporal Thomas Henry CURL MM, 13th Royal Fusiliers, killed in action on 25 April 1917. *Soldiers Died in the Great War* makes no reference to his Military Medal. (A.14)

The cemetery also contains one RAF casualty from the Second World War. Flying Officer David Stuart Harold BURY, 111 Squadron, who had been head boy at Eton, was killed on 19 May 1940, aged 25. His squadron, which had been the first to fly Hurricanes in January 1938, was operating east of Cambrai that day, destroying at least four enemy aircraft, but losing BURY and one other man, Pilot Officer Iain Colin Moorwood, who is buried in the churchyard at Sains-les-Marquion. BURY's father, Captain Edmund William Bury, 11th King's Royal Rifle Corps, was killed in action on 5 December 1915 and is buried in Rue-Petillon Military Cemetery, Fleurbaix.

Naval Trench Cemetery, Gavrelle

The cemetery lies in fields to the west of Gavrelle, just south of the D950. It is reached via a track that runs off the Rue de Fampoux on the south side of the village.

Unlike nearby Chili Trench Cemetery, this one does mainly contain men of the 63rd (Royal Naval) Division, though the majority are not from the attack on Gavrelle on 23 April 1917. The division remained in this sector throughout the summer of 1917 and most of its burials relate to this later period. Petty Officer G.T. HALL MM, Hawke Battalion, is one of only two gallantry award holders buried in this cemetery and is one of just three casualties from the fighting at Gavrelle in April 1917. His MM was gazetted on 26 March 1917.

The cemetery derives its name from a support trench dug by the division while holding this area during the summer months of 1917. Thirty-five men from the division can be found here, all killed or died of wounds during July, August or September that year, including one officer, Lieutenant Austin Pugh COOK, 2nd Battalion, Royal Marine Light Infantry and one NCO, Corporal W. MARSDEN MM. This amounts to well over a half of the total casualties buried in this small battlefield cemetery.

One of the July casualties, Able Seaman Andrew Horn STIRLING, Hawke Battalion, who was killed in action on 29 July 1917 (D.8), lost a brother a year earlier. Serjeant Walter Gray Stirling was killed in action near Longueval on 20 July 1916 whilst serving with the 5th Cameronians. He is buried in Caterpillar Valley Cemetery.

Later burials from 1917 are from the London Regiment, mainly its 21st Battalion. The 47th (London) Division arrived in the Oppy–Gavrelle sector during the last week of September where it remained for two months before the Battle of Cambrai. The division had a fairly quiet time, but did carry out raids, the largest of which took place at 4.30pm on 4 November. The 23rd and 24th Battalions, London Regiment, carried out the operation, each using two companies, assisted by a demolition team of Royal Engineers. Total numbers involved amounted to around 500 men. Within ten minutes the units had penetrated the enemy's forward and support trenches on a frontage of about 1,000 yards where they caused havoc, even taking a German working party of between 150 and 200 by surprise. Some prisoners were taken, but most were killed; probably because the news had just been received that south London had been subjected to an air raid. An unknown number of Germans were burnt or buried alive after they refused to leave their dug-outs when called to surrender. The demolition parties destroyed at least nine dug-outs before everyone retired after a hectic but productive half an hour in the German lines. Before withdrawing, the Londoners left a sign reading: *'We'll teach you to bomb London'*.

It will be noted that none of the casualties buried here relate to either of the battalions involved, though eight members of the 21st Battalion were killed on the same day, almost certainly by shell fire when the Germans retaliated. Casualties for the 23rd and 24th Battalions on the day of the raid amounted to eleven men killed and forty-two wounded, including three officers.

There is also one Second World War grave; that of Captain Robert Duncan MILLER, 2nd Cameronians, who was killed in action on 21 May 1940 and who came from Liverpool. He was killed by small arms fire that evening after taking 'C' Company to defensive positions around Fresnes. The following day his battalion withdrew to Vimy Ridge. Casualties during this period were described as 'slight'. By 26 May his battalion was on the Ypres–Comines Canal in contact with the enemy where it came under increasing pressure the following day. A few days later, his battalion was involved ferrying men to the beach at Dunkirk, before boarding vessels for England. (Row C. Grave 1A)

Gavrelle Communal Cemetery

The cemetery houses just seven burials, and as with most of the communal cemeteries in this area, the graves are from the Second World War. There are four infantrymen, two artillerymen and one man from the Royal Army Ordnance Corps. All were killed during the latter part of May 1940, and though the date of death for two men of the 2nd Royal Inniskilling Fusiliers is shown as between 18 May and 8 June 1940, they are more likely to have died towards the end of May. The cemetery is on the Rue de Plouvain on the east side of the village.

Plouvain Communal Cemetery

There are just five Second World War burials in this cemetery. Two men, Lance-Sergeant Walter MITCHELSON (Grave 2) and Private Cecil Eric HAWKINS (Grave 3), both served with the 5th Yorkshire Regiment and died in action on 20 May 1940. Two of the remaining three, Private Arthur JENNINGS, 2nd Wiltshire Regiment (Grave 4), and Lance-Sergeant Francis QUINN, 2nd Royal Inniskilling Fusiliers (Grave 5), died three days later on 23 May. The final grave is that of Lance Corporal Robert MACMILLAN, also 2nd Royal Inniskilling Fusiliers (Grave 6), who died on 25 May 1940. The men are buried in two separate plots on the western side of the cemetery.

Brown's Copse Cemetery, Roeux

The cemetery lies to the south of the D42, just east of Fampoux. It can be seen from the road, but has to be accessed via the Rue des Etangs, then the Rue Saint-Hilaire. The track from this road to the cemetery is a dead end, but can be reached by vehicle.

Plots I to IV consist almost entirely of burials from the fighting to capture Roeux and Greenland Hill in spring 1917. In this sense it is a battlefield cemetery. However, after the Armistice 850 graves were brought in from areas north and east of here, and these now make up Plots V to VIII. Today, owing to its size, it resembles a concentration cemetery, though I never think of it as such.

This cemetery has a very Scottish character to it owing to a high proportion of burials from Scottish regiments from two divisions, the 9th (Scottish) and the 51st (Highland). Casualties from the 9th (Scottish) Division are mainly from 12 April 1917, while those of the 51st (Highland) Division relate principally to the fighting on 23 April. In total there are 533 burials from Scottish regiments, 488 of which are from the fighting that occurred in this locality between April and June 1917.

A notable feature of this cemetery is the number of officers and men buried here from the 2nd Seaforth Highlanders who, together with the 1st Royal Irish Fusiliers, made an unsuccessful attack on Roeux and Greenland Hill at midday on 11 April. The 2nd Seaforth Highlanders attacked with twelve officers and 420 other ranks, of which all twelve officers and 363 other ranks became casualties. Today, six officers and 113 other ranks are buried in this cemetery, representing a third of the battalion's casualties that day and almost a tenth of the total burials here. The 1st Royal Irish Fusiliers has fewer burials from this attack, just one officer and thirty-six other ranks.

All six officers of the 2nd Seaforth Highlanders are buried separately, strongly suggesting that their bodies were recovered and buried at different times. Among them is Glaswegian and former pupil of Fettes College, Lieutenant Donald MACKINTOSH VC. His father, Donald James Mackintosh MVO CB, held the rank of colonel and was Assistant Director of Medical Services for the Lowland Divisional Area of Scotland. Both father and son had attended Glasgow University.

MACKINTOSH, despite having been shot through the right leg and virtually crippled, led his men forward, capturing a trench. He then collected men from another company whose officers had become casualties and drove back an enemy counter-attack in which he was again wounded, this time to such an extent that he was unable to stand. Still, he remained with his men, who by this time numbered around fifteen. As their final objective had not yet been reached, he ordered them to prepare to advance. With great difficulty, he got out of the trench and was encouraging his men forward when he was again hit and fell mortally wounded, aged 21. (Plot II.C.49)

Second Lieutenant William DAWSON from Lanark (Plot I.E.36) and Second Lieutenant Robert Alexander Cameron MACMILLAN from Ullapool (Plot II.E.7), both 2nd Seaforth Highlanders, were killed the same day as Mackintosh, and were the sons of clergymen. MACMILLAN was one of seven children. He was an excellent academic and had won a bursary to the University of Glasgow, beginning his studies in 1901. He developed a passion for Philosophy and graduated with a First in 1904, having also won a number of other prizes and distinctions. He continued his studies, but turned down an Exhibition at Cambridge so as not to become a burden on his family after the death of his father. His studies took him to Germany, and then into the Church. After spending some time as a minister at Prestwick, he followed his family to South Africa, becoming a minister there. Throughout this time he was torn between the Church and an academic career. In 1912, having returned to Scotland, he gained his Doctorate in Philosophy at Glasgow University. His thesis on Kant was subsequently published and cemented his reputation within academic circles. The book was dedicated to his mother who lived just long enough to see it in print.

When war broke out he volunteered and became an army chaplain. Even this did not satisfy his conscience to 'do his bit', so he chose to enlist as a soldier, eventually receiving a commission in November 1916. His last letter was written from the battlefield at Arras, not long before the ill-fated attack on 11 April 1917. John Buchan, the novelist, was a family friend and spoke fondly of him at his memorial service. He had corresponded regularly with Buchan and his letters are now held in the Buchan Collection at the National Library of Scotland. His family also privately published a memoir of his life.

The remaining officers from the 2nd Seaforth Highlanders buried here are: Second Lieutenant George Thomson Dickson ALEXANDER, aged 22 (Plot I.D.42); Second Lieutenant Philip Cranstoun GROVE, aged 19 (Plot III.D.28), and Second Lieutenant Hugh Price ROSE, a former pupil at Sherborne School who had also studied at Oriel College, Oxford, and Sandhurst, aged 20. (Plot III.F.8)

The only officer from the 1st Royal Irish Fusiliers buried in this cemetery from 11 April is Second Lieutenant Gerald Somerville Yeats CULLEN, aged 19, and from Co. Kerry. He was also the son of clergy and had been with the battalion since the middle of July the previous year. (Plot III.D.6)

After the failures on 11 and 12 April to extend the gains of the opening day, and because only small gains had been made elsewhere on the battlefield, a decision was taken to suspend further offensive action until a more co-ordinated and much bigger effort could be made. It was obvious that the Germans had reacted swiftly and decisively to the opening day and now had fresh troops in good defensive positions ready to meet any further attempts to advance.

Further attempts were made to capture Greenland Hill and Roeux during the final week of April. The first attempt was on 23 April when the task was given to the 51st (Highland) Division as part of a collective attempt to renew the battle which involved eight other divisions attacking on a frontage of 10 miles between Fontaine-les-Croisilles in the south to Gavrelle in the north. Despite countless acts of gallantry, 23 April ended with very little to show other than a casualty roll of around 10,000.

The second attempt occurred a few days later when the 34th Division attempted to capture the same objectives that had eluded the Highlanders. It fared no better and the divisional history notes that twenty-one officers and 213 other ranks were killed in action between 21 and 30 April and that total casualties during this period, including all ranks, amounted to 2,644.

Roeux and Greenland Hill were again attacked at 3.45am on 3 May, this time by the 4th Division and the 9th (Scottish) Division. Their assault was part of another major effort along 16 miles of front aimed at capturing the ground between Arleux in the north to Bullecourt in the south, and particularly objectives not secured at the end of April. The results were again bitterly disappointing. The western edge of Roeux finally fell to the 4th Division in a renewed effort on 11 and 12 May. On the night of 13 May, the 51st (Highland) Division, which had relieved the 4th Division, discovered that the Germans had withdrawn and occupied the entire village the next day.

Among the 34th Division casualties buried here are sixty-five officers and men from its eight battalions of Northumberland Fusiliers, all killed in action on or around 28 April, including Second Lieutenant William Hast WESTHORP, 27th Battalion (Plot II.E.27), Second Lieutenant Douglas James BAKER, 24th Battalion (Plot II.E.48) and Captain John Joseph McCORMACK, 27th Battalion

(Plot III.E.22). There are relatively few from the other battalions of that division, but there are seventeen officers and men of the 11th Suffolk Regiment, all killed on 28 April, including Lieutenant Dudley Melville MILLER (Plot I A.33) and Second Lieutenant Hugh Stevenson GRAND (Plot I.D.29), aged 24, who had also been mentioned in despatches.

Corporal Robert DOUTHWAITE MM, 2nd South African Regiment, was killed in action on 12 April 1917, aged 36. He was wounded as a signaller during the fighting at Bernafay Wood in July 1916 and had been recommended for a DCM, though he was subsequently awarded the MM instead. He and two other men were the first South African recipients of the MM. (Plot I.A.2)

DOUTHWAITE is one of a 122 South African soldiers buried in this cemetery, all of whom were killed in action on 12 April. A number of these men were veterans of the bitter fighting at Delville Wood in July 1916, and some of them had been wounded there, including Private V.J.B. GIBB (Plot I.A.26), Private N. EDWARDS (Plot I.B.29), Lance Corporal John Norman Victor MIDDLETON, aged 19 (Plot I.B.30), and Second Lieutenant W.V. FORTH (Special Memorial I.C.26), all from the 2nd South African Regiment.

Also buried here are Serjeant John Charles HURLIN, 'B' Company, 1st South African Regiment (Plot II.A.42) and Private Christopher Guy PEMBERTON (Plot II.D.18), Private A.A. DAVIS (Plot II.B.27), Serjeant Philip Stephen O'DONOGHUE (Plot II.D.40), Private Percy James ROBINS (Plot II.H.2), Lance Corporal Percival WICKS (Plot III.B.35) and Private Gideon George PRINGLE MM, 'E' Company (Plot III.D.24), all belonging to the 2nd South African Regiment. Second Lieutenant Norman Wilhelm BEDDY, 2nd South African Regiment (Plot III.F.10), had also fought at Delville Wood in July 1916.

Captain Ernest Edgar Daniel GRADY, 'A' Company, 4th South African Regiment, had also served in German South-West Africa in 1914, and then in Egypt, before coming to the Western Front. Another veteran of the German South-West Africa campaign was Private James Chalmers EDMOND, 'A' Company, 2nd South African Regiment. According to the CWGC register, he had served there with the South African Irish Horse and had also seen action in the Boer Rebellion. GRADY had previously been mentioned in despatches and had been wounded at Delville Wood on 19 July 1916. Both men had Irish connections; GRADY was born at Longford in Ireland (Plot II.A.1) and EDMOND had parents who came from Belfast (Plot II.E.15).

Two of the South African casualties, Private Mathew Brown CAMPBELL, 4th South African Regiment (Plot II.D.33) and Private W. DUNN, 1st South African Regiment (Plot III.B.33), fell in action on 12 April, aged just 17. Buried nearby is Private H.G. IND MM, 2nd South African Regiment (Plot III.B.14), the third man from that battalion buried here with a gallantry award. The youngest casualty in the cemetery is Private William August TRANTER, 2nd South African Regiment (Plot III.D.44). He was killed on 12 April, aged 16.

Serjeant Joseph THOMAS DCM MM, 12th Royal Scots, was also killed in action on 12 April 1917, aged 29. His DCM was gazetted on 11 March 1916 and was awarded for conspicuous gallantry as a lance corporal when leading his section in a bombing attack in the face of heavy bomb and rifle fire, setting a fine example by his own personal courage, and holding on until the position was consolidated. (Plot I.A.9)

Lieutenant George Pringle SMITH, who is shown in the CWGC register as serving with the 14th Royal Scots, was killed in action on 12 April 1917. He was actually attached to the 11th Battalion at the time of his death. (Plot I.A.34)

Second Lieutenant Francis Johnston SMITH MC, 7th Gordon Highlanders, attached 6th Battalion, was born in Aberdeen on 25 November 1883 and studied Law at the university there. He enlisted on 25 January 1915, joining the 4th Gordon Highlanders, but some time later he was attached to the 6th Battalion. He gained his commission on 5 August 1916, which brought about a move to the regiment's 7th battalion. He won his MC in March 1917 and fell two months later on 16 May while leading his men in a counter-attack, which succeeded in re-taking the position. The citation for his MC was gazetted on 17 April 1917. It was awarded for an operation during which he was the first to enter the enemy's trench where he personally accounted for two of the enemy garrison. Throughout the operation he set a splendid example and its success was later attributed largely to his courage and leadership. (Plot I.C.39)

Private Duncan CAMERON, 1/7th Gordon Highlanders, was killed in action on 23 April 1917, aged 25. Sometime later his mother received several personal effects found on him when he died, among which were a religious book, a cigarette case and some photographs. His mother returned the last two items believing that they were not his. (Plot I.E.11)

Second Lieutenant Alfred Sydney Borlase SCHIFF, 1st Rifle Brigade, died on the opening day of the Battle of Arras. Having taken Hyderabad Redoubt, the battalion pushed out patrols and tried to establish a series of outposts beyond it, but came under sniper fire from Germans lying out in the open between the redoubt and the Roeux–Gavrelle road. A German machine gun was also operating from the inn situated on that road, no doubt encouraged by the fact that this part of the battlefield was not under fire from British artillery. SCHIFF was in the act of withdrawing his men back into the redoubt under fire when he was shot in the chest. He was 19 years of age and came from Chelsea, London. (Plot I.F.2)

Lieutenant George Canning Staples ARMSTRONG, 3rd Royal Irish Fusiliers, was killed in action on 3 May 1917, aged 29. He had joined the 1st Battalion two weeks before the opening of the Arras offensive. The CWGC register shows his parents resided at Farney Castle, the home of the Armstrong family since the beginning of the eighteenth century, though the castle goes back far longer with its earliest parts dating from just after the Norman Conquest. (Plot I.F.22)

Private James John SIMPSON, 4th South African Regiment, was killed in action on 12 April 1917, aged 28. The book by Ian Uys, *Delville Wood*, makes several references to SIMPSON. He became a 1st Class Lewis gunner in January 1917 and was a veteran of the fighting at Bernafay Wood and Delville Wood in July the previous year. Simpson left several graphic accounts of the fighting there, including how he was wounded in the left forearm on 16 July and how he had to make his way to a dressing station at Maricourt, a journey of six miles, during which he fainted three times. On one of those occasions he was given water by a wounded soldier of the Seaforth Highlanders which revived him. The Highlander appeared happy, as he had received a 'blighty'. Both men remained chatting to each other before SIMPSON decided to set off. He had only gone about 15 yards when a shell burst, killing his companion and leaving his body completely submerged in a shell hole with only the remains of his kilt visible. SIMPSON, fortunately, suffered no further injury and eventually made it to the dressing station. (Plot II.A.32)

A little further along from SIMPSON is Private Henry Braham EDWARDS, 1st South African Regiment. He was wounded at Delville Wood in July 1916 and also died in the South Africans' advance on 12 April 1917. (Plot II.A.37)

Second Lieutenant Hugh Charles ALLEN DCM, 7th Black Watch, was killed in action on 23 April 1917. He had won his DCM as a serjeant and his award was gazetted on 10 January 1917. It was awarded for conspicuous gallantry in action during which he led his platoon with great courage and initiative and, although wounded, he carried on until the capture of the enemy front line was completed. (Plot II.B.28)

Lance Corporal John BUCHANAN MM, 7th Black Watch, was killed in action on 23 April 1917. *Soldiers Died in the Great War* shows his death occurring on 25 April, as does the regimental history. This last source is surprising because the war diary for the battalion shows a comprehensive list of casualties and he is shown as having been killed in action, on 23 April. (Plot II.B.32)

Captain Menotti Campbell MacCORMAC, 7th Gordon Highlanders, was killed in action on 16 May 1917, aged 26. He had originally gone to France in September 1914 as a private with the 14th Battalion, London Regiment (London Scottish). He was then gazetted to the 7th Battalion Gordon Highlanders on 4 August 1915, though his death actually occurred while attached to the 5th Battalion. Judging by his army number it is entirely possible that he was present with the London Scottish during its heroic effort to assist the Cavalry Corps at Messines Ridge on 31 October 1914. (Plot II.C.1)

Corporal Charles Donald Paton EASTON, 7th Black Watch, was killed in action on 23 April 1917, aged 26. His brother, Private Stewart Macalister Easton, was killed in action on the opening day of the Battle of Loos, 25 September 1915, aged 23. He served with the 7th Royal Scots Fusiliers and is now commemorated on the Loos Memorial. (Plot II.C.50)

Second Lieutenant Harry Marslen BUSSEY, 3rd Royal Irish Fusiliers, attached 1st Battalion, was killed in action on 3 May 1917, aged 23, and had been with the battalion for less than a week. He enlisted in August 1914, serving initially with the Royal Fusiliers, and had been wounded twice previously; firstly near Armentières in the summer of 1915, and then in July 1916 on the Somme. His commission came in January 1917. (Plot II.F.7)

Second Lieutenant Hubert Leslie VILLE, 2nd Duke of Wellington's Regiment, was killed in action on 3 May 1917. He had been awarded the Order of St. George, 3rd Class (Russia). *Officers Died in the Great War* shows him under the surname 'Vile'. (Plot II.G.23)

Lieutenant Charles Hamilton Malise GRAHAM, 1st King's Own (Royal Lancaster Regiment) was killed in action on 17 May 1917 (Plot III.C.4). There is a note in the regimental history regarding him. On 3 February 1917 around twenty Germans dressed in white snow suits raided a sap. The skirmish lasted just seven minutes during which the enemy managed to secure four prisoners, all of whom managed to escape and return back to our lines. The raiders had three men killed and left one of their men wounded in the sap. As the remainder withdrew, four more were shot. Lieutenant GRAHAM then went out and brought in one of them.

His grandfather was the late General Sir S. James Graham KCB, who died on 11 May 1917, six days before his grandson. Charles's father, Lieutenant Colonel John Malise Anne Graham DSO and Bar, also served during the war. He began his military career in 1889 with a commission in the Royal Lancaster Regiment. During that career he took part in the Nile Expedition of 1899 where he served for a while as ADC to Kitchener, later Lord Kitchener of Khartoum. He was awarded his DSO in 1901 for services during the South African War. He retired in 1903, but volunteered to serve in the Great War. The Bar to his DSO was awarded in the New Year's Honours List 1918. He retired for the second time later that year.

Second Lieutenant William Marais Boupas TOOKE, 2nd South African Regiment, was killed in action on 12 April 1917 (Plot III.D.8). His brother, Second Lieutenant John Conrad Austin Tooke, also served in the 2nd South African Regiment and died of wounds on 17 June 1917, aged 21. He is buried at Étaples Military Cemetery.

Second Lieutenant Francis George McGIBNEY, 4th Royal Irish Fusiliers, attached 1st Battalion, was killed in action on 3 May 1917. He had only been with the battalion since 15 January 1917. (Plot III.D.11)

Lieutenant Leonard Arthur FULLER, 11 Squadron, Royal Flying Corps, was killed in action on 17 May 1917. His path to the Royal Flying Corps had been via the OTC at the University of London and the 8th Durham Light Infantry. He died in aerial combat by a shot to the head. (Plot III.D.13)

Second Lieutenant Thomas ELWORTHY, 1st King's Own (Royal Lancaster Regiment), was killed in action on 3 May 1917, aged 24, and had formerly served with the Royal Engineers (Plot III.E.30). His brother, Lieutenant Edward Pearce Elworthy, served with the 67th Field Company, Royal Engineers, in Gallipoli. He was killed in action on 9 May 1915 and is commemorated by a special memorial in Green Hill Cemetery.

Serjeant Albert Alexander BUCHAN, 7th Gordon Highlanders, was killed in action near Roeux on 23 April 1917 (Plot III.F.40). His brother, Ralph, died of wounds on 27 July 1917, also serving with the 7th Gordon Highlanders, and is buried at Dernancourt Communal Cemetery on the Somme. Two other brothers, Harry and Marshall served during the war; fortunately, they survived.

Serjeant William KELLY DCM, 6th King's Own Scottish Borderers, was killed in action on 6 June 1917, aged 31. His award was gazetted on 21 June 1916 and was won as a serjeant with the 8th Battalion for consistent good work, frequently carried out in dangerous situations. The citation singles out one occasion when he made a gallant attempt to rescue a wounded officer of another regiment. (Plot III.H.5)

Lieutenant George Ernest WALKER, 11th Royal Scots, died on the 6 June 1917 following a local operation that was the last attack made that year by the 11th and 12th Royal Scots on the Arras front. Each battalion had one officer killed in the attack, which began at 8pm on 5 June, and WALKER died the following day. The attack took place astride the Arras–Douai railway. Casualties were light, largely owing to a decision to wait for twenty seconds after the barrage began, which duped the Germans into believing that no infantry attack was about to take place. This allowed the five companies of Royal Scots to cross no man's land virtually unopposed. New posts were quickly established and the objectives successfully consolidated. (Plot III.H.19)

A small group of fourteen men from the 2nd Lancashire Fusiliers can be found scattered throughout Plots I, II and III. All were killed during an attack on 3 May 1917 in which the battalion's casualties amounted to seventeen other ranks killed, eighty-four wounded and 174 missing. Snipers and machine-gun positions hidden on the Arras-Douai railway embankment and in ruined buildings around Greenland Hill and the north end of Roeux made the Fusiliers' task virtually impossible to achieve.

Private Hubert Charles BARNFIELD MM, 2/5th Gloucestershire Regiment, was killed in action on 15 November 1917 according to the CWGC records. *Soldiers Died in the Great War* records his death as 5 November 1917 and it makes no reference to the award of his MM. (Plot IV.B.10)

It is also noticeable that between September and November 1917 there are burials from second line Territorial units. These belong to the 61st (2nd South Midland) Division. It arrived in France in late May the previous year, taking part in its first offensive action at Fromelles on 19 July 1916. It was then involved in operations on the Ancre in January 1917 and was even in action on 9 April 1917, but at Le Verguier at the southern end of the Hindenburg Line where the British Fourth Army was continuing to press the German withdrawal. Burials are from the 2/7th and 2/8th Worcestershire Regiment, the 2/5th, 2/6th, 2/7th and 2/8th Royal Warwickshire Regiment, the 2/4th, 2/5th and 2/6th Gloucestershire Regiment and the 2/4th Royal Berkshire Regiment.

Private James Arthur ROBERTS, 2/4th Gloucestershire Regiment, formerly South Staffordshire Regiment, was killed in action on 2 November 1917, aged 17. (Plot IV.B.15)

Corporal Arthur William MYHILL MM, 2/6th Gloucestershire Regiment, was killed in action on 24 October 1917, aged 30. He is listed in *Soldiers Died in the Great War* as serving with the 1/6th Battalion at the time of his death, which is not the case. (Plot IV.B.20)

Second Lieutenant William Charles WICKS MC, 4th Sherwood Foresters, attached 10th Battalion, was killed in action on 16 September 1917, aged 20. He had won his MC on 8 August 1917 during an enemy raid on trenches occupied by the 7th Lincolnshire Regiment astride the Arras–Douai railway line near Roeux. The enemy was driven back, but left behind seven boxes of explosives, indicating that the probable intention had been to destroy dug-outs and strongpoints. It was during the raid that Second Lieutenant WICKS killed three of the raiding party with his revolver after they had crept up to No.2 sap and wounded its occupants with bombs. The 7th Lincolnshire Regiment had ten men killed, twenty-five wounded and two remained unaccounted for and were presumed to have been taken prisoner. Sadly, WICKS was killed on 16 September 1917 during a raid carried out by his own battalion and the 12th Manchester Regiment. His MC was gazetted on 27 September 1917, but the citation was not published until 10 January 1918. (Plot V.E.5)

Captain Lionel Sydney PLATT, 57 Squadron, Royal Flying Corps, and his observer, Second Lieutenant Thomas MARGERISON, were both killed on 13 April 1917. PLATT was educated at Eton and Magdalen College, Oxford, before obtaining his commission in 17th (Duke of Cambridge's Own) Lancers in 1905. In 1913 he was appointed as adjutant with the Denbighshire Yeomanry and joined the Royal Flying Corps in September 1916. A month before his death he was gazetted as a flight commander (Plot V.F.4). MARGERISON, his observer, had originally joined the 1/1st Huntingdon Cyclist Battalion, but then transferred to the 5th East Yorkshire Regiment (Cyclist Battalion), with the rank of serjeant. In March 1915 he was gazetted and posted to the 2nd Huntingdon Cyclist Battalion. He later opted for more modern transport and joined the Royal

Flying Corps (Plot V.F.1). He and PLATT were attacked over Vitry-en-Artois on a reconnaissance mission and were shot down over enemy lines.

There are just two Canadian soldiers buried here. Private Frederick Gerald MERRITT (Plot VI.A.8) and Private James Forbes McDONALD (Plot VI.C.30), both from the 85th Battalion, Canadian Infantry, were meant to have been part of a blocking party for a raid planned for the night of 30 July 1918. However, the raid was abandoned owing to an error by our own artillery. The protecting barrage fell on the enemy's front line rather than its support trenches. The raiding party, lying out close to the enemy's wire, was caught in the barrage and had to be withdrawn to avoid casualties. Both men, however, were killed before the withdrawal, presumably from shelling, and several others were wounded.

Two of the Royal Flying Corps casualties are from 1916. Second Lieutenant Morton HAYNE was a pilot with 25 Squadron and was killed in action on 10 October, aged 18 (Plot VI.G.15). HAYNE's observer, Lieutenant A.H.M. Copeland, was taken prisoner. Lieutenant Arthur Lindsay Moore SHEPHERD, 11 Squadron, died of wounds as a prisoner on 3 November 1916, aged 25. (Plot VI.G.13)

The 7th Black Watch was again in action here in August 1918 along with the rest of the 51st (Highland) Division. Its role this time was to capture the tactically important points around Greenland Hill, Hausa Wood and Delbar Wood, east of Roeux, and so protect the left flank of the attacks being carried out south of the River Scarpe. Roeux, in particular, had caused huge problems on 11 April 1917 when its machine guns had been able to fire across the river valley at troops attacking Monchy-le-Preux, causing significant casualties. The lessons learned that year were not lost on those involved in the late summer of 1918.

On 24 August 1918 the 7th Black Watch attacked at 4.30am. The attack went well except for heavy fighting in the eastern part of the Hyderabad Redoubt, but this point was soon secured. The importance of this location is highlighted by the fact that the Germans made several counter-attacks that day to try to dislodge the battalion, followed by a further effort the following morning. Not only was this counter-attack repelled, but the 6th Black Watch also took the rest of the previous day's objectives.

During this fighting the 7th Black Watch had three of its officers killed, along with six other ranks, one of whom was Serjeant James ADAMS MM (Plot VII.A.6.), who was killed in action on 24 August. The regimental history shows ADAMS killed on 28 August 1918, and *Soldiers Died in the Great War* also shows his date of death as 28 August. However, 24 August, as given in the CWGC register, is the more likely date of the two.

According to the CWGC register, Private James B. KIDD, 4th Gordon Highlanders, was killed in action on 31 August 1916. If this were so, this would make him the only 1916 infantry casualty in this cemetery. However, according to *Soldiers Died in the Great War* he was killed in action on 31 August 1918. This latter date makes far more sense, since his battalion was in the Armentières sector at the end of August 1916; whereas, of course, at the end of August 1918 it was in action near Greenland Hill. (Plot VII.C.32)

All the Royal Flying Corps burials, of which there are nine, were brought here after the war from Vitry-en-Artois Communal Cemetery and German Extension, along with eight other soldiers. Among them were Captain Theodore Dawson ADAMS, 10 Squadron, Royal Flying Corps (Plot VII.E.36), and his pilot, Lieutenant Owen Vincent LE BAS, who is buried here with him (Plot VII.F.36). LE BAS had joined the Queen's (Royal West Surrey Regiment) on 31 July 1914 and went to France in September 1914. He was wounded at Langemarck later that year, but returned to the front on Christmas Eve 1914. He joined the Royal Flying Corps as an observer and returned to England in April 1915 in order to gain his pilot's certificate. He was then gazetted as a flying officer in August that year. Both men were killed in action over Douai on 7 November 1915. Captain ADAMS's father served as Senior Chaplain of the 57th (West Lancashire) Division.

Captain Charles Roydon BROWN MC, 1st Essex Regiment, was killed in action on 14 April 1917, aged 25. He had been commissioned from London University OTC in 1914 and had been previously wounded in 1915. He received his captaincy for distinguished service in the field with effect from 1 January 1916 and had also been mentioned in despatches. His MC was gazetted on 17 January 1917 showing him as serving with one of the service battalions of the Essex Regiment. He had served with both the 9th and 13th Battalions. (Special Memorial 4)

Second Lieutenant Richard Evison KIMBELL, 60 Squadron, Royal Flying Corps, was killed two days later on 16 April 1917, aged 19. He had formerly served with the 14th (King's) Hussars. (Special Memorial 5)

Also commemorated by way of a special memorial is Major Hubert Dunsterville HARVEY-KELLY DSO. He was an extremely colourful character. Originally reported as missing, it was later confirmed that he was killed in action on 29 April 1917, aged 26, shot down by Kurt Wolff. He had been seconded to the Royal Flying Corps in 1913 from the Royal Irish Regiment and in January 1916 he became a squadron commander, so he was a very experienced flyer. His DSO was gazetted on 23 February 1915 for services in the field and shows his regiment as the Royal Irish Regiment. He was the first British combatant to land in France when he deliberately touched down ahead of his squadron commander, Charles James Burke.

While flying during the Battle of Le Cateau he drove down an enemy plane. Not content, he landed his own aircraft, got out, and chased the German pilot on foot with his revolver before taking off again. The future British ace, James McCudden, disliked flying with him on account of his unpredictability. On another occasion, after overstaying his leave, the authorities made several enquiries at a number of addresses across England and Ireland where he was known to reside, as well as various haunts in London. Hearing of this, he decided, in typical fashion, that attack was the best form of defence. He bounced into the War Office pretending to be outraged and demanded to be posted back to France immediately. Few could have got away with such a stunt, but he was truly a one-off. (Special Memorial 7)

A further twelve holders of the MM can be found scattered throughout the cemetery. Of note are:

Serjeant William Thomas WILLIAMS MM MSM, 50th Field Ambulance, Royal Army Medical Corps, killed in action on 24 April 1917 (Plot I.G.35). *Soldiers Died in the Great War* shows his death on that date, but not in action or from wounds.

Private Sidney Hall STEVENSON MM, 10th Sherwood Foresters, killed in action on 16 September 1917. *Soldiers Died in the Great War* makes no reference to his MM. (Plot IV.B.60)

Private Sam PADGETT MM, 2nd Duke of Wellington's Regiment, killed in action on 23 March 1918, aged 22. He had been awarded the *Croix de Guerre* (Belgium). (Plot IV.C.29)

Level Crossing Cemetery, Fampoux

The cemetery lies on the south side of the village of Fampoux, just across the River Scarpe and next to the railway line. It was begun in June 1917, mainly to accommodate burials from the fighting south and east of the village during April and May. Even the casual visitor will become aware of the significantly high proportion of burials from Scottish regiments, which come to just over 55 per cent. Men from all three Scottish Divisions that took part in the Battle of Arras can be found here, though burials from the 15th (Scottish) Division are confined to the last four months of 1917 when it was holding the line rather than its earlier involvement in the Battle of Arras. There are 116 from this Division and ninety-eight from the 51st (Highland) Division, the majority of the latter being from the period prior to 23 April. In contrast, there are just six burials from the 9th (Scottish) Division.

The 23rd April 1917 is the date recorded on thirty headstones of the 9th Royal Scots and thirty-five officers and men of the 7th Argyll & Sutherland Highlanders are also buried here from the same attack against Roeux. There are a few casualties, too, belonging to the 34th Division from the final days of April, mainly from the 11th Suffolk Regiment, 10th Lincolnshire Regiment and the 16th Royal Scots.

In amongst the above units are small numbers of soldiers from the 17th (Northern) Division; men from the 6th Dorsetshire Regiment, 12th Manchester Regiment, 7th East Yorkshire Regiment, 8th South Staffordshire Regiment, 7th Border Regiment, 10th Sherwood Foresters, 7th Yorkshire Regiment, and the 51st Signal Company, Royal Engineers, as well as some from the 4th Division, particularly from the summer months.

The earliest burials, two privates from the Duke of Wellington's Regiment, are from 9 April 1917. The CWGC register shows Private Frank THOMPSON serving with the 5th Battalion, but this makes no sense, as neither the 1/5th nor the 2/5th Battalion was on this part of the battlefield on that day. The 1/5th Battalion, which was part of the 49th (West Riding) Division, was in Belgium at the time. A further confusion arises from the fact that the same soldier appears in *Soldiers Died in the Great War* as Frank 'Thomason', though I believe this is a typographical error. In the case of Private Clement SIMPSON, 2nd Battalion, he is shown in *Soldiers Died in the Great War* as having been killed in action on 9 May 1917 rather than 9 April. The 4th Division, to which the 2nd Battalion belonged, was in this sector in May 1917 and it remains difficult to decide which date is correct. The two are buried near each other. (Plot B.67 and 69)

Captain Douglas CUTBUSH MC, 5th Middlesex Regiment, attached 4th Battalion, was killed in action on 10 April 1917, aged 21. His MC was gazetted on 6 March 1917, a few weeks before his death. It was awarded for conspicuous gallantry in action after showing great courage and ability, reorganizing his company and consolidating a newly-won position under very heavy fire, setting a fine example to his men. (Plot I.A. 9)

Second Lieutenant Robert George Innes MAVOR MC, 7th Argyll & Sutherland Highlanders, was killed in action on 23 April 1917, aged 25. His MC was gazetted on 20 July 1917 and was awarded for conspicuous gallantry and devotion to duty, taking command of his company at a time when it was held up by machine-gun fire. He immediately re-organized it and led it to its final objective showing great skill in handling his men. (Plot I.A.11/16)

Private Douglas Eldred YOUNG, 10th York & Lancaster Regiment, had formerly served with the Royal Field Artillery. He was the son of Lieutenant Colonel Walter Douglas Young of Baltimore, USA, where Douglas also lived. He was born in Quebec, but had enlisted in Durham, England. He is one of four men buried here from his battalion, which was part of the 37th Division, and he was killed in action sometime between 9 and 12 April 1917. (Plot I.A.39)

Captain Patrick (Pat) Alexander BLAIR MC, 9th Royal Scots, was killed in action on 23 April 1917, aged 37. He was a chartered accountant by profession and his father was Sheriff of Lothian. His story as a company commander, and his relationship with his men, is told by Jonathan Nicholls in *Cheerful Sacrifice*. His MC was awarded posthumously and was gazetted on 4 June 1917 in the King's Birthday Honours List. (Plot I.B.1)

Lieutenant Simon Fraser ROSS, 4th Gordon Highlanders, was killed on 23 April 1917, aged 28, during the attack on Roeux. He had gained a Master's degree in Classics at Aberdeen University and was the son of a farmer. On the outbreak of war he had been in charge of a church mission in Canada, but by 1915 he had moved back to Scotland where he became a licensed probationer of the

Presbyterian Church of Scotland, showing great promise as a preacher while working around Elgin. His religious beliefs did not prevent him enlisting and in April 1915 he gained his commission. He was promoted in the field to lieutenant on 23 July 1916, having especially distinguished himself during fighting on the Somme where he was severely wounded. He spent much of his convalescence training recruits before they were sent off to the front. (Plot I.B.22)

Captain Alexander TAYLOR, 9th Royal Scots, was killed in action on 21 April 1917. Born at Carrickfergus, Co. Antrim, he held a Master's Degree, as well as a degree in Law, later working for the Sheriff's Office at Forfar. Prior to the main attack on Roeux and the Chemical Works on 23 April 1917, 'A' and 'C' Companies were tasked with capturing a trench that ran just west of Mount Pleasant Wood. They had tried to rush it on the 20th, but were immediately driven back by accurate machine-gun fire. The following day 'A' Company managed to secure the trench and establish a post on the corner of a small copse in front of the main wood. Unfortunately, this position was lost after the decision was taken to push on beyond the initial objective. TAYLOR's men were forced back to their original trenches having been badly cut up by rifle and machine-gun fire. TAYLOR was killed during this latter action. (Plot I.B.27)

Private George TEMPLETON, 9th Royal Scots, was killed in action on 22 April 1917, the day before many of his colleagues lost their lives. He had formerly served with the Lothian & Borders Horse and was one of six brothers who served during the war. Unlike George, the others served with the Seaforth Highlanders, three of them with the 6th Battalion, and unlike George they all survived. The family came from Grantown-on-Spey, Morayshire. (Plot I.B.73)

Lance Corporal George BAKER, 1st South African Regiment, came from Durban. He was killed in action on 12 April 1917 (Plot I.B.79). He was one of three privates who rescued Lieutenant Arthur Craig on 16 July 1916 during the fighting at Delville Wood. Craig was lying wounded in the open with most of his bombing party killed around him. Despite fierce machine-gun fire, Private Faulds went out and dragged Craig back to safety, assisted by Privates BAKER and Estment. BAKER was badly hit twice while doing so. According to CRAIG it took twenty-five minutes to drag him back over the barricade. The hail of machine-gun fire was so heavy that CRAIG later described how he had been hit twice in the left shoulder, his tunic was torn to shreds and all his equipment and his water bottle had been splintered to pieces.

Private Faulds, the man who had taken the lead in this daring rescue, was recommended for the Victoria Cross, which he was duly awarded. BAKER and Estment were recommended for the DCM, but were awarded the MM instead. Faulds went on to gain a commission and won the MC. In March 1918 he was wounded and taken prisoner. Sadly, BAKER was the only one of the four who did not survive and he was buried a month after his death once this part of the battlefield had been cleared. Thankfully, while researching this book, it became apparent that the CWGC record for BAKER did not show his MM, nor did his headstone. The CWGC has since kindly acknowledged the omission and has undertaken to rectify matters in due course. After ninety-three years unnoticed, their records now show his award. (Plot I.B.79)

Serjeant John CHRISTIE DCM, 51st Divisional Signal Company, Royal Engineers, was killed in action on 24 May 1917. His DCM was gazetted on 11 March 1916 and was awarded for conspicuous gallantry and good work on many occasions when repairing telephone wires under shell, machine-gun and rifle fire. He had previously served with the Argyll & Sutherland Highlanders. (Plot I.C.6)

Private Henry John MILSOM, 10th Field Ambulance, Royal Army Medical Corps, was killed in action on 15 June 1917 (Plot I.C.13). His brother, Arthur James Milsom, 8th Royal Warwickshire Regiment, is buried not far away in Valley Cemetery, near Vis-en-Artois, and died of wounds as a prisoner on 29 August 1916; his battalion was fighting on the Somme at the time.

Lieutenant Colonel Utten Lamont HOOKE, 3/4th Queen's (Royal West Surrey Regiment), was killed by a shell on 21 June 1917, aged 36 (Plot I.C.35).

Private J. CAMPBELL, 10th Cameronians, was accidentally shot by Private Frederick Albert Parrish, one of his comrades, on 10 October 1917 (Plot I.D.23). Parrish was later killed in action on 4 July 1918 while serving with the 9th Cameronians. He is buried at La Kreule Military Cemetery, Hazebrouck.

Serjeant Harry WILLIAMS DCM MM, 1st Royal Warwickshire Regiment, was killed in action on 21 June 1917, aged 23. His DCM was gazetted on 18 July 1917 and was awarded for conspicuous gallantry and devotion to duty when, exposed to heavy artillery and machine-gun fire, and in full view of the enemy, he carried on dressing the wounded and carried them to a place of safety showing total disregard for his own safety. (Plot I.E.13)

Second Lieutenant John Mcintyre SUTHERLAND, 9th Royal Scots, was killed in action on 23 April 1917, aged 37 (Plot I.E.21). After gaining an honours degree at Edinburgh University he went on to teach Classics at Glasgow Academy. Like Lieutenant Donald Mackintosh VC, he was educated at Fettes College, Edinburgh.

Second Lieutenant Charles Robert WILSON MC, 88th Company, Machine Gun Corps, was killed in action on 24 May 1917, aged 31, and came from Co. Dublin (Plot I.E.50). His MC was gazetted on 20 June 1917 and was awarded for conspicuous gallantry and devotion to duty, maintaining control of his guns throughout the entire operations, handling them very effectively, inflicting severe losses on the enemy and setting a splendid example of coolness and determination to all. His brother, Lieutenant Arthur Hone Wilson, 4th Royal Fusiliers, also fell while attached to the 7th Battalion. He died of wounds at Étaples on 18 November 1916, aged 21, and is buried at Étaples Military Cemetery.

Christmas 1917 was not kind to the 8th Seaforth Highlanders and several men who were killed between Christmas Eve and Hogmanay now lie here in Plot II, Rows B and C.

Privates Adam MITCHELL (Plot II.B.43), George Peter PEACE MM (Plot II.B.44) and Norman BEATON (Plot II.C.16) were killed in action on Christmas Eve 1917. Private James BIRNIE (Plot II.C.20) and Lance Corporal John MacRAE, aged 18 (Plot II.C.21) were killed on Christmas Day. The following day claimed the lives of Privates John James FAIRWEATHER (Plot II.C.14) and James FRASER (Plot II.C.15), while Private Thomas BOND was killed in action on 31 December 1917, aged 20 (Plot II.B.40).

Lieutenant George Smith Mitchell MILNE, 8/10th Gordon Highlanders, was killed in action on 14 October 1917, aged 23, while leading a daylight raid on enemy trenches near Fampoux. He was the only son of a draper, and another with a Master's degree from Aberdeen University where he had read Law and Economics. He was a native of Aberdeen and was educated at Aberdeen Grammar School before going on to university. On the outbreak of war he joined 'D' Company, 4th Gordon Highlanders, as a private, but in October 1914 he obtained a commission in the 10th Battalion. He served in France from October 1915 until August the following year when he returned to England with a view to joining the Royal Flying Corps. However, he was involved in an accident and his injuries curtailed his training. He returned to the 10th Gordon Highlanders in August 1917. (Plot II.C.32)

A further four holders of the MM are buried here:

Serjeant John TUNSTALL MM, 7th Argyll & Sutherland Highlanders, killed in action on 23 April 1917, aged 33. His MM is not shown in *Soldiers Died in the Great War*. (Plot I.A.60)

Corporal Alexander MILLER MM, 7th Argyll & Sutherland Highlanders, killed in action on 23 April 1917, aged 20. (Plot I.B.42)

Gunner Langham BISHOP MM, 221st Siege Battery, Royal Garrison Artillery; killed in action on 7 May 1917, aged 22. (Plot I.C.6)

Private Henry MASON MM, No.4 Company, 3rd Coldstream Guards, died of wounds on 17 January 1918, aged 33. He is one of twenty-nine men from the Guards Division buried here who fell during January, February and March 1918 and all five regiments are represented. (Plot II.B.37)

Roeux British Cemetery

All 319 officers and men buried here are 1917 casualties and almost all are from the months of April and May. This cemetery is therefore almost entirely connected with the Battle of Arras 1917. This is reflected in the three dates that recur on many of the headstones: 23 April, 28 April and 3 May 1917. Of these three dates, the 28th is the date that is most evident, followed by 3 May, and then 23 April. Headstones bearing these three dates cover nearly half of the cemetery, which lies about 250 yards along the same track as Crump Trench British Cemetery.

The dead are from several divisions, but predominantly from the 4th Division, the 34th Division and the 51st (Highland) Division. Although the 51st (Highland) Division was made up entirely of battalions from a number of Scottish regiments, Scottish battalions also served in the other two divisions; for example, the 2nd Seaforth Highlanders formed part of the 4th Division and the 15th and 16th Royal Scots were part of the 34th Division. This cemetery therefore has a very Scottish character to it, even more so if we take into account the Tyneside Scottish component of the 34th Division.

Second Lieutenant Thomas Geoffrey BOWER, Household Battalion, was killed in action on 3 May 1917. According to CWGC records, the cost of that day's action to the battalion was ninety-eight officers and men killed. The majority of them are now commemorated on the Arras Memorial, but twenty-two who were killed in action on 3 May, including BOWER, are buried in this cemetery or commemorated here by special memorials. (A.26)

Captain Robert James Armstrong DUNN, 4th Gordon Highlanders, was killed in action on 23 April 1917 during the attack on Roeux and the Chemical Works in what was the opening day of the Second Battle of the Scarpe. (A.50)

Serjeant Frank McGREGOR DCM, 8/10th Gordon Highlanders, was killed in action on 17 September 1917. His DCM was gazetted on 21 November 1917 and its citation on 7 February 1918. It was awarded for conspicuous gallantry and devotion to duty as acting serjeant after he found himself in the front line with troops falling back on either flank. He immediately organized a strongpoint and held on all day with about twenty men in spite of determined efforts by the enemy to dislodge him. After dark he went forward with an officer to try to clear out an enemy post. They were out for three hours, but found the post very strongly held. (A.65)

Company Serjeant Major John Simpson WILLOCKS MM, 9th Royal Scots, was killed in action on 27 May 1917, aged 26. Anyone who knew the veteran, Bill Hay, or who has read Jonathan Nicholl's book *Cheerful Sacrifice* will no doubt remember that there was a lot of animosity between Hay and WILLOCKS. Hay would often refer to him as 'B*ll*cks' in order to annoy him and recalled how the two of them almost came to blows in the assembly trench just before going over the top on the morning of 9 April 1917. WILLOCKS's MM was gazetted on 20 June 1917, less than a month after his death. (B.12)

Lieutenant David ANDERSON, 4th Gordon Highlanders, was killed in action on 23 April 1917, aged 23. He had been a law student at Aberdeen University and was the son of William Anderson OBE JP, who served as Chief Constable of Aberdeen between 1903 and 1932, having joined Aberdeen City Police in 1890. (B.14)

Private Thomas Halliday KEDDIE MM, 9th Royal Scots, was killed in action on 18 May 1917, aged 19. He is the youngest of the four holders of the MM buried in this cemetery, all of whom were Scotsmen serving in Scottish battalions. (B.23)

Private George TAYLOR, 2nd Seaforth Highlanders, was killed in action on 3 May 1917, aged 30. He came from Orkney and had enlisted on the mainland at Fort George, just outside Inverness. In the case of men like him, I always reflect on the likelihood that graves such as his may never have been visited by family and relatives. Even now, the journey from Orkney to Arras is not an easy one. After the Armistice the distance, cost and difficulty of travel from places such as Orkney to the Western Front would have proved prohibitive for many people, though the same could be said in the case of the families of Commonwealth soldiers. (B.25)

There are two brothers buried here: Private James BENSON (Special Memorial A.6) and Private John BENSON (B.32). Both men were killed in action on 3 May 1917, aged 22, serving with the 2nd Seaforth Highlanders. They were from Grangemouth, Scotland, and both had previously served with the Argyll & Sutherland Highlanders.

Second Lieutenant James Irvine TAYLOR MC, 10th Lincolnshire Regiment, was killed in action on 28 April 1917. He was the son of a clergyman and was a former pupil of Kingswood School. His MC was gazetted posthumously on 1 July 1917 and was awarded for conspicuous gallantry and devotion to duty in leading the remainder of his company to its objective, where he re-organized the company and consolidated its new position. He then went out on patrol and brought back valuable information. (C.10)

Private Donald SMITH, 2nd Seaforth Highlanders, was killed in action on 3 May 1917, aged 22. He was from Stornoway on the Isle of Lewis, where he enlisted (C.21). Lance Corporal Angus MacIVER, from the same battalion, was killed in action on the same day, aged 26, and also came from Stornoway, where he too had enlisted (D.38). The Lewis War Memorial carries the names of 1,150 men who lost their lives in the Great War out of 6,712 who are known to have served. The total population of Lewis, according to the 1911 census, was 29,603. Fatal casualties for the island as a percentage of those who served therefore amounted to 17 per cent. Even if today's modern and efficient methods of transport are taken into account, there are likely to be very few from Lewis who manage to get to the battlefields of France and Flanders in order to visit the graves of relatives.

There are two men buried in Row C: Private Eli JENKINS (C.16) and Private Albert JENKINS (C.30). Both men served with the 1st Somerset Light Infantry and were killed in action on 3 May 1917. The CWGC records give no clue as to whether they were related, but details in *Soldiers Died in the Great War* strongly suggest that they were not.

Private Robert Garden Forbes LIND MM, 4th Gordon Highlanders, was killed in action on 23 April 1917, aged 22 (C.57). The other three holders of that gallantry medal buried here are from the Royal Scots.

Lance Corporal Henry William HADDON, 10th Lincolnshire Regiment, was only 18 years of age when he was killed in action on 28 April 1917. He was from Kettering and was not one of the original 'Grimsby Chums'. (D.11)

Company Serjeant Major William Urquhart FERGUSON, 16th Royal Scots, was killed in action on 28 April 1917, aged 30. He had enlisted in December 1914 and was wounded on 1 July 1916 near La Boisselle. The wound to his arm had been sufficiently serious to ensure his return to 'Blighty', where he remained until December that year when he was again passed fit for service at the front. (D.40)

Corporal Thomas HOGG MM, 15th Royal Scots, was killed in action on 28 April 1917. HOGG had worked for *The Scotsman* newspaper before the war. (D.41)

Trooper Charles LE FEAVER, Household Battalion, was killed in action on 22 May 1917, aged 30 (D.28). His younger brother, Victor George Le Feaver, fell in action on 29 June 1916 whilst serving with the 8th East Kent Regiment (The Buffs), and is buried in Berks Cemetery Extension in Belgium.

Captain Christopher Cardew CODNER, 'A' Company, 1st Somerset Light Infantry, was killed in action on 3 May 1917, aged 22. Accounts of the fighting and the circumstances of his death were not easily pieced together after the events of that day and he was initially reported missing. The attack broke down almost as soon as it had begun. The battalion account states that the bombardment of Roeux Wood had not been sufficient enough to deal with the many machine guns hidden among its battered remnants and shell holes. The infantry had also experienced great difficulty locating these machine guns owing to the fact that it was still dark when the attack began at 3.45am. Reconnaissance of the area to be attacked had also been inadequate. Not only that, the maps issued were found to be inaccurate in respect of our positions close to the River Scarpe relative to the objectives to be attacked. When CODNER and his men left their trenches they initially advanced towards the river rather than their objectives, which lay to their left at a right angle. (D.52)

Private Alexander McNaughten FARQUHARSON, 9th Royal Scots, was a signaller with his battalion and was killed in action on 25 May 1917, aged 32. He was awarded a 1st Class Honours degree from Edinburgh University and had then gone on to obtain his Master's degree, picking up a prize as medallist in English Literature along the way. He was the eldest of four brothers who served during the war. (Special Memorial C.9)

Roeux Communal Cemetery
The men here are all Second World War casualties and around a third of the thirty casualties are unidentified. Of those identified, eleven are from the

2nd Wiltshire Regiment and there are also two Warrant Officers, Class II, from the 2nd Cameronians, along with four others from that battalion. Other casualties are from the 2nd Royal Inniskilling Fusiliers, 11th Durham Light Infantry and 1/9th Manchester Regiment. All were killed in action in May 1940, but most fell on or around 23 May. The date of death for three of the men is uncertain; in the case of Fusilier James ROBINSON that uncertainty extends to two weeks between 24 May and 4 June.

Another point to note is that this cemetery is not the one referred to in accounts of the fighting in April and May 1917. That cemetery was situated about 250 yards further west, near the crossroads in the centre of the village.

Crump Trench British Cemetery, Fampoux

The cemetery is located against an embankment on the west side of Roeux about 500 yards from the edge of the village and adjacent to the A.1 Autoroute. It is accessible by vehicle, but as the CWGC notes point out, the last 150 yards consists of a stretch of rough track that has to be covered on foot. From Roeux, take the road leading to Fampoux, and vice versa. The small track in question runs parallel to the embankment and is signposted.

The CWGC register notes that the cemetery was made by fighting units between April and August 1917. Until the village of Roeux was captured, Crump Trench became part of the new British front line once the position had been captured and consolidated on 11 and 12 April. Even after Roeux was captured a month later, the location was frequently shelled, and at the end of the war it was found that eighty-five graves had been destroyed by shell fire. The high proportion of unknown burials and the thirty-three special memorials to men believed to be buried here serve as testimony to the destruction caused by the German guns throughout 1917 following the Battle of Arras, and again in 1918, particularly at the end of March when the Germans re-took this position.

The first identifiable burial here is a soldier from the 9th Royal Scots who fell on 21 April 1917, followed by a further twenty-two casualties from the same division, the 51st (Highland) Division, as a result of the attack on 23 April. The majority of these are from the 7th Argyll & Sutherland Highlanders, with one casualty from that date from the 23rd Northumberland Fusiliers, part of the 34th Division. Other battalions from the 34th Division, such as the 20th and 26th Northumberland Fusiliers and the 10th Lincolnshire Regiment, have a few casualties here, but the 4th Division has rather more and these date between May and July 1917. The 1st Royal Warwickshire Regiment, the 1st Royal Irish Fusiliers, the 2nd Seaforth Highlanders and the Household Battalion, all from the 4th Division's 10 Brigade, are well represented, particularly around 3 May when there was a concerted effort to renew operations, and again throughout July when the division was holding the line.

There are quite a few casualties of interest among the 141 identified graves here. In spite of its location, it is well worth a visit.

Private Patrick Bernard McALEAVEY MM, 1st Royal Irish Fusiliers, formerly Royal Inniskilling Fusiliers, was killed while out with a working party on 11 July 1917. He had taken part in a raid a few weeks earlier on 24 June when his skill and gallantry in handling his Lewis gun earned him his MM. The raid had been a minor one, the purpose of which had been to capture a series of shell holes that the Germans had begun to organize into two defensive lines about 50 yards north of the most easterly buildings in Roeux. Some resistance was met beyond the first line of shell holes and it was here that McALEAVEY provided his support to the three officers and sixty other ranks who took part in the venture. One of the officers, Second Lieutenant Norman Eric Lloyd Fitt, was wounded and captured and died two days later. His body was never recovered after the war and he is commemorated on the Arras Memorial. McALEAVEY's MM was gazetted posthumously on 20 August 1917. (Plot I.A.5)

Second Lieutenant Thomas Douglas WILSON, 7th Argyll & Sutherland High-landers, was killed in action on 23 April 1917, aged 26. He had been a student at Fettes College in Edinburgh and served from July 1915. He had been wounded early on in the attack in which he was killed, but had insisted on remaining with his men. Though one of three children, he was the only son of Sir John Wilson of Airdrie, 1st Baronet, and Lady Wilson, his second wife. Sir John Wilson was the MP for Falkirk between 1895 and 1906 and had also held the position of Justice of the Peace in Fife, Glasgow and Lanarkshire before becoming Deputy Lieutenant of Lanarkshire. (Plot I.A.8)

Private Danson William YEOMAN, 1st East Lancashire Regiment, was killed in action on 22 June 1917, aged 19. The parental home is shown as Marsden Hall, Nelson, in Lancashire, which was quite a substantial house and sounds rather grand, though from local records it would appear that his family worked there in some capacity and had lodgings as part of their employment. (Plot I.A.18)

Second Lieutenant Dermot Jepsen HENRY, 5th Royal Irish Fusiliers, attached 1st Battalion, was killed in action on 9 July 1917, aged 24. He died in localised fighting on the northern outskirts of Roeux around some shell holes that were disputed by both sides long after the Battle of Arras had concluded. German trench mortar fire was reported as heavy that day and five other ranks lost their lives with a further ten wounded. (Plot I.C.29)

Captain Harry Eustace HERRICK, 1st Royal Irish Fusiliers, was killed in action on 11 May 1917. He had only been back with his battalion for a few days when he was killed. He was one of the original officers that had disembarked with the battalion on 23 August 1914. By mid-October that year HERRICK was in charge of his battalion's machine-gun section and he was involved in heavy fighting with it at Le Ruage on the 18th when the enemy made several attacks to the north and east of Houplines where his battalion was holding trenches. When his battalion was relieved the following day by the 1st Rifle Brigade, he and his machine-gun section remained behind in order to provide additional protection to the line. He was still in charge of the section when he was seriously wounded on 25 April 1915 during the Second Battle of Ypres. He had been away convalescing from those wounds for two years when he returned to his battalion only to be killed a few days later to the north-west of Roeux. (Plot I.C.33)

Second Lieutenant Claude Alexander HUSKISSON, 6th Hampshire Regiment, attached 1st Battalion, and Trench Mortar Battery, was killed in action on 15 June 1917, aged 22. His elder brother, Second Lieutenant Herbert George Huskisson, died of wounds on 27 January 1917 in Mesopotamia, aged 26, serving with the 6th Hampshire Regiment, and is buried at Amara War Cemetery. Their late father, Colonel John W. Huskisson, served in the Mediterranean and the East Indies as a second lieutenant with the Royal Marines before being promoted to the rank of lieutenant colonel in 1879. Claude's grandfather, Captain Thomas Huskisson, had served in the Royal Navy and had been in action at the Battle of Trafalgar. He ended his distinguished career as Paymaster of the Royal Navy. (Plot II.A.14)

Second Lieutenant Frederick Laurence HISLOP, 6th Argyll & Sutherland Highlanders, was 36 years old when he was killed in action on 23 April 1917. He studied at Glasgow University where he gained a Bachelor of Science degree and was a member of its OTC. He was gazetted in July 1916 and served briefly with the 14th Battalion, London Regiment (London Scottish) before transferring to the Argyll & Sutherland Highlanders. Though shown as 6th Battalion, he would have been attached to the 7th Battalion at the time of his death. (Plot II.B.13)

Captain Reginald Charles RUNDELL, General List, attached 10th Trench Mortar Battery, was killed in action on 3 May 1917, aged 22. He also held a Bachelor of Science degree and was initially gazetted in the Hampshire Regiment, but transferred in June 1916 to the General List from which he was posted to trench mortar duties. (Plot II.B.32)

Second Lieutenant John Edward LOWRIE, Household Battalion, was killed in action on 17 June 1917, aged 21. He is one of sixteen officers and men from the battalion buried here and a number of them are buried in this row, including two other officers. The battalion was formed using reservists from the Household Cavalry, and after a period of training and re-adjustment from cavalry to infantry, it went to France in November 1916 where it became part of 10 Brigade in the 4th Division. The Battle of Arras was its first heavy engagement in the war. Throughout much of April and May the battalion was in trenches very close to this cemetery. (Plot II.C.1)

Lieutenant William Launcelot Collier SHACKLETON, 26th Northumberland Fusiliers (Tyneside Irish), was killed in action on 24 April 1917. He was commissioned in the regiment on 21 December 1914 and went to France with his battalion in January 1916. In May that year he returned to England suffering from shell shock after being wounded, and so was not present with his battalion on the opening day of the Battle of the Somme. Having returned to France, he was again wounded during the attack on 23 April 1917. Once his wound had been dressed he returned to the action, but was mortally wounded the following day. (Plot II.C.3)

Second Lieutenant Cecil Vincent RICE, Household Battalion, was killed in action on 11 May 1917, aged 20 (Plot II.C.6). His brother, Sub-Lieutenant Eric Vyvyan Rice, Nelson Battalion, Royal Naval Volunteer Reserve, was killed in action at Gallipoli on 13 July 1915, aged 24, but has no known grave. He is commemorated on the Helles Memorial. Their father was Sir William Rice KB JP.

Second Lieutenant Norman BONHAM-CARTER, Household Battalion, was killed in action on 3 May 1917, aged 49 (Plot II.C.7). He was a keen cricketer who had played for Balliol College XI at Oxford and was a member of the MCC. He was also one of eleven children. One of his brothers, General Sir Charles Bonham-Carter CMG GCB, became Governor and Commander-in-Chief of Malta. Another brother, Sir Maurice Bonham-Carter, served as Private Secretary to Herbert Henry Asquith between 1910 and 1916, and in 1915 married his daughter, Helen Violet Asquith. Sir Maurice was the grandfather of the actress Helena Bonham-Carter, which makes Second Lieutenant Norman Bonham-Carter her great uncle.

Lieutenant Hugh Valentine GAMBLE, 2nd Seaforth Highlanders, was killed in action on 3 May 1917. He had been a scouting and signalling officer and had also served for a time in the capacity of Town Major, attached to HQ Staff. (Plot II.C.8)

Serjeant Adam Jackson BELL DCM, 2nd Seaforth Highlanders, was killed in action on 3 May 1917. His DCM was gazetted on 1 June 1916 and was awarded for conspicuous gallantry and devotion to duty when covering a working party with his bombers under heavy trench mortar fire and heavy bombing. For five hours he moved among his men, encouraging them, and when his relief arrived he volunteered to remain behind so that he could continue to help. (Plot II.C.9)

There are two more gallantry award holders buried here: Lance Serjeant William LAIDLAW MM, 10th Argyll & Sutherland Highlanders, killed in action on 12 June 1917. *Soldiers Died in the Great War* does not show the award of the MM next to his name (Plot II.A.7). Serjeant Robert STIRRAT MM, 2nd Seaforth Highlanders, was killed in action on 3 May 1917 (Plot II.C.13).

Lieutenant George DONALDSON, 6th Gordon Highlanders, was killed in action on 16 May 1917. Although he is one of only two men from that battalion buried in this cemetery, he is one of thirty-three men from it who fell that day as the attrition around Roeux continued. The Germans had chosen the same day to launch a counter-attack against Roeux and the Chemical Works, using a fresh division. The plan was to infiltrate along the north bank of the Scarpe and along the railway embankment before turning inwards on both flanks in an enveloping movement. The attack was preceded by a heavy bombardment. During the day the 6th Gordon Highlanders were involved in making a counter-attack with the 5th and 6th Seaforth Highlanders south of the Chemical works. (Special Memorial A.15)

Biache-Saint-Vaast Communal Cemetery

The village of Biache-Saint-Vaast sits a couple of miles east of Roeux, just beyond Plouvain. Most of the village is situated south of the Arras-Douai railway line, but a small section extends north of the line, which is where the communal cemetery can be found. The D.43 runs through Biache-Saint-Vaast from north to south and the cemetery lies about 300 yards north of the railway on this road.

There are two airmen from the Second World War buried here. One is Warrant Officer Dennis Cecil BURMAN, Royal New Zealand Air Force, who died on 16 August 1944 after his Spitfire was shot down. The other man, Flight Lieutenant Ian Scovil SODEN DSO, was killed in action on 18 May 1940 when his Hurricane was shot down over Vitry by a German ME 110. His DSO was gazetted on 28 June the same year and is worth citing in full:

This officer's flight was ordered to France at short notice and during two days he acted as leader in many combats against the enemy. He personally shot down five enemy aircraft and possibly two more, whilst his flight destroyed a further seven. On one occasion he attacked single-handed between fifty and sixty fighters, destroying one of them. One evening in May 1940, while his aerodrome was being heavily bombed, he jumped from a shelter trench and climbed into the nearest fighter air- craft, without knowing whether it was fully fuelled or armed, and took off from the aerodrome in smoke. Many delayed action bombs were present. He left the compara- tive safety to make a lone attack on a greatly superior force. The officer displayed great personal dash and courage and his personal influence made his flight into a determined fighting unit.

Chapter Two

A Couple of Poets – Saving Captain Cowan – 'Roodge Veen' and Grenadine

Bailleul Road West Cemetery, Saint-Laurent-Blangy

This CWGC register notes that the village of Saint-Laurent-Blangy adjoins the north-east side of Arras, which is really a way of saying that it now forms part of the town's suburban landscape. Directions for Saint-Laurent-Blangy are very evident on leaving Arras from the north or east sides of the town. I prefer to head out east and to pick up the D.60, which runs north-south through the village. Take the D.60 heading north and pass under the flyover, the D.950, and continue over the roundabout. The D.60 becomes the D.919 and about 400 yards further on the cemetery can be seen out to the left in the fields by two small copses. To reach it take the next left turn, then turn left again. The cemetery is about 250 yards down the track.

The cemetery consists largely of officers and men from three Scottish lowland regiments: the Royal Scots, the Cameronians and the King's Own Scottish Borderers. The majority of the Royal Scots are men of the 11th and 12th Battalions, though a few are from other battalions of the regiment. The 6th King's Own Scottish Borderers and the 9th Cameronians make up the other key element of this cemetery. These four battalions belonged to 27 Brigade, which was part of the 9th (Scottish) Division, and it was this division that had the honour of making the deepest penetration into the German lines on the opening day of the Battle of Arras. All of the burials here relate to 1917 and eighty-four of the ninety-three identified casualties are from 9 April. Although a very small cemetery, there are a number of individuals worthy of note, including some gallantry awards.

Second Lieutenant Maurice HILLIER, 6th King's Own Scottish Borderers, was killed in action on 9 April 1917, aged 19. He was educated at Stonyhurst, the renowned Catholic College, then at Downside School, followed by the Royal Military College, Sandhurst. He was gazetted in the King's Own Scottish Borderers in 1916. He was the son of Edward Guy Hillier CMG of Peking who worked for the Hong Kong and Shanghai Bank. Maurice's grandfather was Charles Batten Hillier, who had served as British Consul in Bangkok. (A.7)

Second Lieutenant John Mann GRANT DCM, 11th Royal Scots, was killed in action on 9 April 1917, aged 27. Prior to the war he had served as a corporal in the Ceylon Planters' Rifle Corps. His DCM was gazetted on 5 June 1916 while serving as a corporal. The very brief citation for the award appeared on the 22nd of that month and states that it was awarded for conspicuous and consistent good work and devotion to duty. His regiment is shown in both publications as the Ceylon Planters' Rifle Corps. (A.12)

Captain Thomas Whittle MARTIN MC, Royal Army Medical Corps, attached 11th Royal Scots, was killed in action on 9 April 1917. His MC was gazetted on 30 May 1917 and was awarded for conspicuous gallantry and devotion to duty, organizing the evacuation of wounded men across no man's land during operations, and it concludes by commenting that he had also done fine work on previous occasions. (B.1)

Serjeant James FINDLAY DCM, 6th King's Own Scottish Borderers, was killed in action on 9 April 1917. His DCM was won as a lance corporal and was awarded for conspicuous gallantry in action, displaying great courage and initiative during a raid against the enemy's trenches. During the raid he carried a wounded officer back to the point of entry, and he himself bombed an enemy dug-out. The award was gazetted on 6 March 1917. Unfortunately, *Soldiers Died in the Great War* makes no reference to the award next to his name. Battalion records suggest that most of the casualties in his battalion on 9 April were caused by our own artillery firing short, though in reality some of these casualties may equally have been caused by men keeping very close to our barrage. It is interesting to note that, in spite of this, the overall success of the division's advance that day was attributed to a good barrage. (B.8)

A further four men were awarded the MM: Corporal James ROBERTS MM, 9th Cameronians, killed in action on 9 April (A.16); Lance Corporal Robert RODON MM, 12th Royal Scots, killed in action on 9th April 1917. There is no note of the MM against RODON's name in *Soldiers Died in the Great War* (B.13). Serjeant Harry GRAY MM, 11th Royal Scots, killed in action on 9 April 1917 (B.20); Corporal John HAMILTON MM, 11th Royal Scots, killed in action on 9 April 1917 (B.25).

Finally, there are five men from the 12th King's Own Yorkshire Light Infantry buried here, one of whom is Serjeant Walter Gordon MACDONALD who had been mentioned in despatches (A.4). All five men were killed during the first couple of weeks in May 1917. The 12th King's Own Yorkshire Light Infantry was raised in Leeds in early September 1914 by the West Yorkshire Coal Owners' Association and until 1 July 1917 it was attached to the 31st Division as its pioneer battalion. From that date until the Armistice it was attached to Fifth Army and was employed specifically on the construction and maintenance of light railways.

Bailleul Road East Cemetery, Saint-Laurent-Blangy
This cemetery lies a short distance from the previous one. From Bailleul Road West Cemetery, pick up the D.919 again and head north towards Bailleul-Sir-

Berthoult. The cemetery is on the right hand side close to the German military cemetery of Saint-Laurant-Blangy, which contains or commemorates over 30,000 men. Although Bailleul Road East Cemetery sits firmly on the 1917 battlefield, it is a concentration cemetery and Plots II, III, IV and V reflect this. Row R, in Plot I, was added in August 1918 while this was still an active part of the front.

Bailleul Road East Cemetery contains 9 April casualties from every battalion of the 34th Division. All but thirteen of the 120 headstones bearing that date are from battalions of this division and the 22nd Northumberland Fusiliers (Tyneside Scottish) account for nearly a fifth of that total. The cemetery was begun by the 34th Division in April 1917, but it was used throughout that year by other divisions, and again after the war when several cemeteries were closed and a number of isolated graves were brought here. There are seven special memorials located near the War Stone adjacent to Plot I. These commemorate men whose graves were lost when Northumberland Cemetery, near Fampoux, was closed. Plot V tells a similar story in that some of its headstones carry the inscription: 'Buried near this spot'. One of these is probably the main reason why many visitors come to this cemetery. The poet, Isaac ROSENBERG, is one of the soldiers known to be buried here, but whose final resting place cannot be precisely located. He was killed in action on 1 April 1918, aged 27, while serving as a private with the 1st King's Own (Royal Lancaster Regiment). He was originally buried along with several other men by the Germans in a single makeshift grave, which was exhumed after the Armistice. (Special Memorial V.C.12)

Among those who fell on the opening day of the Battle of Arras are several officers and men from the 34th Division, some of whom hold gallantry awards. Second Lieutenant Walter Hamilton BRODIE, 15th Royal Scots, was killed in action, aged 25, on 9 April 1917 (Plot I.A.2). He is one of three officers from that regiment buried here, though one of them, Second Lieutenant John Gibson SPEEDIE, fell in June. SPEEDIE, who is buried in Plot V, Row A, had been awarded the French *Médaille Militaire*.

Buried near him is Serjeant Richard HARLEY MM, 11th Suffolk Regiment, who was killed in action on 9 April 1917 (Plot I.A.10). *Soldiers Died in the Great War* makes no reference to his MM. It also makes the same omission in respect of Lance Corporal John CONDON MM, 15th Royal Scots, who was also killed in action on 9 April. (Plot I.A.20)

Lance Corporal Victor Frederick PAMMENT DCM, 11th Suffolk Regiment, was killed in action on 9 April 1917. His DCM was gazetted on 25 September 1916 and was awarded for conspicuous gallantry as part of a machine-gun team. When the gun's commander had been wounded and its second-in-command killed, he collected up the gun and its spare parts and carried them forward unaided, firing the gun as he went. He was 22 years old when he died. (Plot I.A.16)

Two men of the Tyneside Scottish Brigade buried nearby also won the MM, Private Fred Harold GIBSON MM, 20th Northumberland Fusiliers (Plot I.A.28) and Lance Corporal Isaac WAUGH MM, 20th Northumberland Fusiliers (Plot I.D.23). Both men were killed in action on 9 April 1917. Again, *Soldiers Died in the Great War* fails to show the award against GIBSON's name.

Private John Henry Nixon GRAHAM, 21st Northumberland Fusiliers, was another soldier who was killed in action on 9 April 1917 (Plot I.A.31). The CWGC register tells us that he served under the alias 'Nixon'. His younger brother, Robert, was killed serving with the 15th Durham Light Infantry on 1 July 1916 and is buried at Gordon Dump Cemetery on the Somme, though he chose to serve under the surname of 'Graham'.

Second Lieutenant James Arthur HOPPER MC, 26th Northumberland Fusiliers (Tyneside Irish), was killed in action on 10 April 1917, aged 33. His MC was gazetted on 28 April 1917 and was awarded for conspicuous gallantry and devotion to duty after leaving the trenches in company with a NCO and penetrating the enemy lines, bringing back valuable information. His citation suggests that this was not unusual and that he had done similar fine work on previous occasions (Plot I.B.6).

The 24th Northumberland Fusiliers (Tyneside Irish) lost Company Serjeant Major Stephen O'NEILL DCM, on the opening day of the Arras offensive. His DCM was gazetted on 14 February 1917 and was awarded for conspicuous gallantry in action when he assisted another NCO in keeping a sap clear, thereby enabling a bomb post to be replenished with bombs. Later that day he assisted in extricating several buried men. (Plot I.B.8)

Privates Andrew FRASER (Plot I.B.29), George MILLER (Plot I.A.4), William Clayton JACKSON (Plot I.A.7) and Thomas THOMPSON (Plot I.B.17), all of whom served with the 16th Royal Scots, are shown respectively in the CWGC register as: '*He came from … Glasgow, Causewayhead in Stirlingshire, Halifax and Leith*'. This is very unusual and I can only presume that this information was provided by the battalion or regiment rather than their families. Normally, in the absence of any fixed address, the entry in the register is confined to nominal and regimental detail, date of death, and possibly age. All four were killed in action on 9 April 1917.

Among the 9th (Scottish) Division casualties in this cemetery are four men of the South African Brigade who were killed on 9 April 1917. Two of them, Lance Corporal Percy Venables WRIGHTSON and Private J.O. MEDLIN, 3rd South African Regiment, had been wounded at Delville Wood in July 1916; WRIGHTSON on 16 July (Plot I.A.8), MEDLIN on 15 July (Plot I.D.2). WRIGHTSON was 46 years old when he died.

Major Arthur Travers SAULEZ, D Battery, Royal Field Artillery, was killed in action by shell fire on 22 April 1917, aged 33. This was the day preceding the assault on Gavrelle and Roeux by the 63rd (Royal Naval) Division and the 51st (Highland) Division. The CWGC register shows that he had been twice mentioned in despatches and also refers to his brother, Captain Alfred Gordon Saulez, who died on 5 July 1921 while serving in Mesopotamia with the Royal Army Service Corps. He is buried in Baghdad (North Gate) War Cemetery.

Major SAULEZ was instrumental in assisting the infantry of the 4th Gordon Highlanders to progress beyond a troublesome part of the Blue Line that was being defended by a determined machine gunner. Although the artillery was working to a planned timetable, there was sufficient flexibility, according to the Official History, for local commanders to make some adjustments. SAULEZ, who was observing the infantry advance, spotted the enemy machine gunner, and using his discretion, made a telephone call to his battery. He was able to pinpoint the machine gunner and bring direct fire on to the position, destroying the post and eliminating the threat. His action greatly assisted the infantry and no doubt saved many lives that day. (Plot I.E.8)

SAULEZ is one of forty-eight men buried here who fell between 10 and 22 April. Surprisingly, one of them is a Newfoundlander killed in action on the 14th April in defence of Monchy-le-Preux, which lies on the other side of the River Scarpe and is some distance away. (Plot III.G.19)

There are a further thirty-nine burials between 23 April and the end of the month, including a 16-year-old soldier from Walsall, Private Edward Algernon SWINNERTON, 18th Durham Light Infantry. He died of wounds on 30 April 1917 and had formerly served with the Sherwood Foresters. (Plot I.F.8)

As with the soldier from the Newfoundland Regiment, the presence of thirteen Australians on this part of the battlefield is unexpected. They are scattered throughout the cemetery and all of them are infantrymen who fell between March and May 1917. They are almost certainly the ones referred to in the CWGC notes who were originally buried by the Germans in one of their cemeteries near Lagnicourt.

Second Lieutenant Arthur David FLETT, 16th Royal Scots, was killed in action on 9 April 1917 whilst leading a charge to destroy a machine-gun position operating from the railway cutting near Maison Blanche Wood (Plot I.G.1). The German machine gunners also displayed fine gallantry, fighting to the death as FLETT and Second Lieutenant Erik James Ptolemy Thurburn, who was aged just 19, closed in on them. After this gallant act they cleared several dug-outs and captured a number of prisoners. Neither FLETT nor Thurburn were decorated for their courage and leadership during this action. One of the dug-outs was being used as a dressing station, and when cleared it yielded a pleasant surprise; Captain Cowan, who had been taken prisoner during a raid two days earlier, was found safe and well. Some 125 men had taken part in the raid, carried out in order to secure identification and intelligence prior to the Battle of Arras, which resulted in the capture of three prisoners. Thurburn, attached to the

16th Royal Scots from the Cameronians, has no known grave and is commemorated on the Arras Memorial.

In Row N there are two holders of the MM: Lance-Serjeant Walter Moffat CARRICK MM, 18th Durham Light Infantry, killed in action on 28 June 1917 (Plot I.N.4), and, a little further along the row, Lance Corporal Frederick William STACEY MM, 14th Worcestershire Regiment, killed in action on 27 July 1917 (Plot I.N.12).

Private James Ross MOWAT, 6th Black Watch, was killed in action, aged 20, during an attack that took place on 20 August 1918. He had enlisted in October 1915 and had served with the Lovat Scouts before transferring to the 7th Cameron Highlanders. He had then contracted trench fever and spent some time in hospital before returning to the front in September 1917. The attack in which he was killed took place on the north-west slopes of Greenland Hill and was completely successful. (Plot I.R.4)

Lieutenant Francis Wycliffe RUSSELL MC, 16th Battalion, London Regiment (Queen's Westminster Rifles), was killed in action on 27 August 1918, aged 20. His MC was gazetted on 22 June 1918. He was educated at Marlborough College and had then obtained a scholarship to study at Christ Church College, Oxford. His father was a canon and the rector of Dedham in Essex, a village made famous through the works of John Constable, including its parish church, which he also painted. His MC was awarded for conspicuous gallantry and devotion to duty during an enemy attack. Despite being badly shaken by a bursting shell, he led his company with great skill, inspiring his men with confidence by his very fine example. When the trench in front of his position was captured by the enemy, he formed a bombing block in the communication trench, which halted the enemy's advance. He then organized a defensive post in front of the final defensive line and held it until the following day. (Plot II.B.9)

Another interesting feature of this cemetery is the presence of casualties from 1914 and 1915. None of these deaths occurred in the Arras area, as this sector of the Western Front was occupied by the French at that time. They were either buried originally by the Germans, or else they were recovered from isolated graves close to where they fell and brought here after the war. The majority of the 1915 casualties are from the Battle of Loos and are scattered across Plots II, III and IV. They include men from the 2nd Oxfordshire & Buckinghamshire Light Infantry, the 1/4th Lincolnshire Regiment, the 3rd Royal Fusiliers, the 1/5th Leicestershire Regiment, the 10th Highland Light Infantry, the 2nd Argyll & Sutherland Highlanders, the 2nd Cheshire Regiment, the 1/5th South Staffordshire Regiment, and the 1st Grenadier Guards.

The first of the 1914 casualties are to be found near the start of Plot II, Row C. These are two men of the 2nd Devonshire Regiment who fell during a local attack at Moated Grange, near Neuve Chapelle, carried out at 4.30pm on

18 December after a brief fifteen minute bombardment. Although the battalion gained some trenches to the east of the farm, its left flank was unable to negotiate our own wire and here it proved impossible to reach the German trenches. The German garrison in this part of the line was able to beat off the attack easily and inflict heavy losses. The attack was only partially successful and total casualties for the 2nd Devonshire Regiment amounted to six officers and 120 other ranks. Serjeant William WOOLACOTT and Private William Ernest BRAUND are buried next to each other. (Plot II.C.4 and 5)

Second Lieutenant Thomas Edward George DAVIS, 2nd Royal Welsh Fusiliers, was killed in action on 27 May 1917, aged 30. (Plot II.G.17) He was the son of a clergyman and was quite a colourful character. In his book *The War the Infantry Knew 1914–1919*, Captain J.C. Dunn describes a scene in the battalion mess at Lucheux in September 1916 where DAVIS, who was somewhat the worse for drink, shocked his commanding officer by claiming: '*I'm a bastard Saxon myself*'. Having drunk the last pint of champagne belonging to one of his fellow officers, DAVIS wiped his lips and commented with contempt: '*I don't like these light French wines. I prefer roodge veen (vin rouge) and grenadine to that.*' Dunn refers to him in the narrative using the variant spelling of 'Davies'.

DAVIS's battalion took part in an attack on 20th May 1917 to capture Fontaine-les-Croisilles, which lay between the River Sensée and a feature known as 'The Hump'. During this attack a little progress was made by the 5th Cameronians. They managed to capture a section of front trench in the Hindenburg Line between the Hump and the Sensée, but failed to take the Hump itself or Tunnel Trench. In the same attack, the 20th Royal Fusiliers also made slight progress towards Chérisy.

A week later, on Whit Sunday, 27 May, DAVIS took part in a repeat attack aimed at securing Tunnel Trench, which lay about 300 yards away on a reverse slope. In order to protect this position, the Germans had connected up a series of shell holes between the trench and the crest of the reverse slope. The attackers followed the creeping barrage, but a delay occurred as the 2nd Royal Welsh Fusiliers and the 5th Cameronians attempted to close a gap. This resulted in the barrage running away from them before they were able to reach the line of shell holes. When the garrison emerged from cover it reacted swiftly and effectively. It was here that DAVIS was killed, along with Captain Conning. Up to that point the few casualties had come mainly from our own barrage. The attack was already in difficulty, and once the barrage had lifted from Tunnel Trench, the Germans manned their parapet in numbers and the attack was met with even heavier fire. Total casualties among the 2nd Royal Welsh Fusiliers amounted to ten officers and 155 other ranks, half of whom lay dead.

After the failed attack a report was called for by Corps HQ. Lieutenant Colonel Chaplin, the commanding officer of the 5th Cameronians, admitted that his men had halted when they ran into our own barrage, but in their defence, he stated that this had occurred in order to steady the line. Unfortunately the order to halt had been misinterpreted by some as an order to retire. Courageously, he accepted that it was this fatal delay, rather than pressing on with the advance, that had cost the Royal Welsh Fusiliers so dearly. Captain Conning is buried in Croisilles British Cemetery. *The War the Infantry Knew 1914–1919*, which is arguably one of the best collective descriptions of life in and out of the trenches, gives an excellent account of the Welsh attack.

There are further pockets of 1914 casualties in Rows J and K. Private Patrick MACK, 2nd Leinster Regiment, is one of those early casualties. He was killed on 18 October 1914 in a little known action at Prémesques, near Armentières (Plot II.J.9). In the next row there are two casualties belonging to the 1st Devonshire Regiment who were killed in action on 24 and 25 October 1914 during the fierce fighting involving Smith-Dorrien's II Corps around Givenchy and La Bassée (Plot II.K.34 and 37).

Also among the 1914 dead are Lieutenant Ronald Cameron GUTHRIE-SMITH, 1st Highland Light Infantry, and six identified men of that battalion who were killed on 19 December near Givenchy. GUTHRIE-SMITH was blown up when one of a small number of mines was exploded by the Germans prior to launching a savage counter-attack to recover trenches. The 1st Highland Light Infantry, which was part of the Lahore Division, happened to be holding trenches around Givenchy between 19 and 22 December 1914. During that time it lost two officers, as well as fifty-five men killed and sixty-three others wounded. Perhaps even more telling is the fact that a further eight officers and 276 men were recorded as missing in action. No doubt a number of the missing were blown up or buried when the mines were fired, but the exceptionally fierce nature of the encounters in and around the new craters would also have left a good many unaccounted for as the fighting ebbed to-and fro and positions were repeatedly won and lost. Lieutenant GUTHRIE-SMITH's body was recovered after the war, as were the bodies of the other six men who are now buried in the same row next to him or nearby. (Plot II.N.7)

Second Lieutenant Richard Parry EVANS, 1st Royal Welsh Fusiliers, was killed in action on 14 May 1917 along with another subaltern, Second Lieutenant Lewis George Madley, and the Honourable Maurice Berkeley Peel MC and Bar, Chaplain 4th Class, Army Chaplains' Department. They and fourteen other ranks were killed when their battalion was called upon to try to push through Bullecourt village from a forming up point between the old German line and the village cross roads. 'B' and 'D' Companies gallantly tried to press home the attack at 2.10am but were stopped when they encountered a number of enemy strongpoints scattered among the ruins. Despite attempts to bombard these positions with rifle grenades and Stokes mortars, followed by a renewed attack by 'A' and 'C' Companies two hours later, no further progress could be made. The Honourable Maurice Berkeley Peel is buried at Quéant Road Cemetery, Buissy. Second Lieutenant Madley has no known grave and is commemorated on the

Arras Memorial. Another officer, Second Lieutenant Ralph Royds Brocklebank, who also took part in the attack and who subsequently died of wounds two days later, is buried Achiet-le-Grand Communal Cemetery Extension. Second Lieutenant EVANS is the only one buried here from that attack. (Plot III.E.5)

Serjeant Archie Randolph PEACHY MM, 14th Battalion, London Regiment (London Scottish), was killed during a successful operation that took place at dusk on 11 May 1917, aged 28 (Plot III.E.31). During the attack three companies of the London Scottish captured a German position, known as Tool Trench, just north of the Arras-Cambrai Road, while the 4th Battalion, London Regiment (Royal Fusiliers), simultaneously assaulted positions around Cavalry Farm. Both parties moved off at 8.30pm without a preparatory barrage, intending to catch the enemy off guard, which was exactly what happened. Rations for the garrison had just arrived and many of the defenders were found without weapons to hand. For the London Scottish, this was the last time it was engaged in operations around Arras that year. PEACHY was one of five officers and seventy other ranks killed during the second phase of this attack on 11 May by the 56th (London) Division. Most of the casualties occurred among 'D' Company, which overran its objective, which was largely a collection of shell holes that had been so badly damaged that the men had great difficult identifying the position. The company then came under machine-gun fire as it carried out the task of consolidation.

Private William C. RIGGINS DCM, 10/11th Highland Light Infantry, was killed in action on 11 April 1917. His DCM was gazetted on 14 March 1916 where the spelling of his surname is shown as 'RIGGENS'. It was awarded for conspicuous gallantry while serving as a lance corporal with the 10th Highland Light Infantry before its amalgamation with the 11th Battalion in May 1916. The citation records how RIGGINS had carried several messages under heavy fire. He had then tended to an officer who, as it turned out, was mortally wounded. Having dressed his wounds, he remained with him until he died. He then carried the news back to his commander. (Plot III.G.18)

It was mentioned earlier that most of the 1915 casualties are from the months of September and October and are mainly from battalions that were engaged at Loos. The two exceptions are a single casualty from the 2nd Devonshire Regiment, who was killed in action on 9 May 1915 at Aubers Ridge, and Captain Reginald George STRACEY, 1st Scots Guards, who was killed in action on 1 January 1915, aged 33. He fell at Cuinchy, near La Bassée, and had previously been mentioned in despatches. He was one of the original officers that had landed in France with the battalion on 14 August 1914 and had been involved in the desperate fighting to hold the line near Gheluvelt during the last few days of October at the First Battle of Ypres. It was there that he served as adjutant.

On 2 November he had a lucky escape when a shell burst close to him and he was buried alive for an hour and a half. The attack in which he was killed took place at night. Its objective was to recapture an observation post and a machine-gun emplacement. 'C' Company, under STRACEY, was given the task of securing the post, whilst 'B' Company's objective was to recover the gun emplacement. STRACEY and another officer were killed as they came under increasing machine-gun fire after crossing the nearby railway embankment. Although the Scots Guards managed to capture the positions, their right flank and the area to the rear of that flank were heavily exposed to enemy fire. After just an hour, it became increasingly obvious that the new situation was untenable and the battalion was forced to relinquish it before daylight. (Plot IV.F.3)

It is also worth pointing out the four men from the 2nd Royal Irish Regiment. Again, they fell in another of those half-forgotten encounters involving II Corps that seem to have been eclipsed by the First Battle of Ypres. Between 18 and 20 October 1914 the 2nd Royal Irish Regiment took part in fighting around the tiny hamlet of Le Pilly. Having captured the position, the battalion found itself in a small salient, which the Germans then pounded with shrapnel. When the Germans re-took the position they captured 302 prisoners, most of them wounded, and only one officer and 135 men remained after the fighting; too few to remain in the line. They returned to Saint-Omer where they were employed in securing lines of communication until the battalion could be replenished. The four men now buried here were killed in action on 19 October. One of them is Private Daniel CRONIN who was 17 years old when he died (Plot IV.J.2). The other three men are buried close by (Plot IV.J.3, 5 and 6).

Finally, there are two other gallantry award holders buried here. They are: Bombardier William DEEGAN MM, 10th Siege Battery, Royal Garrison Artillery, killed in action on 6 May 1917 (Plot I.H.12) and Serjeant Louis K. MASON MM, 2nd Royal Warwickshire Regiment, killed in action on 4 May 1917, aged 39 (Plot III.B.2).

Highland Cemetery, Roclincourt
The cemetery lies out in open fields to the north-east of the village of Roclincourt, just off the small road leading out to the village of Thélus. The easiest way to get there is to take the D.60. Whether coming from the direction of Écurie or from Saint-Laurent-Blangy and Arras, make for the crossroads in the centre of Roclincourt. If arriving from the former direction, turn left; if coming from the latter, turn right. After about 250 yards there is a track running off to the right and into fields. The track is driveable for part of the way, but it is best to stop before it begins to deteriorate, and in bad weather it may be advisable to avoid it altogether because of difficulties turning. The cemetery is reached by continuing down another small track that is definitely unsuitable for vehicles and which runs at right angles to the main one. In any case, the cemetery is clearly visible in the fields, unless exceptionally foggy.

The CWGC register points out that Roclincourt lay just behind the British lines in April 1917 and that the 51st (Highland) Division and the 34th Division attacked from the direction of the village on the opening day of the Battle of

Arras. It is easy to understand why the cemetery, made after the advance on 9 April, was originally called Roclincourt Forward Cemetery No.1 on account of its location. Graves belonging to the 51st (Highland) Division occupy most of Plot I, Rows A and C, as well as Plot II, Rows A and D. The CWGC register also notes that Plot I, Row B, and Plot II, Row C, were made after the Armistice when graves were brought in from the surrounding battlefield, and that Plot II, Row C contains soldiers from the Canadian Field Artillery and Canadian Railways Troops removed from Fond-de-Vase British Cemetery after the war, which was located about a mile east of Maroeuil.

Whilst many of the burials here are from the 51st (Highland) Division, there are also small numbers from the 4th Division and 9th (Scottish) Division, all of whom fell on or around 9 April 1917. Additional to these are a handful of casualties from the 2nd Division, the 34th Division and the 17th (Northern) Division, as well as thirty-three men of the Canadian Expeditionary Force.

Private William James MIDDLETON, 6th Gordon Highlanders, was killed in action on 9 April 1917, aged 20 (Plot I.A.15). His brother, Private John Middleton, had also enlisted in the same battalion, but it would appear that the two became split up at some later stage. According to *Soldiers Died in the Great War*, John was killed in action on 18 June 1915, aged 21, serving with the 7th Battalion. He is commemorated on the Le Touret Memorial near Neuve Chapelle. Together the brothers had walked the few miles to Aboyne from the family home at Tarland in order to enlist. William MIDDLETON is one of forty-eight Gordon Highlanders buried in this cemetery and all except two are casualties from 9 April. The majority, like MIDDLETON, are from the 6th Battalion and all except one are buried in Plot I, Row A.

Captain John Spence GRANT MC, 6th Gordon Highlanders, was killed in action on 9 April 1917, aged 27. His MC was gazetted on 16 November 1916 and was awarded to him as a second lieutenant for conspicuous gallantry on 22 September that year when he carried out reconnaissance work and took part in a daring raid on an enemy trench, and later rendered valuable assistance in getting the wounded back. He was a popular and well-respected officer who had studied at Aberdeen University before the war, adding a Master's degree to his Bachelor of Divinity degree. Prior to enlistment in 1915, he had practised his ministry at Broughty Ferry near Dundee. He had served with his battalion throughout the Somme fighting in 1916. (Plot I.A.47)

Buried in Plot I, Row B are sixteen men from the South African Brigade; all of its four infantry regiments are represented and all were killed in action on 9 April 1917. At the beginning of the row is Second Lieutenant William DORWARD, 4th South African Regiment, aged 36 (Plot I.B.1). His parents were from Dundee, Scotland, but he was from Cape Town. Further along is Major Howard Church SYMMES, 2nd South African Regiment (Plot I.B.45), and Lance Corporal Harry BOTTERILL MM, also of the 2nd South African Regiment (Plot I.B.50). His was one of twenty-seven MMs gazetted to men of the South African Brigade on 22 January 1917. The South African Brigade had seven of its officers killed in action on 9 April; the remaining five are to be found scattered among four other cemeteries, none of which are too far away. They are Point du Jour Military Cemetery, Mindel Trench British Cemetery, Sainte-Catherine British Cemetery and Saint-Nicolas British Cemetery.

Company Serjeant Major John Thomas MORRISON DCM, 9th Cameronians, was killed in action on 9 April 1917, aged 28. His DCM was gazetted on 26 March 1917 and was awarded for conspicuous gallantry during a raid on the enemy's trenches. He had taken a mobile charge into the enemy's second line to destroy a concrete machine-gun emplacement, which he carried out successfully, and was one of the last men to leave the enemy's trenches. Sadly, his is another example of *Soldiers Died in the Great War* failing to show the award next to his name. (Plot I.B.21)

Captain Geoffrey Laird JACKSON, 1st Rifle Brigade, died of his wounds on 9 April 1917, aged 23. He had previously been mentioned in despatches. He was wounded near Hyderabad Redoubt commanding 'B' Company as it pushed through to the redoubt on the afternoon of the opening day of the Battle of Arras. He died between the Regimental Aid Post and the Advanced Dressing Station. He had fought with the battalion as a second lieutenant at the Second Battle of Ypres and also served as the battalion's adjutant while on the Somme in 1916. (Plot I.B.37)

Plot I, Row B also contains other 4th Division casualties, including men of the 1st Hampshire Regiment, the 1st East Lancashire Regiment and the 1st Somerset Light Infantry. A few graves further along is Serjeant Andrew BUTTERS MM, 9th Northumberland Fusiliers, who was killed in action on 16 May 1917 (Plot I.B.42).

There are just two casualties from 1918 and both men are buried in Plot I, Row B. One is a lance corporal from the 9th Battalion, British West Indies Regiment, killed in action in October (Plot I.B.31), the other is a private from the 7/8th King's Own Scottish Borderers, killed at the end of May (Plot I.B.46). Several battalions of the British West Indies Regiment served on the Western Front as troops for securing lines of communication and as pioneers, but others went on to serve in Italy and Palestine, while the 1st Battalion served in the Cameroons and the 2nd Battalion served in the East African Campaign.

Second Lieutenant Basil Herbert LAST, 17th Middlesex Regiment, was killed in action on 23 April 1917. His battalion was part of the 2nd Division. He had originally enlisted in the 16th Battalion, London Regiment (Queen's West-minster Rifles), in 1914 (Plot I.C.53). Next to him is another officer from that division; Second Lieutenant James Charles BLYTH, 5th King's Royal Rifle Corps, attached 1st Battalion. BLYTH was educated at Eton and University College, Oxford. He was gazetted in the King's Royal Rifle Corps in March 1916 and was posted to the 1st Battalion in August that year. He was killed in action by a shell on 13 April 1917 during the capture of Bailleul-Sir-Berthoult. Although the village was taken without much opposition, the battalion came under heavy shell fire while crossing the ridge near to the railway cutting. His father was Lieutenant Colonel Blyth, who lived in Norfolk Street, just off Park Lane, London, and at Brawith Hall, Thirsk, although the CWGC also shows an address in Iver in Buckinghamshire (Plot I.C.52).

The cemetery also contains eleven men from the Canadian Railway Troops who were killed in action on 4 April 1917. They are buried consecutively (Plot II.C.48 to 58). The men were part of the 5th Battalion, Canadian Railway Troops, which suffered thirty-eight casualties when a single high explosive shell fell amongst them, killing twelve. The twelfth casualty, Sapper Frank Cochrane Hermiston, is commemorated on the Canadian National Memorial at Vimy Ridge.

Second Lieutenant Alexander James DAVIDSON, 4th Seaforth Highlanders, was killed on 8 April 1917, aged 30, during the final preparations for the opening of the Battle of Arras (Plot II.D.3). Chronologically, he is the first of the 120 identified casualties from the Seaforth Highlanders buried in this cemetery, 117 of whom were killed in action the following day. The majority are from the 6th Battalion, but eighteen of them are 5th Battalion men. Apart from DAVID-SON, there are two other 4th Battalion men buried here, as well as two from the 9th Seaforth Highlanders who died in early May 1917. The 9th Battalion was the pioneer battalion of the 15th (Scottish) Division and not part of the 51st (Highland) Division like the other three.

There are further burials from the 51st (Highland) Division and, as well as the familiar date of 9 April 1917, it will be noted that a number of headstones relate to 17 March 1917. This was the date of a second large-scale raid by the 51st (Highland) Division that was carried out by the 8th Argyll & Sutherland Highlanders. It followed a raid a fortnight earlier on 5 March by the 6th Gordon Highlanders. Both raids were carried out primarily to gather information on the garrison opposite and its defences, but they were also intended to cause as much damage as possible. Not only was the raid on the 17th larger in terms of the number of men involved; 378 other ranks compared with 303, but the intention was to remain in the enemy lines longer in order to ensure sufficient time for destruction and mayhem. Both raids were highly organized affairs in which officers and men were allotted specific objectives. Gallon cans of petrol were hurled down into the dug-outs, followed by phosphorous bombs, all with a view to killing those inside. High explosive ammonal charges, each weighing 20lbs, were then used to blow in dug-out entrances.

The first raid had yielded much information, including the location of a large dug-out used as some kind of administrative headquarters and also as an officers' mess. This was designated as a specific objective for the Argyll & Sutherland Highlanders. The second raid proved more costly than the first; casualties amounted to eight officers and 102 other ranks, though most were described as lightly wounded, compared with six and forty-eight in the earlier raid. Today there are eleven men of the 8th Argyll & Sutherland Highlanders buried here who fell during that raid on 17 March 1917, including two officers. They are all buried in Plot II, Row A, but are not buried consecutively.

Such raids were always controversial, and yet a third raid carried out on 31 March by the 6th Black Watch showed the extent to which these highly aggressive tactics had begun to have an effect on the garrison. The enemy trenches and positions were found to be more lightly held than before, no doubt owing to the extensive damage to dug-outs and the number of casualties already suffered during the previous two raids. It was also learned that many of the traverses in the German trenches had been loop-holed. As the raiders made their way through the trench system they were fired at from close quarters through these apertures. Likewise, it was discovered that dug-out entrances often had traverses that had been similarly loop-holed.

The lesson drawn from this latest raid was that movement above the trenches in the open was now preferable to moving through them, and so on 9 April the same trenches were crossed, and crossed successfully, by moving above them in the open. Furthermore, the experience of advancing behind a creeping barrage during the raids provided valuable preparation for the day of the actual offensive when the tactic was again used.

Serjeant Charles Stewart MACKENZIE, 6th Seaforth Highlanders, was reputedly killed while trying to protect a comrade who had been wounded in a bayonet fight. In doing so, MACKENZIE was also bayoneted as he tried to save the man's life. He had also been wounded previously and had spent some time in hospital back in Scotland where the medical staff treating him had decided to amputate his arm. MACKENZIE thought otherwise and went on to make a good recovery. The story is included in the superb book by Derek Bird, *The Spirit of our Troops is Excellent: a history of the 6th (Morayshire) Battalion, Seaforth Highlanders 1914–1919*. A footnote in the book tells how MACKENZIE's great grandson, a musician, wrote a lament as a tribute to his memory entitled, *Sergeant Mackenzie*, which was subsequently featured in the film, *We Were Soldiers*. (Plot II.D.29)

Écurie Communal Cemetery
There are seven burials in this cemetery. Four of them, a signalman with the 5th Division and three privates from the 6th Seaforth Highlanders, were all killed in the fighting around Arras during the last week of May 1940.

Sergeant (Flight Engineer) Maurice John TAYLOR, 427 Squadron, Royal Canadian Air Force, was killed in action on the night of 12/13 June 1944. Three of the squadron's Halifax bombers failed to make it to the target area near Arras, though his aircraft must have come close. Enemy night-fighter activity had been intense on way to the target, and again on the return journey as far as the coast. However, twelve of the squadron's Halifax bombers did return safely from the mission and Royal Air Force records indicate that the raid was carried out with a reasonable degree of accuracy. The Arras raid was one of several that took place that night, involving a total of 671 aircraft. A number of targets had been selected in and around the towns of Poitiers, Caen, Amiens, and Cambrai, mainly railway yards and infrastructure. He and the four men referred to above can be found east of the main path.

To the west of the main path are two Welsh Guardsmen. Guardsmen Gwyn WILLIAMS and William Joseph WILLIAMS, 2nd Welsh Guards, fell on 1 September 1944.

Roclincourt Military Cemetery

The cemetery lies within the village of Roclincourt itself. At the centre of the village is a crossroads where the D.60 meets the Rue d'Arras and the Rue de Thélus, which is now set out as a small roundabout. About 150 yards down from this junction along the Rue d'Arras is a small turning known as the Voie des Croix. The cemetery lies at the end of this small road where there is sufficient space to both park and turn.

At the start of the Battle of Arras it lay just behind the front, close to where the 51st (Highland) Division and 34th Division sectors met and both divisions made use of the existing French cemetery to bury their dead. The French graves were re-located after the war to allow space for the present day cemetery to be laid out.

The 31st Division also used this cemetery for burials, particularly the 12th York & Lancaster Regiment (Sheffield Pals), the 13th and 14th York & Lancaster Regiment (1st and 2nd Barnsley Pals) and the 10th, 11th, 12th and 13th East Yorkshire Regiment (1st, 2nd, 3rd and 4th Hull Battalions). Burials from these units run between September 1917 and February 1918. Smaller numbers of men from the 2/4th and 2/5th York & Lancaster Regiment can also be found here; both of these battalions formed part of the 62nd (West Riding) Division. The York & Lancaster Regiment has a combined total of fifty-three burials in this cemetery and the four battalions of the East Yorkshire Regiment have forty-one.

There are also ninety-eight Canadian soldiers buried here. On 9 April 1917 the right flank of the Canadian Corps was not far from where this cemetery is situated and yet, in spite of the proximity, there are only two Canadians buried here who were killed on 9 April and only a handful from March 1917. Prior to the opening of the Battle of Arras each division already had pre-designated locations for burials and the cemetery at Roclincourt lay within the 51st (Highland) Division's sector rather than that of the Canadian Corps. The vast majority of Canadian burials in this cemetery are actually from April 1918 and can be found in Plots IV, V and VI.

This cemetery also contains a rich array of supporting arms; among the Royal Engineer units we have members of the Tunnelling, Signalling, Railway, and Special Companies. There are also men of the Royal Army Medical Corps, the

Royal Army Veterinary Corps, the Army Chaplain's Department, the Royal Air Force, the Royal Field Artillery and Divisional Ammunition Trains. One such soldier is Serjeant Ernest George PASK, Army Veterinary Corps, attached 170 Brigade, Royal Field Artillery, who died on 5 June 1917, aged 50 (Plot I.C.21). There is also one member of the Tank Corps buried here; Private John Charles CLAREY, 11th Battalion, Tank Corps, died of wounds on 1 April 1918, aged 24. He had previously served with 2nd King Edward's Horse and had also campaigned in British East Africa (Plot V.B.21).

Second Lieutenant James Alison Wilson ADAMS, 'A' Company, 9th Royal Scots, was killed when he was shot through the head while climbing out of the assembly trench at the start of the attack on 9 April 1917 (Plot I.A.41). He was 19 years old and that was his first time in action. Not far away from him lies fellow officer, Second Lieutenant William 'Bill' Percival FERGUSON, also 9th Royal Scots, who was killed on the same day, aged 21 (Plot I.A.4). He was gazetted on 9 July 1915 and had gone to France exactly a year later. Though he had only been abroad on active service for nine months, this was his ninth time in action. Like ADAMS, he was immediately shot as he was climbing out of his trench. Some of their men who fell that day are also buried in Plot I within rows A and B.

Lieutenant Colonel Edward William HERMON DSO, 1st King Edward's Horse, commanding the 24th Northumberland Fusiliers (Tyneside Irish), is one of two battalion commanders buried in this cemetery (Plot I.B.1). He was shot through the chest on 9 April 1917 as he was moving his Battalion HQ across no man's land and following up the advance of his men. An Old Etonian, who went on to Christ Church, Oxford, he left his studies to join the 7th (Queen's Own) Hussars and served in the Boer War from its outbreak. After that he left the regular army and served with the Special Reserve unit, King Edward's Horse. During his military career he was mentioned in despatches on three occasions and his DSO was awarded posthumously for services in the field in the *London Gazette* dated 4 June 1917 as part of the King's Birthday Honours List. He is one of forty-nine identified casualties belonging to either the Tyneside Scottish (102 Brigade, 34th Division), or the Tyneside Irish (103 Brigade, 34th Division), who now rest here after losing their lives on 9 April or in the days either side of it.

Second Lieutenant John Sherbrooke RICHARDSON, 26th Northumberland Fusiliers, was also killed in action on 9 April 1917 and is one of several officers from the Tyneside Irish Brigade killed that day and buried in this cemetery. (Plot I.B.2)

Second Lieutenant George REID, 6th Gordon Highlanders, had served in 'U' Company at Aberdeen University between 1910 and 1914 and went with the 4th Battalion to France when it proceeded there in February 1915. He was wounded in April, and again on 25 September that year at Loos, and was subsequently killed in action on 9 April 1917, aged 25. The grave reference in the CWGC register should show the row as 'B' and not '11'. (Plot I.B.3)

Captain John Archibald AINSLIE, 2nd King's Own Scottish Borderers, had spent most of the war with the regiment's 1st Battalion and was serving in India at the outbreak of war. He was transferred to the 2nd Battalion only three weeks before his death, which occurred on 19 May 1917. He was killed by the same random shell that killed Captain Wilfred Walter LAURIE, who was just 19 years old. AINSLIE had fought with the 1st King's Own Scottish Borderers at 'Y' Beach in Gallipoli and was wounded on 8 May 1915 while supporting an attack near Gully Ravine. He was also the only company commander to have survived the attack by the 1st Battalion near Beaumont Hamel on 1 July 1916; in fact, he was credited with saving many lives that day by directing survivors back to their own trenches across the narrowest section of no man's land after the attack had broken down. AINSLIE and LAURIE are now buried next to each other. (Plot I.C.2 and 3)

Second Lieutenant Frederic Stanley FARMER, 14th Worcestershire Regiment, was mortally wounded on 20 July 1917 when he was hit by a shell as he was supervising a working party. His battalion, which was the pioneer battalion attached to the 31st Division, was based at Saint-Nicolas, a suburb of Arras, from where it provided working parties throughout July to September 1917. The same shell burst also blinded one of the men with him. Even outside a major action, the work of a pioneer battalion was never risk-free, as illustrated by the casualty return for the 14th Worcestershire Regiment in July 1917, which shows seven officers and men killed and twenty-four wounded. (Plot I.D.14)

Second Lieutenant Thomas JACK, who was killed on 9 April 1917, is shown serving with the 6th Royal Scots, but is more likely to have been attached to either the 8th Battalion (Pioneers) or the 9th Battalion. In May 1916 the 6th Battalion merged with the 7th Battalion to form the composite 6/7th Battalion, which was part of the 15th (Scottish) Division. This division fought on the opening day of the Battle of Arras, but south of the River Scarpe, and also included the regiment's 13th Battalion. The regiment's 11th and 12th Battalions were also in action that day with the 9th (Scottish) Division not very far from Roclincourt. (Plot II.A.17)

Second Lieutenant Thomas Bryson WADDELL, 5th Seaforth Highlanders, attached 4th Battalion, was killed in action on the 8th April 1917. He is one of thirty-eight men from the 4th, 5th and 6th Seaforth Highlanders buried here who were killed on 9 April or on a day either side. After graduating from Glasgow University in 1912 with a Bachelor of Science degree, he became a teacher at Dornoch Academy, Sutherland. He enlisted in Glasgow and served with the 14th Argyll & Sutherland Highlanders before obtaining his commission. (Plot II.A.27)

Plot II contains three officers from the Tyneside Irish Brigade who were killed in action on 9 April 1917. Second Lieutenant Henry John JAMES, 24th Northumberland Fusiliers, had served as a serjeant with the regiment's 13th Battalion before being commissioned in January 1917. He was killed in action, aged 34 (Plot II.A.11). A few graves further along is Captain Thomas Watkin BLOTT, 24th Northumberland Fusiliers, who was also killed in action at the age of 34 (Plot II.A.15). Second Lieutenant Harold LECKENBY, 'C' Company, 26th Northumberland Fusiliers, had been commissioned in late January 1916 and served with the battalion on the Somme the previous year. He was not present on 1 July, but joined the battalion on 8 July as the 34th Division began the process of replacing the heavy losses incurred near La Boisselle on the opening day of the Battle of the Somme (Plot II.A.39).

Captain Percy East LONES, 5th Field Ambulance, Royal Army Medical Corps, was killed near Oppy when a shell hit the aid post where he was working on 28 April 1917. He had previously been a member of the University of London OTC. (Plot II.B.11)

Lieutenant Arthur Robert Dick BACON, 1st Royal Berkshire Regiment, was killed in action on 25 April 1917. He and six other men from his battalion were killed in heavy shelling that day and another officer and six other ranks were wounded. He was one of the first pupils to attend the Imperial Services College at Windsor and had been a member of its OTC. Whilst out of the line, his battalion had been providing working parties for salvage duties around Roclincourt. (Plot II.B.12)

Second Lieutenant Stanley Ferns JEFFCOAT, 22nd Royal Fusiliers, was killed in action on 29 April 1917 during operations against the German defences around Oppy. His battalion was one of four Royal Fusilier battalions that took part in the attack, the 17th Battalion supporting the 24th, whilst the 23rd Battalion supported the 22nd. JEFFCOAT and his men came up against dense wire, as well as heavy machine-gun fire, and as casualties began to mount, JEFFCOAT, who had only recently joined the battalion, found a gap in the wire. Gathering up a few men, he led them into the enemy's trench. Throughout the morning, and assisted by some men of the 63rd (Royal Naval) Division, he led his party along the trench, bombing as he went forward. Despite having to dispute almost every traverse, he led his party along a considerable length of the trench, clearing it entirely. His initiative, leadership and courage that day enabled his battalion to achieve all of its objectives south of Oppy Wood. However, he was mortally wounded later on and died the same day. Although recommended for the VC, his gallantry was never acknowledged by the award of any decoration. (Plot II.B.17)

The Reverend Albert Thomas VERYARD, Chaplain 4th Class, attached to 15th Trench Mortar Battery, was killed in action on 28 June 1917. (Plot II.C.9)

Captain Douglas Cumming Paget KINDERSLEY DSO, described as a quiet man with a dry sense of humour, was killed in action on 22 June 1917, aged 45. Although originally commissioned in the Highland Light Infantry, he was killed while serving with the 2nd King's Own Scottish Borderers and had been attached to that battalion for some time. He was one of only two experienced officers remaining after the 2nd King's Own Scottish Borderers had made its successful attack on Morval on 25 September 1916 where it captured 700 prisoners. That success paved the way for the French to capture Frégicourt the following day, which in turn led to the fall of Combles. His DSO was awarded in connection with actions on 9 April 1917 when he showed courageous leadership and dash in clearing a captured German trench at the point of the bayonet. He had also been awarded the French *Croix de Guerre*, almost certainly in connection with the September operations on the Somme in conjunction with French forces. (Plot II.C.10)

Serjeant Joseph MANDEVILLE DCM MM, 1st Cheshire Regiment, was killed in action on 4 August 1917. His DCM was awarded while commanding his platoon and leading it with the utmost gallantry and skill, keeping up the spirits of his men by his unfailing cheerfulness and personal example. The citation notes that he then spent the whole of the following night searching for, and successfully bringing in all the dead from no man's land. (Plot II.D.2)

Second Lieutenant John Henry LAWRENCE, 3rd Duke of Cornwall's Light Infantry, attached 2nd Battalion, was killed in action on 20 August 1917, aged 20. Although the CWGC register shows him attached to the 2nd Battalion, he was actually killed serving with the 1st Battalion, which formed part of the 5th Division and which did spend time in this sector. The 2nd Battalion did go to France with the 27th Division in December 1914, but it moved to Salonika eleven months later. The man buried next to him, Serjeant James HAINES MM, was killed on the same day serving with the 1st Battalion. (Plot II.D.23 and 24)

At the beginning of Row F are two men who were killed in action on Christmas Day 1917. Second Lieutenant Laurence METCALFE is shown as serving with the 16th West Yorkshire Regiment at the time of his death. Second Lieutenant Edwin Lane STUCKEY is shown with the 17th Battalion, London Regiment (Poplar and Stepney Rifles), but was attached to the 4th Battalion, London Regiment (Royal Fusiliers), when he died, aged 20. The two officers are buried side by side (Plot II.F.2 and 3). Neither man is shown in *Officers Died in the Great War*.

Private Harry WILLIAMS, 1/9th Battalion, London Regiment (Queen Victoria's Rifles), was executed for desertion on 28 December 1917. He had already fallen foul of military discipline after going absent, an offence for which he received fifteen years imprisonment, though the sentence was suspended. In November 1917 he refused orders to fall in at a time when part of the line was under attack and his battalion was preparing to move forward. The question remains as to why he was tried for desertion rather than cowardice; the timing of his refusal to obey orders could not have come at a more critical time when his comrades and others were facing the prospect of danger and death, and it should come as no surprise that his trial took a dim view of his conduct. (Plot II.F.4)

Second Lieutenant Douglas Hamlin McKIE, 3rd Northumberland Fusiliers, attached to 27th Battalion, died of wounds on 11 April 1917. He returned from Brazil in order to serve. (Plot III.A.7)

Lance Corporal George William KING DCM, 23rd Royal Fusiliers, was killed in action on 21 May 1917 aged 21. His DCM was gazetted on 17 April 1917 and was awarded for conspicuous gallantry and devotion to duty in rescuing several wounded officers and then bringing in a machine gun under very heavy fire, setting a splendid example of courage and determination as he had done on previous occasions. (Plot III.B.3)

Captain Marcel James MARTIN, 16th Royal Warwickshire Regiment, was killed on 9 May 1917 and was the battalion's adjutant at the time of his death. He was one of several men from that battalion who lost their lives from heavy shelling around that time. (Plot III.B.7)

Second Lieutenant John William Wellesley SUTTON MC, Royal Garrison Artillery, attached 28 Brigade, Royal Field Artillery, was killed in action on 29 June 1917, aged 19. He was gazetted in the Royal Garrison Artillery from the Royal Military College, Sandhurst, on 27 July 1915 where he had been a cadet. His MC was gazetted on 25 November 1916 and was awarded for conspicuous gallantry in action. While under heavy fire he rescued a fellow officer who had been buried. Later, when his battery was under heavy fire, he remained at his post and set a splendid example to his men. (Plot III.C.1)

Another small group of 2nd King's Own Scottish Borderers can be found in Plot III, Rows C and D, all of whom were killed between 1 July 1917 and the end of August 1917, including Second Lieutenant James McKercher LAWSON who before the war had worked at the head office of the Royal Bank of Scotland in Edinburgh. (Plot III.C.4)

Major Arthur John Spencer HAMMANS MC, 1st Duke of Cornwall's Light Infantry, was killed in action on 3 July 1917 aged 25 (Plot III.C.22). He had been made a Chevalier of the *Légion d'Honneur* and also served as adjutant of his battalion in November 1915. He was gazetted as acting major on 8 January 1917. His MC was gazetted on 10 March 1915 and was awarded for gallantry and coolness on 16 December 1914 after filling in a trench 100 yards from the enemy during which he spent three hours under heavy fire. His father, the late Major Arthur William Hammans, also served in the same regiment. He died in England on 13 June 1916 at the age of 76 and is buried at Goring (St Thomas of Canterbury) Cemetery.

Private William Frederick CLARKE, Private Edwin James DICKS and Private William Edward LAKE, who had all formerly served with the Norfolk Regiment, were with 'B' Company, 12th York & Lancaster Regiment, when they were killed on 24 and 25 September 1917. The men had not been with their new battalion very long, having recently arrived as part of a new draft. It is likely that they knew each other quite well. Two of them, CLARKE and LAKE, are buried next to each other (Plot III.D.26 and 27), but DICKS is buried separately (Plot I.E.1).

Serjeant Henry WAKE, DCM, A Battery, 310 Brigade, Royal Field Artillery, was killed in action on 5 February 1918. His unit was part of the 62nd (West Riding) Divisional Artillery. His DCM was gazetted on 17 December 1914 while serving as a Bombardier with the 41st Battery, Royal Field Artillery. The citation states that he had helped to work the telephone for two hours under heavy shrapnel fire after the infantry had been driven back behind his observation station. The fire of his battery had saved the situation and the infantry was able to regain its former positions under its covering fire. (Plot IV.A.5)

Air Mechanic 2nd Class Thornton BROOKE, 5 Squadron, Royal Flying Corps, was killed in action on 5 February 1917, aged 23, while attached to the Royal Garrison Artillery. (Plot IV.A.10)

Second Lieutenant William Henry PEARCE, 13th Battalion, London Regiment (The Kensingtons) was killed in action on 19 February 1918, aged 27 (Plot IV.A.22). The regimental history records that the battalion was inspected that day by the divisional commander at Saint-Aubin. The previous tour of duty in line had ended on 13 February, and although *Officers Died in the Great War* agrees with the date of death in the CWGC register, it is hard to see how he was killed in action under the above circumstances. It is, of course, always possible that for some reason he and a small number of men may have remained behind and not returned to Saint-Aubin, or indeed may have gone up to the Roclincourt sector from Saint-Aubin that day. Another man from the battalion, Private William Horsley, died of wounds the following day, very likely as a result of whatever incident led to PEARCE's death. Private Horsley is buried in Maroeuil British Cemetery, a few miles west of Roclincourt.

Second Lieutenant Benjamin Alfred STARLING, 2nd (City of London) Battalion, London Regiment (Royal Fusiliers), was killed in action on 23 March 1918. STARLING had joined the battalion on 12 March 1917 with a draft of fifty-six men. He was born in Victoria, Australia, and had been a civil engineer before the war. He initially joined the 3rd (City of London) Battalion, London Regiment (Royal Fusiliers), before transferring to the 2nd Battalion in January 1917. (Plot IV.B.1)

Second Lieutenant Frederick James DREW, 230th Siege Battery, Royal Garrison Artillery, was killed in action on 29 March 1918, aged 20. The CWGC information in the cemetery register notes that he was a distinguished scholar and had been educated at King Edward VI Grammar School, Southampton, before going on to Oxford, studying at Queen's College. Two other men from his battery are buried next to him. (Plot IV.B.20)

Private Harry Thomas HENRY MM, 2nd Canadian Light Trench Mortar Battery, was killed in action on 15 April 1918, aged 24. His MM was won on 15 August 1917 at Hill 70 where he performed work as a stretcher-bearer tending to the wounded under very heavy shell fire. On 18 August he again did excellent work with his platoon, guiding and directing it while under a very heavy gas bombardment. (Plot IV.C.16)

Major Arthur PLOW MC MM, 14th Battalion, Canadian Infantry, was killed in action on 19 April 1918, aged 28. His MC was gazetted in the New Year's Honours List on 1 January 1918. His MM was awarded the previous year and was gazetted on 11 October 1916. He had won it while serving as a sergeant, though by the time it was gazetted he had already been promoted to lieutenant; in fact, from 13 June 1916 he served as adjutant of his battalion. (Plot IV.C.22)

A small grouping of men from the 13th Royal Scots can easily be missed. They are buried consecutively, in so far as five are buried next to each other at the end of Plot IV, Row D, followed by the remaining three who are buried at the start of Row D in Plot V. The first five are: Sergeant Duncan McGREGOR, Private James WELLS, Private G. SMITH, Private James MILLAR and Private James Edwards MARSHALL (Plot IV.D.22 to 26); the remaining three are: Private Basil GRETTON, Private Andrew LANDELS and Private John BOYLE (Plot V.D.1 to 3). Their burial during the day had to be abandoned owing to heavy shell fire and the short ceremony was then postponed until nightfall. All were killed during a raid carried out by 'A' Company on German trenches that was led by Second Lieutenant Ross and Second Lieutenant Thomas Smith. A total of nine men lost their lives, and Smith was also killed during the raid when he became cut off from the rest of the party. A further two men were recorded as missing in action and a further sixteen were wounded. Second Lieutenant Thomas Smith has no known grave and is commemorated on the Arras Memorial. Private LANDELS's brother, William, was killed in action on 22 August 1917, aged 25, serving as a private in the same battalion. He is buried at Tyne Cot Cemetery.

Whilst the majority of Scottish casualties in this cemetery are from the 51st (Highland) Division, a small section of Plot IV holds a few burials from the 52nd (Lowland) Division. This division had recently served in Palestine and only arrived on the Western Front in spring 1918. One of its officers, Second Lieutenant Thomas Reekie Morrison TAYLOR, 5th Royal Scots Fusiliers, was killed in action on 14 August 1918 (Plot IV.E.8). The other identified men buried with him can be found between graves E.2 and E.7.

Captain Arthur Lewis CARLISLE, 2nd Royal Berkshire Regiment, was killed in action on 29 August 1918, aged 28 (Plot IV.E.14). His brother, Captain John Edward Gordon Carlisle, was also killed in action on 11 May 1915 serving with the 107th Indian Pioneers and is buried in Béthune Town Cemetery.

Captain Charles THOMSON MC and Bar, 7th East Lancashire Regiment, attached 2nd Battalion, was killed in action on 1 September 1918, aged 24. When the 7th Battalion was disbanded in February 1918 he was one of eight officers and 198 other ranks who were posted to the 2nd Battalion. He was killed shortly after whilst leading a party, with the assistance of two other officers and a Lewis gun section, in a local attack on a German trench south of Gavrelle during which three enemy machine guns were captured. Before the position could be consolidated, the Germans counter-attacked in an attempt to re-gain their lost trench. The counter-attack was repelled, but it was during this phase of the fighting that THOMSON was killed. His body was later brought back to Roclincourt for burial.

His MC, gazetted on 18 July 1918, was awarded for conspicuous gallantry and devotion to duty while in charge of a patrol that successfully raided a machine-gun post after another patrol had previously failed. The success of the operation was mainly attributed to a fine reconnaissance carried out by him and to his courage and leadership during the raid itself. There is no trace of any bar to his MC in any of the Gazettes and *Officers Died in the Great War* also fails to acknowledge the bar. The regimental history makes no mention of it either. (Plot IV.E.20)

Plot IV, Row F contains a small number of burials from 1916. The first of these casualties was caused by rifle grenade when Private Ernest MUNDAY, 1st East Surrey Regiment, was killed on 13 March (Plot IV.F.4). The following day, Second Lieutenant Charles Clarke POCOCK from the same battalion was accidentally killed when one of our own rifle grenades exploded on leaving the muzzle, wounding a fellow officer and one other man (Plot IV.F.5).

The grave of young Private Frank TAYLOR, aged 17, can be found a little further along the row. He was killed in action with the 8th King's Royal Rifle Corps. On 1 July 1916 the Germans fired a large mine, which was anticipated by our own tunnelling engineers, although it turned out to be larger and was detonated sooner than expected. The next day the Germans put down heavy trench mortar fire onto the sector held by the 8th Battalion and three men were killed, one of whom was TAYLOR (Plot IV.F.14). Another man from the same battalion is buried a few graves along from TAYLOR. Corporal Charles SAYSELL MM, 8th King's Royal Rifle Corps, was killed on 22 July 1916 just before the battalion moved down to the Somme (Plot IV.F.17). SAYSELL won his MM in connection with events on 25 April that year when the Germans had put down a heavy bombardment that caused a building to collapse, resulting in nine casualties. Some of these men were buried in the rubble, but Corporal SAYSELL and two other lance corporals succeeded in digging them out, despite being still under shell fire.

Second Lieutenant Frederick William ELLIS, 13th Battalion, London Regiment (The Kensingtons), was killed in action on 3 March 1918. The regimental history makes little reference to this period and notes that the time was chiefly spent in strengthening the defences and putting out wire. There was a growing awareness that the Germans were about to carry out a major offensive and great efforts were being made up and down the front to prepare for increasing activity by the enemy almost anywhere along the British line. (Plot V.A.16)

Captain Ernest Stewart HERON, 5th Cheshire Regiment, is shown in the CWGC register as having been killed in action on 20 March 1918. However, *Officers Died in the Great War* gives the more likely date of death as 28 March 1918, although the German trench mortars were active around 20 March and were particularly concentrating on the wire in front of the division's front. His battalion was the pioneer unit attached to the 56th (London) Division, and at the time of HERON's death it was located between Roclincourt, Bailleuil and Willerval, north of the Point du Jour Ridge, where it was engaged in maintaining and improving defences. (Plot V.B.19)

Plots IV, V and VI each contain burials from the 51st (Highland) Division. For the most part these are men killed between 25 and 28 May 1918, most of whom are from the 4th Gordon Highlanders, the 6th and 7th Black Watch and the 6th Seaforth Highlanders. One of the men is Lance Serjeant Robert McLEISH DCM, 6th Black Watch, who was killed in action on 26 May 1918. His DCM, gazetted on 28 March 1918, was won while he was serving as a lance corporal. It was awarded for conspicuous gallantry and devotion to duty during an attack that was held up by machine-gun fire coming from two enemy dug-outs. After his officers had all become casualties, he took command, rallying the men and leading them in a successful attack on the dug-outs. He had then shown great initiative in con-solidating the position, re-organizing its defences, and repulsing a counter-attack during which he and his men inflicted severe losses on the enemy. (Plot V.D.23)

Second Lieutenant John Capel MAURICE, 2nd Royal Berkshire Regiment, was killed in action on 7 October 1918 (Plot V.E.18). His brother, Second Lieutenant Charles Henry Pryce Maurice, died on 24 January 1917 and is buried at Warlin-court Halte British Cemetery, Saulty. He is shown serving with the 3rd Royal Berkshire Regiment, though this battalion never served overseas and was effec-tively a depot or training unit. It did, however, serve in Ireland from 1917 until the end of the war. *Officers Died in the Great War* simply notes that he died on active service.

Sapper Joseph COUPLAN, 461st Field Company, Royal Engineers, was killed in action on 12 March 1918 (Plot VI.A.8). He previously served in the Royal Army Medical Corps. His brother, Corporal Maurice Couplan, died of wounds on 3 May 1918 while serving with the 1/7th Duke of Wellington's Regiment and is now buried in Boulogne East Cemetery.

Second Lieutenant Lauriston Ross FRASER, 14th Battalion, London Regiment (London Scottish), was mortally wounded on 21 March 1918 aged 22. The battalion history shows him in the casualty returns for the 9–17 April 1917. This is clearly at odds with the entry in *Officers Died in the Great War*, which shows him killed in action on 21st March, and is all the more strange because this date is supported by his medal index card which shows the same date of death. Unfortunately sometimes such inconsistencies and errors do occur. (Plot VI.A.24)

Major James Gordon GOODFELLOW MC, 416th (Edinburgh) Field Company, Royal Engineers, was killed on 23 March 1918 (Plot VI.A.27). His MC was gazetted on 3 June 1918 in the King's Birthday Honours List. Buried in the next row is Captain Frederick William ANDERSON who also served with the 416th (Edinburgh) Field Company, Royal Engineers. He was killed in action on 29 March 1918 (Plot VI.B.11). Major GOODFELLOW's brother, Lieutenant Eric Hector Goodfellow, was killed in action in Mesopotamia on 9 March 1916, aged 23, serving with 28th Battery, 9 Brigade, Royal Field Artillery. He is commemorated on the Basra Memorial.

Second Lieutenant Ernest SMITH, 46 Squadron, Royal Air Force, was killed in action on 28 April 1918 while flying a Camel aircraft. (Plot VI.C.22)

Lieutenant Colonel Rex Hamilton LEYLAND, 2nd Rifle Brigade, was killed in action by a shell around 5am on 24 September 1918, aged 33, while he was visiting part of the line. He had only been the battalion's commander since June that year. That month every battalion of the 8th Division had had to take on a new commanding officer after all the previous ones had become casualties during the previous month's fighting on the Aisne and the subsequent retreat. (Plot VI.E.1)

Captain Kenneth Salwey HOWARD, 1st Sherwood Foresters, was killed in action on 6 October 1918 (Plot VI.E.8). On 3 October the 8th Division had shifted its boundaries, handing over the Willerval sector to the 20th (Light) Division, but at the same time taking over the sectors around Greenland Hill and Plouvain from the 51st (Highland) Division. Preparations were also being made for an attack on the Rouvroy–Fresnes Line on 7 October. On 6 October the 1st Sherwood Foresters carried out an operation in preparation for the following day by pushing forward along the communication trenches that connected with the Rouvroy–Fresnes Line from the west. The 1st Sherwood Foresters made good progress along Oppy Support Trench, so that the village became virtually surrounded, which led to the capture of two officers, thirty-four other ranks, and six machine guns. Lieutenant Percy Horace ADAMS, 4th Sherwood Foresters, attached 1st Battalion, was killed in action a few days before Captain HOWARD on 3 October 1918, aged 20 (Plot VI.E.12).

There are eighteen holders of the MM buried here, two of whom held other gallantry awards and who, along with two other men, Corporal Charles SAYSELL MM, and Serjeant James HAINES MM, have already been mentioned. The remaining fourteen are:

Serjeant John CRAIG MM, 'D' Company, 1/6th Argyll & Sutherland Highlanders, died of wounds on 23 May 1917, aged 33. *Soldiers Died in the Great War* makes no reference to his MM. (Plot I.C.7)

Lance Corporal Thomas Richard VOCKUICH MM, 18th Durham Light Infantry, killed in action on 28 September 1917. (Plot I.E.5)

Serjeant James QUINN MM, D Battery, 165 Brigade, Royal Field Artillery, killed in action on 15 December 1917, aged 29. (Plot I.F.18)

Sapper Joseph William COONEY MM, 3rd Battalion, Canadian Railway Troops, killed in action on the 16th December 1917, aged 19. (Plot I.F.21)

Corporal Sidney Charles WILSON MM, 1st Bedfordshire Regiment, killed in action on 2 July 1917. (Plot III.C.8)

Lance Corporal William HUDSON MM, 2/8th West Yorkshire Regiment; killed in action on 19 January 1918. (Plot III.F.6)

Serjeant William REDFEARN MM, 13th East Yorkshire Regiment, killed in action on 27 January 1918, aged 29. (Plot III.F.22)

Gunner Wilfred Henry NASH MM, 69th Siege Battery, Royal Garrison Artillery, killed in action on 11 February 1918. (Plot IV.A.15)

Sergeant Alfred C. McLATCHIE MM, 10th Battalion, Canadian Infantry, killed in action on 20 April 1918, aged 23. (Plot IV.C.26)

Bombardier John CAMPBELL MM, 5th Trench Mortar Battery, Royal Garrison Artillery, killed in action on 5 April 1917. (Plot IV.F.21)

Sergeant Charles Blair KENNEDY MM, 47th Battalion, Canadian Infantry, killed in action on 21 April 1918, aged 38. (Plot V.C.16)

Lance Corporal William Campbell McINTOSH MM, 'C' Company, 1/7th Argyll & Sutherland Highlanders, killed in action on 19 May 1918, aged 22. (Plot V.D.5)

Lance Corporal Reginald Alfred SOUTHERN MM, 4th (City of London) Battalion, London Regiment (Royal Fusiliers), killed in action on 16 March 1918. (Plot VI.A.18)

Private H. DIXON MM, 14th Battalion, Canadian Infantry, killed in action on 28 April 1918. (Plot VI.C.12)

Roclincourt Valley Cemetery

In contrast to Roclincourt Military Cemetery, which existed before the Battle of Arras, this cemetery was created in the immediate aftermath of the opening day of the battle on 9 April 1917. The earliest burials are from units of the 51st (Highland) Division and it continued to be used until the following August, by which time there were just under 100 graves. This original cemetery is represented today by Plot I, Rows A to E and some of Row F. After the war the cemetery was enlarged to accommodate a number of graves from five nearby cemeteries that were then closed. Three of these consisted mainly of men from the 34th Division, whilst the remaining two contained predominantly men from the 51st (Highland) Division. The cemetery we see today was designed by Sir Reginald Blomfield and 465 of the 518 casualties buried here have been identified.

Today the 34th Division has a large share of the burials here with a total of 128 identified graves. All eight consecutive battalions of the Northumberland Fusiliers that made up two of the division's brigades; the Tyneside Scottish (20th to 23rd Northumberland Fusiliers) and the Tyneside Irish (24th to 27th North-umberland Fusiliers), have men buried here. On 9 April 1917 the 34th Division attacked on the right flank of the 51st (Highland) Division and virtually all its casualties here are from that date. However, the cemetery contains relatively few burials from the 11th Suffolk Regiment, and only one from the 10th Lincoln-shire Regiment which, along with the 15th and 16th Royal Scots, made up the 103 Brigade of the 34th Division.

The fifty-six identified burials here belonging to the Argyll & Sutherland Highlanders are mainly men from the 7th and 8th Battalions who were killed with the 51st (Highland) Division either on or around 9 April 1917, or in the weeks leading up to the battle. However, some of the burials are from the regiment's 6th Battalion, which was the pioneer battalion attached to the 5th Division, and its burials date from May to August 1917. More 51st (Highland) Division casualties can be found scattered throughout the cemetery, particularly NCOs and men of the 4th, 5th and 6th Seaforth Highlanders. Apart from one, all of them were killed on the opening day of the Battle of Arras, or a day either side of it.

Even more numerous are men of the Royal Scots with a total of eighty-eight identified casualties. In almost every case the date of death is 9 April 1917, though a few are from the previous couple of days. Around half of them are from the two Edinburgh Battalions, the 15th and 16th Royal Scots, which were part of the 34th Division. Presumably many of these men would have been brought here from Kite Crater, King Crater and Rab's Road cemeteries, which were closed after the Armistice and which are referred to in the notes in the CWGC register. The remainder of the regiment's dead are men belonging to, or who were attached to, the 9th Battalion, which was part of the 51st (Highland) Division.

Whilst on the subject of the Royal Scots there are a number of entries in the CWGC register here relating to men from the 16th Royal Scots (2nd Edinburgh Battalion) where the only personal biographical information is, '*He came from ...*' followed by a location. This is something I have come across only in relation to men of the Royal Scots Regiment, but it occurs in other cemetery registers. This may have been an attempt by the regiment to fill a gap where no family or next-of-kin details had been provided or recorded. It is, however, unusual.

Second Lieutenant Robert Alexander MONKHOUSE, 6th Gordon High-landers, was killed in action some time between 9 and 11 April 1917. The pre-sumption here has to be that he was originally shown as missing in action and that his body was discovered two days later. (Plot I.A.1)

Second Lieutenant William Farquhar IRELAND, 8th Gordon Highlanders, was killed in action on 9 April 1917, aged 22. He and Second Lieutenant MONK-HOUSE are the only officers among the thirty-one Gordon Highlanders buried in this cemetery. (Plot I.A.26)

The two most senior officers buried here are Major Victor WALROND, 15th Battery, 36 Brigade, Royal Field Artillery, and Major Philip Gerald BAILEY, also of the 36 Brigade, Royal Field Artillery (Plot I.C.1 and 3). Lying between them is Second Lieutenant William Herbert MANIFOLD, who was part of WALROND's Battery, as is a fourth man, Second Lieutenant Howell Thomas BALL (Plot I.C.4). All four were killed in action on the same day, 26 April 1917.

Another small group of artillerymen from this brigade are buried here in Plot I. Row B. Major WALROND was twice mentioned in despatches and was 27 years of age when he died. The Walronds were an aristocratic family from Devon. Sir John Walrond, 1st Baron, married the Honourable Frances Caroline Hood, daughter of the 2nd Baron Bridport. One of their sons, Sir William Hood Walrond, 2nd Baron Walrond and 1st Baron Waleran, served as an MP for two Devon constituencies between 1880 and 1905 and went on to become Chancellor of the Duchy of Lancaster and a Privy Counsellor. His son, the Honourable William Lionel Walrond, died at home serving with the Army Service Corps in November 1915. Major Victor WALROND was his cousin. Another member of the family, Captain George Basil Stuart Walrond, was killed in action near Arras on 19 March 1916 and is buried at Agny Military Cemetery.

Second Lieutenant Harry Elsmore HOWARD, 25th Northumberland Fusiliers (Tyneside Irish), died of wounds on 8 April 1917. He had originally been reported as missing the previous day and was last seen somewhere near Kite Crater. His father, Stephen Howard, served as a quartermaster serjeant with the East Lancashire Regiment. (Plot I.F.19)

Second Lieutenant John Charles MALLORY, 1st Northumberland Fusiliers, attached 26th Battalion, was killed in action on 9 April 1917. In *Officers Died in the Great War* his surname is shown as 'Maloney'. Regimental sources, however, confirm his surname as shown in the CWGC register (Plot I.F.20).

Captain John Fenwick HUNTLEY, 25th Northumberland Fusiliers (Tyneside Irish), was killed in action on 9 April 1917, aged 30. The second objective, the Blue Line, was known to be occupied by several German machine guns. Prior to the assault, HUNTLEY led a party to carry out a reconnaissance of these positions, but was killed by a sniper's bullet (Plot II.A.18). One of the men with him, Lance Corporal Thomas Bryan, went on to silence one of the guns, killing two of the crew with the bayonet and allowing the battalion to take its objectives. The machine guns had been carefully sited so as to catch the attackers as soon as they appeared on the crest of the ridge around 300 yards away. The machine guns were also close to the point where the left flank of the 34th Division joined the right flank of the 51st (Highland) Division and had inflicted casualties on the attacking Scots, particularly the 8th Argyll & Sutherland Highlanders, who had pushed on through the 6th Gordon Highlanders towards the Blue Line. Lance Corporal Bryan was awarded the VC and survived the war. He had played rugby league for Castleford before the war.

Second Lieutenant Layford Kyffin BROWNE, 25th Northumberland Fusiliers, was killed in action on 9 April 1917. He was a chartered accountant by profession and had returned from South America in September 1915 in order to enlist. He had previously served with the Artists' Rifles and was commissioned in May 1916. (Plot II.B.20)

Private Richard EDWARDS, 23rd Northumberland Fusiliers (Tyneside Scottish), who was killed in action on 9 April 1917, had already lost a brother, Private George Edwards, who died serving with the 1st Scots Guards on 17 November 1915. George is buried in Douai Communal Cemetery, presumably after he died of wounds in captivity. *Soldiers Died in the Great War* shows Richard EDWARDS serving with the 26th Battalion, rather than the 23rd Battalion, and states that he had also previously served in the Royal Field Artillery. (Plot II.C.2)

Second Lieutenant Arthur James PROBERT, 25th Northumberland Fusiliers, was killed in action on 9 April 1917. He initially enlisted in the Artists' Rifles, and in civilian life had worked a journalist. (Plot II.C.11)

Second Lieutenant Thomas Guthrie PAUL, 25th Northumberland Fusiliers, was killed in action on 9 April 1917. He had been with the battalion on the opening day of the Somme offensive on 1 July 1916 and was initially reported as missing in action that day. (Plot II.C.14)

Another soldier with a brother buried elsewhere is Private Hubert Vaughan McKINLEY, 22nd Northumberland Fusiliers (Tyneside Scottish). He was killed in action on 9 April 1917 (Plot II.D.8). His brother, William Gordon McKinley, 48th Divisional Ammunition Column, Royal Field Artillery, died on 6 January 1919, aged 25, and is buried in Dueville Communal Cemetery Extension near Vicenza in Italy.

One Northumberland Fusilier has a very different date of death to the rest. Private Edward Thomas MOULDING, 23rd Battalion, was killed in a completely separate attack from the rest of his regimental comrades buried in this cemetery. The CWGC register shows that he was killed on 23 April 1917 (Plot II.E.5). It is surprising that he is the only infantry casualty here from that date, particularly given the cemetery's proximity to the northern end of the bitter and unsuccessful fighting that took place on 23 April 1917. Losses for the 34th Division were high that day. The divisional history does not give daily casualties for the April fighting, but the total for the ten days up to and including 30 April is given as 2,644 for all ranks. In the case of Edward Thomas MOULDING, *Soldiers Died in the Great War* shows him as serving with the 22nd Battalion, rather than the 23rd as shown in the CWGC register. The same source even shows him killed in action on 9 April 1917 rather than the 23rd. It is clear from his army number that both records relate to the same soldier.

Second Lieutenant John Ernest CALKIN, 22nd Northumberland Fusiliers, was killed in action on 9 April 1917, aged 25. He was one of five children, four of whom were boys. His younger brother, Herbert Baptiste Calkin, was 19 years old when the war ended, but did not take part in it. However, he did go on to serve during the Second World War. (Plot II.E.17)

Private Edward BOLTON, 1st Cheshire Regiment, died on 14 April 1916. He was executed that day after he had been brought back to France from England. He had deserted and was found living under a different identity. (Plot II.F.7)

The CWGC register makes no specific reference to Lance Corporal George Storrie CAMPBELL and Private John Mitchell CAMPBELL being brothers who fell on the same day, 9 April 1917, while serving in the same battalion, the 9th Royal Scots. However, the parental details and the family's address in Edinburgh make it clear that they were brothers. They are also mentioned in the book, *Cheerful Sacrifice* by John Nicholls in one of several accounts given to him by Serjeant Bill Hay, one of their fellow comrades who survived the war, and whom I met on many occasions in the early 1980s when the London branch of the Western Front Association met on the first floor of the 'Holloway Castle' public house in Islington. John CAMPBELL, who was 25 years old when he died, was five years older than George. They are buried very close to one another (Plot II.G.13 and 16).

Private Arthur Robert STREETS, 10th Lincolnshire Regiment (Grimsby Chums), was killed in action on 9 April 1917, aged 25 (Plot III.F.2). His brother, Serjeant John William Streets, will be familiar to anyone who has read Martin Middlebrook's, *The First Day on the Somme* and *The Somme Battlefields – A Comprehensive Guide from Crécy to the Two World Wars*. 'Will' Streets was killed in action with the 12th York & Lancaster Regiment (Sheffield Pals) near Serre on 1 July 1916, aged 31. He gave up the chance of attending his local grammar school so that he could work and bring in much needed family income to help support his brothers, one of whom was Arthur. Another brother, Harry, also served during the war. 'Will' Streets is believed to be buried in Euston Road Cemetery, Colincamps, and is commemorated there by way of a special memorial. The CWGC register for that cemetery notes that 'Will' had two works published: one on coal mining, the other being a collection of his poems under the title, *The Undying Splendour*, which was published in May 1917. His headstone bears a line from one of his poems:

'*I fell, but yielded not my English soul; that lives out here beneath the battle's roll.*'

Second Lieutenant Robert Archibald MACNEILL, 21st Northumberland Fusiliers, was killed in action on 9 April 1917. The grave number in the CWGC register should be shown as '4' instead of 'H'. (Plot III.F.4)

Second Lieutenant Owen Bennett Goold JOHNSON, 11th Suffolk Regiment, was killed in action on 9 April 1917 (Plot IV.A.5). His brother, Lieutenant Donald Frederic Goold Johnson, was also killed during the war while serving with the 2nd Manchester Regiment. He died of wounds on 15 July 1916 and is buried in Bouzincourt Communal Cemetery Extension on the Somme.

Second Lieutenant Charles George Gordon WILSON, 3rd Cameronians, attached 9th Battalion, was killed in action on 9 April 1917, aged 29. He is one of just three men from that regiment buried in this cemetery. (Plot IV.C.20)

Although there are few 1916 burials in this particular cemetery, three can be found buried consecutively at the start of Plot IV, Row F. One of them is a South African killed in December that year, probably as a result of shell fire (Plot IV.F.3). After its ordeal at Delville Wood in July 1916 the South African Brigade was withdrawn from the Somme, along with the rest of the 9th (Scottish) Division, and it spent two periods that year holding trenches just north of Arras. Next to him are two New Zealand sappers killed on the same day, 15 August 1916 (F.4 and F.5).

Plot IV.F.6 to 10 contains five men of the 15th Sherwood Foresters. The CWGC register shows the date of death for all of them as 2 November 1916, though *Soldiers Died in the Great War* shows Lance Corporal Frederick JOHNSON (Plot IV.F.9) as having died a month later on 2 December 1916, as does his head-stone. Two other men from the same battalion, Private Ernest Marriott and Private David Spicer, also died on that day and are buried in the Faubourg d'Amiens Cemetery in Arras.

Second Lieutenant Thomas Emery BAINBRIDGE, 29th Northumberland Fusiliers, attached 21st Battalion, was killed in action on 9 April 1917, aged 22. He was killed during his battalion's advance to the Blue Line, which involved crossing 1,200 yards of ground. By 11am his battalion had gained its objective, though at a heavy cost in officers. BAINBRIDGE, who was in charge of No.14 Platoon, was killed with his platoon sergeant as they were establishing a bombing post in the railway cutting just north of Maison Blanche. (Plot IV.G.7)

Private N. LYSELL, 3rd South African Regiment, was wounded at Delville Wood on 17 July 1916 and was subsequently killed in action on 9 April 1917 (Plot IV.G.20). Another man from the same regiment, Private Fred CROMP-TON, who was also wounded during the fighting there in July 1916, was also killed in action on 9 April 1917 (Plot IV.G.17). LYSELL and CROMPTON are among the twenty-one identified South African casualties buried here in Plot IV, mainly in Rows G and H. Most of these men fell on the opening day of the Arras offensive.

Lieutenant Basil Llewellyn Boyd THOMAS is shown in the CWGC register as serving with the 15th Royal Welsh Fusiliers when he died, but he was actually attached to the 27th Company, Machine Gun Corps, 9th (Scottish) Division, when he was killed in action on 9 April 1917. (Plot IV.H.3)

As with 1916, there are few 1918 casualties in this cemetery. With very few excep-tions they are all 4th Division casualties from the 1st Rifle Brigade, the 1st King's Own (Royal Lancaster Regiment), the 1st Somerset Light Infantry and the 4th Battalion, Machine Gun Corps. The division fought and held its ground north of the River Scarpe on 28 and 29 March when the German offensive reached its peak on this part of the Western Front. One member of the 4th Battalion, Machine Gun Corps, Private George Robert GARNHAM, is shown in the CWGC register as having died on 28 March 1919, but that appears to be a typographical error as the headstone shows the year of his death as 1918. As well as making sense, this would appear to be confirmed by his entry in *Soldiers Died in the Great War*. He originally enlisted in the York & Lancaster Regiment.

Finally, there are nine gallantry awards in this cemetery, all of them holders of the MM. They are:

Serjeant Kenneth BALLAM MM, 7th Battery, 34 Brigade, Royal Field Artillery, killed in action on 28 April 1917. (Plot I.C.8)

Private William ROSE MM, 4th Field Ambulance, attached to 34 Brigade, Royal Field Artillery, killed in action on 28 April 1917. (Plot I.C.9)

Private Edward John LOURIE MM, 25th Northumberland Fusiliers, killed in action on 9 April 1917, aged 41. There appears to be no trace of him in *Soldiers Died in the Great War*. (Plot II.A.19)

Lance Serjeant George MILLS MM, 7th Argyll & Sutherland Highlanders killed in action on 9 April 1917. (Plot III.B.2)

Private Thomas HALL MM, 20th Northumberland Fusiliers, formerly East Yorkshire Regiment, killed in action on 9 April 1917. (Plot III.B.13)

Serjeant Austin Arthur WEBB MM, 11th Suffolk Regiment, killed in action on 8 April 1917, aged 33. (Plot III.D.10)

Private Peter Wilson WATSON MM, 7th Argyll & Sutherland Highlanders, killed in action on 9 April 1917. There is no reference to his MM in *Soldiers Died in the Great War*. (Plot III.E.14)

Private James DAVIDSON MM, 16th Royal Scots, killed in action on 9 April 1917. (Plot III.F.9)

Corporal George DENMAN MM, 1st Somerset Light Infantry, killed in action on 28 March 1918. (Plot IV.B.10)

Chapter Three

An Early Bird – Some Epitaphs –
Joy Rides to the Front

Cabaret Rouge British Cemetery, Souchez

One of the main arterial roads leading north from Arras is the D.937, the main Arras-Béthune road. As it runs north it passes through La Targette where there is both a British and a French Cemetery. Cabaret Rouge British Cemetery sits on the west side of the road a little further on, just before the road drops and twists its way into the large village of Souchez. It is impressive and large with just over 7,500 burials, though fewer than half of these have been identified.

The word 'cabaret' in French has several meanings, one of which translates roughly as 'café'. The one that stood here was built of red brick with red tiles for its roof, hence it became known as the 'red café' or in French, '*le cabaret rouge*'. It stood no chance of surviving the war and by March 1915 it had been more or less obliterated by shelling. Nevertheless, its pile of red brick fragments and brick dust still provided a landmark of kinds, at least for a time. The name was then used to refer to the sector and to a nearby communication trench. When the British took over this part of the front, they began to make a small cemetery on the site that formed the beginnings of the present cemetery.

The CWGC register notes that the cemetery was particularly used by the 47th (London) Division in 1916, then by the Canadian Corps in 1917 until August. It then continued to be used until September 1918 by whichever units happened to be holding this part of the front. By this stage the cemetery contained a few hundred burials, but after the war it was massively enlarged to create the cemetery we see today. This 'concentration' process means that there are burials from each year of the war.

After the heavy fighting here by the French in 1915, trench life settled down into a state of 'live and let live'. During the winter and early spring 1916 neither side showed much aggression above ground, though on 8 February the Germans carried out two surprise attacks, capturing a section of trench just south of Zouave Valley. Two weeks later, on 21 February, the opening day of their offensive at Verdun, the Germans also captured the small knoll that lay between Souchez and Givenchy-en-Gohelle, known as the 'Pimple'. When the British took over this sector from the French Tenth Army in March 1916 it initially remained a so-called 'quiet sector', but not for long. Following a week of continuous work, initially to improve the appalling state of the trenches, this sector soon became much more lively. Sniping and mining activity were stepped up and trench raiding became a frequent occurrence, as was the British way.

Although the British only took over this sector in March 1916, even a casual visit to this cemetery, or quick glance at the CWGC register, will reveal that there are a surprising number of 1914 and 1915 casualties buried here. Many of them would have been originally buried by the Germans, but others came from small battlefield cemeteries or isolated graves that were cleared after the war. There are 104 identified casualties from 1914 buried here, 733 from 1915, 656 from 1916, 810 from 1917 and 884 from 1918 up to the Armistice. There are just four dating from 12 November 1918 to the end of 1919.

In the case of this cemetery, it may be more useful to highlight casualties according to their year of death. This is a very large cemetery, and so for most people a systematic visit, plot by plot, will not be practical, or even desirable. Even so, this is a cemetery that is worth an hour of anyone's time. It may look daunting from the roadside, but once inside it is quite possible to cover a surprising amount in a relatively short space of time. And there is always something new to discover.

1914

Second Lieutenant Henry Noel ATKINSON DSO, 3rd Cheshire Regiment, attached 1st Battalion, died of wounds in captivity, aged 25. He was gazetted to the 3rd Cheshire Regiment (Special Reserve) in March 1913. On mobilization he was attached to the 1st Battalion, which at the time was stationed in Londonderry. He embarked with his battalion on 14 August 1914 as part of 15 Brigade, 5th Division. He was involved in the fighting during the Retreat from Mons, including the Battle of Le Cateau, as well as on the Aisne.

He won his DSO in action on 22 October 1914 at Violaines, near La Bassée, where he was wounded, and the award was gazetted posthumously on 1 December that year. 'D' Company had been in a position on the west side of Violaines digging trenches with 'B' and 'C' on either side, but not far enough forward to give adequate cover or warning to those carrying out the work. The Germans made a surprise attack, whereupon 'D' Company managed to withdraw, but 'C' Company was left exposed, eventually managing to conform, but under heavy fire. It was during this retirement that ATKINSON showed conspicuous gallantry while under heavy fire from both flanks. He managed to collect a few men together and succeeded in checking the enemy, thereby facilitating the retirement of the remainder of his company. During this isolated incident 220 NCOs and men, as well as five officers, were killed or died of wounds, including ATKINSON. A further two officers were captured and the battalion virtually ceased to exist, at least in the short term. ATKINSON was also mentioned posthumously in Sir John French's despatch of 14 January 1915 for distinguished service in the field.

Unconfirmed reports claimed that he had been wounded and taken to a French hospital in Douai, which then fell into German hands, but this seems unlikely. He almost certainly died of wounds soon after his capture, particularly as he died on the same date as the action in which he was wounded. ATKINSON was a keen golfer and was the Welsh amateur golf champion in 1913. After the war his father, the vicar of Audlem, erected a private monument to him and his fallen comrades in the civilian cemetery in Violaines. (Plot XIII.E.12)

Lieutenant Charles Hylton VAN NECK, 1st Northumberland Fusiliers, was killed in action on 20 October 1914, aged 21 (Plot XVI.B.17). He was educated at Harrow and gained his commission with the 3rd battalion in October 1913. His eldest brother, Philip, who was educated at Eton, was killed six days later on 26 October 1914 while serving as a lieutenant with the 1st Grenadier Guards. He is buried at Zantvoorde British Cemetery, Belgium.

Major Lord John Spencer CAVENDISH DSO, 1st Life Guards, was killed in action on 20 October 1914, aged 42. He was the son of Lord and Lady Edward Cavendish and grandson of the 7th Duke of Devonshire. His mother, the Honourable Emma Elizabeth Lascelles, had been Maid of Honour to Queen Victoria, and his maternal great-grandfather was Henry Lascelles, 2nd Earl of Harewood. He joined the Life Guards from the Militia in 1897 and between 1899 and 1902 he served in the South African War as a signalling officer at both brigade and divisional level. He was present at the Relief of Ladysmith and at Colenso, Spion Kop, Vaal Kranz, Tugela Heights, Pieter's Hill, Zand River, Diamond Hill, Elands River, Bethlehem and Wittebergen. He was mentioned in despatches on 1 February 1901 and was awarded his DSO for services in South Africa. (Plot XXI.C.26)

Second Lieutenant Sydney Alexander GOLDSMID, 3rd Worcestershire Regiment, was killed in action on 7 November 1914. He was second cousin of the late Sir Julian Goldsmid, 3rd Baronet, a lawyer and one time MP for Honiton, who died in 1896. Sydney was the last of the male Goldsmid line. It seems the family was destined never to have a direct heir to the baronetcy.

He went to Sandhurst in 1911 and received his commission in the 3rd Worcestershire Regiment the following year. He was mentioned in Sir John French's despatch on 8 October 1914 for his reconnaissance work. He was killed during an attack on his battalion's trenches just east of Ploegsteert Wood. The previous day had been dense with fog and his battalion commander had expressed the view that their position was untenable unless further artillery support could be given. German shelling was heavy, but Lieutenant Colonel Stuart was told that further artillery support could not be provided because German artillery positions could not be located in the fog. At 5am on 7 October, when the German infantry emerged through the fog and attacked, his battalion was only able to hold the trenches on its left flank.

A counter-attack was launched that met the Germans just inside the eastern edge of the wood. Fierce fighting then took place as support arrived from companies of the 2nd Royal Inniskilling Fusiliers, the 1st East Lancashire Regiment and later from a company of the 2nd Seaforth Highlanders. The original trenches, however, could not be recovered and a new line was established inside the wood, which fortunately linked up with the left hand section of the original trenches still held by 3rd Worcestershire Regiment. GOLDSMID was one of four officers from his battalion killed in action that day along with forty-two other ranks. Total casualties for his battalion exceeded 200. (Plot XXI.E.24)

Second Lieutenant William Miles SMALLEY, 1st Sherwood Foresters, was killed in action on 9 December 1914, aged 23. Before the war he worked as a demonstrator in the theatre at University College, Nottingham, and after serving a four-year apprenticeship then obtained a position as a lecture assistant in the Chemistry Department. He joined the college's OTC and in February 1914 obtained a commission in the Special Reserve. At the time of his death he was engaged to be married and his fiancée was serving as a Red Cross nurse. He had two brothers who also served during the war. He was killed by a sniper while supervising trenches at 'Port Arthur' near Neuve Chapelle. The fatal shot came from the same house where a fellow officer, Lieutenant Maclean Proctor Dilworth, had been killed the previous month. His commanding officer, Lieu-tenant Colonel Marshall, later commented that SMALLEY's first aid skills and medical knowledge had been of a standard not normally encountered outside the medical professions and that this had made him a valuable member of his bat-talion. Marshall himself had had a close brush with death from the same source after a bullet struck the cigarette case in his breast pocket causing damage to his tunic and grazing his chest just below his heart. (Plot XXVI.A.16)

Lieutenant Maclean Proctor DILWORTH, 1st Sherwood Foresters, was killed in action on 20 November 1914, aged 26. He went to France with his battalion as its machine-gun officer the same month. It was while he was reconnoitring a house about 40 yards in front of his battalion's trenches that he was shot through the neck. One report indicates that the sergeant with him killed the German who shot him. Two nights later, Captain Donald William Auchinbreck Campbell made an attempt to bring back his body, but he too was killed. Campbell was attached to the battalion from the 4th South Staffordshire Regiment. After that, no further attempts appear to have been made and Campbell's body was never found. He is commemorated on the Le Touret Memorial. DILWORTH was an only son and his parents lived in Kensington, London. (Plot XXVI.A.17)

Captain John Mounsey LAMBERT, 3rd Northumberland Fusiliers, attached 1st Battalion, was killed in action near Neuve Chapelle on 28 October 1914, aged 30. He was the only son of the late Major General George Craster Lambert who had risen from ensign in 1845 to become colonel of the 101st Royal Bengal Fusiliers (later Royal Munster Fusiliers) by 1869, and who had fought in India during the 1st Sikh War. George's brother, John, also served with him briefly in India, but was mortally wounded in 1846. (Plot XXVII.E.25)

Lieutenant Duncan BAILLIE, 2/9th Gurkha Rifles, was killed in action on 2 November 1914 near Neuve Chapelle. He was educated at Charterhouse School and the Royal Military College, Sandhurst, passing out first and winning the Sword of Honour. He gained his commission in 1909 and began his soldiering in the Indian Army with a year's attachment to the Highland Light Infantry at Lucknow, followed by his move to the 2nd Gurkha Rifles the following year. BAILLIE was sent forward with two platoons to assist the rest of the battalion, whose trenches had been left vulnerable after the village had been evacuated. As it tried to hold on in the small salient, the battalion came under enfilade fire from a German mortar. Having brought up the reinforcement party, he was killed by a rifle bullet to the head while reconnoitring the situation. (Plot XXVII.E.34)

Lieutenant St. John Alan CHARLTON, 4th Bedfordshire Regiment, attached 1st Battalion, died of wounds on 26 October 1914. *Bond of Sacrifice Volume 1*, states that he was killed on the Aisne, but his battalion was nowhere near the Aisne at the time of his death. The 1st Bedfordshire Regiment was defending the line around Rue d' Ouvert, just east of Festubert. He was an only son and was educated at Eton. His great-grandfather, Henry Thomas Liddell, was 1st Earl of Ravensworth. (Plot XXVII.H.25)

Captain George Bruce LEGARD, 1st Queen's Own (Royal West Kent Regiment), was adjutant of the battalion and was mortally wounded near Neuve Chapelle on 27 October 1914 (Plot XXIX.C.40). He was twice mentioned in despatches; firstly on 8 October 1914, and again on 14 January 1915. He was aged 29 when he died and is now buried next to his commanding officer.

His brother, Lieutenant Geoffrey Philip Legard, was killed in action at Frezenberg Ridge, just outside Ypres, on 8 May 1915 whilst serving with the 2nd Northumberland Fusiliers. He is commemorated on the Menin Gate. Another member of the Legard family, Lieutenant Reginald John Legard, was killed in action the following day, 9 May, serving with the 2nd West Yorkshire Regiment. He is buried in Merville Communal Cemetery. The family came from an old and distinguished lineage dating back to the Norman Conquest.

Major Matthew Percival BUCKLE DSO, 1st Queen's Own (Royal West Kent Regiment), was killed in action on 27 October 1914, aged 45. He was the son of Admiral Claude Edward Buckle, Royal Navy, and the family home was in Lincolnshire. He was gazetted to the Royal West Kent Regiment in 1889 and served as adjutant between 1897 and 1901. BUCKLE was awarded his DSO in the South African War in recognition of services during the campaign. He was present at operations in the Orange Free State and was severely wounded in 1900. He also took part in operations in the Orange River Colony, including action at Wittebergen and in Cape Colony, Transvaal and on the Zululand frontier in Natal. He was mentioned in despatches on 10 September 1901. After South Africa he attended the Staff College, serving also at the War Office, and at Aldershot as brigade major. He was on the list of qualified interpreters in French and also served at the Staff College in India with the temporary rank of lieutenant colonel.

When war broke out BUCKLE was about to take up an appointment in Albania, but returned to his battalion in Dublin instead, sailing for France on 13 August as part of the BEF. He was present during the Retreat from Mons, the Marne and the Aisne and he was twice mentioned in despatches, firstly on 8 October 1914, and again on 14 January 1915. He died whilst commanding his battalion. His leadership in defence of his battalion's position was said to have been exemplary, holding out for eight days without losing a trench. In many ways he epitomised the notion of the perfect regimental officer of his day. He was a Freemason, a keen cricketer, and a good all-round sportsman. (Plot XXIX.C.41)

Lieutenant Duncan Gavin RAMSAY, 2nd Royal Sussex Regiment, attached 2nd Queen's (Royal West Surrey Regiment), was killed in action on 18 December 1914, aged 21. After attending Sandhurst he joined the Royal Sussex Regiment in January 1913. He was one of eight officer casualties when his battalion made a night attack on enemy trenches in support of another battalion. After the action he was reported missing and, despite a local truce in order to bury the dead and bring in the wounded, his body was not recovered. It was believed that his body had already been recovered by the Germans and his commanding officer, writing to his family, told of how two officers had been allowed into the German trench system to see a wounded British officer, whom they believed to be RAMSAY. The two officers had not been allowed to leave and were taken prisoner, so there was no further news. The attack had not gone well and machine-gun and rifle fire had been heavy. RAMSAY had been seen back in the British trenches trying to re-group remnants of his company, then making his way back towards the enemy positions, after which he was not seen again. The hope that he might still be alive, in spite of his wounds, proved unfounded and his body was buried by the Germans.

Prior to that attack, he had carried out a night reconnaissance on the enemy positions and had got to within about 20 yards of the enemy's main trenches, where he came under fire. On the night of 14 December he had taken twenty-three men to attack a German post. The picket was surprised and two of its seven occupants were killed. His party also captured a prisoner and managed to bring back two of its own wounded men. These actions shortly before his death earned him a mention in despatches on 14 January 1915. (Fleurbaix Churchyard Memorial No. 43)

1915

Company Serjeant Major William Stewart ROSS, 'A' Company, 8th Seaforth Highlanders, was killed in action at Loos on 25 September 1915, aged 46. He had served during the Relief of Chitral in 1895 and also held the Long Service and Good Conduct Medal. (Plot VI.H.5)

Lieutenant William Middleton WALLACE, aged 22, and his pilot Second Lieutenant Charles R. GALLIE, aged 24, 2 Squadron, Royal Flying Corps, were killed in action on 22 August 1915 when their BE2c came down near Sainghin whilst on a photographic reconnaissance. Both men are now buried together in the same grave. WALLACE, who had previously served with the 5th Rifle Brigade, came from Edinburgh and had been a Scottish International Rugby player. He made his debut against an England XV at Twickenham in March 1913 and had also played for Cambridge University while studying at King's College. GALLIE formerly served with the Royal Scots Fusiliers. The men were buried behind enemy lines and the Germans subsequently returned WALLACE's cigarette case, some photographs, and an identity disc to his father, via the United States Embassy. (Plot XII.D.11)

In 1915, the Royal Flying Corps was still very much a new fighting arm. Two of its men, Lieutenant Denys CORBETT-WILSON, and his observer, Second Lieutenant Isaac Newton WOODIWISS, were killed in action on 10 May 1915 when their aircraft was shot down, almost certainly by anti-aircraft fire. CORBETT-WILSON had been a member of the Royal Flying Corps (Special Reserve) when war broke out. In 1911 he had travelled to Pau where he attended an aviation school, learning to fly at his own expense. He was also an only son whose father, Carlos Wilson, was a successful lawyer.

Coming from a very comfortable middle class background, and once he had become a qualified pilot, he went out and bought himself a single-seater Blériot. It was CORBETT-WILSON who made the first ever flight across the Irish Sea, though the flight to Ireland was not without incident as rain set in and his engine and compass developed problems. However, he managed to land safely, and back in England, he frequently flew whenever he was visiting friends and family. This was at a time when even travel by private car was restricted to people of means. In 1913 he made another challenging flight, this time over the Jura Alps in a Blériot two-seater aircraft. He often wrote to his mother, who came from Ireland, and in 2006 many of his letters were published under the title, *Letters from an Early Bird – The Life and Letters of Denys Corbett-Wilson*.

WOODIWISS, an only son who had lived with his parents at Trusthorpe Manor, Lincolnshire, was the grandson of the late Sir Abraham Woodiwiss, a prominent railway contractor of his day. Those intrigued by his Christian names will be pleased to know that their suspicions are correct; he was distantly related to Sir Isaac Newton. He had attended Cheltenham College before entering Sandhurst just before the outbreak of war, after which he joined the Lincolnshire Regiment. The family home was transformed by the war. The gardeners joined the army, as did the four coach horses, much to the distress of the coachman, Mr Dakin. The house was frequently used by young officers from a nearby army camp who were invited there to play tennis and enjoy tea with the family. One of his sisters joined the Womens' Army Auxiliary Corps, whilst three others went to London to work in roles that would enable young men to be released for military service. Isaac, who was always referred to in the family as 'Newton', was 18 years old when he was killed with Lieutenant CORBETT-WILSON, aged 32. Both men are buried in the same grave (Plot XV.M.38).

Lieutenant Charles Anderson ALLISON, 2nd East Lancashire Regiment, was one of six officers from that battalion killed in action at Neuve Chapelle between 10 and 14 March 1915. ALLISON died on 12 March, aged 33, when the Germans launched an attack to recover the ground they had lost during the previous two days. Though initially successful, they were driven back by a counter-attack by the 1st Worcestershire Regiment and the 2nd Northamptonshire Regiment, supported by the 2nd East Lancashire Regiment, which managed to secure breastworks and houses near the Mauquissart–Pietre road. Ironically, this had been the objective of a proposed British attack that day, which never took place owing to the German pre-emptive strike at 5am that morning. He had served as regimental sergeant major and was one of five senior battalion NCOs who received their commission shortly after their arrival in France. (Plot XVI.AA.38)

Serjeant John MACDONALD DCM, 4th Black Watch, was killed in action on 8 May 1915. The award was gazetted on 3 June 1915 and was awarded for ability, courage and dash in leading his section during an attack at Neuve Chapelle on 10 March 1915. (Plot XVII.A.5)

Captain John Francis BILL, 1st South Wales Borderers, died of wounds from a sniper's bullet in the Port Arthur sector on 29 March 1915, aged 33 (Plot XXVII.A.7). His brother, Kenneth, also fell while serving with the 11th Battalion, Tank Corps, on 18 April 1918, aged 24. He is buried at Brown's Road Military Cemetery, Festubert, and had previously served with King Edward's Horse.

Captain Duncan CAMPBELL, 2nd Black Watch, was killed in action on 18 May 1915, aged 34. The battalion was holding trenches near Rue du Bois between 16 and 19 May, often under heavy shell fire. His father, Edward Parker Campbell, served as a major in the Black Watch and then as a lieutenant colonel in the Argyll & Sutherland Highlanders. Duncan served in the South African campaign and in the Nigerian Expedition. His brother, Patrick Colin Campbell MC, joined his father's late regiment, the Argyll & Sutherland Highlanders, before transferring to the Royal Flying Corps and winning the MC for coming to the assistance of a cavalry patrol by dropping bombs on the enemy and enabling his observer to enfilade their trench with machine-gun fire. Unlike his brother, he survived the war. (Plot XVII.A.15)

Second Lieutenant Kenneth Rose DENNYS, 2nd Royal Munster Fusiliers, was killed at Aubers Ridge on 9 May 1915, aged 25. He was shot in the head almost immediately while leading his platoon over the top. The British bombardment had failed to subdue the enemy's positions and the Germans were able to man their trenches as soon as the attack began. The attackers met a hail of rifle and machine-gun fire. His father had been Crown Solicitor for Hong Kong and his late grandfather was a major general in the Indian Army. DENNYS had been born in Hong Kong, but was then educated in England where he later began a career as an actor. When the war broke out he enlisted in the 28th Battalion,

London Regiment (Artists' Rifles), before receiving a temporary commission, whereupon he transferred to the 2nd Royal Munster Fusiliers. (Plot XVII.A.17)

Lieutenant the Honourable Keith Anthony STEWART, 2nd Black Watch, was killed in action at Aubers Ridge on 9 May 1915, aged 20. He was educated at Harrow and the Royal Military College, Sandhurst. He was commissioned on 12 August 1914 and had been involved in action at Givenchy and at Neuve Chapelle prior to his death. He was the son of the late Randolph Henry Stewart, 11th Earl of Galloway, whose estate was near Newton Stewart, Wigtownshire. (Plot XVII.A.21)

Private Paxton Malaby DENT, 4th Seaforth Highlanders, was killed in action on 28 April 1915, aged 24. He was educated at Mill Hill School and Worcester College, Oxford. The family lived in Croydon and his father, Joseph Malaby Dent, was a successful book publisher who ran his own company and who was responsible for creating *The Everyman Library*, the plan being to publish a thousand classics at an affordable price. The Copyright Act 1911 restricted the company's ability to publish Victorian works, and the Great War caused further problems in respect of paper supply and inflation. Joseph died in 1926, but the series did eventually achieve a thousand titles in 1956, thus fulfilling his dream. (Plot XVII.A.27)

Captain Guy Greville NAPIER, 35th Sikhs, attached 47th Sikhs, died of wounds on 25 September 1915. He was a very competent cricketer and, as a member of the MCC, played for Lord's Gentlemen. He was a former pupil at Marlborough School and had also attended Cambridge. His father, Thomas Bateman Napier, had been a judge and also served as Liberal MP for Faversham, Kent, between 1906 and 1910. Although there were two daughters, Guy was his only son. (Plot XVII.A.40)

Captain Robert Foster DILL DSO, 129th Duke of Connaught's Own Baluchis, was the brother of Lieutenant John Rowe Dill, who is buried nearby, and both brothers served in the Indian Army. Robert was killed on 11 April 1915 and had held his commission since 1903. He received his DSO for gallantry at Hollebeke, near Ypres, on 31 October 1914 when he had remained with the battalion's machine-gun section until the crew of one of the guns was killed and the other gun had been put out of action, by which time he himself had been wounded. He had also been mentioned in despatches. (Plot XVII.B.1)

Major Frederick COPELAND, 69th Punjabis, had only been in France since 29 May 1915 and only joined the Indian Corps on 5 June, the day before he was killed (Plot XVII.B.13). He and the battalion's adjutant, Lieutenant John Rowe DILL, were visiting some trenches when they were both killed by a shell. Although he had only been in France for a week before his death, COPELAND had served in Egypt and Gallipoli and had been mentioned in despatches. He was 48 years old when he died. DILL, whose brother Robert is also buried in this cemetery, was the son of a prominent member of the Scottish clergy (Plot XVII.B.12).

Captain Robert Charles Wallace ALSTON, 1st Highland Light Infantry, was killed in action on 18 August 1915, aged 35, while inspecting the construction of listening posts. The posts were about 60 yards beyond our front line and were reached via covered ways. *Officers died in the Great War* indicates that he died of wounds, though the above account, taken from *Proud Heritage* by Lieutenant Colonel Oats, which chronicles the 1st and 2nd Battalions during the war, can probably be relied upon. Sources sometimes make no distinction between 'being killed in action' and 'dying soon after being wounded'. (Plot XVII.B.32)

Captain Francis Faith HODGSON, 84th Punjabis, died of wounds on 17 May 1915, aged 34. He served on the North-West Frontier in 1908 and was a career soldier in the Indian Army. He was a married man whose only daughter was born on 15 March 1915. His wife, Katherine, was a descendant of Elizabeth Fry, a Quaker and well known prison and social reformer. (Plot XVII.B.46)

Captain Percy BEATTIE-CROZIER, 4th Prince Albert Victor's Rajputs (15th Ludhiana Sikhs), was killed by shell fire on 19 May 1915. In the late afternoon, the previous day, the Sirhind Brigade had been due to attack Ferme du Bois, but heavy shelling had prevented it reaching a preliminary position along some former German trenches. A simultaneous attack on Cour d'Avoué by the Guards Brigade did go ahead and managed to make some progress. The attack by the Sirhind Brigade was planned for later that night, but never took place, and the next morning Captain BEATTIE-CROZIER was killed. He was an only son. After attending Sandhurst, he was commissioned in the South Staffordshire Regiment. In 1905 he transferred to the Indian Army and took part in two minor operations in 1909. In 1913 he became aide-de-camp to the Acting Governor of Ceylon. (Plot XVII.C.3)

Captain Eric Landon BROWN MC, 'A' Company, 4th Suffolk Regiment, was killed in action on 18 August 1915, aged 26 (Plot XVII.C.6). He had also been mentioned in despatches. The CWGC register refers to his pre-war ties to the 4th Battalion, which began in October 1908 when he was commissioned. His MC was gazetted on 29 June 1915, but I can find no citation for it. His brother, Lieutenant Horace Manton Brown MC, died of wounds on 14 April 1918 and is buried at Mendinghem Military Cemetery in Belgium. His MC was gazetted in the New Year's Honours List on 1 January 1917.

Captain Michael Algernon FITZROY, 4th Seaforth Highlanders, was killed on 17 April 1915, aged 20, whilst supervising improvements to an advanced listening post that was vulnerable to enfilade fire. According to the battalion war diary, he was killed by a sniper on 16 April near Brewery Road, Neuve Chapelle. He was the second son of the Honourable Edward Algernon Fitzroy, MP for Daventry and Speaker of the House of Commons. Michael attended Rugby School, followed by Oriel College, Oxford. When the war broke out he was abroad, but he returned to England and joined the 4/Seaforth Highlanders, obtaining his commission in September 1914. He went to France with his battalion in November 1914 and took part in the Battle of Neuve Chapelle the following March, when he was slightly wounded in the shoulder. He was promoted to captain on 11 March 1915, the second day of the Battle of Neuve Chapelle, a rank he held for barely a month before he was killed. (Plot XVII.C.22)

Lieutenant Maurice Alexander Ross Geraldine FITZMAURICE, 21st Field Company, Royal Engineers, was killed on 6 August 1915, aged 23. He had attended the Royal Military Academy, Woolwich, and had been wounded at Neuve Chapelle while his unit was trying to consolidate a captured position in the village. Before the war he had been a government engineer at Bareilly in India. His father had also been a prominent member of the Indian judiciary. Lieutenant FITZMAURICE had previously been mentioned in despatches. (Plot XVII.C.40)

Private James DEMPSTER, 1st Seaforth Highlanders, was 29 years old when he died of wounds on 9th May 1915 at Aubers Ridge (Plot XVII.D.10). Two of his brothers were also killed during the war. His brother, Frank, 2nd Gordon Highlanders, is commemorated on the Loos Memorial and was killed in action on 25 September 1915, the opening day of the Battle of Loos. His brother, John, who was awarded the MM, was wounded on 7 July 1916 serving with the 58th Company, Machine Gun Corps, but died the following day. He is buried at Bécourt Military Cemetery, Bécordel-Bécourt, on the Somme.

Lieutenant Colonel Frederick Charles FRANCE-HAYHURST, commanding the 4th Royal Welsh Fusiliers, was killed in action at the Battle of Aubers Ridge on 9 May 1915, aged 43. He landed at Le Havre with the battalion the previous year on 6 November. He was killed with others while leaving the breastworks of the support line and few, if any, managed even to reach the British front line trenches owing to the intensity of fire. A second attack later that day also ended in failure. His brother, Commander Cecil Halsted France-Hayhurst, HMS *Patuca*, died at home from illness on 24 February 1915, aged 40. The family came from Middlewich in Cheshire. (Plot XVIII. B. 20)

Major Wilfrid Harry DENT, 10th Yorkshire Regiment, was killed in action at Loos on 26 September 1915, aged 48. He was educated at Harrow and was a keen cricketer and a member of the MCC. His battalion had set off in poor light behind 45 Brigade with the 12th Northumberland Fusiliers on the left. Although the dividing line between the two battalions was a track that ran from Loos to Hill 70 Redoubt, the maps provided were not detailed enough. Dent and his men mistook the Loos Crassier, which was not shown on their map, for Hill 70, which was on it, but was poorly marked. After coming under heavy fire the men began to drift back. Lieutenant Colonel Hadow, DENT's commanding officer, was the first to expose himself to danger when he rose up and encouraged his men to press forward. When he was killed, DENT did exactly the same, but was also cut down, and a further two officers died trying to rally the York-shiremen. By mid-morning, however, they were forced to withdraw to the western slopes of the hill from where the attack had originally begun. DENT had also served in Burma and at the Relief of Peking in 1900. (Plot XVIII.E.1)

Second Lieutenant John (Jock) GAY, 16 Squadron, Royal Flying Corps, was killed in action on 10 October 1915, aged 22. His observer that day, Lieutenant D. Leeson, was taken prisoner. GAY and Leeson had flown together on several occasions and had begun to develop a good understanding as a team. They were involved in a number of encounters with enemy aircraft, and on one occasion, while carrying out a reconnaissance over Courière, they became engaged with an Albatros, which seemed to be manoeuvring as if to fire, but then suddenly dived when fired at. GAY and Leeson dived in pursuit, firing as they went. The German then released a white flare, at which point machine-gun and rifle fire was directed at them from ground troops. The pair realized that it was time to break off, but not before they had attacked an enemy balloon, forcing it to be pulled down. GAY, who was an only son, had begun studying Medicine at St Bartholomew's Hospital in the City of London where he also joined the City of London Yeomanry. He and Leeson were shot down over German lines while on a photographic reconnaissance. (Plot XX.F.9)

Brothers Arthur and Richard FOLLOWS were both killed in action on 25 January 1915 while serving as privates with the 1st Coldstream Guards. Their army numbers show that they enlisted together and it is fitting that they now lie next to each other in death (Plot XXV.B.1 and 2). They came from Ansley, Nuneaton, in Warwickshire and were aged 22 and 23 respectively. Their deaths occurred when the Germans launched a local attack either side of the La Bassée Canal. The fighting was fierce, and although the line was driven back, most of the ground was later recovered by counter-attack. For the 1st Coldstream Guards the cost was heavy and amounted to 202 casualties in total.

Drummer Denis HAYES, 2nd Leicestershire Regiment, was killed in action on 13 March 1915, aged 16. His battalion had attacked a few days earlier, on 10 March, at Neuve Chapelle and was relieved on the 13th when it moved to L'Épinette. The battalion's war diary records that it had succeeded in gaining several of the enemy's trenches and had managed to consolidate them. (Plot XXVI.L.10)

Lieutenant Colonel Victor George Howard RICKARD, aged 40, took command of the 2nd Royal Munster Fusiliers as the battalion was being brought up to strength shortly before the Battle of Aubers Ridge. He was killed immediately on 9 May 1915 when a bullet struck the spinal column in his neck just as he was leaving the trench to follow 'D' Company in support of the initial attack.

The close proximity of his body to our own front line enabled his body to be recovered far more easily than was the case for the many others who are now commemorated on the Le Touret Memorial. The battalion's casualties that day amounted to 379, including forty-nine killed. The day before the attack, as he and his battalion were making their way to the trenches, RICKARD had formed the battalion into a hollow square near a wayside calvary where he spoke to his men about their coming ordeal. The men received general absolution from Father Gleeson before singing a 'Te Deum' and resuming their march to the front.

In 1918 RCKARD's wife published a small book entitled, *The Story of the Munsters*, which covered the battalion's actions at Étreux, Festubert, Rue du Bois and Hulluch, and which she dedicated to her late husband and all his regimental comrades who fell in 1914 and 1915. On the dedication page she refers to the shamrock, which forms part of the regimental cap badge. Her husband had introduced it within the battalion in February 1915 in order to give it a distinctly Irish emblem. The appendix section of her book contains two extracts from a moving and affectionate letter written to her by Serjeant Louis Moore and dated midnight on 25 May 1915. He had just returned from the trenches, and despite the lateness of the hour, he described how he had visited her husband's grave the day before and had '*seen that everything was well*'. He added that he intended to get a photograph of it and send it on to her. The letter continues by saying that a cross had been appropriately inscribed and that '*in case anything should happen to me, I have marked the exact place on my map.*' Before the war the couple had lived together in France, at Parame in Brittany. RICKARD's body was re-buried here at Cabaret Rouge after the Armistice. (Plot XXVII.A.14)

Private Christopher BARRY DCM, 2nd Royal Munster Fusiliers, a native of Cork, was one of five members of the battalion to receive this award for gallantry in defence of trenches at Givenchy, just north of the La Bassée Canal, on 25 January 1915, which was the Kaiser's birthday. The line had given way on the left of the Munsters' position, as it had in several places along the divisional front, which allowed the Germans to get partly behind their position. The 2nd Royal Munster Fusiliers held on throughout the day until a counter-attack was able to restore their left flank. BARRY, described as 'a slip of a boy', had carried messages back and forth all day under heavy fire in an effort to maintain communication. He was killed a few months later at Aubers Ridge on 9 May while rescuing Captain Hawkes who lay wounded out in the open. Astonishingly, this act of gallantry and self-sacrifice earned him a mention, but no posthumous gallantry award was ever made. Given BARRY's slight build, this feat was all the more remarkable since Hawkes was considered to be one of the biggest men in the battalion. His DCM was gazetted posthumously on 29 June 1915. (Plot XXIX.A.61)

Corporal Ralph HILL, 1/5th Leicestershire Regiment, was killed in action on 13 October 1915, aged 19 (Plot XXIX.C.36). His brother, Harold, was also killed during the war and died on 3 May 1917 serving with the 11th East Yorkshire Regiment. He has no known grave and is commemorated on the Arras Memorial.

Lieutenant Colonel Richard Charles DUNDAS, 11th Royal Scots, was killed in action near Haisnes on 25 September 1915 at the Battle of Loos. He went to

France in 1914 as a major with the 2nd Royal Scots, acting temporarily as its commanding officer before transferring to the 3rd Division staff. In due course, he became the commanding officer of the 11th Royal Scots. Some of his battalion, along with others from the 12th Royal Scots, did manage to reach the outskirts of Haisnes under heavy fire, but were later forced to withdraw to Fosse 8. DUNDAS fell near to where Pekin Trench linked up with Haisnes Trench, along the western edge of the village, as his men tried to cut a way through the enemy's wire. His grandmother, the Honourable Mary Tufton Duncan, was the daughter of Admiral Adam Duncan, 1st Viscount Duncan of Camperdown, who fought at the Battle of Cape Vincent in 1780, and who, as commander-in-chief of the North Sea Fleet, defeated the Dutch fleet off Camperdown in 1797. (Plot XXX.H.3)

Lance Corporal Peter SANDS, 1st Royal Irish Rifles, was executed on 15 September 1915 at Fleurbaix. Not only did he manage to desert from his unit, he also succeeded in making it back to England. He was brought back to France where he was tried and found guilty. He was shot near to the churchyard in Fleurbaix where he was buried. After the war his grave could not be located, so Cabaret Rouge British Cemetery was chosen as the location to commemorate him. (Fleurbaix Churchyard Memorial 41)

1916

Second Lieutenant Frank WILSON, 3rd King's Liverpool Regiment, attached 1st Battalion, died on 3 June 1916 while trying to save the lives of two miners trapped in a collapsed gallery in the Vimy Ridge sector after the Germans had exploded a camouflet near Kennedy Crater. Several other men who rushed to assist became casualties from the effects of gas poisoning. (Plot III.D.3)

There are 123 men buried here from the London Regiment who were killed during 1916, the vast majority coming from battalions that made up the 47th (London) Division. This division, which came to the Vimy Ridge sector in March of that year, was involved in some serious fighting between 22 and 24 May that resulted in 1,571 casualties. Although just under 10 per cent were recorded as killed in action on casualty rolls at the time, which is a fairly low percentage, many more of the 461 officers and men shown as missing would have been killed. Quite a few of the 958 wounded would also have died later.

Second Lieutenant George Archibald Colin LOMAS DCM, 20th Battalion, London Regiment (Blackheath and Woolwich), was the son of a clergyman and was the battalion's Lewis gun officer when he was killed in action on 22 May 1916 at Vimy Ridge, aged 28. His DCM was gazetted posthumously. The German artillery had been unusually active for two days before the attack, which then began on 21 May at around 7.45pm. Four hours prior to the attack the Germans put down a very effective box barrage that isolated the area to be assaulted. 'A' Company, under Captain Leslie Alexander YOUNG, managed to hold up the first attack on Ersatz Alley, a communication trench at the northern end of Zouave Valley, but was eventually forced back into a support trench. LOMAS, acting alone, took a Lewis gun out into the open in order to cover the retirement, repelling three counter-attacks as the fighting continued throughout the night until he was eventually killed. (Plot III.E.6)

Captain YOUNG had already been killed, as had Captain Harold Charles Norman TAYLOR of 'B' Company, the son of Sir Frederick Taylor MD FRCS, 1st Baronet. TAYLOR was the battalion's adjutant at the time. On hearing that the Germans had penetrated the line of craters held by his men, he immediately organized and personally led a counter-attack, which succeeded in driving the enemy from the position. Both YOUNG and TAYLOR were killed in action on 21 May, shortly before LOMAS fell. They are buried in Plot III, the former in Row D.21, the latter in Row E.5.

Serjeant W.Z. PORTER DCM, 22nd (County of London) Battalion, London Regiment (The Queen's), was killed in action on 23 May 1916, barely two months after the award of his DCM, which was gazetted on 11 March. It was awarded for conspicuous gallantry carrying sandbags and provisions up to the lines under heavy fire. W.Z. PORTER is, in fact, Serjeant William Sayer PORTER from Deptford in South London. The *London Gazette* shows him as 'W.S.' and not 'W.Z.' PORTER. (Plot III.D.14)

Lance Serjeant Frank Shaw CUSS DCM, 6th Battalion, London Regiment (City of London Rifles), was killed in action on 30 April 1916. His DCM was gazetted on 17 January 1916. The short citation appeared on 14 March that year describing his conspicuous gallantry. Having led a bombing party into the first line of enemy trenches, where they cleared the dug-outs, he then continued to lead the attack up a communication trench. (Plot III.H.5)

A small number of burials can be found relating to the Battle of Fromelles. This action, which took place on a single day on 19 July 1916, was intended as a diversionary attack away from the main fighting on the Somme, but instead resulted in 5,533 Australian and 1,547 British casualties. In 2007 the bodies of 250 Australian and British soldiers who took part in this action were discovered in several pits dug near Pheasant Wood where they had been buried by the Germans on 19 and 20 July in 1916. Exhumation was carried out in 2009 and a detailed forensic investigation took place to identify as many as possible, which has resulted in ninety-seven identifications by name. The Australian units involved that day came from 8, 14 and 15 Brigades, which were part of the 5th Australian Division.

Twenty-three identified casualties from this tragic action were brought here from one or more of the 103 original wartime cemeteries that were closed during the concentration process. Plot XVI contains thirteen men from all three of the Australian brigades that took part in the operation, mainly in Row C, 1 to 12. A further three Australian soldiers lie in Plots XV, XVIII and XXI and seven men of the British 61st (2nd South Midland) Division, belonging to the 2/7th Royal

Warwickshire Regiment, the 2/6th Gloucestershire Regiment and the 182nd Machine Gun Company, and who died in this attack, are represented by special memorials in Plots VIII and XVIII.

There are sixty-nine burials from the 11th, 12th and 13th Battalions, Royal Sussex Regiment, mainly in Plot XV, and mainly from 30 June 1916. There is a small, but interesting footnote in *The Official History of the War, Military Operations, France & Belgium 1916, Volume II*, that points out that between 1 July 1916 and the middle of November that year no fewer than 310 raids were carried out by the British First, Second and Third Armies, none of which, of course, was engaged on the Somme. The same source claims that corresponding German raids amounted to sixty-five. These raids were often relatively small affairs ranging in strength from a couple of platoons to a couple of companies, and were aimed not only at harassing the enemy, but equally importantly, at identifying German units. Confirming which units were not active on the Somme at any one time was as important to the overall intelligence picture as knowing which ones were.

The raid by two battalions of the Royal Sussex Regiment during the early hours of 30 June 1916 was carried out with the aim of capturing the German front line and some support trenches that formed a salient just south of Neuve Chapelle, known to the troops as the Boar's Head. The 12th and 13th Battalions, Royal Sussex Regiment, which belonged to the 39th Division, were selected for the task and began preparing for it a week before it was scheduled to take place.

German machine-gun fire was heavy throughout the entire operation. Some men from the 13th Battalion managed to get into the enemy support trenches, but smoke that had been put down in order to mask the attack drifted across the front and this caused confusion and loss of direction. There was some fighting with the enemy using bomb and bayonet, and initial steps were taken to put the captured trenches into a state of defence. Loss of direction had also led to congestion on the right-hand side of the raided area, whilst on the left-hand side very few of the attackers actually reached the enemy's wire. Ironically, the smoke and darkness that seemed to hamper the British efforts did not seem to hinder the Germans, who put down a heavy bombardment using high explosive shells on the congested section of trenches on the right of the attack. After two hours, Captain Hughes, who was commanding the raid, gave the order to retire. As the withdrawal was taking place the Germans shelled the British front and support trenches causing further casualties.

Despite failing to secure the German trenches, Lieutenant General Haking, commanding XI Corps, in whose area the operation took place, considered it a success. However, the war diary of the 13th Battalion acknowledged it as a failure, citing a number of factors as the cause, including the unfortunate consequences of the smoke, the preparedness of the enemy, the intensity of the enemy bombardment and machine-gun fire, and the failure of our artillery to cut the wire on the left of the attack. It did, however, result in significant numbers of

German dead according to reports compiled after the operation, though it is always hard to arrive at any exact figure to justify such claims.

Total casualties for the two battalions came to 950, almost the equivalent of an entire battalion. Given the circumstances, the bodies of many of those killed in the German trenches, or close to the enemy's wire, would not have been recovered. Those that were can now be found in Plot XV.

Several of the officers from the 13th Battalion who lost their lives in this operation are buried here. They are: Lieutenant Clive SPARKS (Plot XV.R.32); Second Lieutenant George John FENCHELLE, who according to *Officers Died in the Great War* died of wounds as a prisoner of war (Plot XV. R.34); Lieutenant Harold Lancelot FITZHERBERT (Plot XV.R.36), and Second Lieutenant Martin Charles DIGGENS (Plot XV.R.38).

Lieutenant Harold Lancelot FITZHERBERT was the grandson of Sir William Fitzherbert KCMG, the New Zealand politician and MP. Harold was farming in Argentina when the war broke out, but came to England and enlisted with his brother in the 12th Royal Sussex Regiment. He was soon commissioned, but did not go to the front until March 1916. His brother, Captain Wyndham Waterhouse Fitzherbert, later transferred to the Royal Flying Corps and was killed in action with 55 Squadron on 7 July 1917. He is commemorated on the Flying Services Memorial in Arras.

A further nine officers were killed in the raid, eight of whom are commemorated on the Loos Memorial, whilst the ninth is buried at St. Vaast Post Military Cemetery, Richebourg L'Avoué.

From time to time the visitor may notice headstones that show the date of death as 1 July 1916. However, nine of these eleven are not casualties from the Battle of the Somme. They belong to the 2nd Division or to the 14th (Light) Division, and there is also one man from the 13th Royal Sussex Regiment who almost certainly died of wounds received the previous day. Both these divisions subsequently fought on the Somme, as did the 39th Division, but at the outset of the offensive they were both further north, where the 2nd Division was holding the Vimy sector.

Preparations for the Somme meant that the British had been unable to devote time and resources to re-taking the ground lost on 22 May at Vimy Ridge. However, this sector did witness raids on a frequent basis throughout the summer of 1916, including a raid by the 13th Essex Regiment on the night of 1/2 July in the Bethonval sub-sector. It was in the Vimy sector around this time that the Germans first made significant use of lachrymatory shells, the first ones falling on Carency on 2 July.

According to *Soldiers Died in the Great War*, Serjeant Claude Leopold BEAUMONT, 16th Battalion, London Regiment (Queen's Westminster Rifles), was killed in action on 1 July 1916, aged 35. It is likely that he died later that day during the German counter-attack at Gommecourt, which re-took the small gains made by the 56th (London) Division and which forced the

London men back to the positions from which they had started on the opening day of the Battle of the Somme. It is also likely that he was buried by the Germans when they began clearing up their trenches after the fighting. The CWGC register refers to the fact that the original wartime cemetery here was considerably enlarged after the war when graves were brought in from over 100 other cemeteries; BEAUMONT's was one of them. He had been reported missing in action on 1 July, but his body was eventually found in 1928 and he was identified thanks to a locket found with him (Plot XXII.C.16). Presumably, the body of Rifleman Charles George Algernon EDWARDS was discovered at around the same time as BEAUMONT's. He too was killed in action on 1 July and is now buried a short distance from his comrade (Plot XXII.C.11).

Second Lieutenant Derek Sivewright JOHNSON, 25 Squadron, Royal Flying Corps, was killed in action on 4 December 1916, aged 21, while returning with members of his squadron from a bombing raid over Pont-a-Vendin (Plot XVI.D.1). Though in the middle of a tight formation, his machine was attacked in a vertical dive by a Halberstadt Scout and was seen to crash in flames in the Bois de Farbus. The Halberstadt was a particularly robust construction that was capable of withstanding the stress caused by vertical dives. JOHNSON was the son of Colonel Frank Johnson, Royal Sussex Regiment. Nearby is Lieutenant Ivan HEALD, aged 33, who was JOHNSON's observer that day. He was older than JOHNSON and was working towards his pilot's certificate when he died. He had previously served with the 63rd (Royal Naval) Division in Gallipoli and had been wounded there. In civilian life he was on the editorial staff of the *Daily Express* (Plot XVI.D.11).

Second Lieutenant Morden Maxwell MOWAT, 11 Squadron, Royal Flying Corps, who was 25 years old, was known to have left his aerodrome at 4.55pm on 16 May 1916 flying a Bristol Scout, but he never returned. He was shot down by the German ace, Max Immelmann, whilst he was engaged with two other enemy aircraft. When his aircraft crashed it was not severely damaged, but MOWAT was barely alive when he was dragged from it and he died of his wounds before he could reach a German field hospital. Unfortunately, he had been struck by a bullet to the chest. Captain Albert Ball referred to MOWAT in his diary as a 'topping chap', and admitted that his death had upset him. Ironically, MOWAT had had a lucky escape on the morning of his death when he had crashed a Bristol Scout into a hangar at his aerodrome. (Plot XVI.D.4)

On 18 June 1916 Second Lieutenant Clarence Elias ROGERS, 25 Squadron, Royal Flying Corps, and his observer, Sergeant Taylor, were reported to have landed about three miles north-north-east of Arras behind enemy lines. One of the occupants was seen to get out and enter the enemy's trench system. ROGERS is shown as having died that day, and it seems likely that it was Taylor who emerged from the aircraft. ROGERS, who was originally buried by the Germans, is now buried here. Their aircraft was also shot down by German ace, Max Immelmann. Taylor was presumably captured and taken prisoner. (Plot XVI.D.6)

Another officer from 25 Squadron, Royal Flying Corps, is Second Lieutenant John Lewis Pasteur ARMSTRONG who was mortally wounded in aerial combat on 22 June 1916, aged 25. His observer, Serjeant G. Topcliffe, was taken prisoner. Their aircraft came down behind enemy lines near Loos and it would appear that ARMSTRONG, who died some three hours later, was wounded three times during his final encounter. He was originally buried by the Germans, but his body was brought to Cabaret Rouge after the war for re-burial. ARMSTRONG transferred to the Royal Flying Corps from the Royal Army Service Corps and worked at the Vickers Engineering Works in Sheffield before the war. (Plot VII.H.1)

Second Lieutenant Harold Winstone BUTTERWORTH, 18 Squadron, Royal Flying Corps, was killed in action on 22 June 1916, aged 21. The CWGC register shows his date of death as 15 July, as do other records. BUTTERWORTH enlisted locally in New Zealand where he was living, but was unable to go overseas with the first contingent of the New Zealand Expeditionary Force. Undeterred, he travelled at his own expense to England where he joined the Royal Flying Corps and quickly qualified as a pilot. He also worked at training establishments there for a while, but then spent six months on operational flying on the Western Front before his death. Flying with him that day was Captain J.H. McEwan, who was taken prisoner. His diary, which he kept between the end of March 1915 and the end of January 1916, is now held at the Air Force Museum in New Zealand. After that time he would have been in France and may not have had time, or perhaps even felt the inclination to continue with his journal. The confusion over his date of death arises from the fact that he was reported missing in action on 22 June. The Royal Flying Corps communiqué for that day is very clear and specific regarding that fact. However, confirmation of BUTTERWORTH's death, which did occur on 22 June, only reached the War Office on 16 July, which is where records have become confused. (Plot XV.J.25)

Lieutenant Arthur James AUSTEN-CARTMELL, 1st King's Royal Rifle Corps, was killed in action at Vimy Ridge on 1 June 1916, aged 23. He was educated at Eton and Trinity College, Cambridge. He and his battalion that day carried out a repeat of an attack that had previously failed on the night of 29/30 May. This second attack was partially successful and, despite heavy shell fire from both sides, the battalion's casualties were light. At the conclusion of the attack our engineers exploded three mines. Although twenty-one other ranks were wounded in the operation, AUSTEN-CARTMELL was the only fatality and his funeral took place at Villers-au-Bois the following day. His brother, Captain Hugh Geoffrey Austen-Cartmell, 2nd Highland Light Infantry, was also a pupil at Eton and was killed in action just north of Beaumont-Hamel on 13 November 1916 at the end of the fighting on the Somme. He has no known grave and is commemorated on the Thiepval Memorial. Their father was a prominent London barrister and the family lived in very comfortable circumstances in Kensington, north London. (Plot XV.M.12)

Second Lieutenant Gilbert Heron CURRIE DCM, 3rd Argyll & Sutherland Highlanders, attached 10th Battalion, was killed in action on 12 October 1916, aged 21. With regard to his DCM, which was gazetted on 5 August 1915, he won it whilst serving as a private in the 9th Highland Light Infantry (Glasgow Highlanders). It was awarded for great bravery and devotion to duty on 17 May 1915 at Richebourg where Private CURRIE volunteered to carry three messages up to captured German breastworks under heavy rifle fire and shell fire. These messages had previously been passed along the trench from hand to hand, but when he found that they had not gone beyond the end of the trench, he collected them and carried them across 100 yards of open ground under heavy fire where he delivered them. (Plot XVII.AA.29)

Lieutenant Bernard Harold HARTLEY, 20th Lancashire Fusiliers, was killed in action on 4 November 1916, aged 21. He had been head boy of School House at Clifton College, Bristol, where he was a member of the OTC. He then went on to Manchester School of Technology, later to become the University of Manchester Institute of Science and Technology (UMIST). He was an only son and was born in St Petersburg, Russia, where his family had a cotton business. He had originally enlisted in the Inns of Court OTC from which he was commissioned in June 1915. His early days in France were blighted by illness, requiring hospitalization at one point, but he was able to return to his battalion in March 1916. In August 1916 the battalion moved from the Somme to the Arras sector where he was killed while carrying out a reconnaissance of some old trenches in no man's land, which it was hoped might be used for a future raid. According to the intelligence report by the NCO who was out with him that night, it would appear that Lieutenant HARTLEY had at one point ventured very close to the enemy's wire and that the two had then become separated. His body was apparently recovered by the Germans the following day who then buried him. (Plot XVII.J.26)

Lance Serjeant Alfred Edward LENNOX, 1st Regiment, South African Brigade, was killed in action on 18 October 1916, aged 40 (Plot XXX.E.21). During the South African War he had served with the Cape Mounted Police, and also with the South African Mounted Rifles in German South-West Africa in 1914–1915. He is one of twenty-eight South African soldiers buried here, most of whom fell on 9 April 1917. He and the two men next to him, together with another man who is buried elsewhere in the cemetery (Plot XVI.H.40), were all killed in action on the same day, but not in the Arras sector. They fell in an attack to capture the Butte de Warlencourt, near Le Sars on the Somme. Whether they were killed in action or died of wounds, they were probably buried by the Germans and their bodies brought here after the war.

In 1926 a farmer ploughing near the site of Red Dragon Crater, near Givenchy, had to stop work when a piece of timber became caught up in the ploughshare. When he removed it, he discovered a hollow, almost certainly the remains of a dug-out, containing the bodies of two British officers. They were identified as Second Lieutenant Trevor Allington CROSLAND, 2nd Royal Welsh Fusiliers, and Captain Owen PRYCE-EDWARDS, who were attached to 'B' Company of the same battalion from the 18th Royal Fusiliers. They were originally reported missing after the Germans had fired a mine prior to a trench raid in the early hours of 22 June 1916. The subsequent crater became known as Red Dragon Crater by association with the cap badge of the Royal Welsh Fusiliers. CROS-LAND, who was only 19 years old, was described in one account as being 'thrilled' as he had marched his platoon up to the position that evening. It was to be his first and only experience of life in the trenches, for he was killed just three hours later. Both men were subsequently reburied in this cemetery, but for some reason not together. CROSLAND is buried in Plot XXXI.A.27 and PRYCE-EDWARDS is buried in the same plot, but in Row B.3

Second Lieutenant Robert Harold BECKH, 12th East Yorkshire Regiment, died of wounds on 15 August 1916, aged 22. His family lived at Great Amwell, Hertfordshire. He attended Haileybury College, virtually a stone's throw from the family home, before going on to Jesus College, Cambridge. He was killed in action by machine-gun fire near Robecq whilst carrying out a routine night patrol. He was also a minor poet, some of whose work was published in 1917 under the title, *Swallows in Storm and Sunlight*. Perhaps his best known work is 'The Song of Sheffield', with its repeated lines, '*Shells, shells, shells! The song of the city of steel*'. (Marquillies Communal Cemetery, German Extension, Memorial 24)

1917

Private Walter Stewart IRWIN, 78th Battalion, Canadian Infantry, was killed in action on 22 February 1917, aged 16. (Plot II.B.3)

Captain Hugh TOMLINSON MC, 57 Squadron, Royal Flying Corps, was killed in action on 2 April 1917, aged 34, when the FE2d aircraft he was flying came down. His observer, Lieutenant N.C. Dennison, was taken prisoner. TOMLINSON had also been mentioned in despatches. TOMLINSON's MC was gazetted on 26 June 1916 and the citation appeared on 31 July the same year. It was awarded for gallantry and devotion to duty after taking part in two air raids. Despite sustaining serious injuries on two occasions during night flights, he remained undaunted and continued to fly, carrying out most valuable work. (Plot VII.J.3)

Lieutenant Norman FIELD, 25 Squadron, Royal Flying Corps, was killed in action along with his pilot, Second Lieutenant Peter Liddell (Lydell) McGAVIN, who was flying their DH4 on 14 August 1917. McGAVIN was a Canadian who had studied at Toronto University. He was recommended for a commission and initially began training with the artillery. However, he opted to transfer to the Royal Flying Corps where he was commissioned in March 1917. Much of his flying was carried out around Lens and Arras. On the day they were killed, he and FIELD were part of a bombing operation behind German lines south-east of Lens. As they were returning home they were intercepted by a large enemy formation and attacked. Sadly, they were shot down and killed. (Plot VII.H.9 and 10)

Captain Charles John Beech MASEFIELD MC, 'C' Company, 1/5th North Staffordshire Regiment, died from his wounds on 2 July 1917 while in German captivity, aged 35. His MC was gazetted on 25 August 1917 and was awarded for conspicuous gallantry and devotion to duty (as a second lieutenant) in recognition of his leadership during a raid on enemy trenches, which he had carried out with great dash and skill under heavy trench mortar fire. During the raid he attacked a party of the enemy single-handed, personally killing two of them at close quarters. The raid resulted in the killing of at least fifty of the enemy and three prisoners were also captured. Once his objective had been achieved, he successfully withdrew his company. The citation adds that he had shown conspicuous gallantry and good leadership throughout the entire operation. (Plot VI.H.23)

Lieutenant Douglas GORDON, 10 Squadron, Royal Flying Corps, formerly Argyll & Sutherland Highlanders, was killed in action on 14 August 1917, aged 19. His observer, Lieutenant Percy Grant Cameron, was also killed, aged 25, when their Armstrong Whitworth FK 8 aircraft was shot down while on observation duty for the artillery. Cameron's body was never recovered and he is now commemorated on the Flying Services Memorial, Arras. GORDON had gained his pilot's certificate in December 1916. (Plot VII.D.1)

Second Lieutenant Frank ROUX, 10 Squadron, Royal Flying Corps, originally from Clermont Ferrand, France, was killed in action on 26 April 1917, aged 31, flying a BE2e aircraft. His observer, Second Lieutenant J.H. Price, was taken prisoner. (Plot VII.G.15)

Second Lieutenant Herbert Arthur CROFT, 2 Squadron, Royal Flying Corps, was killed in action on 14 February 1917 when his machine was shot down by Manfred von Richthofen near Loos while observing for a battery of the Royal Garrison Artillery. His machine crashed near Cité St. Auguste. His observer, Second Lieutenant Cyril Douglas Bennett, who was born in Moscow where his parents happened to be working at the time, was injured in the crash, but survived the war as a German prisoner. Bennett was an interesting character. In 1919, after his release from captivity, he served briefly in the Caucasus and the Volga region against the Bolsheviks, and then in the Second World War he worked in a liaison role with the Russians in Teheran. (Plot VII.H.11)

Private Gordon Victor MACKIE, 'D' Company, 25th Battalion, Canadian Infantry, was killed in action on 28 April 1917, aged 16. Mackie had previously served with the 112th Battalion along with his brother, Private Everett Mackie. Both had enlisted at the same time, though their attestation papers show that Gordon enlisted the day after Everett, who was 18 years old. There is the intriguing possibility that on 9 December 1915 Gordon went with his brother to join up, but had given his correct date of birth and been turned away. Could he have returned the following day, a few years older? His army record shows his date of birth as 21 May 1897, making him 'officially' 19 years old when he died. (Plot VII.Q.8)

The headstone for Pioneer George Candlish TAYOR, Canadian Pioneers, shows his date of death as 30 April 1917 and records that he was 24 years old when he died. The inscription at the base of the stone is particularly poignant and notes that he was killed on his birthday. His parents lived in Toronto, but he was born in Aberdeen. I came across his grave by chance while carrying out other research in this cemetery in March 2014. (Plot VIII.A.1)

Second Lieutenant Derek Percy COX, 27 Squadron, Royal Flying Corps, was killed in action on 21 August 1917, aged 21. He was shot down near Lille while on a bombing mission and was originally reported as missing in action. News of his death was later confirmed by the Germans via the Red Cross. He was educated at Harrow and Trinity College, Cambridge. When the war broke out he joined the 11th (Prince Albert's Own) Hussars, but having gained a place at Sandhurst, he then decided to serve as a private in the Machine Gun Corps. However, after over a year in the ranks, he accepted a commission in the Royal Flying Corps, serving initially as an observer. He returned home in September 1916, where he qualified as a pilot, and returned to the front in June 1917. (Plot VIII.J.29)

His father was Major General Sir Percy Zachariah Cox GCMG GCIE KCSI and his mother, Lady Cox DBE, was the daughter of Surgeon General, Sir John Butler Hamilton. General Cox had a very interesting military and colonial career. He was originally commissioned in the Cameronians, but then served on the Staff of the Bengal Corps. He was then posted to British Somaliland where he led an expedition against rebels who were disrupting trade routes and carrying out raids along the coast. He subsequently held a series of administrative and political posts in Muscat and the Persian Gulf where he had a hand in the establishment of an effectively autonomous Kuwait. During the war he served in Mesopotamia and Palestine as Chief Political Officer attached to the Indian Expeditionary Force, and towards the end of the war he was involved in negotiations that led to the Anglo-Persian Agreement. His most striking legacy was his involvement in the creation of what we now know as the modern state of Iraq following the revolt there against the British in 1920. He served as High Commissioner there until 1923. He also became a very good friend of the adventurer and archaeologist, Gertrude Bell. He died in 1937.

Lieutenant Hubert Pelham SWORDER, formerly of the Queen's (Royal West Surrey Regiment), and his observer, Second Lieutenant Alfred Henry MAR-GOLIOUTH, formerly 5th King's Own Yorkshire Light Infantry, were both attached to 57 Squadron, Royal Flying Corps, and were killed in action on 2 April 1917 when their FE2d came down (Plot VIII.S.32 and 33). SWORDER's brother, Lieutenant John Perkins Sworder, 2/4th Queen's (Royal West Surrey Regiment) was also killed while attached to 1/1st Herefordshire Regiment on 24 July 1918, aged 28. He is buried in Vauxbuin French National Cemetery near Soissons.

Lieutenant Charles Jesse PULLEN, 25 Squadron, Royal Flying Corps, formerly Royal Garrison Artillery, and his observer Second Lieutenant Eustace Dixon Sharper ROBINSON, aged 19, were killed in action on 4 September 1917. They were reported as missing in action and by the end of the war their bodies had still not been found. Their names were then recorded on the Flying Services Memorial at Arras, but both men are now commemorated in this cemetery. Both headstones now carry the inscription: 'Believed to be'. (Special Memorials VIII.U.5 and 6)

Private Archibald ABERDEEN, 10th Cameronians, was killed in action on 22 December 1917 while carrying out a reconnaissance. *Soldiers Died in the Great War* indicates that he died of wounds. This was a quiet period on the Arras front and along the Western Front in general, though offensive patrols, raids, and re-connaissance never stopped and intelligence gathering continued as usual. (Plot XII.E.11)

Among the forty-two Royal Flying Corps casualties buried here from 1917, there are several from 43 Squadron who fell between March and October. Its first commander was Major Sholto Douglas, who served with distinction during both World Wars and who went on to become Marshal of the Royal Air Force.

Second Lieutenant Herbert John GREEN and Lieutenant Alexander William REID, 43 Squadron, Royal Flying Corps, became their opponent's twenty-third victory when they were shot down over enemy lines on 4 March 1917 by Manfred von Richthofen. Flying a Sopwith two-seater, they were on a patrol flight over the southern part of Vimy Ridge where they became isolated and were attacked by several enemy machines. GREEN, who had been a member of Durham University OTC, was eager to join up, and after training with the Royal Flying Corps he was gazetted. He arrived in France in January 1917, and had only been at the front for a short time before he was killed. Three of his brothers also served in the Royal Flying Corps.

REID, his observer that day, had served as a trooper with the Hampshire Yeomanry before the war, but he too had volunteered to serve overseas without any hesitation. He was gazetted in the King's Own Scottish Borderers towards the end of 1914 and went to France in November the following year to replace losses after the Battle of Loos. He was wounded serving with the 6th Battalion and while at home recovering he was accepted for training by the Royal Flying

Corps. He arrived at his squadron on 23 February 1917 and was killed nine days later. Both men were originally buried by the Germans at a location known as Bois Bernard, about nine miles east of Vimy Ridge, but are now buried side by side here at Cabaret Rouge British Cemetery. (Plot XII.E.3 and 4)

Richthofen's twenty-sixth victory was the shooting down of Second Lieutenant James SMYTH and Second Lieutenant Edward Gordon BYRNE, 2 Squadron, Royal Flying Corps. They were killed on 11 March 1917 whilst engaged on a photographic mission. Their aircraft, a BE2d, came down near La Folie Wood, on Vimy Ridge, and was completely destroyed. SMYTH originally came from the Belfast area, but by the time war broke out he was living with his wife and children in south London and working as an engineer. He joined the Royal Flying Corps and after training in England he went to France where he joined his squadron.

BYRNE had joined the army as soon as he was old enough and had spent twelve years in the Royal Army Medical Corps, serving in India, China and Africa. He re-enlisted at the outbreak of war, having retired some years earlier, and went to France, initially with the Australian Volunteer Hospital Corps in 1914. He was gazetted in the Gordon Highlanders and served in the trenches with the 4th Battalion where he was wounded. He then applied to join the Royal Flying Corps and was accepted. He initially served as an observer and, like many flyers, he had a fear of being shot down in flames. Both men are now buried side by side (Plot XII.E.8 and 9).

Two brothers, Wilfred CHENIER, aged 28, and Olivier CHENIER, aged 27, were both killed in action on 9 April 1917 serving in the same battalion, the Royal Canadian Regiment, when it attacked towards the northern edge of La Folie Wood on the opening day of the Battle of Arras. Their consecutive army numbers show that they enlisted together on the same day, which was 11 March 1916. They are two of the 188 men buried here from the opening day of the Battle of Arras (Plot XII.E.15 and 16).

Second Lieutenant George Harold HEARN, 1st East Surrey Regiment, died of wounds on 12 May 1917 following the action at Fresnoy on 8 May. He was taken prisoner, as were two other wounded officers from the battalion, but he succumbed to his injuries four days later. Fresnoy had been captured on 3 May by the Canadian 1st Division and the new line formed a small salient to the east and south of the village and Fresnoy Wood. During the early hours of 8 May the Germans launched a counter-attack to re-take the position. The initial attack was repulsed, but it was renewed about an hour later and succeeded in making a breach east of the village where 'B' Company's left front joined the right flank of the 12th Gloucestershire Regiment. The Germans were then able to press home their attack on three sides of the salient. The left flank became untenable and HEARN, who was already wounded, was captured at this stage in the fighting. When the Germans entered Fresnoy Wood they found a number of men in a dug-out that was being used to house 'D' Company's HQ. Having tried to bomb its occupants, the enemy threw burning brushwood into it. Fortunately British shells began to fall on the attackers and the Germans retired from the wood, leaving the one officer and seven men to make their escape. (Plot XV.F.10)

Lieutenant Colonel John Herbert RIDGWAY DSO, North Staffordshire Regiment, attached 10th York & Lancaster Regiment, was killed in action on 23 April 1917, aged 41. With the exception of three months sick leave, he had served at the front continuously since September 1914. His DSO was gazetted on 1 January 1917 in the New Year's Honours List. He had held his commission since 1900 and served in the South African War. (Plot XV.G.10)

Lieutenant Colonel John Willoughby SCOTT DSO, Queen's Own Oxfordshire Hussars, commanding the 8th Somerset Light Infantry, was also killed in action on 23 April 1917, aged 38. He was the son of the late Sir John Scott KCMG DCL, who served as Deputy Judge Advocate General to HM Forces. Scott had been a barrister in civilian life, but was also one of five officers from his regiment who had previously fought in the South African War where he had served in the Royal Artillery. The Queen's Own Oxfordshire Hussars landed at Dunkirk on 22 September 1914 with Scott in command of 'A' Squadron. The regiment soon moved to Saint-Omer. One of its duties was to provide guards at Saint-Omer where Sir John French's HQ was located, as was GHQ itself and Sir John's personal quarters.

Scott and two fellow officers, Captain Hermon-Hodge and Lieutenant Gill, had a fortunate escape just as the First Battle of Ypres was getting under way. Several of the officers had brought privately owned cars with them and were using them to 'joy-ride' up to the front, eager to experience action, and no doubt a tremendous buzz after hearing about 'the front line' from airmen based near Saint-Omer whose mess they often visited. On one occasion, whilst driving up the Menin Road, they came across a group of British soldiers who were digging-in. Enquiring where the front line was, they were told by the soldiers that this was it and that the Germans were only a few hundred yards off.

The regiment was itching to become actively involved in the fighting and was becoming tired of carrying out its current duties. On 29 October, a fellow officer, Major John Strange Spencer Churchill, who was socially and politically well-connected, obtained agreement from Sir John French, while the two men were having dinner together, for the regiment to go to the 'real' front. By the first week of November the regiment had moved into trenches around Wulverghem. Major Churchill was the younger brother of Sir Winston Churchill and was later awarded the DSO in the King's Birthday Honours List on 3 June 1918. He was also awarded the French *Croix de Guerre* and the *Légion d' Honneur*.

On 30 June 1915 Scott took over as second-in command of the regiment and six months later he left it to take over as commanding officer of the 8th Somerset Light Infantry. He then remained in command of that battalion until his death leading it in the attack on Greenland Hill on 23 April 1917. Though he had been away from his parent regiment for just over fifteen months, news of his death reached it six days later where his passing was noted with great sadness. Many tributes were paid to him and he was regarded as a very fine and experienced soldier who had been mentioned in despatches three times. (Plot XV.G.11)

Second Lieutenant Philip Lovel WOOD, 43 Squadron, Royal Flying Corps, was killed in action on 4 March 1917, as was his observer, Second Lieutenant Alan Hughes FENTON. Both men were recorded as missing in action and after the war their names were inscribed on the Flying Services Memorial at Arras. However, in 1992, following an investigation into the circumstances of their death, the CWGC accepted that the men were, in fact, buried in this cemetery close to each other. Their names were removed from the memorial and their headstones are now marked: 'Buried near this spot'. (Plot XV.G.23 and 17)

Lieutenant Andrew Ronald LEGAT MC, A Battery, 317 Brigade, Royal Field Artillery, was killed in action on 28 March 1917, aged 29. His MC was gazetted two days earlier on 26 March 1917 and was awarded for conspicuous gallantry in action after he had made his way to a forward battalion HQ under a heavy barrage with valuable information, and for establishing and maintaining communications under heavy fire throughout the operation. (Plot XV.K.18)

Second Lieutenant Kenneth Bassano COOKSEY, 59 Squadron, Royal Flying Corps, formerly 3rd Queen's Own (Royal West Kent Regiment) was killed in action, aged 21, while flying a RE8 aircraft. His observer that day, Air Mechanic Reginald Hansford JONES, also died, aged 20, when their machine came down on 8 April 1917. Both men are now buried next to each other. This was a time of intense pressure for the Royal Flying Corps and huge demands were being placed on air crews, never more so than in April that year, which became known as 'Bloody April'. (Plot XV.K.20 and 21)

Serjeant Reuel DUNN, 43 Squadron, Royal Flying Corps, died from his wounds on 2 April 1917, though his pilot, Second Lieutenant Algernon Peter Warren, survived the war after being taken prisoner. DUNN was shot in the stomach while they were on a sortie to take photographs over enemy lines. Their machine was shot down by Manfred von Richthofen, marking his thirty-third victory. Warren narrowly escaped death when their aircraft was riddled with bullets, damaging the engine, the fuel tank, the controls, the instrument panel and even passing through his clothing. Nevertheless, he managed to bring the aircraft down and then tried to help DUNN, who was still conscious, but clearly very badly wounded. DUNN, who was a motorcycle despatch rider with the Army Service Corps before joining the Royal Flying Corps, died a few hours later in German hands (Plot XV.M.24). Warren went on to finish his education after the war and became an architect. He served with the Royal Engineers during the Second World War.

Lieutenant Hugh POPE-HENNESSY, 49th Battalion, Canadian Infantry, was killed in action on 30 April 1917, aged 31. He was the son of the late Sir John Pope-Hennessy KCMG, and Lady Pope-Hennessy, of Rostellan Castle, Co. Cork. Sir John Pope-Hennessy held a number of posts within the Colonial Service across the Empire, including Governor of Hong Kong and then Mauritius. (Plot XV.M.26)

Second Lieutenant William Henry GUNNER MC, 60 Squadron, Royal Flying Corps, was killed in action on 29 July 1917, aged 26, flying a SE5 aircraft. His MC was gazetted on 20 July 1917 and was awarded for conspicuous gallantry and devotion to duty while carrying out an offensive patrol during which he engaged and attacked nine enemy aircraft, two of which were attacking the rear machine of his patrol. Having convoyed the other machine back to the aerodrome, he again returned to the air with his patrol in response to an urgent call to drive off some enemy aircraft. Although he had been wounded during the initial encounter that day, he insisted on carrying on until the day's work was complete. The citation concludes that on numerous other occasions he had shown great skill and courage in the offensive. (Plot XV.M.28)

Canadian flyer, Second Lieutenant Malcolm Guy Macdonald OXLEY, 43 Squadron, Royal Flying Corps, and his observer, Air Mechanic II Class, Charles Albert BLATHERWICK, are buried next to each other. Both men were killed in action on 19 September 1917. (Plot XV.K.27 and 28)

In the same Plot, but in Row Q, is another officer from 43 Squadron, Second Lieutenant George Page BRADLEY, who was killed in action on 27 October 1917, aged 18, while flying his Camel aircraft. (Plot XV.Q.36)

Lieutenant Harry Alexander Taylor KENNEDY, 40 Squadron, Royal Flying Corps, was killed in action on 22 August 1917, aged 22, flying a Nieuport aircraft. He had previously served with the 13th Battalion, Canadian Infantry. His squadron was involved in a fight with seven enemy aircraft that day. The Royal Flying Corps communiqué covering this period refers to the encounter, but makes no reference to any losses on our side, only to an enemy machine that was driven down out of control. He was mentioned a week before his death when he was credited with driving down an enemy aircraft out of control, as was Lieutenant (later Major) Edward Mannock, who at the time was also serving with 40 Squadron. (Plot XV.R.23)

Lieutenant James Kelvey HOWARD, 13 Squadron, Royal Flying Corps, was killed in action on 11 February 1917, aged 22, as was his pilot, Captain James THORBURN, aged 31, flying a BE2c aircraft. The pair had gone up in order to correct an artillery shoot, but were set upon by two enemy machines. On hearing the news, another member of their squadron, Captain Thomas Maclean, took an aircraft up and flew above the area where they had been seen to fall, but he could find no trace of their machine. He then wrote to HOWARD's father to inform him of his son's death. (Plot XVI.A.21 and 22)

Second Lieutenant Leslie Vincent MUNN, 16 Squadron, Royal Flying Corps, formerly 6th Leicestershire Regiment, was killed in action on 16 February 1917 (Plot XVI.A.23) along with his pilot, Second Lieutenant Ernest William Lindley, formerly 9th Manchester Regiment, when their BE2c was brought down. Lindley is buried at Brown's Copse Cemetery, Roeux. CWGC records for Lindley do not show him serving with the Royal Flying Corps, but under his former regiment. He is buried there in Plot VI, Row G.

Second Lieutenant Arthur Leslie CONSTABLE and his observer, Second Lieutenant Charles Duncan KNOX, were yet another pair who served with 43 Squadron, Royal Flying Corps, and both were killed in action together on 17 March 1917. CONSTABLE is now buried here (Plot XVI.A.30). KNOX, who formerly served with the 10th Suffolk Regiment, was originally thought to have no known grave, but is now believed to be buried in this cemetery a few graves along from his pilot. His headstone records that he is 'buried near this spot' (Plot XVI.A.27). The two graves that separate the men each contain the body of an unknown officer of the Royal Flying Corps killed on 17 March 1917. It is therefore equally possible that KNOX could be in one of those graves.

Lance Corporal Walter Stephen HOLLAND DCM, 21st Northumberland Fusiliers (Tynesde Scottish), died of wounds on 10 March 1917, aged 21. His DCM was gazetted on 10 January 1917 and was awarded for conspicuous gallantry in action. The citation records that he had displayed great courage and determination during a raid on the enemy's trenches and, later on, had rescued a wounded officer under heavy fire. (Plot XVI.B.22)

Second Lieutenant Sydney HARRYMAN, 8 Squadron, Royal Flying Corps, died while he was a prisoner of war on 24 March 1917 from wounds received six days earlier on 18 March. His pilot, Second Lieutenant C.R. Dougall, was also taken prisoner after their BE2d came down over enemy lines. They were shot down by German ace, Werner Voss, and were the eighteenth of his forty-eight victories. (Plot XVI.B.24)

Lance Corporal Allen Mortimer KEMP, 1st Battalion, Auckland Regiment, New Zealand Expeditionary Force, was killed in action on 13 February 1917. He had previously served in Samoa and is one of just five New Zealand soldiers buried here who died between early October 1916 and late August 1918. It is possible that he died following a raid on trenches held by his battalion on 12 February. Realising that the raid was imminent, the New Zealanders withdrew from their position and ambushed the raiders at the appropriate moment with bombs. This occurred while the division was north of Arras, near Fleurbaix. (Plot XVI.E.1)

Two others from the 2nd Canterbury Regiment, who fell on 1 October 1916, are undoubtedly casualties from the fighting on the Somme around Gird Trench and Eaucourt l'Abbaye. It is possible that both men died of wounds while prisoners of war and were re-buried here after the war. (Plot XXX.A.1 and 2)

The casualty from 3 November 1916 may also have died in German captivity as a result of the Somme fighting, but is more likely to have been killed after that when the New Zealand Division was north of Arras. On 12 October 1916, the New Zealand Division moved from the Somme, minus its artillery, to the area around Outersteene, Strazeele and Estaires. Again, he would have been re-buried here after the war. (Plot XVI.C.15)

The 1918 casualty is from the fighting in August when the New Zealanders were operating close to Bapaume. He was almost certainly buried somewhere on that battlefield, but was then brought here for re-burial after the war when many isolated graves were re-located to this cemetery. (Plot VII.F.2)

Lieutenant Justin Morell McKENNA, 11 Squadron, Royal Flying Corps, was killed in action on 2 October 1917, aged 21. His observer, Lieutenant Sydney SUTCLIFFE MM, who was 24 years old, and who had formerly served with the Royal Welsh Fusiliers, was also killed with him that day. The squadron was returning from a bombing mission and was somewhere between Cambrai and Douai when it was attacked by an enemy patrol. Three of the enemy were brought down, but McKENNA and SUTCLIFFE became isolated from their colleagues during the fight and were shot down. They fell behind German lines where their funeral was attended by a number of German airmen. A photograph of the funeral was published in the *Sunday Telegraph* in October 2013. The accompanying article stated that the actress, Virginia McKennna, was Justin's niece. (Plot XVI.F.19 and 20)

Captain William George Sellar CURPHEY MC and Bar, 32 Squadron Royal Flying Corps, was killed in action on 15 May 1917. He won his MC for a series of attacks on enemy aircraft in 1916 and was gazetted on 14 November 1916. The bar to it, gazetted on 14 March 1917, was awarded for conspicuous gallantry in action while on patrol with three other aircraft. It states that he had engaged and attacked an enemy formation of ten aircraft and after a prolonged fight had managed to drive down one of them. Although wounded, he later led an attack on another enemy aircraft, and succeeded in bringing it down. The citation con-cludes that he had done similar fine work on a number of previous occasions.

On 4 February 1917 he was part of an offensive patrol that encountered an enemy formation near the villages of Achiet-le-Grand and Achiet-le-Petit. CUR-PHEY brought down one of them, but several of his squadron's machines were damaged during the fight, so they broke off as a group and returned to base. CURPHEY and Lieutenant W.R. Randall changed their machines and then took off again in search of the enemy unit. They soon became engaged in another fight and, with assistance from his colleague, CURPHEY succeeded in bringing down another enemy aircraft even though he himself had been wounded in the head. He was again in the thick of action three days later, on 7 February, when he brought down another enemy machine.

CURPHEY was eventually killed on 15 May that year after his squadron had successfully carried out an attack on enemy balloons, forcing the occupants to escape by parachute and the balloons to be hastily hauled down. His squadron's de Havilland aircraft were spotted by six German Albatros scouts, and although one was destroyed by another member of the squadron, CURPHEY was driven down and his machine was seen to flip over on landing. (Plot XVI.G.8)

Second Lieutenant Daniel Joseph SHEEHAN, 66 Squadron, Royal Flying Corps, was the eldest son of the Nationalist MP for Mid-Cork, Captain Daniel Desmond Sheehan, often better referred to as D.D. Sheehan. He was largely responsible for raising the 9th Royal Munster Fusiliers and, along with J.L. Esmonde, William Redmond and Tom Kettle, was one of the leading person-alities in the Nationalist Volunteer Movement and the raising of the 16th (Irish) Division. D.D. Sheehan also served in the trenches with the battalion he had done so much to raise. However, he left the front towards the end of 1916 owing to declining health and partial deafness, but he carried on with the 3rd Battalion at home where he assisted with training.

Daniel and his brother Martin were educated at Christian College, Cork, and Mount St. Joseph's College, Roscrea. Both he and Martin were talented rugby players and both had played for Munster in the Senior Colleges Inter-Provincial Rugby Championships. Daniel also showed a keen interest in sailing and in 1912 he joined the training ship, *Medway*, where he won a first prize for navigation and general seamanship. He later transferred to HMS *Hibernia* as a midshipman in the Royal Naval Reserve as a first step towards applying for a permanent com-mission in the Royal Navy. Before transferring to the Royal Naval Air Service, he did actually serve with the 3rd Battle Squadron in the North Sea in 1914–15. He obtained his aviator's licence in 1915 and was wounded whilst flying over Belgium.

Although he was then considered unfit to carry on flying in the Royal Naval Air Service, he obtained permission to transfer to the Royal Flying Corps. Initially, he served for a while as an instructor at Oxford before finally managing to return to active service. He died on 10 May 1917 whilst on a scouting mission. He was intercepted by a group of enemy aircraft and was shot down near Noyelles, though he did manage to land his machine before he died. (Plot XVI.N.16).

His younger brother, Martin Joseph Sheehan, was killed in action on 1 October 1918 while on observation duties with 13 Squadron, Royal Air Force. Before the war he went to Canada where he had a short career in banking before joining the Canadian Expeditionary Force in 1915 as a private. In 1916 he went overseas with his battalion, but then transferred to the Royal Munster Fusiliers, subsequently gaining his commission. He was present at Passchendaele, but then decided to transfer to the Royal Flying Corps as an observer, serving not only in France, but also in Italy. His body was recovered after he was shot down in an RE 8 aircraft near Cambrai and he is now buried in Anneux British Cemetery with his pilot, Second Lieutenant William George McCaig, who came from Fife.

The boys were part of a remarkable family that gave outstanding service during the war. Their sister, Eileen, served as a VAD nurse and ambulance driver and was badly injured during a bombing raid. Another brother, Michael J. Sheehan, later OBE, CBE, enlisted before his sixteenth birthday and was reputedly the youngest member of the British Army to receive a commission. Although he was twice wounded, he survived the war and went on to serve again during the Second World War in Burma. D.D. Sheehan's brother, Private John Sheehan, was badly wounded serving with the Irish Guards during the Great War, whilst his brother-in-law, Serjeant Robert O'Connor, who had also served in the South African campaign, was killed in action on 31 July 1917 whilst serving with the 2nd Leinster Regiment. He is commemorated on the Menin Gate.

Lieutenant Geoffrey Stapleton Rowe ROPER MC, 3rd Yorkshire Regiment, attached 7th Battalion, was killed in action on 12 May 1917, aged 27. His MC was gazetted on 25 August 1916 and was awarded for conspicuous gallantry in action. During an assault he led his platoon with great dash and afterwards had crawled back to the trenches in order to make a report before then making his way back to his platoon under close and heavy fire. The *London Gazette* and *Officers Died in the Great War* show the middle Christian name as 'Stapylton'. (Plot XVII.AA.21)

Second Lieutenant George SUTHERLAND, 7/8th King's Own Scottish Borderers, was killed in action on 9 April 1917. He was the only officer from his battalion killed on the opening day of the Arras offensive. (Plot XVII.G.4)

Private George BURNET, 8th Seaforth Highlanders, was killed in action on 9 April 1917, aged 22, and had formerly served with the Lovat Scouts (Plot XVII.G.9). His brother, Private Donald M. Burnet, also fell while serving with 4th Gordon Highlanders on 15 June 1917 and is buried at Achiet-le-Grand Communal Cemetery Extension.

Buried side by side are two officers from the 13th Royal Scots, killed in action on 9 April 1917. They are Second Lieutenant Fraser Campbell BUCHANAN, aged 23, from 'A' Company, and Second Lieutenant George Lothian STEWART, aged 22, from 'C' Company. STEWART had previously been mentioned in despatches. BUCHANAN was a former pupil at Haileybury College, Hertfordshire, which boasts an impressive roll of honour. (Plot XVII.J.43 and 44)

Lieutenant Colonel Philip Mathew MAGNAY, Royal Fusiliers (Special Reserve), commanding the 12th Manchester Regiment, was killed on 13 April 1917 when a heavy howitzer shell scored a direct hit on his battalion HQ during an enemy bombardment that extended as far back as the British support line. He had been mentioned in despatches on three occasions. His adjutant, Captain Frank TOWER, was also killed in the same incident and is buried next to him (Plot XVII.J.47 and 46). MAGNAY's father, Sir William Magnay, 2nd Baronet, wrote a number of novels before his death in January 1917, and his grandfather, Sir William Magnay, 1st Baronet, once served as Mayor of London.

Captain John MARTIN MC, 'A' Company, 8/10th Gordon Highlanders, was killed in action on 9 April 1917, aged 28. His MC was gazetted on 14 March 1917 and was awarded for conspicuous gallantry and devotion to duty after showing marked courage and ability in organizing and making arrangements for a raid. When the raid took place he personally guided and supervised the assaulting troops. (Plot XVII.J.48)

The Reverend Herbert John COLLINS, Chaplain 4th Class, attached 9th Black Watch, was killed in action on the opening day of the Battle of Arras, aged 35. He was a Roman Catholic chaplain and had joined the battalion before it went to France. It was said of him that he was ever-present in the front line among the men, which he believed was his place. He famously carried a knapsack containing cigarettes for the men and was much respected for his courage and cheerfulness. His posthumous mention in despatches on 8 June 1917 had, in fact, been submitted as a recommendation for the MC. (Plot XVII.K.10)

Serjeant Thomas KITCHING DCM, 15th Signal Company, Royal Engineers, was killed in action on 9 April 1917. His DCM was gazetted on 14 January 1916 and the citation for it appeared on 11 March 1916. It was awarded for conspicuous gallantry whilst laying and maintaining telephone wires under heavy fire, particularly during an assault on the enemy's trenches. (Plot XVII.K.43)

Lance Corporal Alexander Douglas WATT, 1st Gordon Highlanders, was killed in action between 9 and 11 April 1917, aged 22 (Plot XVII.N.4). His brother, Private Charles Watt, originally served with the 4th Gordon Highlanders, but was killed whilst attached to the 1st Battalion. His death occurred on 27 September 1918 and he is buried at Lowrie Cemetery, Havrincourt.

Regimental Quartermaster Serjeant William Thomas FAWN, 6th Dorsetshire Regiment, was killed on 22 April 1917 (Plot XVII.T.28). He was mortally wounded when two shells exploded in Arras after the battalion had returned there from the trenches. Two other men were killed outright and twenty-one others were wounded, many of them part of his staff. The two men killed would appear to be Lance Corporal Frederick William Goldring and Private Edward Berkeley Cross, both of whom are commemorated on the Arras Memorial. Two of the wounded also died later that day: Lance Corporal Thomas Herbert (Bert) PHILLIPS (Plot XVII.T.29) and Private George ARNOLD (Plot XVII.T.30). How the three men came to be buried here rather than at Arras is not easily explained.

Far more attention is generally given to the 'fighting man' than to the unsung heroes whose efforts go towards trying to provide for him. Plot XIX contains the graves of two NCOs and two privates from No.2 Water Tank Company. It is all too easy to forget that the provision of fresh water for troops was an absolute necessity. Water supply in 1917 on the Arras battlefield was not such a challenge as it had been in the chalky landscapes of the Somme, with the exception of the VII Corps area where the Germans had destroyed or contaminated wells during their withdrawal behind the Hindenburg Line. Arras itself was well supplied and the pumping station there, despite some direct hits, suffered no serious damage. A number of watering points, protected by screens, were available in the town, and mains carried water into the system of tunnels and caves at Ronville and Saint-Sauveur.

However, it was often still necessary to move water by road to storage points from where it could be carried forward by water carts to points where cans could be filled; from there it could be taken up to the trenches. During the final advance, the last four months of the war, it was estimated that about 20 million gallons of water had to be transported by road, requiring 633 Ford cars and 118 3-ton lorries, divided between four water tank companies.

The four men of No. 2 Water Tank Company are buried side by side and it is worth bearing in mind the important contribution they made to the war and their value to the everyday life of the fighting soldier. They were killed in action on 3 September 1917. (Plot XIX.E.15, 16, 17 and 18)

Lieutenant George John HATCH, 8 Squadron, Royal Flying Corps, formerly 17th (County of London) Battalion, London Regiment (Stepney and Poplar Rifles), was killed in action with his observer, Corporal Ernest Frank Langridge DCM, in their BE2e aircraft on 6 April 1917. Both men were aged 20 when they died. (Plot XX.F.4) Langridge has no known grave and is commemorated on the Flying Services Memorial, Arras.

Second Lieutenant Ronald Stuart ASHER, 46 Squadron, Royal Flying Corps, was killed in action on 21 September 1917, aged 19, flying a Sopwith Pup. He and his squadron became involved in a fight with several enemy scouts after flying in the direction of a large arrow marked on the ground behind German lines. At first they encountered a lone two-seater enemy aircraft, pursuing it until the other enemy machines appeared. The squadron got the better of them in the ensuing combat and Second Lieutenant ASHER forced one of them to land, whilst his colleagues accounted for a further three. Unfortunately, there is no reference to his death in the Royal Flying Corps communiqué for that day. (Plot XXIV.AA.6)

Second Lieutenant Oswald William BERRY, 48 Squadron, Royal Flying Corps, was killed in action on 8 April 1917, aged 24 (Plot XXVII.F.21). His observer, Second Lieutenant Frank Bowler Goodison, never recovered from his injuries and died six weeks later in Germany. He is buried in Niederzwehren Cemetery. They had left their airfield in the afternoon to carry out an offensive patrol and ran into an enemy formation near Éterpigny, east of Arras. They were shot down by German ace, Leutnant Fritz Otto Bernert, who scored a total of twenty-seven victories, including five in a single day. Bernert was badly wounded in August that year and was unable to fly again. He died soon after the war as a result of the flu epidemic.

Serjeant Daniel Thomas CONWAY, 13th Northumberland Fusiliers, died on 16 June 1917, aged 23. *Soldiers Died in the Great War* suggests that he died from causes other than wounds received in action. He was one of three brothers to serve during the war. (Plot XXVIII.G.29)

Lieutenant Nathan Lewis CHIPMAN, 85th Battalion (Nova Scotia), Canadian Infantry, was killed in action on 16 June 1917, aged 20. He joined the battalion in October 1915 and, despite his young age, he held a Bachelor's degree from Dalhousie University, Halifax, Nova Scotia. His death occurred while his battalion was in trenches close to Lens, each night having to provide large working parties, often under shell fire. (Plot XXVIII.A.27)

Serjeant Frederick Walter ACCLETON DCM MM, 85th Battery, 11 Brigade, Royal Field Artillery, was killed in action on 16 April 1917. He won his DCM for conspicuous gallantry and devotion to duty while serving as a corporal when, with the help of two officers of his detachment, he had kept up a rapid rate of fire at a critical moment, despite being wounded in two places. His award was gazetted on 20 October 1916; his unit was part of an Army Field Artillery Brigade. Sadly, *Soldiers Died in the Great War* makes no reference to either his DCM or his MM. (Plot XXIX.A.28)

Lieutenant Harry Dudley BLACKBURN, 43 Squadron, Royal Flying Corps, was killed in action on 5 April 1917, aged 23, a day on which our offensive patrols proved successful in dealing with enemy aircraft, thus enabling those British machines working closely with the artillery to go about their business with very little hindrance. His squadron had been engaged with enemy aircraft above La Bassée and BLACKBURN's pilot that day, Second Lieutenant C.P. Thornton, was taken prisoner when their machine came down over enemy lines. BLACK-BURN previously served with the 28th Battalion, London Regiment (Artists' Rifles), and the 1st Royal Berkshire Regiment. His grave has since been lost, but he is commemorated here on the Rouvroy Communal Cemetery German Extension Memorial.

Second Lieutenant Henry Scotson RICHARDS, 25 Squadron, Royal Flying Corps, was killed in action on 3 April 1917, aged 21, while observing for his pilot, Lieutenant L. Dodson, who was taken prisoner when their aircraft was brought down. Crews were operating under immense pressure just before the Battle of Arras opened, particularly in relation to the number of photographic missions that were being called for every day. At the same time, the artillery was making huge demands on the Royal Flying Corps, as never before, with regard to artillery registration and observation. All of this was taking place against a backdrop of aggressive enemy opposition. In many cases, crews were operating close to breaking point. (Avion German Military Cemetery, Memorial 18)

Private J. WISHART, 7th Royal Inniskilling Fusiliers, died on the morning of 15 June 1917 when he was executed by firing squad. He had deserted from his battalion while it was in the area between Hazebrouck and Bailleul, making it back as far as Boulogne, where he was arrested. Not only was he arrested at one of the main Channel ports, from which it could easily be inferred that his intention was to leave France, he was also wearing civilian clothing when he was discovered there. Although he put forward mitigation on the grounds that his child was ill, he was found guilty and shot in Merris. Despite being buried in the churchyard there, his grave could not be located after the war.

Julian Sykes and Julian Putkowski point out that he had deserted whilst on the way to join his battalion and note that he is now commemorated here at Cabaret Rouge British Cemetery (Merris Churchyard, Special Memorial 51). The CWGC records show his surname as 'Wishard'. However, *Soldiers Died in the Great War* contains no reference to any soldier by the name of 'Wishart' or 'Wishard' in the volume covering the Royal Inniskilling Fusiliers.

1918

Lieutenant Frederick WILLIAMS, 62 Squadron, Royal Air Force, was killed in action flying a Bristol F2B on 24 June 1918 (Plot VI.H.3). His observer, Second Lieutenant Ernest DUMVILLE, also died that day and is buried next to him (Plot VI.H.2).

Second Lieutenant Thomas Harrison SOUTER, 103 Squadron, Royal Air Force, was killed in action on 4 July 1918. *Airmen Died in the Great War* shows him in the diary page for that day as dying alone, and yet in his biographical entry it shows him as observer. His aircraft that day was a DH9 two-seater bomber biplane and he was killed when he fell from the aircraft while it was in flight. (Plot VII.E.5)

Captain Arthur CLAYDON DFC, 32 Squadron, Royal Air Force, was killed in action on 8 July 1918. He previously served with the Canadian Field Artillery. The citation for his DFC, gazetted on 2 June 1918, states that he went to the assistance of another pilot, single-handed, who was being attacked by eleven Fokker biplanes and six scouts. By skilful manoeuvring, he not only managed to extricate his fellow flyer, but also drove down several of the enemy aircraft. On other occasions he had shown similar gallantry and initiative, particularly in locating, bombing and attacking enemy troop formations on the ground at low altitude. (Plot VII.E.6)

There are thirty-five holders of the MM buried in this cemetery, the youngest of whom is Rifleman Owen Francis FRAY MM, 1/5th King's Liverpool Regiment, who died of wounds on 29 September 1918, aged 18. In early September 1918 there was some doubt as to whether the enemy intended to hold their line between Fromelles and La Bassée or retire to the Haute Deûle Canal. Intelligence from prisoners pointed towards the latter, but stiffening resistance suggested something very different. During the first half of the month every attempt to press forward had been strongly opposed and any ground lost was soon met by German counter-attacks. The experience was the same for the 55th (West Lancashire) Division, which was operating immediately north of the La Bassée Canal, and for the 16th (Irish) Division immediately south of it between Cuinchy and Railway Triangle.

On 17 September both divisions made further attempts to advance. The 1/5th King's Liverpool Regiment was successful in capturing the southern part of Canteleux Trench and Apse House, whilst the 16th (Irish) Division was equally successful south of the canal. A series of forward posts were quickly established, but in the afternoon the enemy counter-attacked south of the canal and retook the positions lost earlier in the day. Later these were restored by the 16th (Irish) Division, but for a time the King's Liverpool men came under heavy machine-gun fire from the railway embankment.

The following day, around sixty of the enemy counter-attacked, this time north of the canal at the junction of Apse Road and Canteleux Alley, driving the 1/5th King's Liverpool men out of a post east of Apse House. It was then that FRAY volunteered to go out alone and locate the enemy's position. He returned with valuable information and later that day he took part in an attack that re-gained the post. His actions earned him the MM. However, just over a week later, he was badly wounded, possibly during his battalion's operation on 27 September to capture the positions of Piano House and the Telephone Exchange near the La Bassée–Estaires road, or perhaps soon after that attack. However, the war diary for this period notes that there were no casualties, although on the 28th the Germans did put down a heavy bombardment, followed the next day by a determined counter-attack when, of course, FRAY is shown as having died. (Plot VIII.H.26)

These were operations carried out under very difficult circumstances, but seem to receive very little attention these days. FRAY's death offers the opportunity to shine a brief light on this neglected part of the final 'Hundred Days'.

Major James Edward CLAYTON MC, B Battery, Royal Field Artillery, was killed in action on 24 June 1918, aged 40. His MC was gazetted on 17 January 1916, but I can find no citation for it. The CWGC record shows that his parents lived in the Saltley area of Birmingham. The family is almost certainly part of the Claytons who operated a large fleet of commercial canal boats around that time. (Plot VIII.K.12)

Plot VIII, Rows K to P, contain seventy-seven burials from the 15th Lancashire Fusiliers (1st Salford Pals) and 16th Lancashire Fusiliers (2nd Salford Pals). In the aftermath of the German March offensive 1918, both battalions found themselves holding parts of the line south of Arras around Boyelles and Boisleux-Saint-Marc. During May, June, and the first few days of July, both sides carried out several raids on each other's trenches. 'C' Company, 15th Lancashire Fusiliers, carried out one such a raid on German positions near Boisleux-St. Marc at midnight on

11/12 June. The party consisted of two officers and fifty men. It was considered successful and several prisoners were captured for identification and intelligence purposes, and the party reported that it had also killed a number of the enemy. As for the raiding party, it reported two of its men killed and ten wounded, including both the officers who took part. Casualty returns show that four men died on the 12th, making it likely that a further two died of wounds shortly afterwards as a result of the operation. Three of the four are buried closely together (Plot VIII.L.16, 20 and 21) and the fourth man is buried nearby (Plot VIII.N.44).

Second Lieutenant Percy William (Peter) HUBBARD MM, 16th Lancashire Fusiliers, was killed in action on 6 June 1918, aged 37. The CWGC register tells us that he had been severely wounded twice and had won the Army heavyweight boxing championship with the 7th Royal Fusiliers in 1914. It goes on to note that he was promoted in the field to the rank of serjeant after the capture of Ovillers in July 1916. In civilian life he had captained the Westminster Bank rugby and cricket teams and was clearly a good all-round sportsman. He had also been a member of the Belsize Sports Clubs. He was killed during a period when his battalion was occupying trenches near Boisleux-au-Mont between 5 and 12 June. (Plot VIII.M.38)

Lieutenant Arthur Granville SHARP MC, D Battery, 72 Army Brigade, Royal Field Artillery, was killed in action on 23 August 1918, aged 20. His MC was gazetted on 1 February 1919 and was awarded while his unit was serving with the Guards Division. On 23 August he was working as a forward observation officer near Hamelincourt where he showed conspicuous gallantry and devotion to duty when for many hours he was under heavy fire, but continued to send back reports on the situation regardless, along with much other valuable information. On one occasion he was isolated with two signallers in a gap between the front line flank companies of two battalions. He succeeded in sending back quickly and accurately the position of those flanks, thereby enabling the gap to be filled. (Plot VIII.N.8)

Lieutenant Colonel Robert Edward Frederic SHAW MC, 13th Battalion, London Regiment (Kensingtons), was killed in action on 23 August 1918, aged 26. He was the son of a clergyman from King's Langley in Hertfordshire. His MC was gazetted in the New Year's Honours List on 2 January 1918. On 23 August that year, his battalion was on the right of the 168 Brigade's attack on the villages of Boyelles and Boiry-Becquerelle, with the 4th (City of London) London Regiment (Royal Fusiliers), and the 14th Battalion, London Regiment (London Scottish), extending the line to the left.

By 7am the brigade had taken its objective, which was a line running beyond both villages. The Kensingtons were then ordered to link up with the Guards Division on their right and capture Boyelles Reserve Trench, which lay in front of them. Despite stronger opposition from this next defensive position, 'D' Company went forward and succeeded in working its way around to Bank Copse where it found the left flank of the Guard's Division. Around late morning, two platoons from 'D' Company, together with men from the 1st Coldstream Guards (2nd Guards Brigade), rushed the Albert–Arras railway embankment and drove the Germans from Boyelles Reserve Trench. Meanwhile, 'A', 'B' and 'C' companies had come under heavy shell fire as they were moving forwards.

By late afternoon the overall situation was still far from clear, not least because no word had arrived as to whether the battalion's left flank was still in touch with the 4th Battalion. In order to try to resolve the matter, Shaw went forward with a runner and a signaller, but unfortunately he was shot by a sniper. His body was recovered and he was buried in Blairville Cemetery in the presence of his battalion. He was deeply respected by his men and had served with the battalion since the early days of the war, firstly as a subaltern, then for the last twelve months as its commanding officer. (Plot VIII.N.11)

Captain Frank Oswald MEDWORTH MC, 2nd Manchester Regiment, was killed in action on 13 May 1918, aged 35. The CWGC register notes that he had previously been wounded whilst serving in Salonika in 1917. His MC was gazetted on 30 July 1917 and was awarded for conspicuous gallantry and devotion to duty while commanding the right company during an assault and leading his men through several barrages with very few casualties. He then consolidated the lines gained with great skill and resource. (Plot VIII.O.1)

Captain Alastair FORBES-MENZIES DSO, 17th Royal Fusiliers, was killed in action on 4 May 1918, aged 25. His DSO was gazetted on 20 February 1918, followed by the citation on 18 July that year. It was awarded for conspicuous gallantry and devotion to duty while serving as a temporary lieutenant after he had held his ground during an enemy attack on a communication trench leading towards the enemy's lines. He brought heavy enfilade fire to bear as the enemy passed his position. His determined action gained vital time to allow the main line of defence to be reorganized. He then organized a bombing attack and re-captured 200 yards of the trench where he established a block. The enemy then made five very determined attacks on his position, suffering great loss on each occasion without gaining further ground. By his courage, coolness and leadership, he saved the situation and assisted in inflicting a severe defeat on the enemy. *Officers Died in the Great War* lists him under the surname 'Menzies'. (Plot VIII.P.9)

FORBES-MENZIES is one of thirty-two men of the 17th Royal Fusiliers buried here. All except one are casualties from March and April 1918 when the 2nd Division was covering the sector south of Arras opposite the villages of Moyenneville, Hamelincourt and Boyelles. The line here was just a ragged and irregular trench system, and sometimes little more than a series of posts constructed around shell holes. Both sides also made great use of the sunken roads that ran through both lines. Often, casualties were the result of shelling, but both sides also patrolled no man's land and raids were not uncommon. The majority of 17th Battalion casualties can be found in Plot VIII, Rows, P, Q and R.

Lieutenant George Francis PAULING MC, 3rd Grenadier Guards, was killed in action on 25 March 1918. His MC was gazetted on 16 November 1916 and was awarded for conspicuous gallantry in action, leading his company forward and establishing a strong point on the left flank in a display of great courage and initiative. Later, he maintained the position for twenty-four hours, causing considerable loss to the enemy until his party was relieved. PAULING had seen action on the Somme in September 1916 during the attacks around Ginchy and Lesboeufs. He was also wounded on 30 July the following year at Ypres while his battalion was moving up to its assembly trenches ready for the attack the following day, the start of the Third Battle of Ypres. He was originally gazetted in the 17th (Duke of Cambridge's Own) Lancers in August 1914, but transferred to the Grenadier Guards in January 1916. (Plot VIII.R.46)

Lieutenant Sidney Reuben PINDER, 80 Squadron, Royal Flying Corps, was killed in action on 19 February 1918 when his Camel aircraft came down. He went to Canada in 1911, but as soon as war was declared he left his job and enlisted with the 3rd Canadian Tunnelling Company. (Plot VIII.S.23)

Private Arthur William COPPEN MM and Bar, 87th Battalion, Canadian Infantry, was killed in action on 18 October 1918. He was in a wooden hut when a shell hit the roof and exploded. Debris from the explosion struck him on the head, killing him instantly. Unusually, there is a citation for his MM. It was gazetted on 8 January 1917 and was awarded for conspicuous gallantry and devotion to duty as a stretcher-bearer. After many of the other stretcher-bearers had become casualties, he carried on working as best he could, although slightly wounded himself. He then remained on duty rendering first aid until his unit was relieved. I could find no trace of the bar to his MM in any of the *Gazettes*, although Canadian records claim that it was gazetted on 14 April 1919. His headstone also refers to both awards. (Plot IX.D.2)

Second Lieutenant Edward Gutherie REYNOLDS, 73 Squadron, Royal Air Force, was killed when his Camel aircraft came down on 8 July 1918. He was South African and an only son, was 19 years old when he died. The Royal Air Force Communiqué for that day makes very little comment on the day's activities and is very brief. It does note that there were heavy thunderstorms during the afternoon. (Plot XV.M.6)

Lieutenant Alexander Hamilton LOCKLEY, 4 Squadron, Australian Flying Corps, was killed in action on 5 September 1918, aged 20, flying a Camel aircraft. He was one of three men from that squadron who fell in action that day. They are Lieutenant Maxwell Hardwicke Eddie and Lieutenant Duncan Campbell Carter. Unlike LOCKLEY, neither of them has a known grave and both men are now commemorated on the Flying Services Memorial, Arras. Eddie had previously served with the 6th Australian Field Ambulance. Enquiry files from the Australian Red Cross Society show that one other member of the squadron, Lieutenant

Taplin, had been traced as a prisoner of war, but that the other three were still missing after their aircraft were attacked by fifteen of the enemy above Douai.

The fight was witnessed by another squadron and although two machines were seen to fall, it was not known whether these were from 4 Squadron or whether they were German aircraft. However, when Lieutenant Taplin was repatriated in February 1919 he was able to confirm that LOCKLEY had been attacked by several of the enemy and that he had seen his aircraft fall out of control from 12,000 feet. Taplin was also told by his captors that LOCKLEY's body had been buried in the German Military Cemetery at Hénin-Liétard, near Lens, and he was even given a note of the grave reference. (Plot XV.M.30)

Captain Herbert HUNTER MC, 6th East Kent Regiment (The Buffs), died of wounds on 23 October 1918, aged 28. His MC was gazetted on 5 February 1919 and was awarded for leadership of his company between 8 and 30 August 1918 during which time he showed conspicuous gallantry and initiative. On 27 August at Favière Wood, when his company was held up by a machine-gun nest, he out-flanked the enemy's position, killing the garrison, thereby saving many lives and enabling his company to reach its final objective. The citation concludes that throughout the whole period he had shown great fighting qualities. (Plot XV.O.16)

Major Leonard Arthur TILNEY MC, 40 Squadron, Royal Flying Corps, was killed in action on 9 March 1918, aged 22, while flying his SE5a aircraft (Plot XV.Q.37). His MC was gazetted on 2 January 1918 in the New Year's Honours List. He had been awarded the Belgian *Croix de Guerre*, and with that had come his appointment as an Officer of the Order of the Crown of Belgium. He had also been mentioned previously in despatches. His father, Colonel Robert Henry Tilney DSO, who lived at Onslow Crescent, South Kensington, served as Colonel of the Duke of Lancaster's Own Imperial Yeomanry during the Great War. His DSO, like his son's MC, was gazetted as part of the Honours List system, but on 4 June 1917. He was twice mentioned in despatches and was also the recipient of a foreign decoration, the French *Croix de Guerre*, which was presented to him in Péronne on 1 April 1917 by the President of France.

Lieutenant Ernest Tilton Sumpter KELLY, 1 Squadron, Royal Air Force, died on 15 June 1918, aged 19, from wounds sustained two days previously while flying a SE5a aircraft. He came from Ontario, Canada, and had scored six victories, placing him among Canada's aces. Canadian records show his date of birth as 20 June 1896, which would make him two years older than the CWGC record. (Plot XV.R.39)

Captain Robert George FERGUSON MC, 1st Royal Scots Fusiliers, died in German captivity on 11 June 1918. His MC was gazetted on 29 July 1918 and was awarded for conspicuous gallantry and devotion to duty. After the enemy had penetrated our lines and had begun to bomb along the trench towards his com-pany's position, he did fine work in setting up blocks where he held off the enemy's advance with accurate fire from rifle grenades until the supply ran out. (Plot XVI.A.4)

Lieutenant William Lloyd BOWEN MC, 3rd South Wales Borderers, attached 6th Battalion, died of wounds on 1 September 1918, aged 36. His MC was gazetted on 26 September 1918 and was awarded for conspicuous gallantry and devotion to duty in May that year during the retirement on the Aisne where he had assisted in the reorganization of scattered units after the enemy had broken through. He then assisted in holding the position throughout the night during which time he used his Lewis guns with great skill, inflicting heavy casualties on the enemy and enabling his men to withdraw once the position had become untenable. His citation shows him serving with the Monmouthshire Regiment. He was fatally wounded at Dranoutre Ridge following a successful attack there. His battalion was in the process of consolidating its newly won position when it came under a counter-attack. He was one of around a dozen casualties sustained by the battalion during that last week of August. (Plot XIX.D.15)

Lieutenant Colonel Eric Gordon BOWDEN MC, 11th Queen's (Royal West Surrey Regiment), was killed in action on 22 July 1918, aged 24. The battalion war diary shows his death occurring on 23 July rather than the 22nd, but states that he was killed by shell fire while riding through Steenvoorde on a day when the battalion's front was described as 'quiet'. He had also been mentioned in despatches and had previously served in Italy. (Plot XIX.E.12)

Lieutenant Victor William SCOTT MC, 18 Squadron, Royal Flying Corps, formerly 13th East Surrey Regiment, was killed in action on 16 March 1918, though his pilot that day, Lieutenant R.A. Mayne, was taken prisoner when their DH4 aircraft came down. SCOTT's MC was gazetted on 10 January 1918 and had been won whilst serving with the 13th East Surrey Regiment. It was awarded for conspicuous gallantry and devotion to duty after he had spent two hours in no man's land under enemy machine-gun fire searching for a wounded man, even though there was every reason to believe that enemy patrols were in the vicinity. Having found the wounded man, he then carried him 500 yards back to our own lines. Afterwards, he organized a search party and went back out into no man's land to within a short distance of the enemy wire in an effort to find two other missing men. The citation concludes that his initiative and complete disregard of danger were deserving of the highest praise. (Plot XXI.D.19)

Lance Serjeant Albert Edward BRIGHT DCM MM, 4th Coldstream Guards, died on 14 April 1918 from wounds. Bright's DCM was gazetted posthumously on 21 October 1918 and was awarded for conspicuous gallantry and devotion to duty during an attack. After all officers of his company had been hit, he displayed great courage and took command of the company. His grasp of the situation at that very critical time was of the utmost value to his commanding officer. During the operation he proved himself a magnificent leader of men. The regimental history makes no reference to this fine NCO in its narrative of events. (Plot XXI.D.20)

Second Lieutenant Richard Curtis WADE, 40 Squadron, Royal Flying Corps, was killed in action on 26 February 1918, aged 19, flying a SE5a aircraft. He was the youngest of three sons who served during the war. He enlisted in the King's Shropshire Light Infantry in September 1914 and spent just over a year at the front before applying for the Royal Flying Corps. He was gazetted in September 1917 and began operational flying the same month. His two brothers served, one in France and Belgium, the other in Mesopotamia. (Plot XXI.F.22)

Second Lieutenant Horace Levick WILSON, 13 Squadron, Royal Air Force, was killed in action on 1 July 1918, aged 19, while observing with Lieutenant Kenneth William MURRAY, aged 21, when their RE8 aircraft came down. As is the case with Canadians attached to either the Royal Flying Corps or the Royal Air Force, MURRAY is shown in the CWGC register as serving with his Canadian unit, though the entry adds that he was attached to the Royal Air Force. His Canadian unit is shown as the Regimental Depot in British Columbia, suggesting that he had little military experience. WILSON was probably also inexperienced, given his age. (Plot XXVI.C.15 and 16)

Lieutenant Dudley Howard HAZELL, 25 Squadron, Royal Air Force, was killed in action on 27 September 1918, aged 23, while flying a DH4 aircraft with his observer, Second Lieutenant David Brown ROBERTSON, aged 18. They were carrying out a reconnaissance flight prior to ground operations against German positions on the Canal du Nord when their aircraft came down. (Plot XXVIII.C.32 and 33)

Lieutenant Colonel Arthur Leonard WRENFORD, Worcestershire Regiment, attached 4th East Lancashire Regiment, was killed in action on 21 March 1918. As a student at Jesus College, Cambridge, WRENFORD had accepted a commission in the Cambridge University Volunteer Rifle Corps, after which, in 1903, he joined the 2nd Worcestershire Regiment. Between then and the outbreak of war he served in Ireland, Ceylon, India and he was also seconded several times during that period to the North Nigeria Regiment. It was while he was serving in Africa in September 1914 that he became a captain. He then re-joined his old regiment and in July 1916 he served on the Somme with its 4th Battalion, though he was transferred for a short time to a Royal Fusilier battalion as a temporary major.

Between April and September 1917 he became an acting major in the Royal Inniskilling Fusiliers, followed by acting lieutenant colonel with the 4th East Lancashire Regiment. The war diary refers to his being wounded and captured on 21 March 1918 near Villeret; his wounds were serious and he died later that day. He was buried nearby at Villeret, which lies in the Département of the Aisne, a very long way from Arras.

After the war his mother erected a stone cross there, inscribed in both English and French. It was erected in a field close to where she believed he had fallen. However, in 1927 his body was found and he was re-interred at Cabaret-Rouge British Cemetery, which was still open for burials, though a very long way from where he fell. In recent years some renovation has been carried out on the original memorial cross, courtesy of the Western Front Association. On 23 May 1918 he was posthumously mentioned in despatches. (Plot XXX.F.17)

Second Lieutenant John Kingham CLARKE and Second Lieutenant Cyril Thomas HOUSTON, both members of 103 Squadron, Royal Air Force, were killed in action on 22 July 1918. CLARKE, an observer, formerly served in the 3rd Connaught Rangers. Both are buried here next to each other. They were killed in action near Houplines during a bombing mission on the main railway junction situated on the edge of the Faubourg de Fives, just east of the centre of Lille. (Plot XXX.H.4 and 5)

1919

There are just two burials dating from 1919 and they are both buried next to each other. They are Aircraftman 1st Class Charles Reginald PEPLOE, 6 Squadron, Royal Air Force, and Aircraftman 1st Class Alfred MACE from the same squadron. Both men died on 23 April 1919. This was a week before the squadron moved to Mesopotamia and was therefore a very busy time for all concerned as aircraft were being moved around and overhauled. At the time of their deaths both men were working at No.1 Aeroplane Supply Depot. Research suggests that both men may have been killed whilst working in a hangar at Tourmignies when an aircraft crashed into it, killing, or at least fatally injuring both men (Plot VIII.H.27 and 28)

1940

Sergeant Herbert ROBINSON, 2nd GHQ Artillery Company, Royal Army Service Corps, was killed in action on 8 April 1940, aged 44 (Plot 29.G.12). His son, Gunner Cyril David Robinson, was killed serving with 3rd Battery, 1st Light Anti-Aircraft Regiment, on 20 August 1942, aged 19. He is buried at Caserta War Cemetery, Italy.

And finally ...

In May 2000 an unknown Canadian soldier from this cemetery was chosen for repatriation and taken to Ottawa as Canada's Unknown Soldier. The site of the grave is marked with a standard CWGC headstone on which is engraved:

'The former grave of an unknown Canadian soldier of the First World War. His remains were removed on 29 May 2000 and now lie interred at the National War Memorial in Ottawa, Canada.'

The soldier was one of a number of men buried here from the 87th Battalion, Canadian Infantry (Canadian Grenadier Guards), killed on 9 April 1917.

Nine Elms Military Cemetery, Thélus

Between Thélus and Roclincourt, some 500 or so yards east of the Arras–Lens Road, a clump of trees was referred to as Nine Elms. Shortly after the capture of Vimy Ridge when a cemetery was made at that location, it acquired the same name. The first burials were from the 14th Battalion, Canadian Infantry, when eighty casualties from the opening day of the Battle of Arras were interred in Plot I, Row A. Subsequent burials were made and the cemetery was enlarged after the Armistice. There are now 430 identified Canadian soldiers among the 484 Canadian graves in this cemetery. Of these, 366 of them were killed in action or died of wounds on 9 April 1917. Additionally, there are 145 British graves, of which 107 are identified, as well as fifty-four French graves from 1914 and 1915. Some French graves were moved after the war, but for whatever reason the others were left in situ.

Private William Milne VC, in 16th Battalion Canadian Infantry (Canadian Scottish), won his VC on the ground just west of the cemetery. On 9 April 1917 he attacked two machine-gun positions, which on each occasion allowed his battalion to continue its advance. He was killed soon after tackling the second position. He has no known grave and is therefore commemorated on the Vimy Memorial.

The 14th Battalion, Canadian Infantry attacked directly west of the cemetery on the morning of 9 April 1917, whilst the 16th Battalion attacked to the north-west of it and the 15th Battalion to the south-west. Captain Walter Willett PICKUP, 14th Battalion, Canadian Infantry, is one of the many here who was killed in action on 9 April; he was 23 years of age. His father, the Honourable Samuel Walter Willett Pickup, was a prominent politician in Canada who had earned significant wealth as a businessman and shipbuilder. (Plot I.A.30)

Two brothers killed on the same day, serving in the same battalion, are buried here in the same grave. Private William James (Bill Jim) WEST, aged 19, and his elder brother, Private Arthur WEST, aged 27, fell on 9 April 1917 while serving with the 14th Battalion, Canadian Infantry (Plot I.A.3). Another brother, Private Lewis Edgar West, who also served with the 14th Battalion, was killed in action on 7 September 1917 and is buried at Lapugnoy Military Cemetery. In spite of their army numbers, which are just eighteen digits apart, Canadian records show the three brothers enlisting on different days between 12 and 26 February 1916. Lewis enlisted on 12 February 1916, William on the 17th and Arthur on the 26th.

Serjeant George Bertrand WYNNE, 'A' Squadron, 19th (Queen Alexandra's Own Royal) Hussars, was killed in action on 20 May 1917, aged 29 (Plot I.A.21). He is one of eight men from his regiment who died that day, six of whom are buried here. He is the only one in Row A, the other five are in Row B. The remaining two died of wounds the same day and are buried next to each other at Aubigny Communal Cemetery Extension. The likelihood is that the men were the victims of enemy shell fire.

Captain John Scatcherd LAYCOCK, 15th Battalion, Canadian Infantry, was killed in action on 11 June 1917, aged 37. He was born in the United States, though his parents are shown residing in Canada. The war diary records that on 10 June the entire battalion was working on Canada Trench on Vimy Ridge. The Germans shelled the area heavily and LAYCOCK was killed by one of the shells. Although there is a discrepancy over his date of death, this could just be a matter of hours. (Plot I.B.1)

An unusual grave is that of Sub-Conductor Francis ROCHE, 5th Division, Army Ordnance Corps. The rank originally referred to a man whose role it was to conduct soldiers to a place of assembly and there is mention of it in early fourteenth century texts. In the late nineteenth century a Royal Warrant created two roles, Conductor of Supplies (Army Service Corps) and Conductor of Stores (Ordnance Store Branch). These roles were effectively the equivalent of staff serjeant major. In 1896, when the Army Ordnance Corps was formed, its staff serjeant majors retained the old title of sub-conductor. In February 1915, with the establishment of warrant officers throughout the army, conductors and sub-conductors became warrant officers class I. There are only eight holders of this rank buried or commemorated on the Western Front, and Sub-Conductor ROCHE is one of only four to be found in France. He is shown in *Soldiers Died in the Great War* as having died on 21 May 1917, though it does not elaborate further. (Plot I.B.15)

Second Lieutenant Edmund JANES, 161st Siege Battery, 70th Heavy Artillery Group, is one of six men from that battery killed in action on 13 May 1917 (Plot I.B.30). Serjeant CAHILL, from Barrow-in-Furness, shown as 166th Siege Battery, is buried amongst them (Plot I.B.31). He was killed the same day, along with the only British gallantry award in this cemetery, Gunner George FAIRCLOUGH MM, 161st Siege Battery, Royal Garrison Artillery (Plot I.B.27). CAHILL and FAIRCLOUGH originally served together with the Lancashire and Cheshire Royal Garrison Artillery on the Western Coast defences back in England. The unit was made up of four companies from Liverpool, two from Seacombe and two from Barrow-in-Furness. Two other men in this group, SPENCE and ARROWSMITH, came from Liverpool and Lancashire and both had enlisted in Liverpool, so they too may have served in the same Territorial Artillery unit before going to France (Plot I.B.28 and 29). It is quite possible that these men may have known each other very well and may have served together for some period of time. All are buried in Plot I, Row B.

There is a small group of pioneers, NCOs and men from 'E' Special Company, Royal Engineers, who died of accidental injuries on 5 October 1917. They are Lance Corporal John JENKINS (Plot I.C.29), Pioneer William Cartwright FORRYAN (Plot I.C.31), and Pioneer Alexander William GIBSON (Plot I.C.32). FORRYAN was one of four brothers who served during the Great War. Second Lieutenant Albert Donald Forryan, 9th King's Own Yorkshire Light

Infantry, was killed in action on 16 September 1916 and is commemorated on the Thiepval Memorial. Corporal John Owen Forryan, 9th Royal Sussex Regiment, was killed seven days before the end of the war on 4 November 1918, aged 24. He is buried at Cross Roads Cemetery, west of Fontaine-au-Bois, near Landrecies.

Private Iwakichi KOJIMA, 10th Battalion, Canadian Infantry, was killed in action on 9 April 1917, aged 38. His parents lived in Japan. He is one of a number of Japanese who enlisted and fought with the Canadian Expeditionary Force. (Plot I.D.32)

The highest ranking casualties buried or commemorated in this cemetery all served with Canadian units.

Major Sydney Lodge THORNE, 60th Battalion, Canadian Infantry, was killed in action on 26 November 1916, aged 37 (Plot I.E.12). He was one of two officers who died when one of our own trench mortars fell short and hit a dug-out being used as a Company HQ. The other officer killed by the explosion was Lieutenant Hubert Gordon PUNNETT (Plot I.E.13) and, according to the battalion war diary, four other ranks were killed in the same incident. They are buried next to their officers and are Private William Thomas GODBEER (Plot I.E.14), Private George BROWNLEE (Plot I.E.15), Private Harold COMPTON (Plot I.E.16), and Private William Smith MOIR (Plot I.E.17).

The same diary also goes on to say that 185 Tunnelling Company carried out a rescue attempt, recovering one officer and three other ranks, all of whom were wounded. One of those men is very likely to be Sergeant Percy Clabburn. He died that same day and is buried at Écoivres Military Cemetery. THORNE had crossed from Canada to England with the first Canadian contingent and had worked in the Pay and Records Office in London before being transferred to the front where he took command of a company of the 60th Battalion.

COMPTON had enlisted whilst under age and his family wrote to the authorities pointing this out. The family later claimed that his battalion received notification that he was to be returned home immediately, but unfortunately it arrived too late; he was killed earlier that same morning. He would have been 17 years old at the time he enlisted, but he was certainly a year older when he was killed, so this version of events may not be strictly true. A month before his death he had written to his family telling how a shell had landed a few yards from him as he was assisting to stretcher a wounded man out of the trenches and how the party had come under sniper fire. His brother, Private Charles Duncan Compton, was killed in action on 9 April 1917 whilst serving with the 18th Battalion, Canadian Infantry. He enlisted a few days after his sixteenth birthday and was 17 years old when he died, making him even younger than Harold.

Private MOIR, who came from Banff in Scotland, served for twelve years with the 16th (The Queen's) Lancers.

Major Robert Eugene WALLACE, 15th Battalion, Canadian Infantry, was killed in action on 9 April 1917, aged 24. (Arras Road Cemetery, Memorial 1)

Major Samuel James BOTHWELL DCM, 1st Canadian Mounted Rifles, was killed in action between 9 and 12 April 1917, aged 41. One record shows his date of birth as 1 June 1879, which would make him younger than he is shown in the CWGC register. He was born in Co. Down, Ireland, but at some stage he moved to Canada where he enlisted in July 1915. Whilst in Canada he served as captain and adjutant of the 66th Battalion. In England he transferred to his new battalion and went to France where he was later wounded. He was an experienced soldier who had also served in the 2nd Life Guards and on the Yeomanry Staff in the South African campaign. It was during his time there that he was awarded the DCM. In 1903 he also took part in the Zulu Rebellion in Natal. (Plot III.F.5)

Sergeant John MIDDLETON, 1st Canadian Mounted Rifles, was killed in action some time between 7 and 10 April 1917 (Plot III.G.6). He was one of seven brothers who served in the Great War, three of whom died, and his brother-in-law also died in the conflict. Of the brothers who were killed, Private Charles Dunn Middleton, 8th Battalion, Canadian Infantry, was the first to die. He was killed in action on 14 June 1916 in operations to recapture Mount Sorrel and Hill 62, near Sanctuary Wood, east of Ypres. Private Archibald Middleton, 49th Battalion, Canadian Infantry, died of wounds on 10 October 1916 and is buried at Contay British Cemetery on the Somme. Brothers Lewis, James, Ernest and Alexander all survived the war and continued to maintain strong ties with the family home at Aboyne in Scotland. Their parents' house in Aboyne was called 'Alberta'.

Sergeant Roy Albert EDMUNDS DCM, 5th Battalion, Canadian Infantry, won his award as a corporal during a bombardment, displaying conspicuous gallantry when a trench mortar bomb dropped into his trench. Without hesitation, he picked it up and rolled it over the parapet where it immediately exploded. This courageous act undoubtedly saved several lives. The award was gazetted on 19 August 1916. He also held the Russian Medal of St. George (4th Class). He was killed in action on 9 April 1917, aged 22. (Plot III.B.10)

There are a number of Canadian soldiers buried here who won the MM. All except one were killed in action on 9 April 1917. Corporal Frank ODD MM, 15th Battalion, Canadian Infantry, was killed in action on 18 April 1917. (Arras Road Cemetery, Memorial 10) The others are:

Corporal John Alexander BERTRAM MM, 14th Battalion, Canadian Infantry. (Plot I.A.26)

Company Sergeant Major John Thomas WRIGHT MM, 15th Battalion, Canadian Infantry. (Plot I.E.40)

Private John BOIS MM, 26th Battalion, Canadian Infantry, was awarded his MM for operations in October 1916 at Regina Trench. (Plot III.F.10)

Sergeant Colin Matson WISDOM MM, 16th Battalion, Canadian Infantry. (Arras Road Cemetery, Memorial 5)

Corporal Thomas MOSLEY MM, 15th Battalion, Canadian Infantry. (Arras Road Cemetery, Memorial 7)

Private Peter CUMMING, 1/4th Seaforth Highlanders, was killed in action on 9 April 1917. (Seaforth Grave, Memorial 8) His brother, Lance Corporal David CUMMING, was killed serving with the 2nd Seaforth Highlanders on 1 July 1916 and is buried at Serre Road Cemetery No.2. The other two brothers, James and John, survived the war.

La Targette British Cemetery, Neuville-Saint-Vaast

Directions to this cemetery from Arras are identical to the ones for Cabaret Rouge British Cemetery. Both lie on the west side of the D.397, which is the main Arras–Béthune road. At the junction with the D.55, turn left, and the cemetery is situated immediately on the right just before the larger French National Cemetery.

The location was very close to a system of underground quarries that were extensively used by the British and Canadians for a number of purposes, but mainly as HQs for a variety of units, especially artillery and medical units based in that area. The location of the quarries was known by its French name, Aux-Rietz, and at one time the cemetery was referred to as Aux-Rietz Military Cemetery. The French cemetery next to it is a reminder that this whole area was a French sector until March 1916 when the British took over.

Plots III and IV each contain a significant number of 8th Division casualties who were killed in action or who died of wounds during the late summer and autumn of 1918 when its battalions were holding trenches between Fresnoy and Méricourt.

Another feature of this cemetery is that several of the headstones have interesting personal inscriptions, some of which offer an insight into the life, death or service of those to whom they refer. The cemetery now contains almost 600 identified burials, nearly half of which are Canadian. Particularly well represented are men from the Canadian Field Artillery, eighty of whom can be found here. Almost 60 per cent of all burials in this cemetery are 1917 casualties, whilst the remainder are mainly from the following year.

Second Lieutenant Patrick McLeod INNES, 111th Siege Battery, Royal Garrison Artillery, was killed in action on 30 April 1917 (Plot I.A.3). He had been a pupil at Haileybury College, Hertfordshire, between 1911 and 1916 and had been head boy there. In 1915 he was awarded a History Scholarship to Trinity College, Cambridge, but that achievement was never fulfilled. The family inscription on his headstone reads: '*Sursum Corda*', which translates from the Latin as: 'lift up your hearts'. It is taken from the opening to the Eucharistic Prayer used in Roman Catholic, Anglican, and many other Christian church services for communion.

His younger brother, Second Lieutenant Donald McLeod Innes, won an Exhibition to read Classics at Trinity College, Cambridge, where he joined the

OTC. He received his commission in summer 1917 and died of wounds on 6 October 1918, aged 19, while serving with the 14th Black Watch. He is buried at Abbéville Communal Cemetery Extension. Their grandfather, Lieutenant General John McLeod Innes, won the VC during the Indian Mutiny while serving with the Royal Engineers. It was awarded for attacking and killing the crew of a field gun single-handed and keeping the enemy at bay whilst under heavy fire.

Lieutenant Herbert Daniel McDONALD MC, 6th Siege Battery, Canadian Garrison Artillery, was killed in action on 28 April 1917, aged 24. His MC was gazetted on 18 July 1917 and was awarded for conspicuous gallantry and devotion to duty while serving as a forward observation officer. It was not for any specific action, but for his conduct over a period of time during which he showed total disregard for danger under fire, setting a fine example to the other officers in his battery, and his work was described in the citation as being of the greatest value. (Plot I.D.25)

Major Alvin RIPLEY, 5 Brigade, Canadian Field Artillery, was killed in action on 2 May 1917, aged 33 (Plot I.E.15). He was an experienced gunner with six years previous military service in the artillery. His only son, Robert, served with the Royal Canadian Air Force in the Second World War and reached the rank of Air Commodore.

Lieutenant Colonel Russell Hubert BRITTON DSO, 5 Brigade, Canadian Field Artillery, was killed in action on 2 May 1917. His DSO, awarded for services in the field during the latter stages of the Battle of the Somme, was one of sixty-four gazetted to Canadian officers on New Year's Day 1917. He enlisted in August 1914, a few days after the war had broken out, and before that he commanded the 8th Field Battery in the Militia. Following his death, his wife requested that his horse be sent back to Canada, but the ship in which it was being transported had the misfortune to be sunk by a German submarine. (Plot I.E.16)

Major Stanley Mott WALDRON, 15th Battery, 6 Brigade, Canadian Field Artillery, was killed in action two days later at Vimy Ridge on 4 May 1917, aged 35. (Plot I.E.18)

Private Adelard BEAULIEU, 22nd Battalion, Canadian Infantry, is shown in the CWGC register as having died on 12 October 1917, aged 23. In fact, he committed suicide. A court of inquiry concluded that he had shot himself in the head during a moment of apparent insanity. The war diary for that day shows the battalion resting at Neuville-Saint-Vaast and taking baths. Prior to that, the period spent in trenches west of Méricourt was described as 'quiet'. (Plot I.G.7)

Major Samuel Henry DOAKE DSO, 52 Army Brigade, Royal Field Artillery, was killed in action on 30 March 1918, aged 25. His DSO was awarded in the King's Birthday Honours List of 3 June 1918. He was commissioned in the Royal Artillery in 1912 after passing out from the Royal Military Academy, Woolwich. He immediately went to France with the BEF in August 1914 and then served continuously at the front for three and a half years. His headstone contains the following inscription from his family: '*Strong, Brave, Gentle, Beloved. In France from August 1914; Fought in Twenty Battles*'. (Plot I.J.1)

Major Harold Egerton Vivian KYNCH, Cheshire Regiment, died on 31 May 1919, aged 37 (Plot I.K.28). His headstone reads: '*He died for Freedom, Honour and England*'. There is one other 1919 casualty buried here; Gunner Anthony Leonard CHRISTIE, 8 Army Brigade, Canadian Field Artillery, who died on 28 March 1919, aged 18 (Plot II.H.9).

Lieutenant Norman SWORDER, 5 Squadron, Royal Air Force, was killed in action on 17 April 1918 (Plot I.J.23). His brother, Lieutenant Malcolm Sworder, died on 18 March 1918 serving with 59 Squadron, Royal Flying Corps, to which he was attached from the Canadian Reserve Cavalry Regiment. Norman had previously served with 'B' Squadron, Lord Strathcona's Horse, before being transferred to the Royal Flying Corps.

There are five graves belonging to men of the 2nd Division Ammunition Column, Canadian Field Artillery, who were killed serving together on 10 May 1917. Gunner Percy Richard ALLABY's inscription at the base of his headstone contains what appear to have been his last words: '*Do what you can for the rest*' (Plot II.A.15). Those killed with him are buried adjacent to him (Plot II.A.14, 16 and 17) or very close by (Plot II.A.9). I have been unable to discover the precise circumstances behind the incident that led to their deaths, but it seems highly likely that they were the victims of shell fire.

The base of the headstone of yet another Canadian soldier, Private Mostyn Scott SANDS, 28th Battalion, Canadian Infantry, carries another very personal inscription; it reads: '*I raised my boy to be a soldier. Mother.*' He was killed in action on 8 May 1917, aged 21 (Plot II.A.12).

Corporal Peter James BARKER DCM (Plot I.K.28), is shown in the CWGC register as serving with the 12th Northamptonshire Regiment. However, the regiment did not have a 12th Battalion, and a further complication is that his DCM was not won with that regiment, nor was it awarded under his full name (Plot II.B.9). He is one of several men in this cemetery from the Northamptonshire Regiment shown as having been killed on 23 May 1917. One of them is shown as serving with the 28th Labour Company. The volume of *Soldiers Died in the Great War* that covers the Labour Corps does, however, provide some answers. Like the others, Private Peter James BARKER was actually serving with the Labour Corps at the time of his death. He had previously served with the East Lancashire Regiment. His DCM was won with the 1st East Lancashire Regiment and was gazetted on 10 March 1915 under the name 'J. Barker'. In January that year, he and Corporal Lindsay had put out a fire at 'A' Company's HQ whilst under heavy fire. All five men shown in the CWGC register as belonging to the

12th Battalion were killed while serving with the Labour Corps (Plot II.B.8 to 11 and 16). In fact, Plot II.B contains twelve men from various regiments, but all were attached to the same unit, 150th Company Labour Corps. All were killed on 23 May 1917, the same day as BARKER.

Flight Sub-Lieutenant John Norquay McALLISTER, 8 Squadron, Royal Naval Air Service, was killed accidentally on 23 June 1917, aged 20. It would appear that one of the wings of his Sopwith Triplane collapsed causing his machine to crash near Neuville-Saint-Vaast. He was a Canadian from Manitoba in Canada. (Plot II.C.15)

Second Lieutenant Walter William GIBBS, Royal Engineers, was killed in action on 22 April 1918 whilst serving with the 1st Field Survey Company (Plot II.J.3). Buried next to him is Sapper Patrick KILLIAN of the same unit (Plot II.J.2). The role of a Field Survey Company was to survey the ground, create maps and identify enemy dispositions. They became increasingly involved with the artillery as the war progressed, particularly in connection with sound ranging. There were eventually five Field Survey Companies in France, one for each Army group.

Major Henry Edward SEWELL, 524th Siege Battery, Royal Garrison Artillery, was killed in action on 4 June 1918, aged 42. His father had worked in the Indian Civil Service. The family lived on the Isle of Wight and quite a few of them had been connected with administrative roles in India. (Plot II.K.14)

Plot II. Row K contains a number of burials of men from Scottish regiments, all killed between 31 May 1918 and 6 June 1918. Private W. HOGG, 'B' Company, 1/4th King's Own Scottish Borderers, who was killed in action on 5 June 1918, was the son of the sculptor William Hogg. (Plot II.K.16)

Plot III, Row A contains three native Indian cavalrymen buried consecutively. All three were killed in action in the summer of 1916. They are: Lance Daffadar Gajraj SINGH, 2nd Lancers; Sowar Babu SINGH, Alwar Lancers; and Saadat KHAN, 17th Indian Cavalry, attached 19th Lancers (Fane's Horse) (Plot III.A.14 to 16). The rank of sowar is the equivalent rank to trooper, and daffadar is the equivalent to sergeant. They are the only 1916 casualties buried in this cemetery and are also the earliest here.

The back row of this cemetery contains eight men of 93rd Battery, Royal Field Artillery who were killed on the opening day of the Battle of Arras. One of the crew from this battery, Corporal John Gottfred ERICKSON, held the MM as well as the French *Croix de Guerre* and was born in Finland, though he enlisted in Goole, East Yorkshire. (Plot III.D.17 to 24)

Lance Corporal William KING, 1st Sherwood Foresters, was killed in action on 28 August 1918 (Plot IV.B.7). The foot of his headstone contains the inscription: '*Also in memory of 16215 Co. Sgt. Maj. Lawrence Leggott KING, MGC, died 9th April 1917*'. Lawrence, who was his elder brother, was killed in action serving with

13th Machine Gun Company on the opening day of the Battle of Arras, aged 23. He is commemorated on the Arras Memorial and had been mentioned in despatches.

Plot IV.A.1 to 9 contains men of the Highland Light Infantry, but not all from the same battalion. Lieutenant John TODD (A.1) and the four men next to him are from the 1/6th Highland Light Infantry, whilst the remaining four are from the 1/5th Battalion. Todd was in charge of a working party on the night of 3/4th July 1918 when it sustained casualties from enemy shell fire that killed Privates George B.D. MARTIN, William BAIRD and David Montgomery HERBISON (A.2 to A.4). TODD died the next day. The CWGC register shows him as serving with the 9th Battalion (Glasgow Highlanders). He joined the 9th Battalion as a private and was one of its original members. He was also wounded at High Wood on 15 July 1916 by a bullet to his chest and spent time in hospital, and in England recovering, before returning to the front. Private Harry BARRACLOUGH was killed in action a few days later on 7 July (A.5). The remaining four Highlanders all died a week later on 13 July.

Lieutenant Colonel Auriol Ernest Eric LOWRY DSO MC, *Croix de Guerre* with Palm (French), 2nd West Yorkshire Regiment, was killed in action on 23 September 1918, aged 25 (Plot IV.C.1). The DSO citation reads:

> '*For conspicuous gallantry and devotion to duty during many days of very fierce fighting when he led counter-attacks against overwhelming odds and restored situations after the enemy had broken through, and finally, when surrounded on all sides, cut his way out, being personally the last to cover the withdrawal. He was overpowered and captured, but during the night escaped from his escort and made his way back across many miles at the greatest personal risk. His fortitude and indomitable courage throughout a memorable twelve days were beyond all praise.*'

These events took place south of the River Somme during the British withdrawal in March 1918, when battalions of the 8th Division were engaged in a fighting retreat, which in my own view, was carried out to the very highest standards.

The circumstances of LOWY'S escape showed remarkable awareness, coolness and quick thinking. The Germans had taken his trench coat, his revolver and other belongings, but in exchange, and perhaps because of his rank, he was given a cape by one of his German captors. The Germans had captured a significant number of prisoners, but on this occasion appear to have been poorly organized in terms of providing for their security. As it began to grow dark, LOWRY'S group appears to have been left unguarded for a time. LOWRY took advantage and slipped away to a nearby heap of potatoes (probably sugar beet) and hid behind it, but before doing so, he also managed to 'acquire' a German steel helmet. He remained hidden until it was dark, but when some German transport came past him on the main Saint-Quentin–Villers-Bretonneux road, he emerged from his hiding place and joined the end of the column. LOWRY accompanied the stream of men and wagons for a while, but then slipped away as he approached Villers-Bretonneux in order to avoid possible detection by units controlling traffic up ahead. After a lengthy detour, he regained the British lines where he was able to give Army HQ a detailed account of enemy gun positions, troop movements and strengths. LOWRY was one of only two officers of the 2nd West Yorkshire Regiment to survive the March fighting, though he was wounded a few days later at Villers-Bretonneux leading the remains of his battalion in a counter-attack.

LOWRY and his battalion were again in the very thick of it in May that year, this time on the Aisne, and again conducting a fighting retreat against high odds. LOWRY himself was wounded by a bullet in the foot; in fact, every battalion commander with the 8th Division became a casualty during that retreat, including Lieutenant Colonel Roberts VC DSO MC, 1st Worcestershire Regiment. LOWRY, though, soon returned to the front and by June he was back in command of his battalion. His *Croix de Guerre* was gazetted on 17 August 1918.

LOWRY'S illustrious military career came to a sad conclusion in rather mundane circumstances when he was struck by a machine-gun bullet whilst visiting outposts. His funeral was attended by an army commander, two corps commanders and three divisional commanders, a clear indication of the respect he had earned for his remarkable courage and leadership. His MC had been gazetted on 17 January 1916.

LOWRY'S two brothers were also killed in action. Second Lieutenant William Augustine Harper Lowry, serving with the 14th (King George's Own) Ferozepore Sikhs, was killed on 4 June 1915 at Gallipoli, aged 25. His younger brother, Captain Cyril John Patrick Lowry, was killed in action on 25 March 1918, aged 20, serving with 'C' Company, 2nd West Yorkshire Regiment which, of course, was commanded by his own brother. Neither has a known grave and so William is commemorated on the Helles Memorial, Cyril on the Pozières Memorial.

Finally, there are twelve holders of the MM buried here, nine of whom are Canadian and six are from artillery units. Some have already been referred to, but the remainder are:

Gunner Patrick Joseph BURNS MM, 1 Brigade, Canadian Field Artillery; killed in action on 10 May 1917. (Plot I.B.15)

Corporal Thomas BOOKER MM, 2nd Canadian Mounted Rifles, killed in action on 1 June 1917. Canadian military records show his date of death as 1 July 1917. (Plot I.C.13)

Gunner J.E. HANSEN MM, 14th Siege Battery, Royal Garrison Artillery, killed in action on 23 May 1917. (Plot I.E.21)

Second Corporal Henry SINKER MM, 9th Field Company, Canadian Engineers, killed in action on 22 September 1917. (Plot I.G.1)

Corporal Robert Frederick LAW MM, 2nd Division Ammunition Column, Canadian Field Artillery, killed in action on 17 September 1917. (Plot I.H.27)

Sergeant Thomas HEAPS MM, 3rd Divisional Trench Mortar Battery, Canadian Field Artillery, killed in action on 30 March 1918. (Plot I.J.4)

Corporal W. BIRRELL MM, 7th Queen's Own Cameron Highlanders, killed in action on 20 May 1918, aged 26. (Plot I.K.19)

Corporal Graham ROGERS MM, Canadian Army Medical Corps, killed in action on 13 June 1917. (Plot II.C.8)

Sergeant George RUSSELL MM, 1st Field Company, Canadian Engineers, killed in action on 17 June 1917. (Plot II.C.10)

Sergeant Frank James NICKLE MM, 8 Brigade, Canadian Field Artillery, killed in action on 28 March 1918. (Plot II.H.9)

Corporal Edward Hayes SMITH MM, 2 Brigade, Canadian Garrison Artillery, killed in action on 5 September 1918, aged 30. (Plot III.C.2)

Arras Road Cemetery, Roclincourt

The cemetery is situated between what were the German first and second lines in April 1917. About 500 yards to the south was where the 5th Battalion, Canadian Infantry attacked on the southernmost flank of the Canadian Corps. Here the Canadian Corps joined up with the 51st (Highland) Division, the left flank of the British XVII Corps, just north of the German first line defensive position known as the Labyrinth.

The CWGC register points out that the original cemetery was made by the Canadian 2nd Brigade very soon after 9 April 1917 and that, initially, it contained only men of the 7th Battalion, Canadian Infantry; in fact, just over seventy of them in what is now the rear of the current cemetery. Obviously, today's cemetery is far larger owing to the post-war concentration of at least sixteen other sites, many of them village cemeteries, but clearly some larger ones too. Even taking into account the concentration from other burial sites, most of the casualties here fell between 8 and 10th April 1917, although a very small number are from later dates.

Several officers of the 7th Battalion, Canadian Infantry, are buried among the NCOs and men, the highest ranking being Major Anquetil Philip NORMAN, killed in action on 9 April (Plot I.B.2). Either side of him is Captain Claude Llewellyn HARRIS, son of the Chief Constable of Wakefield, who was shot through the head while leading his men, and Lieutenant William George ROSS. Major William Ferguson BRADLEY, 1st Battalion, Canadian Infantry, who was killed in action on 3 May 1917, is buried in an adjacent plot (Plot II.B.5 to 7). There is one gallantry award holder among the 7th Battalion men; Sergeant Albert CHAMBERLAIN MM, who was killed in action on 28 April 1917. (Plot I.A.4)

The concentration of other cemeteries into this one after the war has given rise to the inclusion of quite a number of 1914 casualties. Among these thirty-two NCOs and privates is Private Louie LEWIS, 1st Highland Light Infantry, who was killed in action on 19 December 1914, aged 16 (Plot II.A.7), and Boer War veteran, Company Serjeant Major Richard HOLT, 2nd South Lancashire Regiment, killed two months earlier on 20 October in fighting north of La Bassée (Plot II.K.33).

With one exception, the October 1914 casualties are from battalions of the 3rd Division who fell during the fighting around La Bassée, an episode that has often been overlooked by military historians. Another group of 1914 casualties come from battalions that formed part of the Lahore and Meerut Divisions of the Indian Army, namely the 1st Highland Light Infantry (Sirhind Brigade), the 1st Connaught Rangers (Ferozepore Brigade), the 1st Manchester Regiment (Jullundur Brigade), the 2nd Leicestershire Regiment (Garwhal Brigade) and the 1st Seaforth Highlanders (Dehra Dun Brigade). These units were involved in fighting in late November and throughout December between Rouge Bancs and La Bassée, as was the 14th Battalion, London Regiment (London Scottish), in December that year; it also has a couple of its men buried here. Private Thomas Henry BROOM, 1st (King's) Dragoon Guards, attached 1st Life Guards, is the only cavalryman among them. He was killed in action on 2 November 1914 (Plot III.P.14).

There are also sixty-two identified casualties from 1915 who were reburied here after the war. Many of them would have died behind German lines from wounds, often as prisoners of war; others, however, would have been killed in action in captured positions that were later retaken in counter-attacks and then buried by the Germans. Some bodies may also have been buried, lost, and then recovered after the war. A number of these casualties are of interest.

Second Lieutenant Harry ALEXANDER, 1st Grenadier Guards, was killed in action on 17 October 1915, barely a week after his arrival on 9 October. He was killed whilst taking part in a bombing attack on Slag Alley, a communication trench on the south-east side of the Dump behind the Hohenzollern Redoubt. Described as a promising young officer, his was a very short war that started and ended on the Loos battlefield. (Plot II.C.18)

Private John GRIERSON, 8th Seaforth Highlanders, a veteran of the South African Campaign, was killed in action on the opening day of the Battle of Loos, 25 September 1915. He originally enlisted in 1900, but had already left the army before the outbreak of war in 1914. However, he immediately re-enlisted in August 1914 and was 35 years old when he died. (Plot II.H.3)

Lieutenant Malcolm Eyton LAWRENCE, 6th King's Royal Rifle Corps, attached 2nd Battalion, is the first of the 1915 casualties buried here (Plot II.L.33). On New Year's Eve 1914 the 2nd Battalion was driven out of some observation posts and a machine-gun position in front of the main trench line near La Bassée; immediate attempts to retake the position failed. The following day a further attempt was made by the 1st Scots Guards, and although the position was recaptured, it proved untenable. On 10 January 1915 the 2nd King's Royal Rifle Corps made yet another attempt, which this time was successful, and despite three German counter-attacks, most of the positions were recovered and subsequently held. It was during this fighting that LAWRENCE fell, aged 25.

His father, the Honourable Henry Arnold Lawrence, played rugby union for Richmond in 1873 and went on to captain the England Rugby XV in subsequent years, playing in the first ever international match between England and Ireland. LAWRENCE's grandfather, 1st Baron Lawrence, was Viceroy of India between 1864 and 1869.

On 25 January 1915, another small-scale action was fought on either side of the La Bassée Canal. On this occasion the German attack penetrated as far as the keeps and strongpoints behind our support lines. North of the canal, at Givenchy, the lost positions were immediately counter-attacked and recovered, but south of the canal, near Cuinchy, the counter-attacks were delayed, allowing the enemy to consolidate and retain the trenches there. The headstones belonging to men of the 1st Scots Guards and 1st Coldstream Guards are a reminder of this minor encounter that was so typical of the early fighting in this sector. Again, in mid-June, Givenchy was the scene of further fighting. A few men from the 1/4th Loyal North Lancashire Regiment are buried here, although it was not the only unit involved in that action.

Second Lieutenant Edward Offley Rouse WAKEMAN, 1st Grenadier Guards, was killed in action on 16 May 1915 at the Battle of Festubert, aged 25. WAKE-MAN was killed as he advanced with the leading platoon of No. 4 Company, which was cut to pieces by machine-gun fire from a ruined house in front of it. He was the son of Sir Offley Wakeman, 3rd Baronet. An only child, he had graduated from St. John's College, Oxford, and was then commissioned in the Grenadier Guards (Special Reserve). During his brief service he was mentioned in despatches. (Plot III.N.2)

Arguably, the best-known casualty in this cemetery, and probably the most visited, is Captain Arthur Forbes Gordon KILBY VC MC, 'C' Company, 2nd South Staffordshire Regiment, who was killed in action on 25 September 1915, aged 30. There appears to be no citation for his MC, but it was gazetted on 18 February 1915. He was a graduate of the Royal Military College, Sandhurst, and was also a gifted linguist, fluent already in German and Hungarian, who was learning Spanish when the war broke out. His VC was won leading a charge along the canal towpath at La Bassée against a strongly-held enemy position. He was wounded in the attack, which was met by murderous machine-gun fire. On reaching the enemy's wire, KILBY and those still with him were met by a shower of bombs, one of which blew his foot off. Despite this, he continued to urge his men forward, firing his rifle at the enemy as he did so. The award was gazetted on 30 March 1916. (Plot III.N.27)

With the notable exception of one Australian soldier killed in action on 19 July at Fromelles (Plot II.F.12) and three from the 53rd Battalion who died of wounds in German captivity a few days later, who were also involved in the same action (Plot III.C.4 to 6), the 1916 casualties are all from British or Canadian units. One of them, Rifleman Reginald Harry LARKIN, 'B' Company, 9th Battalion, London Regiment (Queen Victoria's Rifles), is buried a long way from where he was wounded, which was at Gommecourt on 1 July 1916. *Soldiers Died in the Great War* shows him as having been killed in action that day, but his burial here seems to suggest that he died of wounds behind German lines, possibly even a day or two later. If he did die on 1 July he would have been buried far closer to Gommecourt. His burial here, even allowing for the post-war concentration of other cemeteries, is unusual and certainly unexpected. (Plot II.D.18)

Private Alfred Leonard JEFFERIES, 6th Somerset Light Infantry, who died on 1 November 1916, had lost his brother, Private Arthur Thomas Jeffries, a few weeks earlier on 16 September 1916. Arthur served in the same battalion as his brother, but has no known grave and is commemorated on the memorial at Thiepval. Alfred, sadly, was executed by firing squad. He went to France with his battalion in May 1915 and was wounded the following month. A couple of months later, having returned to his battalion, he suffered a breakdown and he was allowed a further period in which to recuperate. He never quite recovered and deserted shortly before his battalion was due to take part in an attack at Delville Wood in August. While under arrest and awaiting trial he would probably have learned of his brother's death. (Plot III.O.1)

Sergeant George Simpson TURNER DCM, who was killed in action on 12 March 1916, had won his award for conspicuous gallantry and determination as a lance corporal with the 28th Battalion, Canadian Infantry. Prior to a night attack on the enemy's trenches, he and a corporal crawled out into no man's land, and over a period of four and a half hours cut a passage through the enemy's wire just in front of a machine-gun post. When the assault began he joined the attack and was one of the first to enter the enemy's trenches showing great courage throughout the operation. The award was gazetted on 15 March 1916, just three days after his death. (Plot III.P.15)

There are British casualties from 1917 stretching between January and November, as well as a small number of Australians brought in from other cemeteries. There are also two officers of the Royal Flying Corps, Lieutenant Hugh WELCH, 1 Squadron (Plot II.F.11), and Second Lieutenant John Lowick RICHARDSON, 55 Squadron (Plot II.F.12). They were killed in action on 21 August 1917. WELCH had been flying for quite some time, first as an observer between October 1915 and September 1916, then as a pilot from December that year. He had enlisted in 2 London Brigade, Royal Field Artillery, in August 1914 and was commissioned within the month, but then transferred to the Royal Flying Corps in September 1915. He was brought down in aerial combat. RICHARDSON previously served with the 3/4th Gloucestershire Regiment.

Among the men who fell during the final year of the war, there are two officers, one of whom has a gallantry award.

Second Lieutenant Frank Willard FERGUSON, 87 Squadron, Royal Air Force, was killed in action on 3 September 1918, aged 24, flying a Dolphin aircraft. He was one of thirty-three Royal Air Force casualties that day. He was a Canadian flyer from Saskatchewan, though he was born in North Dakota. (Plot II.A.14)

Captain James GASTON MC, Royal Army Medical Corps, attached 4th Suffolk Regiment, died of wounds on 5 November 1918, aged 36. His MC was gazetted on 24 July 1917 and was awarded for his tireless efforts and splendid example to all those around him as he tended the wounded of five different units, as well as his own. The following day he led a party out of the trenches and recovered a further twelve wounded men who were lying out in front of his unit's position. (Plot II.N.38)

Private Charlie HAMILTON MM, 55th Company, Machine Gun Corps, formerly of the Cheshire Regiment, was killed in action on 19 October 1918. He is one of thirty-three machine gunners killed in action or who died of wounds on the Western Front that day. Their role, supporting the infantry as it advanced against German rear guard units, was a vital one. (Plot II.P.17)

The CWGC register shows Private E.J. PARMENTER, 12th Battalion, Machine Gun Corps, as dying on 14 January 1919, and his headstone carries the same date. Most of the other headstones in that row relate to unknown soldiers, but show no further details, although there are two men buried there who were killed in 1915. There is no reference to Private PARMENTER serving with the Machine Gun Corps in *Soldiers Died in the Great War*, though he may, of course, be listed under a former regiment in which he served. (Plot III.K.31)

Private Loal SINGH, 75th Battalion, Canadian Infantry, died of wounds on 24 October 1918. He was born in the Punjab, but had evidently moved to Canada at a later date because he enlisted at Smith's Falls, Ontario, in September 1915. He was one of a small number of Sikhs living elsewhere other than India who volunteered to fight during the war. He would appear to be the only Sikh to have died overseas serving with the Canadian Expeditionary Force. (Plot III.O.26)

Finally, there is the sad reminder of how close some men came to surviving the war. There are three such men buried here: Serjeant Douglas Roland HARRISON, 7th Battalion, London Regiment, died of wounds on 7 November 1918 (Plot II.N.29); Gunner Edward WILLIAMS, B Battery, 276 Brigade, Royal Field Artillery, also died of wounds on 8 November 1918 (Plot III.P.2); and Private George WATSON, 'C' Company, 7th Northamptonshire Regiment, killed in action on 9 November 1918, aged 19 (Plot III.O.24).

Chapter Four

A Beehive and Two Craters – Curiosity and a Nose Cap – Cousins Divided by War

Arleux-en-Gohelle Communal Cemetery

There are only four graves in this communal cemetery situated on the north side of the village. All are Second World War casualties from the 2nd Battalion, Cameronians (Scottish Rifles). They are:

Rifleman Robert COOPER, 2nd Cameronians, died on 23 May 1940. (Grave 1)

Rifleman Alfred George Samuel VINCENT, 2nd Cameronians, died on 23 May 1940, aged 32. (Grave 2)

Rifleman William SIMMONDS, 2nd Cameronians; died on 10 October 1940, aged 30. His family was from Whitechapel, London. In November 1940 the regimental magazine, *The Covenanter*, still referred to him as missing in action, but believed that he had been killed. Even today, the regimental roll of honour merely shows his death occurring in October 1940 without specifying any date. This suggests two things: first, that there is no certainty regarding his date of death because no reliable record exists, and second, that there is a strong possibility that his body, wherever it lay, was only discovered in October 1940 and that the CWGC record reflects the date of burial rather than any precise date of death. (Grave 3)

Rifleman Ronald MACDONALD, 2nd Cameronians, from Leeds, died on 24 May 1940, aged 17. (Grave 4)

What seems odd is why the chronological order of death is not reflected in the consecutive numbering of the graves. This begs the question as to when and how this plot was made.

Albuera Cemetery, Bailleul-Sir-Berthoult

The cemetery is on the west side of the railway embankment to the north-west of the village of Bailleul-Sir-Berthoult. The easiest approach is to follow the D.919 as it emerges from the suburbs at the north end of Saint-Laurent-Blangy. Continue past Bailleul Road West Cemetery towards Bailleul-Sir-Berthoult. The cemetery lies out in the fields in front of the embankment and is clearly visible. To reach it there is a road to the left about 250 yards beyond the embankment. This road is the one that leads to the cemetery, which is reached via a footpath once over the level crossing. The village of Bailleul-sir-Berthoult was captured on 13 April 1917 by troops of the 2nd Division. Once in British hands, the railway embankment offered a good measure of protection from shelling and was used extensively as shelter for a variety of units, notably medical units, engineers, and HQs up to and including battalion level.

The cemetery is divided into two plots and they are referred to, not as Plots I and II, but as Plot North and Plot South, which is highly unusual. Of the 253 burials, 110 are unidentified, though fifteen men are known to be buried some-where in this cemetery and are now commemorated by special memorials. The only 1918 casualties are eight men commemorated by special memorials near to the entrance to the cemetery, five of whom are from the 14th Battalion, London Regiment (London Scottish), along with one man from the 13th Battalion, London Regiment (Kensingtons), and two from the 4th (City of London) Battalion, London Regiment (Royal Fusiliers). All were killed in action on 28 or 29 March 1918. (Special Memorials A.8 and B.1 to 7)

The York & Lancaster Regiment has a significant number of burials here with twenty-two men buried either in Plot South or commemorated by special memo-rials (Special Memorials A.1 to 5). All of them are 1917 casualties from May and June, and all but one are from the 13th Battalion (1st Barnsley Pals). A few of them are from the end of June 1917 when the battalion was consolidating its gains following a successful attack on Oppy Wood, in which the 14th Battalion (2nd Barnsley Pals) also took part. The attack, which took place on the evening of 28 June, resulted in relatively few casualties. The ground over which the attack took place was personally reconnoitred on 26 June by the 13th Battalion's com-manding officer, Lieutenant Colonel George Boothby Wauhope DSO. He was accompanied by his Intelligence Officer, Captain Lewis Dudley Richard HUG-GARD, who was born in County Tyrone. HUGGARD was killed instantly by metal splinters when a shell burst near to him. He was 23 years old (South C.11). His father, Captain the Reverend Richard Huggard, served as a chaplain with the 14th Battalion and was involved in the recruitment drive for both battalions of the Barnsley Pals in 1914.

Captain Charles Harold ROBIN, 2nd Battalion, Royal Jersey Militia, was killed in action near Oppy on 11 May 1917, aged 31, attached to the 14th York & Lancaster Regiment (2nd Barnsley Pals). He was adjutant of the battalion at the time of his death, which occurred when he was caught by a shell blast. He was educated at Charterhouse School and University College, Oxford, and had been commissioned in the Royal Jersey Militia in 1907. He then transferred to the Royal Fusiliers. He was unfortunately invalided in 1910 and had to leave the regular army, but remained an officer in the Royal Jersey Militia. When the war broke out he was able to persuade the army that he was fit for overseas service and eventually joined the York & Lancaster Regiment's 14th Battalion. He was originally buried in Bailleul-sir-Berthoult, but was brought here after the war. (South C.3)

Second Lieutenant Reginald Douglas BERRY, 12th York & Lancaster Regiment (Sheffield Pals), was killed in action on 12 May 1917 near Gavrelle. His battalion had taken over trenches near the ruined windmill on 9 May and it spent much of the next few days under bombardment. Casualties soon began to mount with nine on the first day and five the following day. On 11 May there were five more fatalities and twenty-nine wounded, including two officers. Second Lieutenant BERRY and three other ranks were killed the following day when another officer, Second Lieutenant Jarvis, and twenty-three other ranks were also wounded. The battalion was then relieved, but not before attrition had claimed three more lives and a further nine officers and men were wounded. (South C.6)

Other battalions from the 31st Division can also found in this cemetery. There are thirteen officers and men of the 11th East Lancashire Regiment (Accrington Pals), who were killed in action during the middle of May 1917. All are in the South Plot, and mainly in Row C. There are also fifteen officers and men from the four Hull battalions of the East Yorkshire Regiment, 10th, 11th, 12th and 13th Battalions, which made up 92 Brigade of the 31st Division. Among this group of casualties is Captain William CARROLL MC, 12th East Yorkshire Regiment, who was killed in action on 3 May 1917. On 22 November 1916 CARROLL had been promoted to second lieutenant for services in the field. Prior to this promotion he had been a regimental serjeant major with the 1st Royal Irish Rifles and it was while he was serving with that battalion that he was awarded the Medal of St George, 1st Class (Russia), gazetted on 27 August 1915. His MC had been gazetted two months earlier on 29 June. (North C.15)

Second Lieutenant Harold WINDER, 10th East Lancashire Regiment, was killed in action on 15 May 1917 (South C.19) and Second Lieutenant Richard Walter JAMES, 11th East Lancashire Regiment (Accrington Pals), had been killed in action on 8 May 1917 (South B.1). WINDER had been one of nine officers and thirty men who joined the 11th Battalion in March that year. Several other men from the battalion were killed on 15 May, very probably during a raid carried out on the night of 14/15 May to capture a German strongpoint about 500 yards south of Oppy Wood. Further attempts were made on each of the following two nights. On 15/16th the position was captured but could not be held, and the raid on the night of 16/17 was broken off because the Germans, who by then were highly alert, reacted as soon as the assault began. The Germans had tried to raid the battalion's trenches on 8 May, but had been driven off. These casualties illustrate perfectly the attritional nature of the fighting that was taking place about this time in the trenches around Arras. Limited in scale and always of a localised nature, such operations were usually carried out to straighten out small sections of the line or to eliminate troublesome strongpoints.

Lieutenant Thomas Arthur ARIS, 23rd Royal Fusiliers, was killed in action on 16 April 1917, aged 40. He served with the South African Mounted Rifles, which was formed in April 1913 by the amalgamation of several South African policing

A soldier tending the grave of a fallen comrade near Blangy, 3 May 1917, the opening day of the Third Battle of the Scarpe (Battle of Arras 1917). (*IWM*)

Canadian troops maintaining the graves of fallen comrades somewhere on Vimy Ridge. (*IWM*)

The grave of Lance Sergeant Ellis Wellwood Sifton VC, 18th Battalion, Canadian Infantry. He was killed in action on 9 April 1917, the date on which he won his VC. He is known to be buried in Lichfield Crater, where he is now commemorated. (*IWM*)

Lichfield Crater, Thélus. The crater, which was conveniently used by the Canadians to bury some of their dead soon after the position was captured on 9 April 1917, is really a mass grave. (*Goodland Collection, CWGC*)

The King visiting a soldier's grave on Vimy Ridge, 11 July 1917. (*IWM*)

Villers Station Cemetery, Villers-au-Bois. The graves of Lance Corporal Albert Edward Dodson, aged 19, and Private John Victor Chapman, aged 20, are clearly identifiable (Plot II.B.1 and 2). Both men were killed in action on 14 October 1916 whilst serving with the 9th Battalion, East Surrey Regiment. (*CWGC*)

Stone mason engraving the headstone of a Canadian soldier. Note the template. A keen eye, a steady hand, a mallet and a chisel; old-style skill and craftsmanship. (*CWGC*)

Écoivres Military Cemetery, situated about five miles north-west of Arras. Although work on the perimeter wall of the cemetery has yet to begin, the cemetery itself appears to have been completed. The River Scarpe lies in the valley in the middle of the photograph, close to the buildings over to the left. The photograph was taken in 1925. (CWGC)

A very early post-war photograph of La Targette British Cemetery, Neuville-Saint-Vaast. (Peter Taylor Collection)

Cabaret Rouge British Cemetery prior to construction work. (*Peter Taylor Collection*)

Cabaret Rouge British Cemetery as it nears completion. The spur of Notre-Dame de Lorette, which is visible to the right of the entrance to the cemetery, was captured by the French in 1915, but at a heavy cost. (*CWGC*)

The entrance to Duisans British Cemetery, Étrun, a few miles north-west of Arras. Today the entrance carries the scars of fighting from May 1940. (*CWGC*)

A single grave on Vimy Ridge containing men from a Canadian battalion. This may once have been part of a communication trench. (*IWM*)

The Cross of Sacrifice at Zivy Crater, Thélus. The shape of the crater is still clearly defined and the human figures provide a good indication of its size. Like Lichfield Crater, it is a mass grave. (*CWGC*)

(*Left*) The headstone of Lance Corporal George Frederick Baker, 1st Regiment, South African Infantry, killed in action on 12 April 1917, aged 26. He is buried at Level Crossing Cemetery, Fampoux. The photograph was taken on 18 February 2011 by the author. For 93 years the CWGC register contained no reference to Baker's MM. In March 2014 the MM had still not been added to the headstone. His gallantry award was won at Delville Wood on 16 July 1916 in one of the most celebrated actions in South African military history. (*J.P. Hughes Collection*)

(*Right*) The Cross of Sacrifice being erected inside a cemetery. The exact location is not known. (*Goodland Collection, CWGC*)

units. His widow is shown as living in Mafeking, which no doubt accounts for his military service in South Africa, and the CWGC register also points out that his father had served in the army, attaining the rank of captain. (North A.19)

The 63rd (Royal Naval) Division also spent much of the summer of 1917 in this area after it had captured Gavrelle. There are burials here from the division's 188 and 189 Brigades, battalions with familiar names such as Nelson, Hawke and Drake, as well as the 1st Royal Marine Light Infantry, which emphasized their association with the Royal Navy, but also the 4th Bedfordshire Regiment and the 10th Royal Dublin Fusiliers, which also made up part of this unique division. There are also quite a number of 1917 burials from Royal Fusilier battalions, most notably the 7th Battalion, which was another that formed part of the 63rd (Royal Naval) Division.

Private James LANGTRY DCM, 10th Royal Dublin Fusiliers, was killed in action on 23 May 1917, aged 31. LANGTRY served and won his DCM under the name of J. FORD while serving as a private in the 1st Royal Dublin Fusiliers. His award was gazetted on 16 November 1915 and was awarded for conspicuous gallantry between 23 and 29 August 1915 at Suvla Bay where he had volunteered to go out alone virtually every night to reconnoitre the ground between our trenches and the Turkish positions. He brought back accurate reports containing valuable information, and even managed to recover about sixty abandoned rifles. The citation concludes that he had shown a splendid example of bravery and devotion to duty. (South A.25)

There are several other 10th Royal Dublin Fusiliers buried near LANGTRY, including an officer attached to that battalion from the 5th Battalion, Second Lieutenant Frederick Ennis BOYD, who was killed in action on 20 May 1917. The battalion had left its billets in Écoivres and had marched up to relieve the 13th York & Lancaster Regiment after dark. The relief was carried out without incident and BOYD was the only battalion casualty that day, though even the war diary fails to note how he was killed. (South B.22)

Air Mechanic 2nd Class Reginald HICKLING and his pilot, Second Lieutenant Iorwerth Roland Owen, 13 Squadron, Royal Flying Corps, were killed in action in their BE2c on 7 May 1917. HICKLING is buried here (South C.1), but Owen, who subsequently died of wounds, aged 20, is buried at Sainte-Catherine British Cemetery. They were on a photographic mission when they were attacked and shot down by German ace, Karl Allmenröder. They were his tenth victory and he went on to score a further twenty before he was shot down and killed near Zillebeke in Belgium on 27 June 1917.

Beehive Cemetery, Willerval
Beehive Cemetery is essentially a Canadian burial ground and is linked almost entirely to the fighting in 1917. Ten different Canadian infantry regiments have

burials here, so that it can also be said to represent all corners of the former Dominion. None of the casualties buried here are officers and there is just one 1918 casualty, a Canadian soldier from the 43rd Battalion who fell in late March that year.

There are just five British graves, all of them privates, three of whom were from units of the 31st Division, the other two coming from pioneer units of the 46th (North Midland) Division and the 63rd (Royal Naval) Division. Two graves are of particular note.

Private Angus Alexander McLEOD, aged 23, and his brother, Private Kenneth Angus McLEOD, both served with the 14th Battalion, Canadian Infantry and were killed in action on the same day, 27 June 1917 (A.2 and A.3). The battalion war diary is useful in so far as it tells us that on 27 June 1917 a working party consisting of two officers and 210 men was shelled whilst at an engineer dump, killing three men and wounding one other. The McLEOD brothers account for two of these deaths. Private Reginald Frederick ELLISON, 14th Battalion, Canadian Infantry, is almost certainly the other fatality referred to in the narrative (A.1).

After the capture of Vimy Ridge, and particularly once the Battle of Arras had come to a close, the Vimy–Lens sector was held by each of the four divisions of the Canadian Corps on a rotational basis until they were called upon in October 1917 to take on the final phase of the Third Battle of Ypres around Passchendaele. Many of the casualties buried here are a reflection of the day-to-day attrition involved in holding the line.

This is a very small, yet very pleasant cemetery with just forty-seven identified casualties and one soldier, a private from the Royal Canadian Regiment, whose grave was lost and who is now commemorated by a special memorial. The name of the cemetery, as the CWGC register points out, derives from the fact that this was a location that once housed a number of German machine-gun emplacements, so the comparison with an angry beehive seems particularly appropriate. The metaphor is brilliantly striking and very much reflects the darker side of trench humour.

Bois Carré British Cemetery, Thélus

The cemetery lies about half a mile or so east of the village of Thélus on the D.49. The cemetery derives its name from the small square wood that stands about 100 yards east of it. Once Thélus was captured on the opening day of the Battle of Arras it remained in our hands for the rest of the war. The cemetery was begun by the 1st Canadian Division, but it was greatly enlarged after the war when other cemeteries were closed and the bodies brought here. Quite a number of men are commemorated by way of special memorials. Two of the cemeteries that were incorporated in this one are Bumble Trench, CD.186, and Canadian Grave, CD27, Neuville-Saint-Vaast. There is a special memorial relating to each of these former burial grounds located near the Cross of Sacrifice. The one for Bumble Trench commemorates five, the other, six Canadian soldiers. All Canadian cemeteries were originally designated by the prefix 'CD', followed by their own unique number.

The ground to the south-west of where today's cemetery lies is where the 1st, 3rd and 4th Battalions, Canadian Infantry, attacked on 9 April 1917. The 31st Battalion, Canadian Infantry, attacked to the north-west towards Thélus along with the 28th Battalion, whilst the 27th and 29th battalions, Canadian Infantry, continued the attack, passing through the 3rd and 4th Battalions and advancing north-east of the cemetery.

The cemetery contains men from all four Canadian divisions, as well as a number from British regiments, including artillery units, and six officers who fell whilst serving with the Royal Flying Corps. There are also six graves of men who died in 1940. Today there are over 500 burials, 454 of which are identified. Around 75 per cent of these are Canadian.

There are two holders of the MM to be found in Plot I. Sergeant Frederick George ALDRIDGE MM, 3 Brigade, Canadian Field Artillery, was killed in action on 25 April 1917. He had enlisted at Valcartier in September 1914 (Plot I.B.7). Private Thomas McQUATER MM, 4th Battalion, Canadian Infantry, was killed in action on 11 April 1917 (Plot I.C.12).

Lieutenant Percival William MURRAY and Second Lieutenant Duncan John McRAE, both from 16 Squadron, Royal Flying Corps, died from their wounds and injuries on 2 February 1917. McRAE, who was the observer, previously served with the 50th Battalion, Canadian Infantry, while MURRAY was at Ypres with the 6th Durham Light Infantry before joining the Royal Flying Corps. They became Manfred von Richthofen's nineteenth victory after setting off on a photographic mission over Vimy Ridge on 1 February, crashing, according to Richthofen's own account, in the German barbed wire along the front line. MURRAY, the pilot, was 20 years old when he died and McRAE was four years his senior. Both men were recovered from their aircraft by the Germans, but died the following day. McRAE's brother was killed in action in 1916, but the CWGC records provide no obvious match. McRAE and MURRAY are now buried in a joint grave. (Plot I.D.1/2)

The CWGC register notes that there is one Canadian soldier buried here who died accidentally in 1919. This is Private Wilfred Acey NICKERSON, whose entry in the register shows him simply as 'Canadian Infantry'. He had actually served with the 1st Depot Battalion, Nova Scotia Regiment, but after the war he worked for the Canadian War Graves Detachment. He was killed accidentally on 4 June 1919. He had gone for a walk after work with two of his colleagues, heading towards Roclincourt. Curiosity got the better of him when he found a nose cap, which he tried to dismantle. The resulting explosion was enough to cause serious injury to him and he died soon after the accident occurred. By trade, like many from Nova Scotia, he was a fisherman (Plot I.F.20). There is another man buried in this cemetery with the same surname, acting Bombardier Arthur

Nickerson, 4 Brigade, Canadian Field Artillery, who was killed in 1917 (Plot III.E.6) but there is no known or obvious family connection between the two men.

Captain Lancelot Lytton RICHARDSON MC, and Second Lieutenant Douglas Charles WOLLEN, both from 25 Squadron, Royal Flying Corps, were killed in action on 13 April 1917 when they were shot down. RICHARDSON, who was an Australian, came from New South Wales. He was posted to 25 Squadron on 3 June 1916 and was soon involved in several aerial combats, one of which left him wounded on 20 July in a fight over Lens that is reported to have lasted three quarters of an hour. During the fight RICHARDSON scored two victories, bringing his total to five. He returned to his squadron as a flight commander in early 1917 and added two more victories to his score before his death. His final victory had been secured with WOLLEN as his observer. His MC was gazetted on 14 May 1917 and was awarded for conspicuous gallantry after he had attacked a formation of five enemy scouts and brought one of them down. On another occasion, although wounded, he destroyed two hostile machines and drove down and damaged at least two others. This last part of the citation clearly refers to the encounter on 20 July 1916. (Plot II.C.14 and 15)

Among the 500 burials are two that tend to get lost: Private Howard WRIGLEY, 2/7th Duke of Wellington's Regiment (Plot II.C.15) was killed in action on 21 March 1918, while Private Henry BOOKER, 4th (City of London) Battalion, London Regiment (Royal Fusiliers), was killed a week later on 28 March 1918 (Plot II.C.7). These are the only two casualties buried here from the time of the German March offensive.

Corporal Arthur Wilfred PETTY DCM, 80th Battery, 15 Brigade, Royal Field Artillery, was killed in action on 22 May 1917. His award was won while serving as a bombardier with the same unit. It was awarded after he had displayed conspicuous gallantry during heavy fighting in the Ypres Salient between 17 April and 11 May 1915 when he had repeatedly repaired the telephone wires under heavy rifle and shell fire. On the latter date he was wounded whilst repairing the wires, but he continued with his work until communication had been restored. The excellent work performed by the 80th Battery during this critical period was largely attributed to his unflagging zeal and devotion to duty. The award was gazetted on 5 August 1915. Sadly, the DCM does not appear next to his name in *Soldiers Died in the Great War*. (Plot II.D.4)

Company Sergeant Major Alfred BROOKES DCM is one of twenty-three confirmed members of the 1st Battalion, Canadian Infantry, buried in this cemetery, the majority of whom were killed in action on 9 April 1917, as was BROOKES. His award was gazetted on 13 February 1917 and was awarded for conspicuous gallantry and devotion to duty. The citation goes on to state that he had displayed great courage and determination on several occasions, leading his men under fire, and at all times had set a splendid example (Plot III.A.3). Sergeant Leslie J.

ELDERKIN MM, also from the same battalion, is buried close by and was killed on the same day (Plot III.A.5).

Private Alexander Neil Mackenzie MORRISON, 'C' Company, 1st Battalion, Canadian Infantry, was killed in action on 9 April 1917, aged 19. For whatever reason, he chose to serve under the assumed name of 'Payne'. His parents back in Sydney, Australia, subsequently named their home 'Roclincourt', presumably in memory of their son. (Plot III.A.9)

Second Lieutenant Keith Ingleby MacKENZIE, aged 18, and his observer, Second Lieutenant Guy EVERINGHAM, aged 22, were killed in action on 8 April 1917 serving with 16 Squadron, Royal Flying Corps. EVERINGHAM, from the Colwyn Bay area, had originally enlisted with the Royal Welsh Fusiliers in October 1914, but after receiving his commission in February 1915 he became a signalling officer. Shortly after arriving in France he became a bombing officer with a trench mortar battery, but transferred to the Royal Flying Corps in September 1916 where he soon became an observer. In February 1917, whilst on leave, he got married, but returned to the front just two days later. Both men are now buried next to each other (Plot III.B.12 and 13). MacKENZIE and EVER-INGHAM were actually shot down by Manfred von Richthofen. They were his thirty-ninth victory and his second victory that day. Their machine, a BE2g, fell just inside the German lines near Vimy Ridge and it appears that the Germans made no attempt to recover their bodies for burial. They were only buried some days later, after the opening of the Battle of Arras, once this part of the line had been captured and consolidated. After bringing down their aircraft, Richthofen was just one victory away from reaching Boelcke's score of forty, a tally which he equalled a few days later on 11 April. EVERNGHAM's younger brother, Robin, was killed serving with the Welsh Horse at Gallipoli on 15 December 1915, a week before the evacuation of the peninsula. He is buried there in 7th Field Ambulance Cemetery.

Two other Canadian recipients of gallantry awards can also to be found in Plot III: Private Gaston PELLETIER MM, 22nd Battalion, Canadian Infantry, who was killed in action on 28 April 1917; and Corporal James D. TAIT MM, 1st Battalion Canadian Mounted Rifles, who fell on 10 April 1917. PELLETIER is buried in Row E.14 and TAIT in Row C.3.

The cemetery also includes five privates from the Canadian Light Horse, all of whom were killed on 9 April 1917, though only two are buried next to each other (Plot III.F.19 and 20). Two troops left Neuville-Saint-Vaast just before 2pm, followed by the rest of 'C' Squadron, with orders to push out to the village of Willerval and hold it if they were able. Although the party that approached the village from the north reached the centre of the village, the party to the south encountered opposition from Germans lying out in the fields, who made it quite clear that they were prepared to put up a defence. After taking casualties and with half of the horses injured or killed, the attempt to secure the village was abandoned and the cavalrymen withdrew. Only one of the five men, Trooper John BLUNDELL, was Canadian by birth; the other four had emigrated from England. The three that are not buried together can be found close to one another (Plot II.A.4, 8 and II.D.10).

Two 1918 casualties have already been mentioned, but there are a further five buried here who fell that year. One of them, from the North Staffordshire Regiment (Plot III.E.4), had transferred to the 211th Company, Labour Corps, when he died on 18 August 1918, though this is not shown in the CWGC register. The remaining four, all privates in the 2nd Devonshire Regiment, were killed on 27 September 1918 and are buried next to each other (Plot III.F.13 to 16).

Lieutenant Reginald Lawrence SLADEN, Princess Patricia's Canadian Light Infantry, was just 19 years old when he was killed in action on 9 April 1917. He was the son of Arthur French Sladen CMG MVO, who served as Private Secretary to the Governor General of Canada. In his letters home, Lieutenant Colonel Agar Adamson wrote of him barely a month before his death, noting that: '*Of all the young subalterns, I think young Sladen shows more promise than any.*' He was one of three officers from Princess Patricia's Canadian Light Infantry who were killed in action on 9 April and one of its ten officer casualties that day (Plot V.A.12). *The Letters of Agar Adamson*, published in 1997, offer a valuable insight into the life of a battalion at the front.

Major John Lovell DASHWOOD MC, 58th Battalion, Canadian Infantry, was killed in action on 13 April 1917. His MC was gazetted on 20 June 1917 and was awarded for conspicuous gallantry and devotion to duty while in charge of a raiding party. The success of the raid was attributed in large measure to his coolness and initiative. According to Canadian records he had previously served in the Royal Flying Corps between December 1915 and April 1916. He then joned his infantry battalion on 2 July that year and was wounded a month later. Prior to the war he was a lecturer in English. His brother, Frederick, also served during the war, but survived and went on to practise law as a barrister in Canada. (Plot V.A.14)

There is one casualty dating back to the summer of 1916, when the 60th (2/2nd London) Division made its brief acquaintance with the Souchez area after it had arrived in France. Private Harry BARRELL, 2/20th Battalion, London Regiment (Blackheath and Woolwich), was killed in action on 22 July 1916. The division subsequently went to Salonika. (Plot V.B.6)

Lieutenant Alexander MALCOLM, 43rd Battalion, Canadian Infantry (Cameron Highlanders of Canada), previously served as company sergeant major and as regimental sergeant major before obtaining his commission as an officer in June 1916. He was promoted to acting captain after the Somme, but was killed in action leading a bombing raid into the German trenches on 5 April 1917 (Plot IV.A.10). This was one of many such raids that took place along the British and Canadian fronts in the days leading up to the Battle of Arras. MALCOLM was in charge of the raid, the objective of which was to penetrate the enemy trenches in three places. However, the raiders soon ran into considerable opposition. MALCOLM was shot in the head and was seen to fall in one of the enemy trenches, reputedly shouting to his men: '*Go on, lads*'. He was initially posted as missing, leaving some room for hope that he might have survived and been taken prisoner. When the same trenches were captured a few days later, the battalion organized a search party under Sir Charles Tupper and discovered his body and the bodies of four other men who were killed with him. Later that day his revolver was found in a German dug-out. It is entirely possible that the other four are the men buried elsewhere in this cemetery (Plot IV.A.8, A.15, B.4 and B.5).

There is just one holder of the MM from a British regiment. Lance Corporal Thomas WHITE MM, 11th East Yorkshire Regiment, formerly Manchester Regiment, was killed in action on 19 July 1917, aged 27. (Plot III.D.10)

All the 1940 casualties are buried in Plot 5, Row C, with the exception of one man from the Royal Army Ordnance Corps who, chronologically, was the last of the six to die on 19 April 1940 (Plot 4.C.1). All the others died sometime between the last few days of March and the middle of April 1940. These men would almost certainly have died at No.8 Casualty Clearing Station, which was situated nearby. Their graves can be found next to the Cross of Sacrifice. The grave references for the five men in Plot 5, Row C, are: 11, 13, 15, 17 and 19. The gaps between the headstones suggest that the graves with even numbers may have been removed at some stage.

Canadian Cemetery No. 2, Neuville-Saint-Vaast

Finding this cemetery is straightforward enough. It lies within the same Memorial Park as the Canadian National Memorial on Vimy Ridge. It is set back off the D.55, which passes through the western edge of the park. It can be reached on foot through an avenue of trees opposite the car park nearest the visitor centre and tunnels. It also has car parking spaces.

The ground where the cemetery is located is where the attack by the 87th Battalion, Canadian Infantry, was brought to a halt on 9 April 1917 with the 75th Battalion behind it in support. The consequence of this setback forced the 54th Battalion, Canadian Infantry, to withdraw, which in turn left the 102nd Battalion not just stalled, but pinned down in shell holes under heavy machine-gun fire. These events are reflected in this cemetery where many of the casualties are from the 87th Battalion, Canadian Infantry, which suffered 299 casualties that day, as well as the 102nd Battalion, Canadian Infantry, which sustained 341.

Like one or two others near Arras, this cemetery contains burials from 1914, 1915, 1916, 1917 and 1918, including many from British regiments. Again, as with Cabaret Rouge British Cemetery, I have opted to cover this cemetery by dealing with each year of the war in turn, though within that format I have tried to keep to the various plots in ascending numerical order. Another unusual feature of this cemetery is that the plots are not denoted in Roman numerals, probably dating back to its origins as a Canadian burial ground before other graves were introduced after the Armistice.

1914

The majority of the thirty-seven burials are from late October 1914 and are mainly the result of fighting by the 3rd and 5th Divisions, which made up II Corps, and the 4th and 6th Divisions, which constituted III Corps. The area covered by these divisions stretched from La Bassée to Armentières. The burials are very scattered and are spread throughout the cemetery. There are only two officers within this group of 'Old Contemptibles'.

Major Fleetwood George Campbell ROSS, 2nd King Edward's Own Gurkha Rifles (Sirmoor Rifles), was killed in action at Neuve Chapelle on 2 November 1914, aged 45. The Gurkhas had already made an initial counter-attack to recover lost trenches, but were driven back yet again. ROSS then led some of his men forward in a further counter-attack and was last seen in hand-to-hand fighting during which he was killed. As with most of the men from 1914, if not all of them here, ROSS was very likely buried by the Germans and would have been brought to this cemetery for reburial once the battlefields were cleared sometime after the Armistice. He had originally served with the Militia, but was gazetted in the Wiltshire Regiment in 1890 before joining the Indian Army. While serving in India he took part in the Tibet Expedition in 1903–1904 where he was mentioned in despatches (Plot 8.E.1). His father, Colonel George Campbell Ross, also served in the Indian Army, but as a cavalry officer.

The other officer is Captain Robert John Blatchford OLDREY, 4th (Royal Irish) Dragoon Guards, who was killed in action on 29 October 1914, aged 31. After the Retreat from Mons and the subsequent battles on the Marne and the Aisne, 2 Cavalry Brigade, with the rest of the British Expeditionary Force, began to move closer to the coast, and it was during this phase of operations that OLDREY became involved in the fighting that took place north of the La Bassée Canal. On 28 October 2 Cavalry Brigade took up positions to cover trenches vacated by Indian troops. Following success at Neuve Chapelle, the Germans were threatening to break through, and all three cavalry regiments of 2 Cavalry Brigade were deployed in an infantry role to help stem the enemy's advance. OLDREY fell the next day which, ironically, was the last day on which the Germans made any serious attempt at a breakthrough, though officially the Battle of La Bassée continued until 2 November 1914. (Plot 12.H.16)

OLDREY's brother, Lieutenant Gerald Vivian Oldrey, died while on active service on 19 February 1919 serving in the 1/1st South Nottinghamshire Yeomanry. He is buried in Cairo War Memorial Cemetery.

1915

Fighting continued on either side of the La Bassée Canal throughout 1915 and it was one of the first locations where mine warfare was carried out. In the early hours of 25 January a German deserter indicated that an attack was to take place later that morning in the sector south of the canal near Cuinchy. An hour later the Germans exploded a mine, followed by a further twenty, though none were large by later standards. They then followed up with infantry attacks north and south of the canal, penetrating as far as the strongpoints or 'keeps' that lay behind our support lines where they were eventually stopped. North of the canal the enemy was driven back by early counter-attacks made by troops from the reserve lines, but south of the canal, where the line was held by 1 Brigade, and to its right by the French, our counter-attacks were delayed and the lost trenches were not recovered, though some were retaken in early February.

For the 1st Scots Guards, the attack on their trenches came on Burns' Night when twenty-seven other ranks were reported to have been killed in the fighting, although the battalion posted 235 as missing in action in addition to the 120 who were wounded. One officer and four other ranks of the 1st Scots Guards are buried here from that day's fighting and all five are buried in Plot 12, Rows E and F. One identified private from the 1st Coldstream Guards who was also killed that day can be found in a joint grave. (Plot 10.C.9 to 10)

There are also casualties here from all the major battles on French soil involving British and Dominion forces that year: the Battle of Neuve Chapelle in March 1915, the Battles of Aubers Ridge and Festubert in May, and the Battle of Loos in September and October 1915. As with the 1914 casualties in this cemetery, those from 1915 are also widely scattered between the different plots and amount to fifty-nine in total. All belong to British regiments.

Second Lieutenant Louis Herbert Cullen SMITH, 1st Monmouthshire Regiment, was killed outright on 13 October 1915 during the final phase of the Battle of Loos. Forward positions near the Hohenzollern Redoubt had become untenable owing to machine-gun fire from the direction of Fosse 8 and the 1st Monmouthshire Regiment, which was the pioneer battalion of the 46th (North Midland) Division, was involved trying to erect defences there to counter the threat. Nevertheless, a withdrawal was ordered, but as it was being carried out, the Germans launched a counter-attack. Second Lieutenant SMITH and his men became caught up in the fighting and he was shot dead as they tried to repel the attack. (Plot 9.A.18)

Captain Leslie John ROBINSON, 2nd Northamptonshire Regiment, was killed on the third day of the Battle of Neuve Chapelle, 12 March 1915, aged 31. (Plot 12.C.1)

Second Lieutenant Arthur Horace LANG was killed while defending a forward trench with the 2nd Grenadier Guards on 25 January 1915 at Cuinchy. He was originally gazetted in the Grenadier Guards in August 1914. His father, Basil, had been Advocate-General in Bombay, but Arthur was educated in England, firstly at Harrow, then at Trinity College, Cambridge. He was also a member of the MCC and was 24 years old when he died. (Plot 12.E.22)

Lieutenant Arthur Conway Osborne MORGAN, 4th Battery, 3 North Midland Brigade, Royal Field Artillery, was attached to the 1/5th Lincolnshire Regiment when he was killed in action on 13 October 1915, aged 30. His battalion was part of the 46th (North Midland) Division. His father held a Doctorate in Divinity and was Master of Jesus College, Cambridge. Arthur had also been a gifted student who had achieved distinction at Winchester School and at Trinity College, Cambridge, where he was President of the Union Society. After Trinity he became a barrister at Lincoln's Inn, London. He was 30 years old when he died and had been mentioned in despatches. (Plot 13.C.7)

Serjeant Albert Alfred WHITE, 2nd Lincolnshire Regiment, who was killed in action on 13 March 1915, aged 30, was already an experienced soldier and a veteran of the South African Campaign. He is listed in *Soldiers Died in the Great War* as Drummer-Serjeant. (Plot 14.E.4)

1916

There are relatively few burials from this middle period of the war, just thirty-two officers and men from British regiments and a mere handful of Canadians from October and December. There are, however, five Australian burials, one of whom is a sergeant from the 59th Battalion, Australian Infantry, who was killed at Fromelles on 19 July 1916 (Plot 12.B.18). For some reason, his body was re-interred here rather than at Cabaret Rouge British Cemetery where several other Australian casualties from this attack can be found.

The Commonwealth character of this cemetery is also enhanced by the presence of four New Zealand soldiers, two of whom died in October 1916. It seems odd to find two men from the 3rd Battalion, New Zealand Rifle Brigade, buried here, especially as they were fighting on the Somme on 1 October 1916, the date recorded on their headstones. It is quite likely that they died of wounds as prisoners of war and were buried by the Germans somewhere between the Somme and Arras. Their graves were obviously found after the Armistice and brought here for reburial, though it appears unlikely that their bodies were recovered at the same time or location, as they are now buried in different plots (Plot 14.A.56 and 19.A.55). The other two New Zealanders, both artillerymen, are buried next to each other and were killed in action on 5 September 1918 (Plot 10.C.12 and 13).

There are also two members of 11 Squadron, Royal Flying Corps, buried together following their deaths on 15 September 1916. Second Lieutenant Frank Edwin HOLLINGSWORTH, formerly Argyll and Sutherland Highlanders, and his observer, Lieutenant Henry Maurice Watkins WELLS, formerly Royal Berkshire Regiment, were initially reported missing on 15 September, but their deaths were later confirmed as having occurred the same day when their FE2b came down. WELLS was a student at Magdalene College, Oxford, where he gained a Bachelor of Arts degree. (Joint Grave 10.C.17 and 18)

Lieutenant Victor Charles Moore MAYNE, 1st South Wales Borderers, joined his battalion in the trenches on 23 March 1915 and went on to serve with it until he was killed in action on 19 February 1916 (Plot 13.F.1). Although the Battle of Loos had closed by the middle of October the previous year, fighting still went on there as both sides tried to secure local advantages, or at least deny such advantages to the other side. The 1st South Wales Borderers was given very short notice regarding an attack it was to carry out to seize two mine craters near the Double Crassier, known as Hart's Crater and Harrison's Crater. MAYNE was shot dead as he neared the top of Harrison's Crater at the head of a party of men who, in spite of his death, managed to secure the position. Hart's Crater was not captured that day, but was taken in a renewed assault a week later on 26 February. Victor's brother, Second Lieutenant Jasper Moore Mayne, who was killed on 9 May 1915 at the Battle of Aubers Ridge while serving with the Royal Field Artillery, aged 20, is buried at Rue Petillon Military Cemetery, Fleurbaix. Their father, Colonel Charles Blair Mayne, served with the Royal Engineers, but died in 1914.

1917

It will come as no surprise to find that the 1917 burials are dominated by units from all four divisions of the Canadian Corps. However, there are still 179 identified casualties from British regiments who fell that year.

The original burials in Plot 1 are men of the 4th Canadian Division, particularly from the 75th Battalion and the 87th Battalion following their attack on Hill 145 on 9 April where the Canadian National Memorial now stands. Other battalions of the 4th Canadian Division are also significantly represented. There are thirty-eight soldiers from the 44th Battalion, most of whom were either killed while consolidating Hill 145 on 10 April, or attacking 'The Pimple' on 12 April. There are also thirty-two men from the 54th Battalion, twenty-eight from the 50th Battalion and twenty-five from the 102nd Battalion.

Of the 467 identified Canadian burials in this cemetery, 291 were killed or died of wounds on 9 April 1917 in connection with the assault on Vimy Ridge; this equates to just over 62 per cent. One of them is Private Percival MOORE, 38th Battalion, Canadian Infantry, who was just 16 years old when he was killed in action (Plot 10.C.28).

There are also some casualties from an unsuccessful raid carried out by the 4th Canadian Division on 1 March 1917, particularly men from the 73rd Battalion, though they are scattered across the various plots. There are also a small number of casualties killed in early June 1917. The 44th Battalion, Canadian Infantry, carried out an attack on 2 June that resulted in 138 of its men being wounded. The attack reached the edge of La Coulotte, a village on the Lens–

Arras Road, which had previously formed part of the original German third line. However, since April, its defences had been strengthened considerably. After the attack, the new Canadian position formed a small pocket in the German line, but this was soon found to be untenable and a withdrawal was then ordered to prevent the newly won position becoming surrounded. However, seventy-eight men, most of them wounded, had to be left behind when the battalion pulled out. Earlier attempts had been made to capture this part of the German line in late April, and again in May, but the village had already been heavily reinforced and was now considered an important outlying part of the Lens defences. Any future attempts were likely to be met by stiff opposition.

Bombardier Bedford COOMBES DCM, 121st Battery, 27 Brigade, Royal Field Artillery, was killed in action on 10 April 1917, aged 20. His DCM was awarded for conspicuous gallantry on 12 March 1915 at Neuve Chapelle where he had repaired telephone wires under heavy rifle fire. (Plot 2.B.4)

Lieutenant John Thomson McCALLUM DCM, 50th Battalion, Canadian Infantry, was killed in action on 10 April 1917. He had won his DCM as a company sergeant major prior to gaining his commission, though it was gazetted on 17 April 1917, seven days after his death. It was awarded after taking command of a raiding party. Having steadied the men, he then led them through what is described in the citation as 'a difficult location' to their objective. The citation goes on to note that his bravery and fine leadership were responsible for the success of the raid. (Special Memorial 3.C.5)

Buried next to each other are two men from 25 Squadron, Royal Flying Corps, who were killed in action together on 17 March 1917. Aircraftman 2nd Class Frederick KING, aged 22, and Lieutenant Arthur Elsdale BOULTBEE, aged 19, became Baron von Richthofen's twenty-seventh victory when they were shot down over Oppy. They were escorting aircraft on a photographic mission when a strong enemy formation set about them, and in the ensuing fight there were casualties on both sides. Before the war BOULTBEE was a student at St Catherine's College, Cambridge, but left university to join up after just one term. He was initially commissioned in the Northamptonshire Regiment, but then transferred to the Royal Flying Corps. He joined his squadron on 1 January 1917 and therefore spent just ten weeks flying operationally before being killed. KING previously served with the Lincolnshire Regiment before going on to join the Royal Flying Corps as an observer. (Plot 11.A.1 and 2)

Private Daniel MARRS DCM, 73rd Battalion, Canadian Infantry, was killed in action on 1 March 1917 during the large scale raid at Vimy Ridge that was a failure. His DCM was gazetted on 3 March, just two days after his death, and was awarded for conspicuous gallantry in action on a previous occasion when he had displayed great courage and determination while dressing two wounded men in the open under very heavy fire. He later assisted in bringing both men back to our trenches. (Plot 11.F.11)

Second Lieutenant Henry Hamilton SHERIDAN, 1st Royal Irish Fusiliers, was killed in action on 3 May 1917, aged 35. Other officers and men from his battalion killed in the same attack are buried elsewhere, such as Brown's Copse Cemetery, Level Crossing Cemetery, Crump Trench British Cemetery, and on the Arras Memorial. (Plot 17.E.17)

One of the post-war reburials here is Private Charles MILLIGAN, 10th Cameronians, who was executed for desertion on 3 June 1917, aged 20. His grave had been lost, but was subsequently located after the Armistice and brought here. His grave can be found at the far end of the cemetery against the wall on the right-hand side. MILLIGAN's disciplinary record had been poor ever since joining the battalion in February 1916 and he had already been sentenced to a year's imprisonment with hard labour, though the sentence was suspended. A further act of disobedience had resulted in Field Punishment No. 1. Then, prior to the Battle of Arras, he went missing for five days before being arrested. The fact that he had deserted in the run up to a major offensive, and particularly one in which his battalion was involved, left little room for leniency once the facts were accepted. When combined with his previous disciplinary record, there was only ever going to be one outcome. (Plot 19.A.14)

Eleven of the thirteen holders of the MM buried in this cemetery are Canadian soldiers, one of whom was also awarded a bar. All of the Canadians are 1917 casualties, whilst the two from British regiments fell the following year.

Private Owen Harold DAVIES MM, 54th Battalion, Canadian Infantry, killed in action on 9 April 1917. He was born in Wales where his parents still lived. He had enlisted in September 1915. (Plot 1.A.26)

Corporal William Robert VOHMAN MM, 75th Battalion, Canadian Infantry, killed in action on 9 April 1917. He was born in London, though by the time he enlisted in August 1915, he and his parents were living in Toronto. His mother was born in Germany and she had family still living there when the war broke out. Consequently, one of his uncles served as a captain in the German Army and a cousin served in the German Air Force. Canadian records spell his name as 'Vohmann'. (Plot 1.B.19)

Private John Donald CALDER, MM, 75th Battalion, Canadian Infantry, killed in action on 3 January 1917. He enlisted in January 1916, having previously spent a short time serving with the Governor General's Foot Guards. His MM was won on 18 and 19 November 1916 on the Somme at Desire Trench, near Courcelette. Despite being ill and suffering from the effects of exposure, he insisted on taking part in his battalion's advance. He went forward in the second wave of the attack and then went on to help dig a trench and assist with the wounded, some of whom he carried in from the open, giving them water. By the end of these operations he was so weak that he was required to spend time recovering in hospital. The citation concludes that his cheerful example inspired all those around him. (Plot 1.B.51)

Sergeant George Elrick RAINEY MM and Bar, 44th Battalion, Canadian Infantry was killed in action on 10 April 1917. He was one of twelve men killed from this battalion as it moved forward to consolidate positions on Vimy Ridge. As it did so, casualties were incurred from sniper fire coming from Bois de la Folie. Four officers and seventy-one men from the battalion were wounded in these operations and a further ten were marked as missing in action. (Plot 2.C.7)

Private Leonard SWAN MM, 75th Battalion, Canadian Infantry, killed in action on 9 April 1917. (Plot 5.B.5)

Lance Corporal James Frederick GATES MM, 42nd Battalion, Canadian Infantry, killed in action on 9 April 1917. He enlisted in August 1916 and was reported to have been killed instantly during his battalion's advance at Vimy Ridge. (Plot 5.B.15)

Corporal Herbert SWINDELL MM, 44th Battalion, Canadian Infantry, killed in action on 12 April 1917. He had enlisted in June 1915 in Winnipeg where he lived, although he was born in Manchester where his parents still resided. (7.C.23)

Sergeant William Randall RIBBANDS MM, 1st Battalion, Canadian Mounted Rifles was, like several men from his battalion, killed in action sometime between 7 April and 10 April 1917. (Plot 6.C.12)

Private John Buchanan WILSON MM, 72nd Battalion, Canadian Infantry, killed in action on 9 April 1917. (Plot 8.F.7)

Private Herbert Victor GOLDEN MM, 18th Battalion, Canadian Infantry, killed on 15 August 1917 during operations to capture Hill 70 on the old Loos battlefield. (Plot 19.C.16)

Private John O'ROURKE MM, 87th Battalion, Canadian Infantry, killed on 9 June 1917. (Special Memorial 27) Canadian army records show a soldier, Private John O'Rourke, who has the same army number as the John O'Rourke in the CWGC register. However, the Canadian record indicates that he survived the war. It also shows him as having served with the 40th Battalion rather than the 87th Battalion and makes no reference to the award of the MM. It does note that he was born in Nova Scotia and that his next of kin also lived there. There is a Lance Corporal John O'Rourke MM, who served with the Newfoundland Regiment. He was killed in action in October 1918 and is buried at Vichte Military Cemetery in Belgium, but his army number is completely different. His parents, however, are shown in the CWGC register as living in Cape Breton, Nova Scotia. It does appear that the name and connection with Nova Scotia has led to the two records becoming confused.

1918

There are thirty-four identified burials from 1918, including the two New Zealand Division casualties already mentioned. Some are from the latter half of 1918, but the rest are from March and April. Two holders of the MM lie among them: Corporal William Edward JARVIS MM, 16th Royal Warwickshire Regiment, died on 17 September 1918, aged 25 (Plot 10.C.14), and Serjeant Albert Edward THOMAS MM, 1/8th Middlesex Regiment, was killed in action on 28 March 1918 (Plot 16.B.22).

Lieutenant Dennistoun Hamilton YATMAN was just 19 years old when he was killed on 11 April 1918 whilst serving with the 1st Northumberland Fusiliers. His father, Brigadier General Clement Yatman CMG DSO, served throughout the war and also served in the South African War. It was during this latter campaign that he was awarded the DSO, which was gazetted in 1901 for services in the field. He was twice wounded during the 1914–1918 conflict and was awarded the CMG in 1918. In 1915 he was the commanding officer of the 1st Northumberland Fusiliers, the battalion to which his son was attached when he was later killed.

Givenchy-en-Gohelle Canadian Cemetery, Souchez

The CWGC register suggests reaching this small cemetery via the village of Souchez. It can also be reached by driving along the D.55, through the Memorial Park, and beyond the car park in front of the Canadian National Memorial. About 400 yards beyond the car park is a track to the left. The cemetery lies about 600 yards down this track, adjacent to the A.26. The track is narrow. There are just 126 identified casualties buried here.

The cemetery sits at the northern end of Vimy Ridge where the 4th Canadian Division carried out its raid on 1 March 1917 that ended in failure. This is also near the area that was mopped up after the capture of the Pimple on 12 April 1917 when the 44th, 46th and 50th Battalions swept forward and eliminated this small, but significant rise that had caused many casualties on 9 April, particularly among the 72nd, 38th and 78th Battalions.

This is predominantly a Canadian Cemetery and very few burials come from British units. Among the British dead are two cavalrymen from the 15th (The King's) Hussars who were killed in action on 12 April 1917 (C.16 and 20). At the opening of the Battle of Arras the 1st Cavalry Division had been waiting for the opportunity to push on towards Hénin-Liétard and the crossing points over the Haute-Deûle and Sensée Canals. However, this advance was conditional and depended on whether the Germans decided to fall back that far; in the event, the opportunity never came.

There is also one British officer, Captain John Douglas DRAYSON MC, 93 Brigade, Royal Field Artillery. He was killed on the opening day of the Battle of Arras. His MC was gazetted on 4 June 1917 in the King's Birthday Honours List. (C.6)

The remaining British casualties here from 1917 are three men who served with the 1st Cheshire Regiment who were killed in action on 13 April 1917. Although the 1st Cheshire Regiment was part of the 5th Division's 15 Brigade, it was attached to the Canadian Corps at the opening of the Arras offensive.

Finally, from a British perspective, there are two casualties from the previous year: one man from the 1/15th Battalion, London Regiment (Prince of Wales's Own Civil Service Rifles), and one from the 1/18th Battalion, London Regiment (London Irish). Both battalions were part of the 47th (1/2nd London) Division, and both men were killed during the fighting in the Souchez sector in late May 1916. (B.10 and 16)

Ninety-one of the 118 identified Canadian burials here are from 9 April 1917, whilst the remainder come from the days that immediately followed. Most are from battalions of the Canadian 4th Division, which attacked the northernmost part of the ridge on the opening day. One of them is Major Gordon Ruthven HERON, 78th Battalion, Canadian Infantry (F.3). The CWGC register notes that he came from Ottawa and had won a Royal Humane Society Medal at the age of 15 for saving the lives of five people. His battalion is well represented here with twenty-nine burials, as are the 72nd Battalion with twenty-seven, and the 38th Battalion, with sixteen. According to the CWGC register, one of the men from the 72nd Battalion, Private Andrew Bennett THOMSON, was born in China (E.8). The note goes on to explain that his parents had worked as missionaries at the China Inland Mission. He, like the majority from his battalion, was killed on 9 April 1917.

There are five graves that relate to the failed raid undertaken by men from the 4th Canadian Division on 1 March 1917. They are somewhat scattered, but are easily found as follows: (B.9) 73rd Battalion; (E.5) 2nd Field Company, Canadian Engineers; (F.13) 87th Battalion; (F.21) 75th Battalion; and (F.22) 72nd Battalion.

With regard to gallantry awards, Corporal Charles BALL MM, 38th Battalion, Canadian Infantry, was one of the many men killed on 9 April 1917. He is the second of the two recipients of British bravery awards buried in this cemetery (Plot F.15). Sapper John GILLEN, 2nd Field Company, Canadian Engineers, who was killed in action on 1 March 1917, was awarded the Italian Bronze Medal for Military Valour (E.5).

The two youngest soldiers buried here are Private Edward J. NELSON, 46th Battalion, Canadian Infantry, who was just 16 years old when he fell on 12 April 1917 (F.10), and Private J. FURLOTTE, 42nd Battalion, Canadian Infantry. He was a year older when he was killed in action on 9 April (B.8).

Givenchy-en-Gohelle Communal Cemetery
The cemetery lies on the eastern outskirts of the village, which is situated on the D.55. If approaching from Arras and the south, this is the road to follow. Just after entering the village the road bends noticeably to the right. About 500 yards

further on there is a junction to the left. This is the Rue de la République. Turn left here and after about 100 yards it splits. Take the right fork, which is Rue de la Chapelle. Continue to the end of the road and turn right at the junction into Rue de l' Égalité; the cemetery is on the right-hand side about 200 yards further on.

The ten burials relating to the Second World War include two airmen from 434 Squadron, Royal Canadian Air Force. Pilot Officer (Air Gunner) Richard Edward John CAMPBELL, aged 20, and Flying Officer (Air Gunner) Robert Bradford LEARN, aged 24, were both killed on 13 June 1944. They are buried next to each other. On 13 June 1944 the Royal Air Force had targeted the railway yards at Arras and Cambrai. The bombing, which was considered to have been reasonably accurate, and therefore successful, was carried out in order to disrupt German efforts to transport men and material to the battle in Normandy. Flying Officer LEARN and his colleague are just two of the sixty-seven members of the Royal Canadian Air Force buried in French cemeteries who were killed in action that night during operations; a further nineteen are buried in the United Kingdom, most of whom died of wounds. (Graves 1 and 2)

The men who flew with LEARN and CAMPBELL that night also died and are buried together at Calais Canadian War Cemetery, Leubringhen. One of them, Wing Commander (Pilot) Christopher Smales Bartlett, had been awarded the DFC and Bar. His DFC was awarded in connection with an operation to destroy a bridge in Syria in May 1942. He landed a demolition team near the bridge and waited while the engineers destroyed it. As he was taking off, with the team safely on board, he came under fire from an armoured vehicle, but managed to get airborne and escaped. The bar was awarded for bringing back his badly damaged aircraft following a raid on Berlin in March 1944, thereby saving the lives of his crew.

The remainder are all 1940 casualties. Among them are four men killed on 23 May 1940 who were attached to 141st Field Ambulance, Royal Army Medical Corps, though the regiment ascribed to two of them is actually the Royal Army Service Corps. Both of these men were evidently drivers attached to the medical unit's transport. (Graves 3, 4, 8 and 10)

Another two men who died serving with the same unit are buried in Graves 5 and 9, this time from the 9th Field Regiment, Royal Artillery. For men killed during the spring and summer of 1940 it is fairly common to find the date of death recorded as 'between' certain dates. Lance Bombardier, George Arthur SINCLAIR (Grave 5) is shown as having died between 10 May and 23 June 1940, but Gunner Joe BAYFORD (Grave 9) has the exceptionally long period of between 24 May and 10 October 1940, which is unusual, but not unique.

Finally, Grave 6 is that of a private who served with the 8th Durham Light Infantry and who died on 23 May 1940; Grave 7 is that of Gunner Charles Robert HEATH, 65th (Norfolk Yeomanry) Anti-Tank Regiment, who died on the same day.

Givenchy Road Canadian Cemetery, Neuville-Saint-Vaast

This cemetery consists entirely of Canadian soldiers, all of them privates or NCOs. Remarkably, there is only one unidentified grave among the 111 burials here. The majority of burials come from two battalions: the 102nd Battalion and the 54th Battalion, both of which belonged to the Central Ontario Regiment and fought as part of the Canadian 4th Division. All eighty-nine men from these two units fell on 9 April 1917 as they attacked either side of Broadmarsh Crater, to the south of where the cemetery now stands. Among them are two recipients of gallantry awards, both in Row A: Private Thomas GODCHERE MM, 102nd Battalion, a Native American and a sniper from Thunder Bay (A.25), and Private Andrew Paterson MELROSE MM, of the 54th Battalion (A.45). GODCHERE's MM was awarded posthumously and was gazetted on 11 July 1917. MELROSE's MM was awarded in February that year.

A few graves along from GODCHERE lies Private Frank Donald AISH, 54th Battalion, Canadian Infantry, who was killed on 9 April 1917, aged 16. He had lied about his age when he enlisted in Vancouver in January 1916. He gave his age as 18, consequently his Canadian army record shows him as 19 when he died. He was born in Warrington, England, but went to live in Canada sometime later with his adopted family where he worked as a farmhand. (A.28)

The cemetery contains the grave of Private George BRONQUEST DCM, Princess Patricia's Canadian Light Infantry, whose death is shown as having occurred between 9 and 10 April 1917. On 9 April his battalion attacked towards the north end of La Folie Wood. The citation for BRONQUEST's DCM does not mention any particular action, but refers generally to his conduct, conspicuous gallantry and excellent service. It goes on to state that he had always shown great bravery and coolness in the performance of his duties, often at very critical moments.

The 87th Battalion, Canadian Infantry, which attacked immediately to the north of the cemetery, also has a handful of its men buried here, as does the 85th Battalion (Nova Scotia Highlanders), which attacked Hill 145 during the afternoon of 9 April 1917 across the ground that lies between the cemetery and the Canadian Memorial on Vimy Ridge. The 85th Battalion was the pioneer battalion allocated to the Canadian 4th Division.

Other units with casualties buried here are: the 75th Battalion with eight burials, the 47th Battalion, with two of its dead from 11 and 13 April 1917, and three members from the 10th Company, Canadian Machine Gun Corps, killed on 10 and 11 April. This is a very good example of a battlefield cemetery.

La Chaudière Military Cemetery, Vimy

The most direct way to reach the tiny hamlet of La Chaudière is to follow the N.17 north passing between Écurie and Roclincourt. Carry on beyond Nine Elms Military Cemetery and Arras Road Cemetery and under the flyover that carries the A.26. At the roundabout follow the route of the old N.17 and continue beyond Thélus and Petit Vimy. Turn left at the roundabout taking the D.51 towards Givenchy. Go under the new N.17 and almost immediately turn right; the cemetery is reached on the left after some 600 yards.

It will come as no surprise, given its location, that Canadian burials figure largely in this cemetery. Here 508 of the 594 identified casualties are Canadian soldiers. A significant number of casualties here are unidentified: a total of 314. Of the 508 identified Canadians, only twelve are from 1918. The remainder are from 1917, of whom 149 fell between 9 and 12 April during the capture and consolidation of Vimy Ridge.

The majority of the British infantry casualties come from battalions of the 5th Division, notably the 1st Duke of Cornwall's Light Infantry; also from the 1st Devonshire Regiment, the 1st Bedfordshire Regiment, the 1st Norfolk Regiment, the 1st East Surrey Regiment, the 12th Gloucestershire Regiment and the 14th, 15th and 16th Royal Warwickshire Regiment. The most frequently recorded date on their headstones is 23 April 1917, but all of these casualties fell within a week either side of that date, which marked the opening of the second main phase of the Battle of Arras, known as the Second Battle of the Scarpe.

A particularly distinctive feature of this cemetery is the fact that there are very few officers buried here, just nine Canadian lieutenants and nine officers from British battalions and the Royal Flying Corps. A number of graves are worthy of note, including several gallantry awards.

Lieutenant Sidney COLLIER MC, 5 Squadron, Royal Flying Corps, formerly 6th Manchester Regiment, was killed in action on 28 March 1918, aged 22 (Plot I.C.1), whilst observing for his pilot, Lieutenant Percy Wilfred WOODHOUSE, who was aged 20 (Plot I.B.1). COLLIER won his MC while serving with the Manchester Regiment, the award being gazetted on 2 February 1916. Their aircraft was flying over Méricourt, near Lens, when it became involved in a fight with five enemy machines. The combat was witnessed from below by Canadian troops of the 43rd Battalion, who even succeeded in bringing down one of the German aircraft by ground fire. The 43rd Battalion's war diary for that day records the action and notes that the RE8 flown by the two British airmen was shot down by a German machine.

Private W.T. Guy, 'D' Company, 6th Queen's (Royal West Surrey Regiment), was killed in action on 11 October 1918 (Plot II.A.16). The CWGC register notes that his father, W.A. Guy, held the DCM. A search of the *London Gazettes* reveals a possible candidate for the award: Sapper (861) A. Guy, Royal Engineers, whose award was gazetted on 3 June 1915, though this cannot be considered as conclusive evidence that they are one and the same person.

A search of the CWGC register will indicate that there are five officers of the Royal Flying Corps buried in this cemetery. However, there is a sixth member, Lieutenant Wilfred Earl McKISSOCK, who was Canadian. He had originally served with the Central Ontario Depot Battalion, but went on to serve with 16 Squadron, Royal Flying Corps. He was killed in action on 1 June 1917, aged 26, along with his observer that day, Lieutenant Arthur William Lennox NIXON. Canadian aviators are nearly always shown in the CWGC registers under the Canadian army unit with which they had previously served. Both men are buried side by side (Plot III.B.3 and 4).

Private John Edward AINSWORTH MM, 1st Norfolk Regiment, is the only British holder of the MM buried here. He was killed in action on 23 April 1917. (Plot III.D.1)

Lieutenant Ralph Douglas REID, 85th Battalion, Canadian Infantry, was killed in action on 5 May 1917, aged 24. He was promoted from the ranks after joining the battalion on 17 September 1915. On 16 September 1916, a year to the day after joining the battalion, he was promoted to lieutenant. He was wounded during the early evening of 9 April 1917 as fighting continued around Hill 145 on Vimy Ridge. His death occurred less than a month later while fighting near Fresnoy. (Plot IV.C.2)

Captain Bertram William Heyman WREFORD, 1st Devonshire Regiment, was killed in action on 23 April 1917, aged 22. His brother, Wilfred Heyman Joynson Wreford, provided financial support for Captain Walter George Raymond Hinchcliffe DFC AFC, when he attempted to cross the Atlantic by aeroplane in 1927 and 1928. Hinchcliffe had scored six victories during the war and had injured himself badly in a crash while landing his machine at night, losing the sight in his left eye as a result of the accident. Despite his injuries, Hinchcliffe went on to fly aircraft for KLM and other commercial airlines. Unfortunately, Hinchcliffe and his co-pilot, the Honourable Elsie Mackay, daughter of the 1st Earl of Inchcape, were killed on 13 March 1928 after they had taken off in an attempt to cross the Atlantic. The wreckage of their aircraft was washed up off the west coast of Ireland several months later. WREFORD's father was a Member of the Royal College of Surgeons and the family home was in Exeter. (Plot IV.F.19)

Private Kost MANOLES MM, 85th Battalion, Canadian Infantry, was a sniper. The battalion history, *The Eighty-Fifth Canadian Infantry Battalion in France and Flanders*, pays tribute, referring to him as a man who knew no fear and whose skills were often utilised. On one occasion, when a Lewis gun team was being prevented from setting up by a German sniper, MANOLES quickly dealt with the threat, silencing his opponent. MANOLES is credited with single-handedly clearing up many similar situations, all of which posed a significant threat to his comrades. The battalion history makes no specific mention of any single act of gallantry that led to the award of his MM, and it is therefore likely that it was awarded for his cumulative record as a sniper and in recognition of his skill, bravery and coolness. Sadly, he was killed in action on 28 April 1917 when he was himself shot by an enemy sniper. (Plot IV.C.17)

The CWGC register shows that his parents were from Athens, but the battalion history refers to him as a Russian. His enlistment papers show his place of birth as Athens and his religion is noted as Greek Orthodox. He was 40 years old when he died and is one of fourteen Canadians buried here who were awarded the MM, including Sergeant John Stewart Sutton SWAIN MM and Bar, 44th Battalion, Canadian Infantry, who was killed in action on 3 June 1917. (Plot VI.C.10)

Lieutenant Fred Creighton COLEMAN, 3rd Norfolk Regiment, attached 1st Battalion, was just 19 years old when he was killed in action on 23 April 1917. (Plot IV.D.8)

Several battalions that came from Alberta are well represented here. Among their ranks is Private Evan MACDONALD, 50th Battalion, Canadian Infantry, who was killed in action near Liévin on 10 May 1917. His brother Hamish died serving as a lieutenant with the 13th Hussars in Mesopotamia, aged 23, having previously served with the Lothian & Borders Horse. Hamish went to France in August 1914 with the original British Expeditionary Force and had also served in Salonika. He was awarded the MC for leading a cavalry charge on enemy positions after his party had come under heavy fire from a knoll some 600 yards away whilst forming part of a scouting line. In doing so, they captured four machine guns and their crews, which had been holding up the advance for some time. The award was gazetted on 17 October 1918. His death came after the war was over on 14 July 1919. He is now commemorated on the Basra Memorial. He was deployed in Kurdistan where he was in charge of a force of local gendarmes. The family memorial in the churchyard at Linlithgow notes that he was 'killed by Kurds', but does not go into any further detail. Evan, like his brother, also served with the Lothian and Borders Horse. (Plot VI.A.8)

Serjeant Hope TRAVIS DCM, 95th Battalion, Machine Gun Corps, formerly Manchester Regiment, was killed in action on 23 April 1917, aged 38. His DCM was gazetted on 14 November 1916 and was awarded for conspicuous gallantry in action while in charge of two machine guns. Serjeant Travis invariably exhibited the greatest coolness and courage in the management of his guns and when the whole team of one of his guns had become casualties, he continued to fire it himself, finally bringing it safely out of action. The 95th Battalion, Machine Gun Corps, was part of the 5th Division and many of the British casualties in this cemetery belonged to that division. (Plot VI.A.16)

Private John George PATTISON VC, 50th Battalion, Canadian Infantry, was born in Woolwich, south London, but then moved to Canada in 1906. At the time of his death on 3 June 1917 he was aware that he had been recommended for the VC, but he was killed in action before it could be confirmed or gazetted. He had survived the opening attack on Vimy Ridge and the days of fighting that followed. The action for which he won his VC occurred on 10 April 1917. An enemy machine gun had been holding up the line of advance and was causing heavy casualties. Without considering his own safety, he went forward, dashing from one shell-hole to another, to within 30 yards of the machine gun's position. Its crew were aware of his presence and had concentrated their fire in his direction as he advanced. He then bombed the post, killing and wounding some of the crew. He then ran forward and bayoneted the remaining five. In doing so, he undoubtedly retrieved a difficult situation and saved many more casualties.

He was killed in action on 3 June 1917, aged 42, during an attack on an electricity generating station near Lens in which his battalion again sustained heavy casualties. He was initially wounded in the foot and had been sent back to have it dressed. Unfortunately, a shell exploded close to where he was resting, killing him instantly. Later, the enemy succeeded in regaining the position where his body lay and for three months he was recorded as missing in action. However, his body had been found by the Germans, who buried him and marked his grave with a wooden cross. Fortunately, it was located by Canadian troops during a subsequent advance. His father, Harry, served in the same battalion from August 1917 and survived the war. (Plot VI.C.14)

Captain George Barclay LOCKHART, 2 Squadron, and Lieutenant Alexander Philip WILSON, who was his observer that day, are the third pair of Royal Flying Corps casualties buried here. They were killed in action on 14 April 1917 in a BE2c aircraft. LOCKHART had previously served with the Highland Cyclist Battalion, Army Cyclist Corps. Both men came from Fife in Scotland. (Plot VI.D.17 and 18)

Private John Henry BROOKES, Royal Canadian Regiment, was killed in action on 9 April 1917. His name is one of several carved on the outside wall of the village church at Écoivres. The village was one of many locations used for billeting troops. (Plot VII.B.13)

Serjeant Walter Thomas COOPER DCM, B Battery, 76 Brigade, Royal Field Artillery, was killed in action on 23 April 1917, aged 27. His DCM was gazetted on 25 November 1916 and was awarded for conspicuous gallantry in action after he had organized a party of NCOs to accompany him to a neighbouring ammunition dump to extinguish a fire that had broken out. He and his party accomplished this dangerous task while under heavy shell fire. (Plot VII.E.7)

Private Ernest Frederick RAMPTON DCM, Royal Canadian Regiment, won his award serving as a stretcher-bearer during an operation in which he worked single handed for seventy-two hours without sleep, dressing men of four different regiments, and evacuating all the wounded from a casualty post. Finally, he collapsed with exhaustion, but after a short rest he went out again in broad daylight and succeeded in bringing in a wounded man under very heavy fire. The award was gazetted on 19 August 1916. (Plot VIII.A.9)

Lichfield Crater, Thélus
To reach this cemetery, follow the D.55 through Neuville-Saint-Vaast as if heading for the Canadian National Memorial on Vimy Ridge. Near the centre of

the village the road splits off to become the D.49. Continue left along the D.55 and take the third turning on the right (Rue de Vimy), which leads over the A.26 Autoroute. Immediately after crossing the A.26, take the track immediately on the right and follow it for about a quarter of a mile to the cemetery. It can also be reached from the direction of Thélus. After passing through the village from east to west along the D.49 there is a crossroads controlled by traffic lights. The Canadian Artillery memorial also stands on the junction. On the other side of the junction there is a small track. Take the metalled track and follow it as it runs towards the A.26 and then runs parallel to it. The cemetery is on the left.

The area around Lichfield Crater formed part of the 2nd Canadian Division sector on 9 April 1917. The 24th Battalion, Canadian Infantry, made its attack that day across the ground that lies to the south of the cemetery, whilst the 26th Battalion attacked to the north side of it. Both units then pushed on to the German second line defences that lay directly ahead of them and which ran north-south about 100 yards west of where Thélus Military Cemetery now stands. The 24th Battalion, Canadian Infantry, has the most number of casualties commemorated here with a total of twelve.

In the immediate aftermath of battle, shell holes and trenches were often used to bury the dead. This was a convenient and expedient way of dealing with significant numbers of burials. The location of such sites was then noted with a map reference. Such records were a vital source of information when the Imperial War Graves Commission began its work after the war. Lichfield and Zivy Craters provided an opportunity for mass burial and both are essentially mass graves, even though the majority of the men interred in them are identified. There are just fifteen unidentified casualties among the fifty-seven men known to lie in Lichfield Crater. Each identified casualty now recorded on the panels in front of the Cross of Sacrifice was killed in action on 9 April 1917.

The cemetery is a small but beautiful creation by the architect W.H. Cowlishaw. It is perhaps best appreciated in summer, when the scent of lavender from the flower beds and the gentle humming of bees provide a peaceful backdrop for quiet reflection, especially on a warm sunny day. Despite its proximity to the motorway it is a very pleasant spot. All the men commemorated here are NCOs or privates.

There is just one headstone within the cemetery and it marks the grave of Private Albert STUBBS, 8th South Lancashire Regiment, who was killed in action on 30 April 1916 and whose body was found after the war, presumably when the cemetery was under construction. The grave could easily have been moved to another more conventional cemetery, particularly as this is a Canadian burial site. However, the effect is all the more poignant for its standing alone very close to the original burial site.

The 8th South Lancashire Regiment, which was part of the 25th Division, took over part of the line east of Neuville-Saint-Vaast on 28 April 1916. The following day the Germans blew a mine under the trenches occupied by 'C' Company, burying three men and wounding two others. Although the explosion was preceded by a heavy trench mortar bombardment, the Germans did not follow it up with any infantry attack. The close proximity of the enemy, however, made it impossible to try to rescue the men, whom it was assumed must have been killed in the explosion. The regimental history does say that the next day, 30 April, bombing took place and 'D' Company's position was shelled heavily.

The CWGC records show just three men from the South Lancashire Regiment killed in action in France between 28 and 30th April 1916, one of whom is STUBBS. The other two men, Private Arthur Mellor and Private Robert Travis, are buried at Cabaret Rouge British Cemetery. Though there is uncertainty over the precise date of death for these men, it seems reasonable to suggest that the incident to which the regimental narrative refers is the one in which STUBBS and the other two men were killed. The eventual resting place of each man perhaps suggests that they were not found at the same time; even Mellor and Travis are buried in different plots at Cabaret Rouge. Travis, incidentally, left behind a widow and six children.

There are two gallantry award holders buried in the crater: Private John Le PAGE MM, 21st Battalion, Canadian Infantry, aged 20, and Lance Sergeant Ellis Wellwood SIFTON VC, 18th Battalion, Canadian Infantry, who was shot dead by a wounded German on 9 April 1917, aged 25.

Le PAGE's MM was gazetted on 12 March 1917, less than a month before his death. He is commemorated here along with eight other men from the 21st Battalion, Canadian Infantry. One of them, Lance Corporal Arthur Alexander ADAMSON, enlisted in November 1914, making him an early member of the Canadian Expeditionary Force. (Panel 3, Column 1)

SIFTON enlisted in October 1914. His VC was gazetted on 8 June 1917 and was awarded for most conspicuous bravery and devotion to duty during an attack after his company was held up by machine-gun fire that had already inflicted heavy casualties. He identified the position where the machine gun was located and then charged it single-handed, killing its crew. Later, when an enemy party was advancing down a trench he kept it at bay until his men had secured the position. It was during this stage of the fighting that he was killed, but in the aftermath it became quite obvious that his actions had undoubtedly saved the lives of many of his men and had contributed significantly to the success of the attack within his sector. (Panel 3, Column 2)

Private Henry Edwin GRATTO, 26th Battalion, Canadian Infantry, was killed on the opening day of the Battle of Arras. He was one of the many snipers employed by the Canadians in their daily quest for supremacy over the Germans during their time on the ridge. He was 27 years old when he died. (Panel 2, Column 3)

Orchard Dump Cemetery, Arleux-en-Gohelle

The cemetery lies between the villages of Bailleul-Sir-Berthoult and Arleux-en-Gohelle on the D.919. It is on the left hand side of the road, about half a mile south-west of Arleux-en-Gohelle. The fields in which it is situated are marked on the French IGN maps as 'Le Cimetière Anglais'. This is a reference to the note in the CWGC register stating that the burial ground was granted by the widow of a captain of the French 72nd Regiment who was killed in 1914.

The area was captured in April 1917 and the cemetery was used until the end of the year. The original burials, as the CWGC register points out, are those in front of the Cross of Sacrifice in Plot I, Rows A to F, which are irregularly set out, and those in Plot IV, Row K, which lies against the wall between the two entrances. The cemetery was greatly enlarged after the war. Over 80 per cent of the burials are unidentified and there are a number of special memorials, including some graves in Plots VII, VIII and IX that are collective burials where the headstones bear the inscription, 'buried near this spot'.

The CWGC register also informs us that in 1940 No. 2 Casualty Clearing Station was stationed at Rouvroy and that the cemetery was again used to bury men who died there from wounds. This concentration cemetery now contains just over 3,000 burials, of which just 756 are identified.

In late April 1917 the 8th, 10th and 5th Battalions, Canadian Infantry, attacked across the fields to the east of where the current cemetery stands towards the village of Arleux-en-Gohelle, which was defended by trenches that ran around its western edge. These defences were originally part of the German third line that looped around the village. East of the village these trenches connected up with a position known as the Rouvroy–Fresnes position via a switch line. The Canadians' objective was to capture Arleux and establish themselves beyond the village. The 25th Battalion, Canadian Infantry, continued the line of attack about 1,000 yards north of the cemetery.

On 28 April the 10th Battalion began its attack astride the Willerval–Arleux road, with the 8th Battalion on its right and the 5th Battalion to its left. The attack began at 4.45am and by 6am the village had been captured, but it was the only real gain of the day. Further south, around Oppy, the attacks made by the 2nd Division met with little success and the 63rd (Royal Naval) Division at Gavrelle made virtually no headway against the defences on Greenland Hill. Not surprisingly, the 2nd Division and the 63rd (Royal Naval) Division make up a significant proportion of the dead here, but there are also casualties from units belonging to other divisions, such as the 34th Division, the 5th Division and the 31st Division, all of which spent time in this sector in 1917. The East and West Ridings of Yorkshire are quite well represented by virtue of the 31st Division's casualties.

On 28 June 1917 an attack was carried out by eight battalions of the 5th Division. The limited objective was to seize the German front line trench system in front of Oppy Wood in order to deny the enemy observation over our lines. The operation was assisted by an elaborate ruse, which included setting out dummy trenches. Dummy tanks were brought forward and dummy infantry, manipulated by ropes and pullies, were also deployed in what was known as a 'Chinese attack'.

The German trenches were captured, but the enemy responded by putting down a heavy barrage. The 1st Bedfordshire Regiment, which had captured Oppy Wood, managed to hold it against counter-attack, but at the cost of two officers and 117 other ranks.

It was also hoped that the operation would divert German attention away from preparations for the forthcoming offensive at Ypres in the aftermath of the Battle of Messines Ridge. There are now nineteen casualties from this attack buried here, but they are all fairly scattered. Most of them are from the 1st Cheshire Regiment, though there are also a few men from the 1st Bedfordshire Regiment, the 16th Royal Warwickshire Regiment and the 12th Gloucestershire Regiment.

Lieutenant Harry Saxon PELL, 40 Squadron, Royal Flying Corps, was killed in action on 6 April 1917. He came from Toronto. At the outbreak of war he became a member of the Governor General's Body Guard, but in the summer of 1915 he transferred to the Royal Flying Corps. He came over to England in 1916 where he continued his training, and eventually went to France in August that year, where he initially served as an observer and gunner with 40 Squadron. On the day of his death, which was Good Friday, he was successful in driving down an enemy machine south of Bailleul, although his original task had been to attack enemy balloons behind Vimy Ridge. He never returned from that flight and was reported as missing in action. His body was buried by the Germans and was discovered after the war by the parents of another airman who had come over to France to look for their son's grave (Plot I.B.6). Harry's younger brother, Lieutenant Willard Augustus Pell, joined the Royal Flying Corps once he heard that Harry was missing, presumed killed. He served in France with 80 Squadron, Royal Flying Corps and was involved in aerial combat and other operations during the German March offensive. He was reported missing in action on 12 April 1918 after he and his colleagues were attacked by a larger enemy formation. The squadron decided to break off, but Willard was last seen engaged in aerial combat and is believed to have been shot down by an enemy machine. He has no known grave and is commemorated on the Flying Services Memorial at Arras.

Second Lieutenant Claude Neville MADELEY, 43 Squadron, Royal Flying Corps, was killed in action on 19 January 1918 whilst flying a Camel aircraft. He was 23 years old when he died. *Airmen Died in the Great War* shows his place of burial as Quiéry-la-Motte, France, which lies about 12 miles north-east of Arras. Quiéry-la-Motte British Cemetery was one of those closed after the war. He and twenty-six others were then brought back here for reburial. (Plot I.B.7)

Company Serjeant Major Walter James SUMMERFIELD DCM, 1st Bedfordshire Regiment, was killed in action on 28 June 1917, aged 28. His DCM, which was gazetted on 3 June 1915, was won as an acting serjeant. It was awarded for conspicuous gallantry and ability in the trenches in April that year at Hill 60 where he had shown great courage and resource defending a crater after thirty of his thirty-five men had been killed or wounded. (Plot I.D.2)

Corporal Herbert THOMPSON DCM, 'A' Company, 1st Queen's Own (Royal West Kent Regiment), was killed in action on 9 May 1917, aged 26. His DCM was gazetted on 26 March 1917 and was awarded for conspicuous gallantry and devotion to duty during a raid in which he handled his machine gun with great courage and determination while covering the advance of the party on his left. Later, he remained alone with his gun in an exposed position under very heavy fire. The citation concludes by adding that he had also done fine work on previous occasions. (Plot I.F.9)

Air Mechanic 2nd Class George PAWLEY, 25 Squadron, Royal Flying Corps, was killed in action on 25 April 1917, aged 19 (Plot III.B.47). His pilot that day, Second Lieutenant Charles Verdon Darnell, formerly Connaught Rangers, has no known grave and is commemorated on the Arras Flying Services Memorial.

Lieutenant James Mitchell SOUTER, 59 Squadron, Royal Flying Corps, was killed in action on 11 April 1917, aged 23 (Plot III.C.9). His pilot, Lieutenant George Tod MORRIS, who was flying a RE8, is buried next to him (Plot III.C.10).

Private John James GILMORE, 13th Company, Canadian Machine Gun Corps, was killed in action on 3 May 1917, aged 21 (Plot III.F.28). The CWGC register records that he was a member of the Loyal Orange Lodge of Canada, one of many from that organization who served and died during the conflict. Some Lodges became dormant during the war owing to the large number of members who had gone overseas to serve.

Second Lieutenant Horace Austen GIBBS (Plot III.E.7), and Second Lieutenant Marcel André SIMON (Plot I.C.7A), 1st Royal Berkshire Regiment, were killed in action on 29 April 1917. SIMON was 18 years old when he died and had enlisted under age by claiming to be a year older. He went to France in February 1917 and celebrated his birthday over there on 1 March. He died in action near Oppy Wood where his grave was marked and recorded, but subsequently lost. However, in 2000 local residents discovered his body along with his revolver, holster and other metal objects that had been buried with him. He was then finally laid to rest with full military honours in the presence of members of his surviving family here at Orchard Dump.

Lieutenant Augustus John JESSOPP, 56 Squadron, Royal Flying Corps, was killed in action flying a SE5 aircraft on 12 May 1917, aged 23. (Plot III.G.30)

According to the CWGC register, Captain Valentine Otto TODD, 1st King's Own (Royal Lancaster Regiment), was killed in action on 9 April 1917, though the regimental history insists that he died on the 10th. He was killed leading 'A' Company in an attempt to secure the railway bridge on the Arras–Lille railway line between Fampoux and Roeux. The plan was to use the position around the bridge to provide cover for the other three companies to cross the embankment before they advanced on Roeux itself. After the bridge was captured by 'A' Company, three of its platoons occupied the embankment north of the bridge, whilst the other platoon dug in on the southern side. However, the position soon came under heavy fire and when the remaining three companies subsequently advanced they were stopped by machine-gun fire from the direction of the Chemical Works. TODD's correct date of death is 10 April, as is clear from contemporary accounts of the fighting. (Plot III.H.36)

Lieutenant William Samuel SPENCE, 16 Squadron, Royal Flying Corps, was killed in action on 26 April 1917 (Plot III.J.30). His observer that day, Lieutenant William Archibald CAMPBELL, a Canadian who had previously served with the 16th Battalion, Canadian Infantry, was also killed and is buried next to him. (Plot III.J.29)

Serjeant Harry VICKERS DCM MM, 2nd East Lancashire Regiment, was killed in action on 14 October 1918, aged 26. The citation for his DCM records his surname as 'Bickers'. The award was gazetted on 15 November 1918 and was awarded after he had taken command of his platoon in an attack and captured two machine guns in the face of strong opposition. He then went on to reorganize his platoon for defence and repelled four determined counter-attacks, maintaining the defensive line throughout whilst under heavy fire. The success of this operation was largely attributed to his courage and determination. (Plot III.K.41)

Serjeant Archibald STORIE (Plot III.K.15), Private Edward QUIGLEY (Plot VI.F.43), and Australian-born Private Ronald Keith INCE (Plot VII.J.15), 2nd Highland Light Infantry, were killed in action on 28 April 1917. It is impossible to determine whether these three men were killed when the battalion's HQ received a direct hit from a shell shortly before the battalion made an attack that day, or whether they were killed in the attack itself. From this battalion 103 officers and men are shown as killed in action on 28 April 1917; all but seventeen of them have no known grave and are therefore commemorated on the Arras Memorial. The fact that the three men are buried in different plots suggests that they were probably killed during the attack rather than together in the dug-out. Their battalion was part of the 2nd Division, which attacked south of Arleux-en-Gohelle on 28 April. The 2nd Highland Light Infantry's position was just north of Oppy Wood. During the attack it came up against uncut wire and heavy machine-gun fire from inside the wood. The 2nd Division made only a few small gains as a result of the fighting on 28 and 29th April and it left the battlefield in a far weaker state than when it had arrived, having sustained just over 3,000 casualties.

Second Lieutenant William George HAMM MC, 13th East Yorkshire Regiment, was killed in action on 2 May 1917, aged 20. HAMM won his MC in early March that year. On 1 March he had taken part in a fighting patrol against a German trench known as Slug Street, which ran between Rossignol Wood and La Louvière Farm at the northern end of the Somme battlefield. The object of the patrol was to find out whether the Germans were still holding the position in any strength. The group left its position at 2am but found that the wire was still strong and it was unable to penetrate any further. The operation was repeated a week later, but failed yet again, and on this occasion the German response strongly suggested that they were not yet willing to give up their defences in this sector. Despite a lack of success in terms of outcome, it was recognized that he had shown great initiative in organizing patrols and bombing parties during these operations, and for his gallantry and leadership HAMM was awarded his MC, which was gazetted on 27 April, just days before his death. (Plot V.D.30)

Private John DREW MM, 8th Battalion, Canadian Infantry, was killed in action in the attack on the Arleux on 28 April 1917, aged 24. He was killed by a sniper whilst acting as a stretcher-bearer. He enlisted at Valcartier in September 1914 and went to France with the 8th Battalion in February 1915 where, at his own request, he reverted from lance corporal to private. His MM was awarded posthumously and was won at Vimy Ridge on 9 April 1917 after he had gone out into no man's land as soon as the attack was under way and dressed wounded men under heavy shelling. He then worked tirelessly, tending the wounded for thirty-six hours without rest. In the six days that followed he worked continuously and carried out much similar work, often under difficult conditions. (Plot V.J.18)

Captain Eugene Gilbert SULIVAN, 4th East Surrey Regiment, attached 1st Battalion, was killed in action on 8 May 1917, aged 23, whilst defending his battalion's position east of Fresnoy. He was killed around 6.30am that day, three and a half hours into a bitter fight during which the section of front on his left, held by 'B' Company, collapsed under a third German assault on the battalion's positions. Before 'B' Company's position fell, it was SULIVAN who realized the seriousness of the situation. He quickly reorganized the left flank of his own company, throwing it back under the cover of a counter-attack made against the Germans in Fresnoy Wood. His actions undoubtedly ensured that his own company's position was not enveloped, at least for the time being, and the counter-attack on the enemy positions in the wood enabled him skilfully to withdraw the remainder of his company into the old German line that skirted the western edge of the wood and village, which was the best available position from which to carry on the fight. SULIVAN was an experienced soldier who had spent fifteen years with the regiment, but he was soon cut off when the Germans renewed their attack. He died as he and the remainder of his men gallantly lined the parapet and parados of their trench in an attempt to fend off the enemy's assault from three sides. (Plot VI.C.15)

Private Gordon HUNTER and Private Allan Ethelbert Gordon SANDERSON, Eaton's Motor Machine Gun Battery, Canadian Machine Gun Corps, were killed in action on 28 April 1917. The unit was named after Timothy Eaton, a Ballymena man, who had set up a chain of department stores in Canada under the family name. The firm employed a large number of people from Ballymena who had gone to live in Canada, and on the outbreak of war many of the male employees went off to fight. The Eaton Battery was one of three such units that became part of the 1st Canadian Motor Machine Gun Brigade, the other two being the Yukon Motor Machine Gun Battery and the Borden Motor Machine Gun Battery, the latter taking its name from the Canadian Prime Minister, Sir Robert Borden. Despite their titles, much of their time on the Western Front involved little mobility until August 1918. Some of their static work included anti-aircraft duties. (Plot VI.K.3 and 4)

Private Arthur HOLMES MM, 16th Battalion, Canadian Infantry, was killed in action on 30 April 1917. He came from Ballymena and was killed by shell fire whilst tending the wounded. He was awarded his MM for his work on 9 April 1917 at Vimy Ridge, but did not survive long enough to receive it. His brother David served with the 1st Royal Irish Rifles. He died of wounds on 20 July 1918, aged 21, and is buried at Bertenacre Military Cemetery, Flètre. (Plot VIII.B.22)

There are five officers from the 14th Royal Warwickshire Regiment buried here. Four were killed by shell fire on 8 May 1917 whilst holding trenches near Arleux. Three of them, Second Lieutenant Charles Arthur POCOCK, Second Lieutenant Edmund Sproston Knapp BARROW, and Captain William Lang VINCE, are buried next to each other (Plot IX.A.45 to 47). Captain Bernard TURNER is buried in the same row, but in grave 23. POCOCK had returned from working in Borneo in order to enlist; VINCE had graduated from Magdalene College, Oxford, in 1913 and BARROW, who had formerly served with the regiment's 4th Battalion, was the son of Major Knapp Barrow CMG, who served with the old 57th Regiment of Foot, and also as Colonial Secretary of the Gold Coast Colony. The fifth officer buried here from the 14th Royal Warwickshire Regiment is Second Lieutenant Cecil Roland SALISBURY, who fell sometime between 8 and 9 May 1917 (Plot IX.A.39).

The Royal Warwickshire Regiment has fifty-four of its men in this cemetery, mainly from the 14th, 15th and 16th Battalions, including two 2nd lieutenants from the 15th Battalion: Second Lieutenant Horace Thomas Royston EVANS and Second Lieutenant Thomas Leslie NICHOLS both fell between 8 and 9 May 1917 and are buried next to each other (Plot I.E.1 and 2). EVANS was the son of Thomas Henry Royston Evans OBE, a solicitor and part-time magistrate from Gunnersbury in south-west London.

The Canadian dead come mainly from the fighting around the Arleux Loop and Fresnoy in late April and early May 1917. Among them is Lieutenant Clifford Almon WELLS, 8th Battalion, Canadian Infantry, who was killed in his first significant action, and whose collection of letters was published after his death under the title, *From Montreal to Vimy Ridge and Beyond*. (Plot IX.J.1)

Captain Richard Morris Stanley BLEASE, 15th West Yorkshire Regiment, was killed in action on 3 May 1917, aged 23 (Plot IX.J.7). He was born in Queensland, Australia, and held a Bachelor of Arts degree (Honours) from Leeds University where he was a member of the OTC. He was killed in action during the attack on Gavrelle, near Gavrelle Trench and Gavrelle Support Trench. In response to the attack, which began at 3.45am, the Germans put down a heavy barrage on their own front line as it was being captured in order to prevent further penetration, causing significant casualties among the attackers.

Lieutenant Douglas Monteith Farquhar SINCLAIR, 40 Squadron, Royal Flying Corps, was killed in action on 30 March 1917 flying a Nieuport 17 single-seater aircraft. He had previously served with the 63rd (Royal Naval) Division. He is now commemorated in this cemetery and is the casualty referred to in the CWGC register as the British airman originally buried in Fresnoy Churchyard by the Germans in March 1917. (Fresnoy Churchyard Memorial 1)

There are relatively few men with gallantry awards buried here, even allowing for the fact that the majority of soldiers are unidentified. All of them have been mentioned already, apart from the several holders of the MM listed below.

Serjeant Charles JONES MM, 6th Battalion, Machine Gun Corps, formerly South Staffordshire Regiment, killed in action on 28 April 1917. His unit, which was part of the 2nd Division, should read 6th Company rather than battalion. (Plot II.E.1)

Private William Alfred ROBINSON MM, 1st Cheshire Regiment, killed in action on 28 June 1917. (Plot III.G.10)

Private John DONKIN MM, 2nd Battalion, Royal Marine Light Infantry, killed in action on 10 July 1917. (Plot VI.B.49)

Serjeant Robert Stanley TEMPLE MM, 'C' Company, 13th East Yorkshire Regiment, killed in action on 3 May 1917. (Plot VI.F.6)

Lance Serjeant William GUEST MM, 16th Royal Warwickshire Regiment, killed in action on 26 August 1917, aged 23. (Plot VIII.A.12)

Private Alexander GLENNIE MM, 6th Black Watch, killed in action on 25 August 1918, aged 21. (Plot VIII.E.39)

Serjeant Ernest WILKINSON MM, 10th York and Lancaster Regiment, died on 21 April 1917. *Soldiers Died in the Great War* does not show the award of the MM against his name. He had served with the Worcestershire Regiment. (Plot IX.E.35)

Private Arthur Roy DUNN MM, 5th Battalion, Canadian Infantry, killed in action in the attack on Arleux on 28 April 1917, aged 22. He was awarded his MM at Vimy Ridge on 9 April 1917 after he had advanced up a German communication trench, bombing his way to the second objective. The trench contained several enemy dug-outs and a number of prisoners were captured as a result of his actions. On reaching the second objective, he reorganized his platoon after the sergeant and officer in charge had been killed. The citation concludes that he was instrumental in consolidating the position. (2nd Canadian Division Memorial 10)

The cemetery also contains twenty casualties from the Second World War, the earliest of which are from October 1939. One of the men buried here is Major Anthony Frederick Halliday GODFREY, 2nd Survey Regiment, Royal Artillery, who died while on active service on 17 October 1940, aged 38. His father had also had a military career and reached the rank of colonel (Plot 3, Row D, Grave 41). The last of the burials is from 25 March 1940. These twenty burials make up quite a diverse group, which includes men from the Infantry, Royal Engineers, Royal Army Medical Corps, Royal Army Service Corps and Royal Army Ordnance Corps, as well as gunners, all of whom can be found in Plot 3, Rows D to G.

Petit Vimy British Cemetery

This small cemetery lies just to the west of the village of Vimy on the east side of the ridge. It is tucked away against the tree line that covers most of the eastern edge of Vimy Ridge and can be reached from the D.917, the main Arras–Lens road. A small road leads to it from the Rue Sedi Carnot in the village of Petit Vimy about 100 yards from the junction with the D.917. At the end of this small road is a track across some fields that leads to the cemetery. It is not the easiest cemetery to find.

Nearly all the burials here are Canadian casualties from May and June 1917, notably from the 4th and 5th Battalions, Canadian Mounted Rifles, but there are also casualties from the 43rd and 52nd Battalions, Canadian Infantry. All of these units formed part of the Canadian 3rd Division. There are now ninety-four burials, but only seventy-one have been identified.

The cemetery contains just four men from British units, an infantryman from the 21st Battalion, London Regiment (First Surrey Rifles), killed in action on 23 May 1917 (B.3), a lance corporal from 182 Tunnelling Company, Royal Engineers, killed in action on 18 June 1917 (E.7) and two members of the Royal Flying Corps.

The two casualties from the Royal Flying Corps were killed in action together on 23 April 1917. Serjeant Amos George TOLLERVEY and Second Lieutenant Eric Arthur WELCH, both members of 16 Squadron, had taken off on a photographic reconnaissance that morning with another aircraft from their squadron. However, they were intercepted and shot down over Méricourt by Manfred von Richthofen, becoming his forty-seventh victory. The other aircraft from 16 Squadron was shot down by his brother, Lothar, shortly afterwards. WELCH, who enlisted at the outbreak of war, was gazetted in the 10th King's Own (Royal Lancaster Regiment) in May 1915 and was later posted to the 7th Battalion. On transferring to the Royal Flying Corps, he initially served with 53 Squadron, but then moved to 16 Squadron shortly before his death.

Serjeant TOLLERVEY was a gunsmith before the war and joined the Royal Flying Corps as a mechanic where he was able to utilise his engineering skills. He progressed within the service and eventually became an observer. At the time he was shot down TOLLERVEY should have been on leave, but had allowed a fellow NCO to return home instead so that he could be present for the birth of his baby. This touching detail is narrated by Norman Franks, Hal Giblin and Nigel McCrery in their book, *Under the Guns of the Red Baron*. Second Lieutenant WELCH and Serjeant TOLLERVEY are buried next to each other (A.4 and A.5).

There is only one gallantry award buried here: Lieutenant Edward DAVISON MM, of the 4th Canadian Mounted Rifles who was killed on 6 June 1917 (C.7). A little further along the row is Private Harry Alvin CARR, 5th Canadian Mounted Rifles, who was killed four days earlier, aged 17 (C.10). DAVISON had previously served as a sergeant with the Governor General's Body Guard which was a cavalry militia unit. He was killed in action by a shell near Méricourt as he was returning from the trenches with mules after taking up the rations.

Private Kenneth Wallas McRAE, 5th Canadian Mounted Rifles, was killed in action on 4 June 1917, aged 19. Two of his brothers served in the same regiment, one of whom was also killed. There is no trace of any obvious candidate in the CWGC records under that surname. (D.8)

Vimy Communal Cemetery, Farbus

The cemetery can be found to the south of the village of Vimy on the D.51. It is not tucked away and is difficult to miss. The CWGC register notes that it was initially used by the Germans until the village was captured in April 1917 by the Canadians. The German graves were removed after the war.

There are thirty-four identified burials in this cemetery and all of them are from 1917, apart from three men who died on 1 April 1918 while serving with the 52nd Battalion, Canadian Infantry (D.3, D4, and D.5).

Several other Canadian infantry units are represented, including eight men from the 14th Battalion, all killed in trenches east of Vimy Ridge as a result of shelling during the first week of June 1917. One of the men, Private George JONES, was killed by a shell as he was speaking to the battalion's adjutant. The war diary states that the officer was wounded in the explosion, but carried on with his duties in spite of his injuries (E.6).

The most senior officer buried here is Major Joseph McBRIDE, 27 Brigade, Royal Field Artillery, who was killed in action on 23 April 1917 (A.1). Several men from the same artillery brigade are buried here with him in Row A.

Next to him is Second Lieutenant Cecil Victor PERRY MC, 120th Battery, 27 Brigade, Royal Field Artillery, who was also killed on 23 April 1917 (A.2). His MC was gazetted on 14 November 1916 and was awarded for conspicuous gallantry in action as a forward observation officer, carrying out his work with the same courage, determination, coolness and initiative as he had shown on many previous occasions, often under intense fire.

There are two more officers from 27 Brigade buried among this group of casualties. One of them is Second Lieutenant Harold HUGHES. The CWGC record makes no reference to the fact that two of his brothers fell during the war. Second Lieutenant George Augustus Hughes MC and Bar, 6th Duke of Wellington's Regiment, attached 9th Battalion, was killed in action near the Forest of Mormal on 4 November 1918, aged 30. He is buried at Caudry British Cemetery. His MC was gazetted on 11 January 1919 and the bar to it on 15 February 1919. Both awards were for very fine acts of gallantry. The other brother, Lieutenant William Hughes, was killed on 19 November 1918 whilst serving with the Royal Air Force and is buried in the Cairo War Memorial Cemetery. The family came from Hawnby, near York, where their father was a clergyman. (A.3)

The other officer in the row is Second Lieutenant Harry HILDAGE, who was killed in action a week or so earlier on 15 April 1917. (A.10)

The fourth grave in Row A is that of Captain George Douglas FERGUSON DSO, Royal Army Medical Corps, attached 27 Brigade, Royal Field Artillery. His DSO was awarded was for conspicuous gallantry and devotion to duty at Delville Wood on 15 July 1916 where he had tended the wounded under very heavy fire, bringing in over fifty wounded and showing the greatest courage and determination. He enlisted in August 1914 and was a graduate of Edinburgh University. He was also mentioned in despatches. FERGUSON was killed in action on 23 April 1917. (A.4)

The third gallantry award holder in this cemetery is Private Alexander Morrison DICK MM, 27th Battalion, Canadian Infantry, who was killed in action on 23 May 1917, aged 26. (C.3)

Zivy Crater, Thélus

This cemetery can be found on the D.49 between Thélus and Neuville-Saint-Vaast, just to the west of the A.26 Autoroute. It is set back slightly from the road and is easily accessible via a small track. If coming from the direction of Neuville-Saint-Vaast it lies just over half a mile to the east of the village. It is well sign-posted and is easy to find. Although there are no headstones in this cemetery, it is a cemetery rather than a memorial; essentially, like Lichfield Crater, it is a mass grave.

This is one of the many mine craters that ran along much of the front line at Vimy Ridge prior to the Battle of Arras in April 1917. In the aftermath of battle it was convenient and often necessary to use large shell holes and craters to bury groups of dead soldiers. There are a number of precedents for this along the Western Front, one of which is Hunter's Cemetery on the Somme. Fifty-three men were buried in Zivy Crater, all of them NCOs and privates, all of them Canadian, and almost all of them from the Canadian 2nd Division. Apart from one soldier who died on 15 May 1917, the forty-eight men who are now identified on panels by the Cross of Sacrifice fell in action on 9 April 1917.

There is just one gallantry award holder commemorated here: Sergeant Harry LIEB MM, who served with the 18th Battalion, Canadian Infantry, under the name of 'LEARY'.

Rather than name their cemeteries, the Canadians originally chose to designate their burial sites by way of lettering and numerals, this one being known as CB.1. After the war the architect, W.H. Cowlishaw, used the idea of the crater as the inspiration for his design. He was also responsible for creating Lichfield Crater, which is very similar in appearance to this one.

Zouave Valley Cemetery, Souchez

This is not a particularly easy cemetery to reach. Possibly the best way to reach it is to take the D.55 as it heads out of Neuville-Saint-Vaast towards Givenchy-en-Gohelle. About 250 yards before the A.26, there is a track (sometimes of poor quality) running off to the left, which eventually runs parallel and very close to the A.26 on the west side of the Autoroute. Take this track and follow it as it runs north. About a mile along this track is the cemetery. The CWGC signage indicating the 'official' access route is to be found in Souchez.

Zouave Valley lay behind the British front line in 1916 and 1917 and formed part of the support line. In and around it were ammunition, engineer and ration dumps, as well as battalion headquarters and dug-outs that served as company headquarters for engineering field companies, signalling companies and forward medical units. A light railway ran from the direction of Carency eastwards into the valley, where it branched off north and south enabling it to feed the front line along the ridge by bringing up supplies.

Today the cemetery contains 178 identified casualties, but around a quarter of the total burials are soldiers whose identity is unknown. The CWGC register points out that eight British and three Canadian soldiers, known or believed to be buried here, are commemorated by special memorials. Similarly, five casualties in Plot II are identified as a group rather than individually and their headstones are inscribed with the words, 'Buried near this spot'. There is still one German grave remaining here, even though there are German military cemeteries nearby. Although there seems to be no logic behind this, it is as well to remember that this small battlefield cemetery was never under any pressure to create space in which to accommodate large numbers of graves; the removal of one German grave was unlikely to make any difference, and so this soldier's final resting place was able to be respected.

The name of the cemetery originates from the days when the French occupied the ridge in 1915 and the first few months of 1916 before British troops took over. The word 'Zouave' refers to a type of native light infantry soldier originally from Algeria, who served in the French army by virtue of its colonial system, which was very similar to ours.

A recurrent date in this cemetery is 1 March 1917; it is inscribed on twenty-nine Canadian headstones. All of them relate to privates or NCOs from the 75th (Mississauga) Battalion, Canadian Infantry. Two men from other units who also fell that day are buried here with them; one from the 73rd Battalion, Canadian Infantry, and a sapper, Chester Adrian RODGERS, 11th Field Company, Canadian Engineers, who had also served in the Boer War.

Just before dawn on 1 March 1917 an artillery barrage was put down on the German trenches near Hill 145 where the Canadian National Memorial now stands. This was the prelude to a raid in which the 75th Battalion, Canadian Infantry, took part. Gas was used and Bangalore torpedoes were also deployed to cut gaps in the enemy's wire. However, a sudden change of wind direction caused the gas to blow back towards the Canadian lines. The discharge of gas also served to alert the German artillery, which then began its reply. When the Canadians left their trenches, machine guns opened up a deadly fire and those attackers who managed to get close to the German wire were met with a hail of bombs causing havoc and heavy casualties, especially in the gaps where the wire had been cut. Many of the wounded, some of them dying, lay out in no-man's land the entire day.

The raid was a costly failure and a truce was later arranged, which allowed the Germans to bring many of the Canadian dead half way across no man's land so that they could be collected. It proved a bitter experience for the Canadians, who were no strangers to hard fighting, but the complete lack of success was difficult to take. Despite the need for intelligence regarding the enemy's defences prior to 9 April, no more raids on this scale were attempted during the next six weeks, though patrols and smaller raids did take place up and down the Canadian line in the run up to the offensive. This is one of several nearby cemeteries where casualties from the raid can be found.

In terms of casualties from the opening day of the Battle of Arras, there are surprisingly very few burials here; just nine Canadians, six of whom share the same grave reference (Plot II.D.18). All six men are sappers from the 11th Field Company, Canadian Engineers. Captain Robert Frederick AITKEN, 78th Battalion, Canadian Infantry, who was killed in action on 9 April 1917, is the only Canadian officer buried here (Plot II.E.8).

Another similar plot contains four men from the 102nd Battalion, Canadian Infantry (Plot II.H.8). One of them is Private John Rennie BALLINGAL, aged 35, who came from Islay, off the west coast of Scotland. All four were killed on 9 January 1917. According to the war diary there were six casualties that day, five of whom were killed whilst attached to the 87th Battalion in front line trenches.

Privates Donald CROSS, 50th Battalion, Canadian Infantry (Plot I.F.6), and Private Frederick William CLARKE, 72nd Battalion, Canadian Infantry (Plot II.F.17), had the misfortune to be killed on Christmas Day 1916. The 50th Battalion's war diary for Christmas Day 1916 merely states that it relieved the 47th Battalion in the front line during the course of which there was one fatality and six men were wounded. The 72nd Battalion war diary is not specific as regards casualties that day, but states that after moving into the front line it had put out defensive patrols during the evening and that their trenches were subjected to a heavy bombardment for about an hour.

It will probably come as a surprise to find that two of the headstones relate to soldiers killed in 1914. Private William PATTINSON, who was 18 years old, and Private Charles Alfred WOOLGER were killed on 18 December 1914 when 'A' and 'C' companies of the 2nd Border Regiment carried out an unsuccessful raid on German trenches near Cordonnerie Farm with men from the 2nd Scots Guards. The raid began at 6.15pm and though the raiders managed to reach the German trenches, they came under heavy fire, not only from the enemy, but also from their own artillery. The survivors withdrew 50 yards and lay out in no man's land for an hour before resuming their attack. This second attempt to penetrate the enemy's trenches met with failure. Two platoons from 'B' Company, supported by a renewed bombardment, made yet another attempt, but ran into uncut German wire, at which point the entire attack broke down.

Later, Private Abraham Acton and Private James Smith each won the VC by going out into no-man's land and rescuing the wounded, including one man on 21 December who had been lying out in the open for seventy-five hours. Smith, whose real name was James Alexander Glenn, survived the war, but Acton was killed on 16 May 1915 during the Battle of Festubert. He is now commemorated on the Le Touret Memorial.

PATTINSON and WOOLGER are among the 110 other ranks recorded by the 2nd Border Regiment as casualties of the raid. They were brought here after the Armistice and may well have been buried originally by the Germans. The fact that they were reburied here rather than in one of the larger concentration cemeteries, such as Cabaret Rouge British Cemetery, still strikes me as somewhat odd. The action in which they died took place near Neuve Chapelle, north of the La Bassée Canal.

There are also three casualties from the Battle of Loos buried here. Serjeant Lewis DAWSON, 6th King's Own Scottish Borderers, is one of them (Plot I.E.4). He was killed on 25 September 1915, the opening day of the battle. According to *Military Operations in France and Belgium 1915, Volume II*, the battalion lost all twenty of its officers who took part in the attack in addition to 630 of its other ranks; when it came to the roll call that evening, it was answered by just one corporal and forty-six other men. The other two casualties are Private John PATERSON, 9th Cameronians, who was also killed on the opening day at Loos (Special Memorial 4), and Lance Corporal Ellis BARLOW, 26th Field Company, Royal Engineers, who was killed in action on 30 September 1915 (Plot I.A.6). PATERSON was born in Pittsburg, USA, but had enlisted in Blantyre, Lanarkshire.

Another 1915 casualty is Captain James BROWN, 6th Cameronians, who was killed on 15 June 1915, aged 38. He was killed in action during an attack just north of Givenchy aimed at assisting the French Second and Tenth Armies, which were still engaged in the Second Battle of Artois, well south of the La Bassée Canal. His battalion captured some ground that day near Violaines and managed to hold on until a company of 6th Seaforth Highlanders finally got through, but the position was found to be untenable and around 4am the next morning this gallant group of men were forced to withdraw back to their original line. The attack was repeated by other units on 16 June, but the small gains were nullified when the Germans launched a strong counter-attack. BROWN was probably buried by the Germans and brought here after the Armistice (Plot I.G.15).

The cemetery also reflects the early days of spring 1916 when the British took over this part of the front from the French Tenth Army. When the British assumed responsibility for the 20 mile stretch, including the entire length of Vimy Ridge, the trenches consisted largely of a series of shell holes and joined-up craters protected by poor, inadequate wiring, often without traverses, and where dead bodies remained unburied after months of decay. The British and the Germans used the first week of the relief to improve their respective defences before hostilities resumed. The French and the Germans had also tunnelled and undermined each other's trenches, but under British occupancy this activity increased dramatically.

At 8.30pm on 15 May 1916 the British blew five mines in the Berthonval sector in order to obtain better observation from the lips of the craters over the German lines. German retaliation came several days later after a careful bombardment of the British communication trenches and gun batteries. Not only was Zouave Valley subjected to terrific bombardment, the HQ of the 47th (2/1st London) Division at Château de la Haie, 4 miles west of Souchez, and even billeting areas 8 miles from the front, also came under fire. On 21 May the German bombardment intensified; then, just after 7.45pm, the German infantry attacked. They soon overran the British front and support trenches, stopping only when they ran into their own barrage. Many of the defenders who fell back gathered in the shallow depression of Zouave Valley where the reserve line ran, and it was from here that men from the 1st/3rd, 1st/4th and 2nd/3rd Field Companies, Royal Engineers manned trenches on the west side of Zouave Valley in an effort to stem the attack. The 1/20th Battalion, London Regiment (Woolwich and Blackheath), and the 10th Cheshire Regiment from the 25th Division were able to limit the extent of the attack by manning their communication trenches and forming a defensive flank, but by then the enemy had seized all the mine shafts in the area with the exception of one.

Some of the ground lost was recovered during the early hours of the 22nd, but only in the 25th Division's sector. The 2nd Division took over from the 47th (2/1st London) Division, the 22nd Royal Fusiliers and the 1st Royal Berkshire Regiment relieving the 17th Battalion (Poplar and Stepney Rifles) and 7th (City of London) Battalion, of the London Regiment, whilst the 1st King's Royal Rifle Corps and the 23rd Royal Fusiliers took up new support positions around Cabaret Rouge.

A British counter-attack to recover the lost support line and, if possible, the original front line, was scheduled for the evening of 23 May. The Germans, however, anticipated the attack and began to shell any likely assembly areas where counter-attacking troops might be forming up. Three distinct barrages fell: one during the late morning, one in the afternoon, and one just before 8pm. One fell in front of the Royal Berkshire's assembly trenches, but behind those of the 22nd Royal Fusiliers, who were lying out on the eastern slopes of Zouave Valley; the second fell on Zouave Valley itself, and the third one concentrated on the communication trenches in that area. In the circumstances the commanding officers of both battalions decided not to go ahead with the counter-attack, but one company of the 22nd Royal Fusiliers never received the cancellation order, nor did a section of the 226th Field Company, Royal Engineers, attached to it. In spite of efforts by two officers to reach them in time, the men advanced at 8.25pm as originally planned. In the face of murderous machine-gun fire, the result was annihilation and the company was virtually wiped out. After that it was decided to completely abandon any further attempts to regain the lost ground. The British simply could not afford to divert the necessary artillery away from the Somme, where preparations were now under way for the proposed offensive scheduled for the end of June.

These events in May 1916 are reflected in some of the burials here There are casualties from the 1st King's Royal Rifle Corps and the 22nd Royal Fusiliers, as well as fourteen men of the 1st Royal Berkshire Regiment who were killed in action on 23 and 24 May; all belonged to the 2nd Division. This division continued to hold the line throughout June and July 1916. There are casualties from the 2nd Oxfordshire and Buckinghamshire Light Infantry who fell between 3 and 12 June; from the 2nd Highland Light Infantry, between 9 and 16 June; from the 1st King's Liverpool Regiment, between 27 June and 3 July; from the 17th Middlesex Regiment on 4 July; and seven men of the 13th Essex Regiment who were killed in a raid on an enemy strongpoint on 1 July 1916. There are also casualties from the 17th Royal Fusiliers, killed on 9 July, as well as several from the 22nd and 23rd Royal Fusiliers. This sequence of burials not only gives a very clear picture of the rotational nature of successive tours of duty, it also demonstrates the daily attrition involved in merely holding the line.

Surprisingly, very few of the 47th (2/1st London) Division's casualties are buried here, despite holding the Souchez sector between 16 March the end of July 1916. Between 21 May and 18 July 1916 there are just three (Special Memorials 2 and 3, and Plot II.D.11). Many of those killed during the German operation on 21 May have no known graves and are commemorated on the Arras Memorial. Many would simply have been blown to pieces during the German artillery barrage.

A small group of men from the South African Brigade can be found in Plot II, Row F. The brigade came to this part of the front, along with the rest of the 9th (Scottish) Division, after its mauling at Delville Wood in July 1916. All of those buried here fell between 24 August and 6 September 1916. Although the group consists of only eight identified burials, all four regiments are represented. Before taking over trenches here on 23 August, the brigade received new drafts totalling forty officers and 2,826 other ranks, all of them replacements for the losses incurred at Delville Wood. Though this was a fairly quiet sector compared with the Somme, the brigade's first casualty on this new part of the front occurred the following day, 24 August, when Private ROBERTS, 4th South African Regiment, was killed (Plot II.F.3).

Second Lieutenant Douglas Edward HOOD, 1st Bedfordshire Regiment, was killed in action on 14 July 1917, aged 21. The battalion had moved into some reserve trenches in Zouave Valley during the early morning of 14 July, where it was deployed on the construction of a mule track between Tottenham Tunnel and Givenchy-en-Gohelle. The war diary refers to this track as Hood Track and seems to infer that the track was a new one. It is entirely possible that it was named after Second Lieutenant HOOD, though this is not specifically stated. The distance between here and Gavrelle, with its connection to the 63rd (Royal Naval) Division, makes it very unlikely that the track had anything to do with the Hood Battalion. (Plot II.A.27)

Second Lieutenant Harry EMMS, 8th Somerset Light Infantry, was killed in action on 6 August 1916. His battalion had until recently been part of the 21st Division and had gone into action on 1 July near Fricourt. However, a week later, the entire brigade was transferred and became part of the 37th Division. Second Lieutenant EMMS had been with the battalion since at least 9 October 1915, the date from which his commission became effective. He was the battalion's only casualty on 6 August, though the circumstances of his death remain obscure. (Plot II.E.5)

Regimental Serjeant Major Charles ELDRIDGE, 1st Cheshire Regiment, was unintentionally killed at the battalion's HQ near La Coulotte on 14 April 1917. His battalion was acting as advance guard to 15 Brigade as it moved up through La Coulotte towards the outskirts of Lens where the German positions now consisted of well-wired trenches and ruined houses which had been converted into strongpoints. During the afternoon of 14 April a party from the 1st Devonshire Regiment was approaching the battalion HQ of the 1st Cheshire Regiment and mistook it for an enemy position. The party opened fire and ELDRIDGE was tragically killed before the error was realized. He had only recently come out from England. (Plot II.A.25)

Serjeant Raymond DREW, 22nd Royal Fusiliers, was killed in action on 24 May 1916, aged 32. The CWGC register notes that his father was an assistant master at Eton College. Raymond, however, did not attend Eton College. His father died when Raymond was still a young boy and he was educated at schools in Oxford before gaining a scholarship to Rossall School in Fleetwood, Lancashire, where he boarded. He went on to Pembroke College, Oxford, but at some stage while he was studying he began working for the Bombay Burmah Trading Corporation. Although he returned to Oxford he never completed his degree. He went back out to the Far East and resumed working for the same company. In 1914 he returned to England to enlist and initially served as a private before gaining promotion. (Plot II.B.17)

The youngest casualty buried here is Rifleman Edward MILLER, 1st King's Royal Rifle Corps. He was killed in action on 24 May 1916, aged 17. (Plot II.E.14)

Chapter Five

Maple Leaves and Shamrocks – Oeufs Frites on his Birthday – An Old French Trench

Aix-Noulette Communal Cemetery

The cemetery contains just five graves from March 1917. One of them is a private from the 7th Northamptonshire Regiment and the remaining four are from the 9th Royal Sussex Regiment, one of whom is a lance corporal. All five were killed in action on 11 March 1917 and their battalions belonged to the 24th Division. Although the five headstones suggest separate burials, the four men from the Royal Sussex Regiment are buried in a communal grave.

Aix-Noulette Communal Cemetery Extension

The cemetery is located off the main Arras-Béthune road, the D.937. On entering Aix-Noulette from the south, the point to look out for is the church. Turn right here onto the D.58, which is the road out to Bully-Grenay. The communal cemetery and its extension are situated on the left, just a couple of hundred yards up the road. The extension still contains around 500 French graves, but British and Commonwealth troops began using it from February 1916 and continued to do so until well into 1918. During this time the area around the two cemeteries was taken up by a number of field ambulance units and the British and Commonwealth section is largely the result of their presence. The extension part of the cemetery continued to grow after the Armistice and now contains 688 identified casualties and a further sixty-one burials of unknown soldiers.

Almost 70 per cent of the headstones in this cemetery carry the maple leaf, the emblem denoting Canadian war dead. Of the 482 Canadian soldiers buried here, 330 of them are 1917 casualties. However, there are no Canadian casualties here from the opening day of the Battle of Arras and there are only three Canadian burials for the entire month of April 1917. All three are privates from 2nd Battalion, Canadian Infantry, who fell on 12 April and all three are buried in the same grave (Plot I.V.28).

Private Gustave COMTE and Private Joseph LA LANCETTE died on the same day, 3 July 1917, when they were executed by firing squad at Aix-Noulette. Both men were from the 22nd Battalion, Canadian Infantry. The battalion's war diary makes no reference to their deaths and restricts its comments mainly to the relief of the 46th (North Midland) Division in trenches near Lens. COMTE already had a history of misconduct, including an incident in late December 1916 for which he was awarded twenty-one days Field Punishment No. 1. Shortly into that punishment he went missing for a short period, after which he went on to complete the rest of his sentence, to which was added an additional week in respect of his absence. However, in April he disappeared again, just before the Battle of Arras, and was only discovered the following month after he had made his way as far as Le Havre. He was tried on 7 June 1917 and his death sentence was confirmed at the end of the month. LA LANCETTE also had a history of short periods of absence, once from a working party, and again whilst on trench duty. As a consequence of the latter occasion he underwent a period of Field Punishment No. 1 which appears to have had a detrimental effect on his health. Like COMTE, he too went missing before the Battle of Arras. It seems unlikely that either man would have escaped a death sentence, but the fact that both cases were heard consecutively, and the fact that both men were from the same battalion, merely sealed their fate; both men were undoubtedly shot as well 'for the sake of example'. (Plot I.F.20 and 21)

It was only in July 1917 that the Canadians began to use this cemetery to bury their dead. The twenty-three Canadian burials that month are mainly from battalions of the 2nd Canadian Division. Among this group of men are two brothers, buried side by side: Private Benjamin Alfred RIPPINGDALE, who was 22 years old, and Private Stanley Horace RIPPINGDALE, who was three years older. Both men were killed on the same day, 16 July 1917, serving with the same battalion, the 20th Battalion, Canadian Infantry. The battalion war diary for that day refers to a Lewis gun crew being wiped out by a direct hit, either from a shell or by a trench mortar round, as German artillery responded to a discharge of gas by 'B' Special Company, Royal Engineers, that had taken place along the battalion's front. No other casualties are referred to that day and it is therefore entirely possible that the brothers were part of that crew. (Plot I.G.11 and 12)

Lieutenant Francis Peter COLLINS, 2nd Battalion, Canadian Infantry, who came from Newfoundland, was killed in action on 23 July 1917, aged 25. His brother, Corporal John Joseph Collins MM, died of wounds later that year, on 6 December, serving with the Newfoundland Regiment. He too was 25 years old when he died and is now buried at Rocquigny–Equancourt Road British Cemetery. His MM was awarded in connection with actions at Cambrai on 20 November 1917 and was posthumously gazetted on 13 March the following year. (Plot I.G.16)

Another July Canadian casualty is Private Emilien GRIGNON, 22nd Battalion, Canadian Infantry, who was killed on 23 July, aged 17. (Plot I.G.20)

The month of August 1917 also features prominently among the headstones and there are now 175 identified casualties from that month buried here. This was the month during which the Canadian 1st and 2nd Divisions captured Hill 70 from the Germans, though at the cost of 304 officers and just over 8,000 other ranks.

The attack took place on 15 August 1917 and many of the casualties occurred during the following few days when the Germans made a number of strong counter-attacks. The loss of this important position committed the Germans to making several determined attempts to recover it, all of which failed and resulted in heavy losses for them as well as for the Canadians. The capture and retention of Hill 70 was not only a great achievement in itself, it also posed a significant future threat to the German positions around Lens. Thirty-three officers and men killed on the day of the initial assault on Hill 70 can be found here, including several officers and men from battalions of the Canadian 2nd Division.

Lieutenant Arthur Garnet Slane FLEMING, 26th Battalion, Canadian Infantry, was killed in action on 15 August 1917, aged 46 (Plot I.K.14). He was born in Dublin in 1870, and fearing that he might be considered too old to enlist, he understated his age by five years when he returned from the United States of America to join up at the outbreak of war. Before being commissioned in the 26th Battalion he served with Princess Patricia's Canadian Light Infantry. He was wounded during fighting on the Somme in 1916 and had also fought at Vimy Ridge in April 1917. In May 1915 near Bellewaerde in the Ypres salient, while serving as a private with Princess Patricia's Canadian Light Infantry, he had covered a withdrawal by his company using bombs, an action for which he received a mention in despatches. Some accounts indicate that he was awarded the DCM for this act of gallantry, but there is no trace of it in any of the *Gazettes*, and it is certainly not listed in the recognized authority on the subject: *The Distinguished Conduct Medal awarded to members of the Canadian Expeditionary Force 1914–1918*. His father had also served in the army as a captain. Buried next to him is Lieutenant Hubert Sydney RITCHIE, 24th Battalion, Canadian Infantry, who is one of two men in this cemetery who was promoted in the field (Plot I.K.15).

Two other Canadian lieutenants, both considerably younger than FLEMING, are also buried nearby. Lieutenant Austin Arlington BECKETT, 20th Battalion, Canadian Infantry, was killed in action during operations to take Hill 70 on 15 August 1917, aged 20 (Plot I.J.2); so too was Lieutenant John Hewitt LAIRD, 24th Battalion, Canadian Infantry, who was 19 years old when he died (Plot I.N.22).

Private James Vance NEILL, 21st Battalion, Canadian Infantry, also died on 15 August 1917 during the assault of Hill 70, aged 38 (Plot I.J.22). His brother, Private William Neill, served in the same battalion and was killed in action later that year between 3 and 4 November near Passchendaele in Belgium. He is buried in Plot II in Tyne Cot Cemetery. Another brother, Private Andrew Cloakie Neill MM, 12th Royal Scots, is also commemorated on the memorial wall at Tyne Cot Cemetery. He fell on 25 April 1918, aged 27.

Among the remaining Canadian casualties from August 1917 there is another officer who, like Lieutenant RITCHIE, was commissioned in the field.

Lieutenant Donald Ryerson MACDONALD, 'B' Company, 18th Battalion, Canadian Infantry, was killed in action on the second day of operations at Hill 70, 16 August, aged 19 (Plot I.K.12). The CWGC register notes that he had twice reverted to the ranks in an effort to get to the front. He was killed after he had gone forward with two other officers and four NCOs to carry out a reconnaissance prior to an attack on enemy trenches between the Lens–Grenay railway and Lens-Saint-Pierre. As they were returning a bomb was thrown at them, killing Lieutenant MACDONALD and wounding another of the officers. The information brought back by Lieutenant Dougall, one of the other officers in the group, proved so valuable that the original orders for a frontal attack were altered. The amended plan, which was successfully carried out the next day, enabled further ground to be taken, but sadly, and rather ironically, Dougall was mortally wounded in the attack and later died at No. 6 Casualty Clearing Station at Barlin where he is buried.

Two other officers buried here who fell during this period are Lieutenant Parker Alonzo FULTON, 26th Battalion, Canadian Infantry, who was killed on 17 August (Plot I.K.13) and Lieutenant John Thompson FISHER, 43rd Battalion, Canadian infantry, who died on 30 August (Plot I.P.2).

There are also three men killed in August 1917 who held the MM:

Sergeant Frederick Washington WILLIAMS MM, 20th Battalion, Canadian Infantry, killed in action on 18 August 1917. (Plot I.J.6)

Lance Serjeant James Donald GRAHAM MM, Princess Patricia's Canadian Light Infantry, killed in action on 30 August 1917. His MM was gazetted on 12 March 1917 and was awarded for his role in a daylight raid on an enemy post. During the initial part of the raid he killed one of the sentries and captured another single-handed. He then destroyed the position by throwing a Stokes mortar bomb and covered the withdrawal of the rest of the party by protecting its flank. He had also been wounded twice; once in November 1916, and again in March 1917. Prior to the outbreak of war he was studying to enter the church as a Presbyterian minister. (Plot I.P.17)

Private Yoichi KAMAKURA MM, 52nd Battalion, Canadian Infantry, killed on 26 August 1917. He was born in Hiroshima, Japan. He won his MM as a Lewis gunner, which he had fired from the hip as he and his platoon advanced. He gave covering fire to the platoon as it made its way through some heavy wire entanglements, and in doing so he personally inflicted many casualties on the enemy who retired in disorder, enabling the platoon to continue its advance. (Plot I.L.19)

There are a further 126 Canadians buried here who fell between September 1917 and the end of the year. One notable casualty among this group is Private Horace James STOKES, 1st Battalion, Canadian Infantry, who was killed in action on 19 September 1917, aged 40 (Plot I.T.2). His son, Private Stanley Tom Stokes, who also served with the 1st Battalion, Canadian Infantry, was killed in action on the opening day of the Battle of Arras, 9 April 1917, and is buried at Écoivres Military Cemetery.

Another grave of note is that of Major Hal Charles FRYER MC, 52nd Battalion, Canadian Infantry, who was killed in action on 4 September 1917, aged 22 (Plot I.D.24). His body was recovered after a raid on enemy trenches and a strong point near Lens. After two unsuccessful attempts, his body was eventually located and brought back for burial by Corporal Tom Hurley, who won the MM for his gallantry in carrying out the recovery. Hurley went on to win a bar to the original award and survived the war.

Private James Laidlaw GOWANLOCK, 116th Battalion, Canadian Infantry, who was killed on 24 August 1917 (Plot I.L.13), also lost a brother. Private Robert George Gowanlock, 2nd Battalion, Canadian Infantry, was killed in action just six days earlier on 18 August. His body was never found and he is commemorated on the Canadian Memorial at Vimy Ridge.

Captain Lewis Brock HENRY, 58th Battalion, Canadian Infantry, who was killed in action on 30 August 1917, near Lens, was an only son. He had previously served as a musketry instructor between May 1916 and July 1917 and had therefore not been with the battalion very long before he died. He is reported to have been killed instantly by a shell splinter at around 1.30pm. He had been a student at the university in Toronto. (Plot I.P.3)

The Canadians continued to bury their dead here during the first part of 1918 and there are 128 burials dating from January that year through to the end of March. The most senior casualty within this group is Major Victor John KENT, 13 Brigade, Canadian Field Artillery, who was killed on 4 March 1918. Canadian army records show that he had previously served with the Canadian Field Artillery as a private and that he had graduated from the Royal Military College in Kingston, Canada, in 1902. (Plot II.A.17)

Plot II, Rows B and C, contain fifteen men from the 5th Battalion, Canadian Infantry, who were killed on 12 March 1918. The war diary that day tells us that a dug-out on Hill 70 was hit during the afternoon, resulting in thirty-three casualties from 'B' Company, many of whom were suffocated. The record shows fifteen dead and twelve wounded, whilst a further nine were reported to have been evacuated suffering from the effects of gas or suffocation. The battalion was unable to remove the bodies for two days, but on 14 March two NCOs and twenty-four men were detailed to bring the bodies back for burial. It is extremely likely that those fifteen dead are the soldiers who are buried here.

One of these men was a veteran of the South African Campaign, Sergeant Frederick ADAMS, who was 37 years old when he died. (Plot II.B. 19)

Another man, Corporal James ALLAN, held the MM, which was awarded for his actions near Passchendaele on 10 November 1917. He was in charge of a Lewis gun team there and when all of its members became casualties and the gun had been buried twice, he dug it out on both occasions and continued to operate it alone until relieved (Plot II. C.6). ALLAN's brother, Private Alexander Allan, had also served in the 5th Battalion and was killed in the attack on Hill 70 on 15 August 1917. His body was never recovered and he is commemorated on the Vimy Memorial.

The same day, 12 March 1918, the 7th Battalion, Canadian Infantry, carried out a raid on enemy trenches and although very little opposition was encountered, Lieutenant Newell Holland BATE was mortally wounded. The war diary shows him dying on the 12th, but the CWGC register shows his death as the following day. (Plot II.B.15)

Among the March 1918 Canadian casualties there are three holders of the MM, all of whom are buried in Plot II:

Sergeant James Arthur MAXWELL MM, 50th Battalion, Canadian Infantry, killed in action on 29 March 1918. (Plot II.E.2)

Sergeant Edward Hercule MEGILL MM, 8th Battalion, Canadian Infantry, killed on 9 March 1918. (Plot II.A.19)

Lance Corporal Frank Wilson HONEY MM, 38th Battalion, Canadian Infantry, killed on 24 March 1918. There is no obvious family link to the VC winner, Samuel Lewis Honey, who is buried at Quéant Communal Cemetery British Extension. (Plot II.D.13)

There are also British casualties buried in this cemetery; in fact, 207 identified officers and men. The earliest of these casualties appears to be Private Albert HURST, 7th Northamptonshire Regiment, which was part of the 24th Division. The CWGC record shows his date of death as 23 March 1915. However, there are two difficulties with this entry. The 7th Northamptonshire Regiment was in France in 1915, but did not arrive until September that year, just in time to take part in the Battle of Loos. More importantly though, *Soldiers Died in the Great War* gives his date of death as 23 March 1917, which I believe is the correct date when all the circumstances are taken into account. (Plot I.C.15)

The remaining four burials from 1915 are genuine Loos casualties, although one of the men, Private Archibald JAMIESON, 8th King's Own Scottish Borderers, was killed when his battalion was holding the line there after the battle had officially ceased. All four are privates and all of them are buried in Plot I. Private Daniel McLAREN, 2nd Highland Light Infantry, is buried in Row V. The other three: Private John FLEMING, 7th King's Own Scottish Borderers; Private John James NICHOLLS, 1st Welsh Guards and, of course, Private JAMIESON, are buried in Row W. These are men whose bodies were brought in either from German cemeteries or from isolated graves after the Armistice.

There are forty-three British casualties here from 1916. Major Laurence Aylmer HALDANE DSO, was killed in action with the 2nd Northamptonshire Regiment on 2 April 1916, aged 32. His DSO was gazetted on 14 January 1916 and was awarded for distinguished service in the field. There does not appear to be any obvious or direct family link between him and Lieutenant General James Aylmer Lowthorpe Haldane. (Plot I.A.6)

Another British officer buried here is Second Lieutenant Thomas Grueber FOLINGSBY, 7 (London) Brigade, Royal Field Artillery. According to the CWGC register, he died on 22 June 1916, aged 20, though there are two other possible dates. *Officers Died in the Great War* shows his death occurring from wounds on 23 June 1916, but the war diary indicates that he was wounded on 21 June and died the same night, as did another officer wounded with him when the enemy scored a direct hit on their trench mortar battery. The other officer, Lieutenant Henry Cyril Dixon Kimber, is buried at Barlin Communal Cemetery Extension. (Plot I.C.9)

Lieutenant William James LOWE, 8th Cameron Highlanders, was killed in action on 27 April 1916 whilst attached to a trench mortar battery. The 8th Battalion was a reserve battalion and never served overseas. He would therefore have been serving with one of the regiment's other battalions on the Western Front when he died. (Plot I.B.5)

Private Joseph HALLS, 99th Company, Machine Gun Corps, was killed in action on 3 May 1916. His brother, Private Leonard Halls, 11th Essex Regiment, died at home on 11 May 1915 and is buried near the family home in Radwinter (St. Mary's Churchyard), Saffron Walden. Another brother, Private Frederick George Halls, was killed in action on 27 May 1918 while fighting with the 2nd East Lancashire Regiment on the Aisne. He is commemorated on the Soissons Memorial. It also seems likely that the three brothers were related to at least two other men killed during the Great War, probably cousins. The CWGC database shows a Corporal Godfrey Henry Halls, 88th Company, Machine Gun Corps, killed in action on 25 May 1917. His parents also lived at Radwinter, Saffron Walden. He is buried at Orange Trench Cemetery, Monchy-le-Preux. There is also a Corporal James John Halls DCM, 1st Rifle Brigade, who was killed in action on 1 July 1916. He also came from Saffron Walden in Essex and is buried on the Somme in Sucrerie Military Cemetery, Colincamps.

There are fifteen men from the 9th Royal Sussex Regiment and twelve men from the 7th Northamptonshire Regiment who were killed in action during March and April 1917. Both battalions belonged to the 24th Division, which in early March 1917 took over the northern part of the Canadian Corps sector between Givenchy to the outskirts of Loos. This released the 1st and 2nd Canadian Divisions to prepare for the Battle of Arras along with the other two Canadian divisions. On 12 April 73 Brigade, 24th Division, attacked the Bois en Hache, whilst 10 Brigade from the 1st Canadian Division attacked the Givenchy spur and Hill 119, otherwise known as The Pimple. The 9th Royal Sussex Regiment and the 2nd Leinster Regiment, some of whose dead are now buried here, led the 24th Division's attack that day, advancing the line as far as Angres on the outskirts of Lens. The 24th Division rarely receives any attention when it comes to the Battle of Arras. It is true that it did not fight on the main part of the 1917 battlefield, but it did cover the northern flank and sustained over 1,200 casualties whilst doing so during the month of April 1917.

Lieutenant Michael Aloysius HIGGINS, 2nd Leinster Regiment, who was killed in action on 31 March 1917 near Vimy Ridge, was an officer friend of Captain Francis Clere Hitchcock whose excellent account of life at the front, *Stand To – A Diary of the Trenches 1915–1918*, was first published in 1937. Thankfully, it has since been re-published, allowing this outstanding work to reach a wider reader-ship in recent years. In 1918 HIGGINS's brother, Kevin, a member of Sinn Fein, was imprisoned in Ireland for making a speech against conscription. He later went on to become Minister for Justice and External Affairs in the Irish govern-ment, which placed him in a position of conflict with many Republican sup-porters. He defended the execution of Republicans by the Irish Free State during the troubles in 1922 and 1923 and was a firm believer in a united and free Irish State, but set within the context of the British Commonwealth. For some this proved too much and he was eventually assassinated on 10 July 1927 by Repub-lican gunmen whilst on his way to mass. (Plot I.D.14)

Buried nearby is Second Lieutenant William Falkland Geordie RICKETTS, 2nd Leinster Regiment, who was killed in action the following day, 1 April 1917, aged 19. The war diary notes that the Germans had put down a heavy artillery bombardment the previous day, but that 1 April was quiet. RICKETTS was recorded as having been killed during the night, along with two other ranks, when another eighteen men were also wounded. (Plot I.D.16)

Battalions of the 24th Division continued to use the cemetery throughout 1918. On 7 September 1918 officers and men of the 9th East Surrey Regiment paraded at the cemetery for the funeral of Captain William Henry LINDSAY MC and four of their comrades who were killed in action during a series of German counter-attacks a few days earlier. One of the men was Lance Corporal Jesse HAYES, who held the MM.

On 1 September the battalion had sent patrols into the suburbs of Lens in order to test whether or not rumours of a German withdrawal from Lens were true. They established a series of posts there, which was the first time that British or Commonwealth troops had set foot in the town since the Germans had taken Lens in 1914. The Germans, however, had not yet abandoned the town and on the morning of 3 September they launched counter-attacks on the East Surrey's posts, driving some back at the third attempt, though these positions were even-tually retaken. It was during this fight that Captain LINDSAY was killed (Plot II.G.20). His body was brought back by Lieutenant Colonel Cameron and Private McNamara. The latter was killed in action several weeks later on 16 October, but was awarded the VC for his actions during the fighting at Lens. Captain LINDSAY won his MC on 25 January 1917 for his part in a successful raid on enemy trenches near Hulluch. Several other casualties from the 9th East

Surrey Regiment can be found here as the 24th Division pushed on through Lens during the last week of September.

An earlier casualty from the 9th East Surrey Regiment is Serjeant James DUG-DALE DCM MM, who was killed in action on 23 June 1918, aged 33, by machine-gun fire whilst leading a patrol (Plot II.G.23). DUGDALE won his MM during the German offensive between 21 March and 5 April 1918, but it was gazetted posthumously on 13 September 1918. He had won his DCM back in 1917 whilst serving with the Loyal North Lancashire Regiment. A British aircraft had crashed in no man's land and its pilot appeared to be trapped. Under heavy rifle fire, DUGDALE left his post in front of our main trench and rushed forward to rescue the man, accompanied by two stretcher-bearers. When one of the stretcher-bearers was hit, he took his place and helped to carry the pilot to safety. The action was witnessed by many of his colleagues and his amazing display of courage and coolness was an inspiring example to all. (Plot II.G.10)

Another holder of the DCM is Bombardier Sidney COUSINS, 5/8th Heavy Trench Mortar Battery, Royal Garrison Artillery (Plot II.G.13). Two other men from the same unit, his friend, Corporal Charles Henry CLARK (Plot II.G.12), and Lance Bombardier Leonard SNELL (Plot II.G.15), were killed with him on 9 July 1918 when they rushed to extinguish a fire that had broken out in a gun pit. Unfortunately, the fire reached the ammunition as the party was struggling to put out the fire and all three men died in the subsequent explosion. The CWGC register notes that Lance Bombardier SNELL had been wounded twice during his service, once in July 1917, and again a few weeks earlier in May 1918. COUSINS's DCM, gazetted on 3 September 1918, was awarded after members of his trench mortar detachment had become casualties. He then kept it in action with assistance of some infantry stragglers until the enemy drew close to his emplacement, at which point he put the mortar out of action. Just as he was about to retire, he saw an officer who was nearly surrounded and, at great personal risk to his own safety, he managed to warn him of the danger, so that the officer was able to get away. Later that day he assisted some infantry details to organize a defensive position.

Other holders of the MM buried here are:

Serjeant James BELCHER MM, C Battery, 107 Brigade, Royal Field Artillery, killed in action on 10 April 1917. (Plot I.E.11)

Private William ADAMSON MM, 10th Battalion, Canadian Infantry, killed in action on 5 October 1917. His MM was won at Hill 70 on 15 August 1917 when he and another man bombed a German machine-gun post that had been holding up the right flank of his company's advance, capturing its crew. At some point, he also appears to have served as a quartermaster sergeant in the 9th Battalion, but for some reason he clearly reverted in rank. (Plot I.J.26)

Private John Randolph SCOREY MM, 3rd Battalion, Canadian Infantry, killed in action on 7 February 1918. His parents came from Southampton and the

CWGC records show a number of men of that surname with family living in and around that location. It would be highly surprising if none of these were related to him, but there appears to be no conclusively clear match. (Plot I.S.18)

Private Joseph MORIN MM, 7th Battalion, Canadian Infantry, killed in action on 30 September 1917. He previously served with the 54th Battalion, Canadian Infantry. (Plot I.U.17)

Lance Corporal Edward Alexander HOWEY MM, 38th Battalion, Canadian Infantry, killed in action on 24 March 1918. (Plot II.D.13)

Private Percy MALKIN MM, 1st North Staffordshire Regiment, killed in action on 7 August 1918. (Plot II.G.17)

Serjeant Frederick RUTTER MM, 1st North Staffordshire Regiment, killed in action on 8 September 1918. (Plot II.H.1)

Bois De Noulette British Cemetery, Aix-Noulette

The CWGC register points out that this cemetery was made by field ambulance units between April 1916 and May 1917. It derives its name from the large wood next to it. From the cemetery it is possible to look up towards the Notre-Dame de Lorette spur on which sits the impressive French National Cemetery and Ossuary. It is probably best approached on the D.937, the Route d'Arras. About a mile and a half north of the turning for the French National Cemetery at Notre-Dame de Lorette is the Rue Zeffe, which runs west from the main D.937 towards the Bois de Noulette. Take the left turn, then the next right. The road now skirts the very edge of the south-eastern side of the wood. About half a mile down this road turn right, then right again. The cemetery lies tucked away in a cutting on the wood's southern edge. It is a small cemetery containing just 130 identified casualties. The location is extremely peaceful and is worth a visit.

The first burials, from the 1st Worcestershire Regiment, occurred here on 9 and 10 April 1916 (Plot I.A.1 to 3). Lance Corporal Cecil James BEDDARD, 'C' Company, 1st Worcestershire Regiment, was just 17 years old when he died of wounds on 10 April. Subsequent burials within this cemetery can be found more or less in chronological order, starting with the 1st King's Royal Rifle Corps, the 2nd Northamptonshire Regiment, the 12th and 13th Durham Light Infantry, the 10th Duke of Wellington's Regiment, and later on, various battalions of the London Regiment and the 63rd (Royal Naval) Division. These latter casualties are buried in Plot I, Rows F, G and H.

Serjeant Kayley EARNSHAW DCM, 10th Duke of Wellington's Regiment, was killed in action on 9 June 1916. His DCM was gazetted on 15 April 1916 and was awarded after one of his guns had been blown into a crater during a heavy and continuous bombardment. He then went out into the open and brought it back and within a short space of time had it in action again. (Plot I.D.3)

One of the officers buried here, Second Lieutenant John White SOMERVILLE, 2nd Royal Marine Light Infantry, who was killed in action on 22 June 1916, had been a talented young Scottish sculptor before the war and had exhibited several times at the Royal Scottish Academy. Other members of the same battalion are buried either side of him. (Plot I.E.4)

Another gallantry award can be found in Row E. Second Lieutenant William Harper BRANTOM DCM, 15th Battalion, London Regiment (Prince of Wales's Own Civil Service Rifles), was killed in action on 4 July 1916. His DCM was gazetted on 3 August 1915 and was awarded for conspicuous gallantry on 24 and 25 May 1915 at Festubert when assisting as a bomber in an assault on an enemy trench carried out by the 8th Battalion, London Regiment (Post Office Rifles), after it became short of bombers owing to casualties. He was one of a group of eight bombers, four of whom were killed in the operation. BRANTOM and three others survived, though two of them were wounded during the raid. However, all four were subsequently awarded the DCM and became the first men from the Civil Service Rifles to win gallantry awards in the war. The *Supplement to the London Gazette*, dated 11 October 1915, records BRANTOM's promotion from private to second lieutenant when he was commissioned in the field. (Plot I.E.9)

Although the CWGC register gives no family details, there are two men buried side by side who were almost certainly brothers. Rifleman Arthur MEAD and Rifleman William MEAD were killed in action on the same day, 18 July 1916, serving with the 17th Battalion, London Regiment (Stepney and Poplar Rifles). Their consecutive army numbers show that they enlisted together. (Plot I.G.1 and 2)

Lance Corporal William James STANBRIDGE, 4th Middlesex Regiment, fell in action on 11 October 1916 (Plot II.B.3). The CWGC records show that his brother, Private Henry Charles Stanbridge, was also killed during the war. Henry was killed in action on 26 September 1915, aged 21, serving with the 9th East Surrey Regiment. He is commemorated on the Loos Memorial.

The remaining British casualty buried here from 1916 is Company Serjeant Major Henry Charles BISS MM, 8th Somerset Light Infantry, who was killed in action on 15 October 1916. His MM was gazetted on 28 August 1916. (Plot II.B.6)

There are ten Canadian soldiers buried here, all from battalions of the Canadian 2nd Division who fell in November and December 1916. They can be found in Plot II, Rows B, C and D. A further eight privates who fell in January and February 1917, some of them from the Canadian 1st Division and some from the Canadian 2nd Division, are also buried with them.

British casualties from 1917 are few and far between, just fifteen in total, including eight men of A Battery, 282 Brigade, Royal Field Artillery, who were killed in action on 8 April. They are buried together in sequence (Plot II.E.1 to 8), though the CWGC register shows one man, Lieutenant Roy Douglas John MONIE, as dying on 18 April 1917 (Plot II.E.1). First thoughts are that this is almost certainly a misprint and should read 8 April 1917, but 18 April is also given in

Officers Died in the Great War. MONIE studied Medicine at the University of Sydney in Australia. The date of death for each of the other men is corroborated by entries in *Soldiers Died in the Great War*.

Camblain l'Abbé Communal Cemetery

The three men buried here were all killed in action or died of wounds on 22 May 1940 serving with the 12th Royal Lancers, Royal Armoured Corps, and they occupy Graves 1, 2 and 3. The eldest is Lance Corporal Harold Albert SMITH, aged 31, then Sergeant Ronald Edward JOHNSON, aged 25, and finally Trooper Bernard Frank HUDSON, aged 20. The 12th Lancers was equipped with small armoured cars, which were no match against German tanks. The regiment did carry out much valuable work in May 1940, scouting and blowing up bridges with the help of small detachments of Royal Engineers who were attached to it. It was also involved in several skirmishes with enemy advanced guards and gave assistance to the Allied forces near Arras in an attempt to slow down the German advance through northern France.

Cambligneul Communal Cemetery

There is just one burial here, that of Trooper Henry James WESTROPP, 12th Royal Lancers, Royal Armoured Corps, who was killed in action on 21 May 1940. That day the HQ of the 12th Royal Lancers was located nearby at Mont-Saint-Éloi. The following day it came under heavy shell fire and was forced to re-locate.

Gouy-Servins Communal Cemetery

From Arras take the D.341 out towards Mont-Saint-Éloi. About two miles beyond Mont-Saint-Éloi, take the turning on the right towards Villers-au-Bois, which is also known as Grande Rue. At Villers-au-Bois, take the left turn, which is the D.65. About a mile and a half further on is Château de la Haie. It sits on the right-hand side of the road, set back within an area of woodland known as Bois de la Haie. This was the Canadian Corps HQ for the Battle of Arras. Gouy-Sevins is to the right at the next junction.

The cemetery is on the north side of the village and although the entrance sits on the main road, it is easily missed. The cemetery itself is a very narrow strip that stretches back from the road. The two CWGC graves are easy to spot once inside the cemetery and are set within a long row of French graves. The CWGC register points out that many of the original French graves within the cemetery and its former extension were removed, presumably to the large cemetery at Notre-Dame de Lorette, which lies east of the village.

There are two graves here, both from late April 1917. They are to be found in the north-west corner of the cemetery. Both are privates; one from the 13th Company, Machine Gun Corps, the other from the 15th Royal Warwickshire Regiment.

Liévin Communal Cemetery Extension

Liévin today is really part of the western suburbs of Lens, but during the war it was a small outlying town in its own right. It was captured by Canadian troops on 14 April 1917 and it remained in Allied hands for the rest of the war. Only 300 men within this cemetery have been identified, leaving almost 400 unidentified.

Probably the easiest way to reach this cemetery from the direction of Arras is to take the N.17 until you go under the A.26 and come to a roundabout. The 'new' N.17 goes off to the left; keep straight on passing through, or close to, Thélus and Petit Vimy. At the roundabout take the D.51 to Givenchy and Liévin. Follow this road to the outskirts of Liévin where the Rue Georges Clemenceau joins the Rue d'Avion. Turn right into the Rue d'Avion and then take the fourth turning on the left towards the Université d'Artois. The first turning on the right is the Rue Jean Caron. Turn right here and the large communal cemetery, the Cimetière de la Tourelle, is on the right-hand side 300 yards up the road. The CWGC extension sits in the south-west corner of the main cemetery. Just before the main cemetery is the Rue Diderot on the right. Take this road and the entrance to the extension is about a 150 yards further on.

Situated close to the southern end of the British battlefields of 1915, the proximity of Liévin to Lens explains the presence of the fifteen casualties buried in this cemetery from that year. The earliest burials are twelve men from the 1st Loyal North Lancashire Regiment who were killed in action on 26 January 1915 when a high explosive shell landed in Beuvry, on the east side of Béthune, where the men were billeted.

Two of the above men, Company Serjeant Major Frederick William MARSH, aged 24, and Regimental Serjeant Major Thomas John HODGSON, aged 38, had each won the DCM and are now buried next to each other. MARSH's DCM was gazetted posthumously on 30 June 1915 and was awarded for conspicuous gallantry and coolness on many occasions, but especially during operations at Givenchy and Cuinchy between 27 December 1914 and 29 January 1915. The citation states that he had displayed a fine example of courage, resource and cheerfulness at a time when it was much needed, adding that he had also shown great devotion to duty in his work. (Plot IV.G.3)

Regimental Serjeant Major Thomas John HODGSON DCM was killed with MARSH and the others when the shell destroyed their billet. At 9.30am orderly room was being held in a paved yard surrounded by buildings where an unusually large number of officers and other ranks were gathered. A high explosive shell fell almost perpendicularly in the middle of the yard, exploding with great violence and causing many casualties. Second Lieutenant Geoffrey Eric BURDEKIN, five NCOs, and seven other ranks were killed outright, and Lieutenant J.G. HAL-STED, Second Lieutenant Malcolm Ernest Callard, and Regimental Serjeant Major HODGSON were severely injured. Callard and HODGSON died of wounds later that day, though Callard was taken to nearby Béthune where he later died; he is now buried in Béthune Town Cemetery. The CWGC records show that Callard's death occurred on 25 January, which is incorrect. Another of the wounded men also died on the 26th. HODGSON's DCM, gazetted on 27 September 1901, was awarded to him for services in the field during the South African Campaign, where he served with the Loyal North Lancashire Regiment as a lance sergeant (Plot IV.G.4). BURDEKIN, who is buried in the same row (Plot IV.G.2), is shown in the CWGC register as serving with the Sherwood Foresters, but he was attached to the 1st Loyal North Lancashire Regiment at the time of his death.

Lance Corporal Edwin EDWARDS, one of the NCOs killed in the same incident, had already been awarded the DCM. His award was gazetted on 16 January 1915, just ten days before his death. It was awarded for gallant conduct near Ypres between 31 October and 14 November 1914 when he had shown the greatest devotion to duty in attending to the wounded whilst under fire, particularly on 31 October at Gheluvelt. His rank is listed as bandsman in the citation. (Plot III.G.14)

The remaining men who were killed are buried consecutively in Plot III, Row G, including Company Serjeant Major John MELIA. Private William GIBSON, who is buried at the start of the next plot, forms part of that unbroken sequence (Plot IV.G.1). GIBSON is shown in the CWGC register as serving with the regiment's 14th Battalion, but was evidently in France with the 1st Battalion when he died.

What is not easily explained is why twelve of the thirteen officers and men who were killed outright in the explosion are buried here rather than in Beuvry Communal Cemetery close to where they died. The communal cemetery there was in use at the time; in fact, three of those who died in the incident are still buried there. There appears to be no easy or logical answer as to why the twelve men ended up here. The CWGC notes mention that a number of cemeteries were closed after the war and that the graves were moved here to Liévin, but Beuvry Communal Cemetery was not one of them.

The remaining three burials from 1915 are from the 8th Seaforth Highlanders, the 10th Cameronians and the 9th East Surrey Regiment, and are casualties from the fighting at Loos in the autumn of 1915.

Of the thirty-nine burials from 1916, Captain Sydney James Drever JOICEY, adjutant of the 10th Northumberland Fusiliers, is the most senior in rank. He was one of four sons born to Sir James Joicey, 1st Baronet, who had made his money in coal mining in the north of England. Sydney was killed in action on 20 March 1916 and fell just 20 yards in front of the German parapet. Nevertheless, a daring rescue was made and his body was recovered at the third attempt by Serjeant Daniel Green. This was deemed worth the risk in order to prevent the Germans from bringing in his body and gathering intelligence, or at least identifying his unit. Green won the MM for his selfless act of bravery. (Plot IV.F.1)

The 23rd Division did not spend very much time in the Arras area, but the 11th West Yorkshire Regiment, which was part of that division, has five burials spread between Plot III, Row D and Plot IV, Rows E and F. All were killed towards the end of March and during the first two days of April 1916. The battalion had taken over trenches near Souchez from the French 17th Division on 3 March and then remained there until the middle of April 1916. The 2nd East Lancashire Regiment, the 1st Worcestershire Regiment, the 7th Royal Sussex Regiment, the 17th and 23rd Royal Fusiliers, the 1st King's Royal Rifle Corps, the 1st Royal Berkshire Regiment, the 2nd Northamptonshire Regiment and the 1st Sherwood Foresters all lost men on the northern part of Vimy Ridge at the start of spring 1916 when they took over trenches from the French. Shelling was a daily occurrence and sniping was rife, and incoming troops unfamiliar with their new trenches were particularly vulnerable. Some of the battalions referred to belonged to the 2nd Division and the 12th (Eastern) Division, both of which spent far longer on this part of the Western Front than did the 23rd Division.

Private Norman SLINGER, 1st Loyal North Lancashire Regiment, died of wounds on 1 July 1916. His battalion, which was part of the 1st Division, was holding the line near Loos at the time of his death, although it did move to the Somme very soon after that, arriving at Candas on 7 July and going into action on 15 July near Bazentin-le-Petit. The division's 2 Brigade had made an attack at the 'Triangle' on 30 June. This was one of a number of local initiatives carried out along the front, partly intended to distract attention from the Somme, but also to take the opportunity to make small local tactical gains. SLINGER was almost certainly a casualty of the operation that took place the day before his death. (Plot I.F.6)

There is just one Canadian burial from 1916 and that is Lieutenant John Soden COOKE, 27th Battalion, Canadian Infantry. He was killed in action on 19 November 1916 and came from Balham in London. He was 26 years old when he died. (Plot III.A.18)

Serjeant James DEMPSTER, 1st King's Royal Rifle Corps, was occupying a sap when he was shot through the head by a sniper on 9 March 1916. He enlisted in 1914 and had already been invalided home after being gassed and suffering a gunshot wound, but had then returned to the front (Plot IV.F.16). A few graves along is Lance Serjeant James LARKMAN MM, also 1st King's Royal Rifle Corps, who was killed in action on 20 April 1916 (Plot IV.F.11).

There are twenty-two officers and men of the 2nd Leinster Regiment buried here, all but one of whom were killed in action on 12 April 1917 during an attack on the Bois en Hache, which lies on the eastern edge of the Lorette spur. The 2nd Leinster Regiment faced the southern and central section of the wood, whilst the 9th Royal Sussex Regiment was to attack its northern section. Their objectives were the capture the German first trench, and then the second trench, which lay 200 yards further down the slope. The Leinster Regiment faced heavy machine-gun fire and all the officers in the leading wave became casualties. The 9th Royal Sussex Regiment also took heavy casualties, but the survivors from both battalions were able to hold on to the second trench and were even able to repel a number of weak counter-attacks. All twenty-two officers and men of the 2nd Leinster Regiment can now be found in Plot IV, Rows A and B.

All four officers killed that day from the 2nd Leinster Regiment are buried here along with eighteen of the forty-eight other ranks who were also killed in the action. Captain John James KELLY, 2nd Leinster Regiment, had been chief sub-editor of the *Continental Daily Mail* and was 26 years old when he was killed in charge of 'A' Company. KELLY kept a small Kodak camera with him in the trenches and had used it to take photographs of enemy positions, even though cameras were officially forbidden. (Plot IV.A.11)

Captain William PROSPER-LISTON is another of the officers from the 2nd Leinster Regiment killed in action on 12 April 1917, though he is shown as 5th Battalion in the CWGC register (Plot IV.B.10), as is Second Lieutenant Harry Charles OULTON, 4th Leinster Regiment, attached 2nd Battalion. OULTON joined the battalion on 20 January 1917 while it was in the Loos area and was affectionately known as 'Zulu' because he had served in the 1906 Natal Rebellion (Plot IV.B.5).

The fourth officer of the 2nd Leinster Regiment buried here is Lieutenant John Hawkins SMYTH. According to the CWGC register he was killed two days earlier, on 10 April. However, this is contradicted by regimental records, which show him as one of the four killed in action on 12 April. He also fought with the battalion on the Somme in 1916. (Plot IV.A.10)

Among the other ranks, Corporal John McSWEENEY, 2nd Leinster Regiment (Plot IV.A.4), was regarded as one of the battalion's 'toughs' and was a veteran of many raids and other actions. Despite being an eager and very capable NCO, he was never decorated for gallantry, but he was promoted in the field to the rank of serjeant. Serjeant Laurence BOYLAN, who was killed the same day as McSWEENEY, was another reliable and capable NCO (Plot IV.A.15). Both had taken part in a successful raid on a German trench system known as The Triangle, adjacent to the Double Crassier, near Loos, earlier in January. An excellent account of the raid can be found in *Stand To – A Diary of the Trenches 1915–1918* by Captain Francis Clere Hitchcock.

There are just a handful of men from the 9th Royal Sussex Regiment buried here from the attack on 12 April 1917, though its casualty list amounted to just over 100, including five officers, none of whom are buried here. The 13th Middlesex Regiment is another of the battalions belonging to the 24th Division with a scattering of burials here dating to the middle part of April. Although the 24th Division played only a minor part in the Battle of Arras, its role should not be forgotten, not least because it sustained just under 1,500 casualties during the two months of April and May 1917.

Another division that was drawn into the fighting on the northernmost sector of the Arras battlefield was the 46th (North Midland) Division. Again, its role was minor, but if it is remembered at all, it is on account of the part played by two of its battalions from 139 Brigade that took part in a local operation either side of the River Souchez during the early hours of 23 April 1917 at the start of the Second Battle of the Scarpe. The attack also involved units from the 5th Division. Although there are no casualties from the actual attack buried in this cemetery, there are some from the 1/6th North Staffordshire Regiment and the 1/6th South Staffordshire Regiment, as well as the 1/6th and the 1/7th Sherwood Foresters, all of whom fell while holding this part of the line opposite an old mine shaft, known as Fosse 3 bis de Liévin, and Hill 65 during late April to July 1917.

Being close to Vimy Ridge, one would expect to find men of the Canadian Corps buried here; in fact, there are ninety-nine of them in this cemetery. Around a third of them were killed during fighting around Vimy Ridge in April 1917, but an almost equal number relate to the fighting in mid-August that year at Hill 70 on the former Loos battlefield.

Approximately half of the April casualties come from one battalion, Princess Patricia's Canadian Light Infantry, whilst almost all the August casualties are from the 4th Canadian Division. The remaining burials are almost entirely from May, mainly from the middle to the end of the month when fighting continued around Arleux and Fresnoy.

Among those who fell during May is Captain Arthur Holford ARDAGH, 20th Battalion, Canadian Infantry, who was killed in action on 10 May 1917 (Plot III.A.15). His handwritten diary is now kept at the Grey and Foresters Museum in Canada. The battalion war diary for that day records that it had been quiet, apart from an enemy bombardment that had lasted forty-five minutes. There is no specific mention of how he died, but it seems likely that he was killed by shell fire along with a number of other men who are listed only as casualty statistics. However, it does record that three officers were among those killed during this brief episode. All three happen to be buried here, the other two being Lieutenant John Haines HANNAFORD (Plot III.A. 14) and Lieutenant Joseph John WATERS (Plot III.A.16).

There are also three gallantry awards among the Canadian May casualties buried here:

Lance Corporal Harry GARRISON MM, 31st Battalion, Canadian Infantry, killed in action on 22 May 1917. (Plot II.E.19)

Lieutenant Wilfred Robert BARNES MC, 31st Battalion, Canadian Infantry, killed in action on 3 May 1917 near Fresnoy-en-Gohelle. His MC was gazetted on 26 May 1917 and was awarded for conspicuous gallantry and devotion to duty during a trench raid in which he led his men with great gallantry capturing two prisoners. The citation concludes that he had always set a fine example. He was killed in action by machine-gun fire while advancing on enemy trenches near Acheville, a small village between Arleux-en-Gohelle and Rouvroy. (Plot II.F.15)

Private Augustin BELANGER MM, 52nd Battalion, Canadian Infantry, killed in action on 25 May 1917 (Plot III.A.7). Next to him, and killed in action the same day and from the same battalion, is a veteran of the South African War, Private Robert Esplin DONALDSON, who was 48 years old when he died (Plot III.A.8). Canadian army records show that another man, Private Peter Belanger, also served with the 52nd Battalion, Canadian Infantry. His army number is consecutive to that of Augustin, and it is quite likely that the two men were related, probably brothers.

There are three Royal Flying Corps casualties buried in this cemetery. Second Lieutenant Norman Alan LAWRENCE and Second Lieutenant George Ronald Yorston STOUT MC, both members of 16 Squadron, were killed in action on 30 April 1917 while flying together. LAWRENCE previously served with the Royal Fusiliers and STOUT with the 8th Argyll & Sutherland Highlanders before taking to the air. STOUT was awarded his MC after he had twice flown at low altitude, on each occasion for a period of two hours, in order to report on the situation of an attack. On both occasions he managed to bring back a very detailed report and the citation concludes that at all times he had shown great skill and courage. The award was gazetted posthumously on 25 May 1917. Both men are buried together in the same grave. (Plot IV.B.19)

Air Mechanic II Class, Thomas ASPINALL, 2 Squadron, Royal Flying Corps, attached Royal Garrison Artillery, was killed in action on 25 April 1917. Forty-eight targets were dealt with that day as a result of co-operation between the Royal Flying Corps and our artillery. (Plot IV.C.6)

After the Canadian success at Hill 70 in August 1917 there was not much activity in that sector until late 1918 when the centre and left wing of the First Army advanced through the southern suburbs of Lens towards Douai. Between 8 and 19 October 1918, the 58th (2/1st London) Division was involved in fighting immediately north of Lens as it advanced towards the Haute Deûle Canal, which formed a natural line of resistance for the retreating Germans.

There are now a number of casualties here from the various battalions of the London Regiment that formed part of the 58th (2/1st London) Division. There are also a number of men whose regiment is shown either as the Rifle Brigade or the King's Royal Rifle Corps, but these are soldiers who had been transferred to the 8th Battalion, London Regiment (Post Office Rifles), or the 6th Battalion, London Regiment (City of London Rifles). Every battalion of the London Regiment was affiliated to a regiment in the British Army and this explains the arrangement under which the above transfers occurred.

The majority of the London Regiment casualties date to or around 14 October 1918 when the division met resistance along the canal line. All thirty men buried here are NCOs or privates, though one of the men, James Charles STANDING (Plot IV.B.12), is shown in the CWGC register under the old rank of bugler. There is one gallantry award holder among them from the Post Office Rifles: Serjeant Percy SIMONS MM (Plot I.F.15).

Finally, there are two officers of the Royal Air Force among the 1918 casualties. Lieutenant Carl Hastings HEEBNER and his observer, Second Lieutenant Douglas DAVENPORT, 103 Squadron, were killed in action together when their DH9 aircraft was shot down on 24 September 1918. HEEBNER and others from 103 Squadron were carrying out a bombing raid behind enemy lines when they were attacked by a large formation of enemy machines. The men are buried in adjacent graves (Plot VI.A.5 and 6).

Sucrerie Cemetery, Ablain-Saint-Nazaire

The village of Ablain-Saint-Nazaire lies at the foot of the Notre Dame de Lorette Ridge on its south side. By October 1915 it lay completely in ruins after fierce fighting had taken place there in May, extending into June of that year. The destruction continued from shelling until the French managed to push the Germans off the summit of the ridge during the fighting in September and early October 1915. By then, the village had been more or less reduced to rubble. There used to be a French military cemetery here until after the war when the graves were removed to the French National Cemetery at Notre Dame de Lorette.

The cemetery lies on the D.57 set back from the road in fields on the south-eastern side of the village. The D.57 is the road that runs west from the main road through the village of Souchez, the D.937. The cemetery contains 381 burials and gets its name from a nearby sugar refinery that was destroyed during the war.

Here 162 of the identified burials are from the Canadian Expeditionary Force. Most are 1918 casualties, though there is still a significant number who fell in the previous year amounting to around 40 per cent. The same percentage holds true when considering the overall split for 1917 and 1918 in respect of all casualties buried here. There is also one Canadian soldier, Lance Sergeant Colin FINNIE, who is shown as having died on 1 May 1919, aged 38, while serving with the 42nd Battalion, Canadian Infantry. Canadian military records do not show the cause of his death (Plot V.A.8).

Captain Douglas Eckley LANGDON, 1st Duke of Cornwall's Light Infantry, was killed in action on 23 April 1917, aged 33. Before the war he worked in Argentina where he was employed by the Buenos Aires and Pacific Railway. He was born in Spain, but had been educated at Ipswich Grammar School. After leaving school, he went to work with the Great Western Railway Company before deciding to move to Argentina. When he returned home to enlist he joined the 18th Battalion, Royal Fusiliers (1st Public Schools Battalion), and was commissioned in 1915. He was wounded in 1916 whilst out supervising a wiring party and was killed in action the following year, clearing some ruined buildings during his battalion's attack on 23 April. (Plot I.A.18)

LANGDON's battalion was part of the 5th Division. Although a few casualties from this division are buried here, the majority of the forty-one British casualties from 1917 are from the 59th (2nd North Midland) Division, and include men of the 2/5th South Staffordshire Regiment, the 2/5th North Staffordshire Regiment, the 2/7th and 2/8th Sherwood Foresters, the 2/4th and 2/5th Leicestershire Regiment and the 2/4th Lincolnshire Regiment, as well as from supporting arms of the division, such as its artillery units.

Two men from the 2nd Leinster Regiment, killed in action on 12 April 1917, are buried here. They are now separated from the majority of their comrades who fell that day, most of whom are either buried in Liévin Communal Cemetery Extension or commemorated on the Arras memorial. The two men, Corporal Robert Henry PURDIE and Private Pierce POWER, are at least now buried next to each other. (Plot I.B.11 and 12)

Sergeant William WARD MM, 13th Battalion, Canadian Infantry, was killed in action on 25 November 1917 (Plot II.B.6). His brother, Herbert, also fell during the war. Herbert was killed in action on 9 April 1917, aged 26, serving as a sergeant with the 15th Battalion, Canadian Infantry, and is commemorated on the Arras Road Cemetery, Memorial 39, at Nine Elms Military Cemetery, Thélus.

Private Archibald Webb PALMER, 4th Battalion, Canadian Infantry, was killed in action on 17 December 1917, aged 28. The CWGC register informs us that he relinquished his commission in the 220th Battalion, Canadian Infantry, in order to enlist over in England as a sergeant so that he could get to the front more quickly. He was born in Toronto, though his parents are shown residing in Bath at the time of his death. (Plot III.A.2)

Private Arthur WHITEHEAD, 31st Battalion, Canadian Infantry, was killed in action on 6 February 1918 (Plot III.C.5). One of his brothers, Private George Whitehead, also served in the battalion, but he was killed in action on 30 March 1917, aged 26. He is buried at Écoivres Military Cemetery. Another brother, Private Robert Whitehead, was just 20 years old when he died in England on 17 July 1916 serving with the 95th Battalion, Canadian Infantry. He is buried at Shorncliffe Military Cemetery, Kent. Throughout the war Shorncliffe was home to a number of Canadian military facilities, including a machine-gun school and later, No. 9 and No. 11 Canadian General Hospitals. Shorncliffe Military Cemetery now contains over 300 Canadian soldiers of the Great War, a number of whom were killed or died of wounds as a result of German air raids on the town and its surrounding area. However, an examination of CWGC records for Shorncliffe Military Cemetery suggests that in Robert Whitehead's case he almost certainly died from causes other than enemy action.

Among the Canadian dead there are just five officers, all of whom served as lieutenants. One of them, Lieutenant Aubrey MACKINNON, 85th Battalion, Canadian Infantry, was killed in action on 21 March 1918. He had not been with the battalion for very long; in fact, he only joined it on 12 November the previous year. (Plot III.D.3)

There is a particular sadness attached to the grave of Private Thomas George GOLDSMITH MM, XVIII Corps Cyclist Battalion, Army Cyclist Corps, who was killed on 14 May 1918 (Plot IV.B.9), which was his 21st birthday. There are a few lines in the unit history of the 60th (London) Divisional Cyclist Company telling us that Private Goldsmith had spent part of that day celebrating his birthday with some of his pals, tucking in to that soldiers' favourite, served up at every estaminet behind the lines: egg and chips. Here was a young man who was trying to enjoy a few hours away from the rigours of war, but fate had other ideas and he was killed later that day. He is one of eighteen holders of the MM buried in this cemetery, half of whom are men of the Canadian Expeditionary Force.

Corporal Gordon Stewart BUCKINGHAM DCM, 84th Field Company, Royal Engineers, was killed in action on 22 May 1918, aged 21. His DCM was gazetted on 21 October 1918 and was awarded for conspicuous gallantry and devotion to duty in handling his men and getting work done on a number of occasions whilst under fire. During enemy attacks he had shown exceptional coolness and had set a fine example to the men of his section. The 84th Field Company, Royal Engineers, was part of the 20th (Light) Division. (Plot V.B.6)

Major Frederick BUTCHER, A Battery, 92 Brigade, Royal Field Artillery, was killed in action on 22 May 1918, aged 35. His battery had not long arrived in the Avion sector, south of Lens, before he was killed. He was in an observation post on Hirondelle Hill, about a mile and a half behind the British lines, when it was subject to a direct hit. Again, his battery was a component part of the 20th (Light) Division. (Plot V.B.8)

Although Private Sidney COPE is shown in the CWGC register as serving with the Herefordshire Regiment at the time of his death, which occurred on 5 October 1918, he and many other men of the Herefordshire Regiment had already been transferred and were actually serving with the 6th King's Shropshire Light Infantry. This battalion was also part of the 20th (Light) Division. (Plot VII.A.6)

Another burial in Plot VII is Captain Lawrence Hilton HOPKINS, who is shown as having been killed in action on 7 October 1918, aged 26, whilst serving with the Huntingdonshire Cyclist Battalion (Plot VII.A.10). *Soldiers Died in the Great War* shows only four overseas deaths from this unit in France and Flanders, all of whom fell in late August or early September 1916, whilst *Officers Died in the Great War* shows just ten deaths, and two of those were killed in action attached to the Royal Flying Corps. The 1/1st and 2/1st Huntingdonshire Cyclist Battalions never left England and were stationed on the east coast throughout the war. The 3/1st Battalion was eventually divided up between the other two battalions and the Machine Gun Corps in March 1916. Clearly Captain HOPKINS was killed while attached or posted to some other unit.

Second Lieutenant Francis Hall BUCHAN, 11th Rifle Brigade, died of wounds on 7 August 1918, aged 20. (Plot IV.E.7) He is one of nineteen men buried here from the regiment who were killed in action or who died of wounds in the summer of 1918 or early autumn. All nineteen belonged to either the 11th Battalion or the 12th Battalion. Two of BUCHAN's brothers also fell during the war, but the CWGC records provide no exact match with regard to them. The brothers were, in fact, Lieutenant David Buchan, 1st Gordon Highlanders, killed in action on 9 April 1917, who is commemorated on the Arras Memorial, and Second Lieutenant John Crawford Buchan VC, 7th Argyll & Sutherland Highlanders, killed in action 22 March 1918, who is buried at Roisel Communal Cemetery Extension.

The cemetery also holds twenty-two men of the 11th and 12th King's Royal Rifle Corps, who, like the men of the 11th and 12th Rifle Brigade, were killed in action during the summer or early autumn of 1918. Many of these men were 18 or 19 years old, and it is noticeable that many battalion war diaries around that time contain references to the arrival of drafts made up of significant numbers of soldiers of a similar age. Second Lieutenant Eric William Bristowe MAGGS, 11th King's Royal Rifle Corps, was killed in action on 20 August 1918, aged 23 (Plot V.E.6). MAGGS was educated at Charterhouse School and had gone on to study Medicine at University College, Oxford. He originally served with the Honourable Artillery Company and had been wounded twice previously.

The 11th and 12th King's Royal Rifle Corps and 11th and 12th Rifle Brigade formed part of the 20th (Light) Division and over half of British burials from 1918 in this cemetery are from this division. The 7th Somerset Light Infantry, the 7th Duke of Cornwall's Light Infantry and the 12th King's Liverpool Regiment are all well represented, together with other elements of the division, such as Royal Engineer Field Companies and units of the Royal Field Artillery that were attached. Six of the nine MMs awarded to British soldiers in this cemetery are from battalions belonging to the 20th (Light) Division.

The 2nd Cameronians became part of the 20th (Light) Division at the start of February 1918, having previously served with the 8th Division. The battalion also has a number of its men among the British dead of 1918. No particular date stands out among the headstones, which are spread across Plots IV, V and VI, and the dates vary between May and October 1918. Private James J. MORRISON, 2nd Cameronians, who was killed in action on 10 September 1918, had been awarded the MM. (Plot IV.F.11)

Apart from Private MORRISON, there are quite a few holders of the MM buried in this cemetery, in fact, a further seventeen. Reference has already been made to two of them, and the remainder are listed below.

Second Lieutenant Ronald William STEVENS MM, 8th Worcestershire Regiment, killed in action on 31 October 1917, aged 24. (Plot II.A.3)

Private William Shannon HODGSON MM, 5th Battalion, Canadian Infantry, died of wounds on 27 November 1917. Before the war he had been a farmer in Saskatchewan and enlisted in December 1915. (Plot II.B.13)

Private Fred CROXFORD MM, 1st Battalion, Canadian Infantry, killed in action on 9 December 1917. (Plot II.C.11)

Sergeant Samuel George DEANE MM, 46th Battalion, Canadian Infantry, killed in action on 31 December 1917, aged 24. (Plot III.A.8)

Lance Serjeant Neil C. McLEAN MM, 47th Battalion, Canadian Infantry, was killed in action with two other men, Private Sheppard James BARWIS and Private Herbert William WADE, when a trench mortar bomb scored a direct hit on the post they were occupying on 8 January 1918. The battalion war diary notes that McLEAN had recently been recommended for a commission and was due to return to England the following day to undergo officer training. McLEAN also served with the 104th Battalion, Canadian Infantry (Westminster Fusiliers of Canada). All three men are buried next to each other. (Plot III.A.11, 12 and 13)

Sergeant Alexander Eugene ROSS MM, 47th Battalion, Canadian Infantry, was killed in action on 9 September 1918. Like Lance Sergeant McLEAN, ROSS previously served with the Westminster Fusiliers of Canada and both men would probably have known each other. ROSS was killed with another man from the battalion, Private William BREWER, though the war diary does not go into detail as to how they were killed. The diary also refers to another man killed that day but according to CWGC records, the only deaths in the battalion on 9 September were ROSS and BREWER, who are buried consecutively, though in different rows. (Plot III.A.15 and B.1)

Private Henry James DOWDING MM, 78th Battalion, Canadian Infantry, killed in action on 1 February 1918. (Plot III.B.15)

Corporal Ernest Walter CUTMORE MM, 31st Battalion, Canadian Infantry, killed in action on 7 February 1918, aged 34. (Plot III.C.8)

Lance Corporal William McLEAN MM, 31st Battalion, Canadian Infantry, killed in action on 9 February 1918. (Plot III.C.13)

Company Serjeant Major William Henry MOTTASHAW MM, 7th Duke of Cornwall's Light Infantry, killed in action on 5 October 1918. (Plot IV.A.14)

Lance Corporal Thomas Morecraft GUSTERSON MM, 'A' Company, 7th Duke of Cornwall's Light Infantry, killed in action on 2 June 1918, aged 22. (Plot IV.C.4)

Corporal William HAWKINS MM, 12th King's Liverpool Regiment, died of wounds on 30 June 1918. (Plot IV.D.7)

Colour Serjeant Frederick Robert WELLS MM, 7th Duke of Cornwall's Light Infantry, killed in action on 3 July 1918. (Plot IV.D.10)

Company Quartermaster Serjeant Frank THOMAS MM, 6th King's Shropshire Light Infantry, killed in action on 2 August 1918, aged 29. (Plot IV.E.5)

Private Robert Einion WILLIAMS MM, 61st Field Ambulance, Royal Army Medical Corps, killed in action on 19 September 1918, aged 27. (Plot V.F.3)

Tranchée de Mecknes Cemetery, Aix-Noulette

The cemetery lies just over a mile outside Aix-Noulette in open fields east of the village. It sits roughly half way between the D.937, which runs through Aix-Noulette, and the D.58, and can be reached via either of these approaches.

The area covered by the cemetery is divided between French burials and a slightly greater number of British and Canadian burials; a couple of German graves also remain. Only three of the 196 British and Commonwealth graves are unidentified. The cemetery takes its name from its French origins. 'Mecknes' Trench is a variation of 'Mequinez' Trench, a name given to it by Moroccan troops during the war. In the same way that many British and Commonwealth troops named trenches after familiar locations back home, the Moroccan soldiers, some of whom came from the town of Mequinez and its surrounding area, gave their trench a name that reminded them of home. The cemetery acquired various other names once the French had handed over this sector to the British, but it has since reverted back to something like its original name.

This is essentially a 1916 cemetery and it was used extensively by the 63rd (Royal Naval) Division from its arrival in the trenches here in June that year until its move to the Somme in early autumn in preparation for its role in the Battle of the Ancre in November. Just under a quarter of all the burials here are from the various battalions that made up the division, including twenty-five from both battalions of the Royal Marine Light Infantry.

There is just one gallantry award among the men buried here. Lieutenant William Harold ARMITAGE MC, 9th Yorkshire Regiment, was killed in action on 22 May 1916, aged 24 (D.5). The CWGC register tells us that he was an only son. His MC was gazetted on 15 March 1916 in recognition of his conspicuous gallantry leading a wire cutting party prior to an attack on the enemy's trenches. The wire was successfully cut in spite of the enemy's Very lights and searchlights, which had made the work particularly dangerous and difficult. Two nights prior to this, he went out to assist a wounded man returning from in front of the enemy wire. Both the 8th Battalion and the 9th Battalion, Yorkshire Regiment, have a number of burials here from the spring of 1916.

Two Petty Officers, John F. THORPE and Henderson M. WILKES, Nelson Battalion, Royal Naval Volunteer Reserve, were killed in action on 4 July 1916. They are buried close, but not next to each other. The division suffered very few casualties that day, though most of the seven men who died were from Nelson Battalion. (G.11 and G.8)

Second Lieutenant Frederic William CATON, Royal Engineers, was killed in action on 28 June 1916 with two other Royal Engineer NCOs of the 2nd Battalion, Special Brigade. Second Lieutenant CATON, who was 31 years old when he died, held a Bachelor of Science degree and a Master's degree from Oxford University. He is buried in the same grave as one of the other men who died with him, Serjeant Douglas HARTLEY (G.14 and G.13). Corporal James Leonard COLE, who was the other NCO killed with CATON, is buried in the same grave as two other Royal Engineers who died the following day, possibly as a result of wounds from the same incident in which CATON and the others lost their lives.

Just before the 63rd (Royal Naval) Division moved away from the area, Private Frank FORDE, 10th Royal Dublin Fusiliers, was killed in action at the age of 16 (J.10). An older member of the battalion, Private Michael MOORE, aged 29, is buried next to him. (J.9) Both were killed in action on 10 September 1916.

There is an interesting collection of graves in Row K. Sergeant George Brandreth INGHAM, 25th Battalion, Canadian Infantry, died on 25 December 1916, together with nine other men. They were killed in action following a raid that was carried out by the battalion at 2.45am on Christmas Day 1916. The battalion's war diary makes specific reference to the death of INGHAM, who was killed in the enemy trenches during the raid (K.14). The diary notes that the raiders accounted for twenty-five of the German garrison, including seven prisoners. Later on that day, the Germans retaliated with a bombardment of the Canadian trenches, killing three men belonging to the 25th Battalion and six from the 22nd Battalion, which was occupying an adjacent part of the line. INGHAM's Canadian army records show his middle name as 'Bearnerd' and also as 'Bernard.'

The cemetery contains forty-five identified Canadian soldiers, twenty-one of whom are 1916 casualties. The only officer among them is Lieutenant Joseph Omeril HUDON, 22nd Battalion, Canadian Infantry, who was killed on 3 November 1916, aged 28. The battalion war diary gives no hint as to the circumstances of his death. (K.19)

Other British units with significant numbers of men buried here are the 17th and 24th Battalions, Royal Fusiliers, which between them have fifteen casualties dating from 29 February to 7 May 1916. There are also fourteen men from various battalions of the London Regiment, mainly in Row G, all of which date from late June to mid-July 1916.

Just twenty-seven of the casualties here are from 1917. The majority of them are Canadian NCOs and privates who were either killed or died of wounds during January and February that year. Almost all are buried in Rows L and M.

Villers Station Cemetery, Villers-au-Bois

Villers-au-Bois is situated at the crossroads where the D.58 meets the D.65. About a mile and a half north-west of the village along the D.65, is another crossroads; turn left here. This is the old track bed of the railway line to Carency. The cemetery lies roughly 200 yards further on the right-hand side. A little over a quarter of a mile away to the north-east is Château de la Haie, which was used extensively throughout the war as a divisional HQ and by the Canadian Corps as its HQ for the Battle of Arras.

This cemetery is another one that was originally made by the French. When the British took over the line in 1916 they continued to use the cemetery until September 1918, after which time the Allied advances progressively distanced it from the actual battlefield. The cemetery was enlarged after the Armistice when many of the French graves were removed to the French National Cemetery at

Notre-Dame de Lorette, though thirty-two German graves still remain. Today the maple leaf is the dominant emblem on the headstones. There are now just over 1,000 identified Canadian soldiers here out of a total of 1,208 burials. Casualties relating to the fighting around Vimy Ridge in April 1917 can be found in Plots V to X.

1916

The earliest Canadian casualty here is Private Andrew Arthur HYNES, 3rd Battalion, who died on 26 October 1916 (Plot II.B.12). He is one of a hundred Canadian casualties buried here who were killed or who died during the months of November and December that year while holding the line on or around Vimy Ridge.

Aside from the dangers of shelling and mine explosions, sniping was a significant occupational hazard on both sides of the line. A typical scenario was played out on 13 December 1916 when Lieutenant Lincoln George HUTTON, 1st Battalion, Canadian Infantry, was mortally wounded near Montreal Crater whilst carrying out a reconnaissance. He was gallantly recovered by one of his men, Private John Miller Douglas, who won the MM for his bravery in carrying out the rescue. However, HUTTON died a few hours later and his funeral took place here in this cemetery at 11am the next day. HUTTON was killed by a sniper's bullet (Plot IV.C.2). Douglas survived another eighteen months on the Western Front, but sadly died of shrapnel wounds to his lower limbs on 4 May 1917 at No. 42 Casualty Clearing Station. He is buried in Aubigny Communal Cemetery Extension in Plot II, Row F.

Another victim of sniper fire was Company Sergeant Major George Hyde PATRICK, 3rd Battalion, Canadian Infantry, who was killed a week earlier on 6 December 1916. (Plot II.C.19)

Shelling and trench mortar fire were also everyday occurrences. Lieutenant William Hamilton MITCHELL and seven other ranks from the 8th Battalion, Canadian Infantry, were killed or mortally wounded on 27 November 1916 during a bombardment. With the exception of one man, Private Frank RABY (Plot IV.B.1), the group is buried together in Plot III.B.12 to 19.

Christmas 1916 was somewhat tarnished for the men of the 44th Battalion, Canadian Infantry. The battalion had recently relieved the 46th Battalion in trenches in the right section of the Carency sector. Unfortunately, Privates Percy CROSSWELL and Hans RONNIE were killed on 25 December 1916. Both men, who were 25 years old when they died, are now buried next to each other (Plot VII.C.25 and 26). Although 25 December is shown in the CWGC register, they may have been killed by shelling during the early hours of Boxing Day. The war diary notes that two men were killed that day, but makes no mention of casualties on Christmas Day.

When the British took over trenches from the French in the Vimy sector in spring 1916, they continued to adopt an aggressive policy with regard to patrolling, raiding and underground warfare, but it was still possible to spend successive tours of duty without ever encountering the enemy face to face. Most of the casualties that did occur were the result of shelling. Although the trenches inherited from the French were improved by means of hard work and regular maintenance, shelling was by far the biggest threat to the lives of British soldiers holding the line here. Today the cemetery contains sixty identified British casualties from 1916, a reminder of those early days of warfare for many British battalions.

Arras was the destination for several divisions following their exertions on the Somme in 1916. At the time, Arras was a far less active sector and was considered somewhere suitable for exhausted divisions to go in order to reorganize, absorb and train new drafts, and also enjoy a certain amount of rest and recreation. The 9th (Scottish) Division was one such formation that moved here, taking over from the 37th Division on 12 August 1916 and setting up its divisional headquarters at Camblain l'Abbé. The South African Brigade, which formed part of the 9th (Scottish) Division, has twenty of its officers and men buried here, all but one of whom fell during September 1916. All four battalions of the South African Regiment are represented, including one officer, Second Lieutenant Cyril Jephson BOUCHER, 'B' Company, 2nd Regiment (Plot II.A.14), and Private Ebenezer PERKINS, 'D' Company, 3rd Regiment, who was 45 years old when he was killed and who had previously served in the South African War (Plot III.A.16).

1917

In 1917 the cemetery was used far more extensively, particularly by the four divisions that made up the Canadian Corps. The period of January and February passed in much the same way as the two previous months. This was still essentially a period of active patrolling, interspersed with occasional trench raids and frequent shelling, sniping and mining. Although the winter months were invariably quieter, activity was still encouraged to maintain keenness, initiative and ascendancy over the enemy. A great deal of effort also went into maintaining and improving trenches, which in the winter months always proved uncomfortable, though frost and intense cold was often preferred to the rain.

Private Victor TALLIS, 46th Battalion, Canadian Infantry, was killed in action on 19 February 1917 (Plot VII.B.22). TALLIS had already lost one brother during the war. Private Edgar Alfred Tallis, was killed in action on 19 September 1916 and is buried in Bailleul Communal Cemetery Extension. He had served with Victor in the 46th Battalion. However, the family suffered further tragedy when two more of Victor's brothers lost their lives in the last year of the war. Private Arnold John Tallis was killed in action on 2 September 1918, aged 24, and is commemorated on the Vimy Memorial. Lance Corporal Harold William Tallis, aged 27, was killed in action on 1 November 1918 and now rests in Aulnoy Communal Cemetery, near Valenciennes.

There are now 147 Canadian burials here dating to the first two months of 1917, most of them from battalions belonging to the Canadian 4th Division. Among them is Sergeant James Henry EDMONDSON DCM, 72nd Battalion, Canadian Infantry, who was killed on 25 February 1917, aged 32. His DCM was awarded for conspicuous gallantry and devotion to duty after reorganizing three bombing squads that had become temporarily disorganized as a result of heavy hostile shell fire. Later, with the help of another man, he protected the flank of the whole raiding party until it had successfully withdrawn. The award was gazetted on 17 April 1917. (Plot VII.C.20)

March 1917 was an interesting time for the British Army as the Germans began their withdrawal back to the Hindenburg Line. As the main body of the German army carried out its orderly retreat, it left behind rearguard detachments, consisting mainly of machine-gun crews and some supporting infantry, whose role it was to harass and delay the advancing British (and French further south) as they edged forward across a wasteland of destruction south of Arras.

This was not the case for that part of the Third Army in front of Arras, where the lines remained more or less as they were, or for the First Army around Vimy Ridge, where it was also very much business as usual. However, preparations were now well under way for the coming offensive that would become known as the Battle of Arras. Patrols were stepped up and raids took place on a greater scale and with such frequency that they almost became predictable. On 1 March the Canadians carried out a large raid that began and ended badly. Many of the casualties from this raid can be found throughout the various cemeteries dotted around Vimy Ridge, as well as those close to casualty clearing stations behind the lines. Villers Station Cemetery contains sixty-seven men who died as a result of the operation on 1 March. The Canadian battalions that took part in the raid were the 38th, the 44th, the 46th, the 50th, the 54th, the 72nd, the 73rd and the 75th Battalions. Their casualties are now located in Plots V, VI, VII, VIII, Rows D and E. A number of senior officers are among the dead.

Lieutenant Colonel Arnold KEMBALL CB DSO, 54th Battalion, Canadian Infantry, was killed in action during the failed raid, which took place at the northern end of Vimy Ridge. He was 56 years old when he died. Prior to the raid, gas was released from several hundred cylinders. However, the wind changed just after its release, leading to the same disastrous results that had occurred at Loos in 1915. Not only were Canadian troops badly affected by the gas, it also alerted the enemy to the pending attack without in any way hindering their response. The German artillery replied with a heavy barrage and machine-gun fire stopped the attack in its tracks. His body could not be recovered in the immediate aftermath of the attack, and even later that evening, all attempts to recover the wounded and the dead had to be abandoned owing to the alertness of the enemy. Efforts were renewed to collect casualties from no man's land the following day, but it was only when a truce was arranged for the morning of 3 March that KEMBALL's body was finally recovered along with the bodies of many others. He was then brought here to the cemetery at Villers-au-Bois where he was buried the next day. (Plot VI.E.1)

KEMBALL's DSO, gazetted on 10 January 1917, was awarded for conspicuous gallantry in action, leading his battalion in attack with conspicuous success
and carrying out every task allotted to him. The citation adds that he had set a
splendid example of courage and good leadership throughout operations.

He was the son of a major general and was educated at Wellington College and
the Royal Military College, Sandhurst. He was gazetted as a second lieutenant in
the Royal Scots Fusiliers in 1880 and went on to serve in India with the
5th Gurkha Regiment. He was promoted to full colonel in 1907, retiring in 1912.
During this first period of service he was twice mentioned in despatches. At the
outbreak of war in 1914 he again volunteered his services.

Major Frederick Travers LUCAS, 54th Battalion, Canadian Infantry (Plot
VI.E.2), and Captain Noel Longfield TOOKER, 54th Battalion, Canadian
Infantry (Plot VI.E.3), were also killed in action on 1 March 1917. As with their
commanding officer, their bodies were only recovered on 3 March when a truce
was observed so that no man's land could be cleared. The truce allowed some
bodies to be recovered, but not all of them. Hopes that a new truce might be
arranged for the following day came to nothing. However, later that night,
several of the remaining bodies were buried in no man's land under the cover of
darkness. The 54th Battalion's losses amounted to six officers killed and seven
wounded, one of whom subsequently died. Casualties amongst the other ranks
came to seventy-seven killed, 126 wounded and ten missing in action.

Another battalion commander, Lieutenant Colonel Samuel Gustavus BECKETT,
75th Battalion, Canadian Infantry, was also killed in the raid. He had previously
been mentioned in despatches. At the start of the raid he took up a position in the
front line to observe the attack by his men. On the battalion's right flank where
heavy opposition was encountered, the German lines were only penetrated at
isolated locations. When the Germans countered by bombing these locations, all
the officers soon became casualties and the men began to fall back. Seeing this,
BECKETT climbed over the parapet, and in spite of heavy machine-gun fire,
went forward to rally his men. He had only gone 40 yards before he was hit just
above the heart by either a rifle or a machine-gun bullet, killing him instantly. An
attempt was made to rescue him, but he was found to be dead, after which all
efforts were concentrated on rescuing the wounded. On the battalion's left flank
the attack fared somewhat better, but the overall results were poor. Just one
prisoner was captured and only four dug-outs were bombed, though it was
thought that the enemy had also sustained fairly heavy casualties. (Plot VII.D.1)

Major James Miles LANGSTAFF, 75th Battalion, Canadian Infantry, also fell
that day. He was the senior officer in charge of the battalion's raiding parties and
it was for this reason that he took up a position in the centre of the advance. He
and a few others managed to enter the German trenches, but were stopped and
bombed back by determined opposition. In spite of this, it was the centre party
that brought back the prisoner captured in the raid. The gaps in the wire soon

became blocked with wounded men, preventing reinforcements reaching LANG-STAFF and his party, which led to rumours that the Germans had blown mines between the gaps. After the raid it was felt that they might have been able to hold their position if only support could have reached them. LANGSTAFF's body was recovered that evening and taken back to Villers-au-Bois for burial together with Lieutenant Colonel BECKETT and others. Their funeral took place on 4 March. Apart from the loss of BECKETT and LANGSTAFF, one other officer was reported to be wounded and missing, whilst a further six were wounded, but had managed to return. Sixty-eight other ranks were killed in the attack, thirty-one were reported to be missing in action, and 112 men had been wounded. (Plot VII.D.2)

Major Russell Kerfoot JOHNSTON, 72nd Battalion, Canadian Infantry, was one of two officers from his battalion killed in the raid. The battalion's other casualties amounted to one officer wounded, who was believed to have been taken prisoner, one officer missing, and two slightly wounded. Fifteen other ranks were killed in action that day and three of the forty-three wounded subsequently died. Twenty-four men were still missing, though it was believed that some had been taken prisoner. (Plot V.F.3)

Private Frederick SUTCLIFFE MM, 72nd Battalion, Canadian Infantry, also fell during the raid on 1 March. A local newspaper back in Vancouver reported that he had been killed by enemy shell fire whilst bringing back a wounded comrade. (Plot VI.D.7)

There are also 139 Canadian dead buried here who fell during the rest of March 1917. Among them is Private Nelson ENTWISTLE, 47th Battalion, Canadian Infantry, who previously served with the 11th Regiment, the Irish Fusiliers of Canada. He had been a shoemaker before the war and originally came from Darwen in Lancashire. He was killed in action on 16 March 1917, aged 50. (Plot VII.E.30)

The first fatality suffered by a newly-arrived battalion at the front always had a sobering effect on the rest of its members. Private Lenley Roy POTTER, 85th Battalion, Canadian Infantry, was the first man in his battalion to die in action when a shell burst amongst a working party, wounding three others. His death occurred on 4 March 1917. Another man from the battalion, Piper Alex Gillis, was also wounded on 23 February while billeted at Château de la Haie. Up to that time its buildings had suffered relatively little damage from shell fire. There are also a further thirty-eight casualties in the cemetery whose deaths occurred between 1 April and 8 April 1917, the final week of preparations for the assault on Vimy Ridge. Many of these casualties occurred from shelling.

Captain Harry Stewart BOULTER, 'B' Company, 124th Battalion, Canadian Infantry, was killed in action on 4 April 1917, aged 24 (Plot VII.H.34). Next to him are two privates from his battalion. The 124th Battalion, Canadian Infantry, was also known as the Governor General's Body Guard. Back home in Canada, BOULTER had been a passionate cricketer.

Although the Canadian fatalities for 9–12 April 1917 came to around 3,600, the cemetery here contains just thirty-eight of them. However, a glance at the CWGC register reveals that twenty-four of the thirty-eight are officers, including eight majors. Once the majority of the ridge had been cleared on the opening day, the wounded could be collected relatively easily, but it also enabled some of the senior officers killed that day to be brought back for burial rather than be buried where they fell. The eight majors are located in Plots VIII or IX, Row A, and are:

Major Harry Frank SARE, 'D' Company, 87th Battalion, killed in action on 9 April 1917. He was born in Gloucestershire. His son, Lieutenant Colonel Francis Lionel Sare, went on to serve during the Korean War. Major SARE's sister, Gladys Irene Sare, is commemorated on the Halifax Memorial, Nova Scotia. She was a Nursing Sister and was one of the fourteen nurses who drowned when their hospital ship, HMHS *Llandovery Castle*, was sunk by a German U-boat off the coast of Ireland on 27 June 1918. The ship was en route to Liverpool from Halifax, Nova Scotia, when the tragedy occurred; 234 lives were lost and only twenty-four survived. (Plot VIII.A.14)

Major Edward Ware JOY, 87th Battalion, killed in action on 9 April 1917 (Plot VIII.A. 16). He was buried here at Villers-au-Bois on 14 April with Major SARE, Lieutenant SAVAGE, and Lieutenant ROOKE.

Major John Hales SWEET, 72nd Battalion, killed in action on 9 April 1917. Before the war he had worked as a lawyer and the CWGC register points out that his father was an archdeacon back in Victoria, British Columbia. (Plot VIII.A.23)

Major Thomas Hugh CALLAGHAN DCM, 72nd Battalion, killed in action on 9 April 1917. CALLAGHAN was one of five officers from his battalion killed that day. A further five officers were wounded and two were reported missing but were believed to have been killed. Among the battalion's other ranks, thirty-three were killed in action, 112 were wounded and forty-five were missing, though most of these were believed to have been killed. Of the thirteen officers and 249 men who took part in the attack that day, the battalion's total casualties came to 202. (Plot VIII.A.24)

Major Edward Cecil Horatio MOORE, 38th Battalion, killed in action on 9 April 1917. He was one of four officers from his battalion killed in action that day and nine others were wounded. Fifty-four other ranks also fell with them, along with 214 who were wounded and forty-four who were recorded as missing in action (Plot IX.A.1). Buried next to Major MOORE are the three officers who fell with him: Captain Harold Frederick HILL (Plot IX.A.2), Lieutenant Reginald Heber Manning JOLLIFFE (Plot IX.A.4), and finally, Lieutenant Andrew Warwick

DUNCAN MC (Plot IX.A.3). All four men were buried together on 16 April. Lieutenant DUNCAN, who had been born in Co. Antrim, was awarded his MC for conspicuous gallantry and devotion to duty when in command of a raid in which he had gallantly led his men into the enemy's trench, in spite of heavy fire, and had carried out the tasks allotted to him with conspicuous success. He was one of seven brothers, two of whom served during the war.

Major Charles Simpson SHIPMAN, 78th Battalion, Canadian Infantry, was in charge of 'A' Company during the attack on 9 April. According to battalion sources he was killed early in the attack at Vimy Ridge (Plot IX.A.15). Battalion casualties are reported in the war diary as six officers killed, eleven wounded, and three missing, with sixty-nine other ranks killed, 258 wounded, and 159 missing. The brief report on the operation by Lieutenant Colonel James Kirkcaldy, the battalion's commanding officer, has since become much quoted. He stated that the losses were regrettable, but that all ranks had been eager for the attack and that he was satisfied that the sacrifices had been cheerfully made.

Major Robert George Howie BRYDON, 102nd Battalion, Canadian Infantry, was initially reported as missing in action on 9 April 1917. However, his body was found the next day and from its position it was determined that he had been killed very early on during the attack (Plot IX.A.16). He was one of four officers killed in action from his battalion that day. Nine others were wounded, one of whom died two days later; 113 other ranks were killed and a further six subsequently died of wounds. Twenty-seven men were recorded as missing in action and 180 were wounded. BRYDON, who before the war was a civil engineer, was shot dead during the attack. He had served with the battalion on the Somme the previous year, and although he had been recommended for the MC, the award was never made. When news of his death reached his family back in Kenora, Ontario, his mother suffered what we would today call a stroke and died just two weeks after Robert's death. His brother, John, also served and survived the war. Oddly enough, BRYDON's runner, Private Herbert Marrison, was found by his side, and yet Marrison is buried in Givenchy Road Canadian Cemetery. Herbert's brother, Private Fred Marrison, also served in the 102nd Battalion, but was killed on 24 October 1916 on the Somme near Regina Trench. Both men enlisted in December 1915 and originally came from Oldham in Lancashire.

Major Arthur McKay ROSS, 87th Battalion, Canadian Infantry, killed in action on 9 April 1917 (Plot IX.A.20). He was one of six officers to be killed that day from his battalion. Another officer subsequently died of his wounds and four more were wounded. Amongst the other ranks, 110 men were killed, 157 were wounded and twenty-five were recorded as missing in action. Lieutenant Edwin George SAVAGE, from the same battalion, was another of the officers killed that day. (Plot VIII.A.15) As one of the battalion's scouts, he had been reconnoitring an advanced position when he decided to attack an enemy strongpoint with three other men. One of the men, Private Peter Marshall McLellan, was killed in the attempt along with SAVAGE and is now buried in Canadian Cemetery No. 2 Neuville-Saint-Vaast. Buried just along from SAVAGE is fellow officer, Lieutenant James Alfred ROOKE, who was killed on the same day (Plot VIII.A.17). Major ROSS's brother, Lieutenant George William Ross, also served in the same battalion, but was lucky enough to survive the war.

Lieutenant Joseph Harold WILSON, 102nd Battalion, Canadian Infantry, died on 11 April 1917 as a result of wounds received two days earlier whilst taking acting command of 'A' Company in the attack on Vimy Ridge. He was found alive in a shell hole, but his leg was badly broken. Initially, he was thought likely to survive, but despite receiving medical attention at the casualty clearing station at Villers-au-Bois he never recovered. He had previously been wounded on the Somme during the fighting at Regina Trench in October 1916. (Plot VII.J.18)

Lieutenant John Douglas ARMSTRONG, 11th Field Company, Canadian Engineers, was also killed in action on 9 April 1917. He was mentioned in despatches and had been a civil engineer before the war. His date of enlistment is shown as New Year's Eve 1916. As an engineer he worked for the Surveyor General's Department back in Canada, and after the war a mountain in the Rockies, formerly known as Table Mountain, was re-named 'Mount Armstrong' in memory of him. Of all the memorials to individual soldiers of the Great War, his must surely be the largest and most impressive. (Plot VII.J.35)

Sergeant Charles Albert OWSTON DCM MM, 42nd Battalion, Canadian Infantry, was killed in action on 9 April 1917. OWSTON had won his DCM as a private for tending and rescuing the wounded under very heavy fire and displaying great courage. When his battalion was subsequently relieved, he remained behind so that the wounded could be evacuated more quickly. The award was gazetted on 14 November 1916. He had also won the MM, which was gazetted on 27 October 1916. (Plot VIII.A.7)

Lieutenant Robert Alexander STALKER, 102nd Battalion, Canadian Infantry, had been wounded previously at St Éloi, in Belgium, on 8 July 1916. He was another of the battalion's officers killed on 9 April 1917. His death had occurred early in the attack, according to the battalion war diary, and was confirmed by two runners at 8.10am. (Plot IX.A.17)

Lieutenant Everett Boyd Jackson FALLIS, 102nd Battalion, Canadian Infantry, was killed in action on 9 April 1917. He was a battalion scouting officer. Initial reports on the fighting that day had indicated that progress was being made, but then news started to filter back that things were not going quite so well on the right flank. He was sent forward to clarify the situation and came back with his report at around 9am, but was killed soon afterwards. (Plot X.A.11)

Much attention is focused on 9 April 1917 when the Canadians stormed Vimy Ridge, and on the following day when they completed the task. Relatively little attention is given to those who fell during the remainder of the month. The continued fighting throughout April and May was often heavy in nature, but has always been overshadowed by events on 9 April. This cemetery contains a further 139 Canadian casualties who were killed or died of wounds between 10 April and 31 May 1917. Another five majors who fell within that period are buried here.

Major Gordon D'Arcy LEE, 46th Battalion, Canadian Infantry, was killed in action on 3 May 1917. A minor operation was carried out in the early hours of 3 May, which was successful in achieving its objectives. During the day the advanced position was held by a platoon of 'C' Company. Captain LEE, who was an acting major at the time, was killed by a sniper whilst the platoon was taking up its new posts (Plot V.F.10). It appears to have taken the German artillery a little time to work out the exact position of these posts, but it eventually located them and put down a bombardment. At the same time, machine-gun fire from the direction of Fosse 3 intensified. Although the operation was purely of local significance, it still proved quite costly. In addition to LEE's death, seven other ranks were killed and another officer and twenty-eight other ranks were wounded in the space of thirty-six hours. A working party of around 150 men was due to dig a new trench overnight on 3/4th May, but it was shelled as it was making its way to the assembly point causing further casualties. Very few men from the working party actually reached the assembly point, by which time there was bright moonlight and the digging was therefore cancelled. Private John Edward LEES, who was one of the men killed with Major LEE on 3 May, is now buried next to him (Plot V.F.11). Private Leroy Archer WIGGINS, who was part of LEE's original patrol, was also killed and is buried in the next row (Plot V.G.10).

Major Richard William Fisher JONES, 124th Battalion, Canadian Infantry, was killed in action on 15 April 1917. He was in charge of a working party repairing the Souchez–Angres road when a shell burst a few feet away, killing him instantly. His battalion was the pioneer battalion assigned for the battle to the Canadian 4th Division. It had originally been the Governor General's Body Guard, but on 1 February 1917 it began its new role as pioneers and joined the division in March where it remained until June 1918 when it joined the 4th Canadian Engineering Brigade. (Plot VIII.A.1)

Major Charles Stuart BELCHER MC, 44th Battalion, Canadian Infantry, was killed in action on 11 May 1917. He had also been mentioned previously in despatches. His MC was gazetted on 14 August 1917 and was awarded for his role during an attack in which he established an advanced HQ in the German lines, and from where he carried out fine work under shell fire. During the early hours of 11 May he and another officer from the battalion rallied a group of men and then led them in a counter-attack, despite the fact that the enemy was using flame throwers. Having made the counter-attack, he withdrew the men to a suitable defensive position. Later on, he led his men in another counter-attack, re-gaining all the ground that had been lost, but he was killed just as the operation was reaching its conclusion. (Plot VIII.B.21)

Major John Francis COSTIGAN, 50th Battalion, Canadian Infantry, was killed in action on 10 April 1917 (Plot X.A.12). His battalion was not involved in the attack at Vimy Ridge on 9 April, but it did go into action the following day near Hill 145 where there were still some enemy positions to be cleared up. He was in command of the assault parties on the left flank of his battalion's front for the attack, which began at 3.15pm. The objectives were quickly taken and consolidated, but casualties were heavy and amounted to eleven officers, five of whom were killed, and over 200 other ranks. A newspaper report in Calgary claimed that COSTIGAN was killed attacking a German gun battery with his revolver, though the battalion's war diary for that day does not go into any details regarding his death. He does not appear to be directly related to Captain Charles Telford Costigan DSO MC who was killed in action in November 1917 and who is buried at Passchendaele New British Cemetery.

Major Anthony Lavelle McHUGH, 3rd Battalion, Canadian Railway Troops, was killed in action on 19 May 1917, aged 53. He had worked on the railways back in Canada before the war and no doubt his experience and knowledge proved very useful while he was serving in France. His middle name is shown as 'Larelle' in the CWGC register. (Plot X.B.1)

Lieutenant Norman Howard PAWLEY MC, 44th Battalion, Canadian Infantry, was killed in action on 12 April 1917 (Plot V.E.4). His MC was awarded for gallantry during a raid on enemy trenches in which he led his party with great dash, personally capturing an enemy machine gun. Having done so, he then detailed a prisoner to bring the gun back to our lines. The machine gun was one of four taken by his battalion, together with three trench mortars and seventy-seven prisoners. The award was gazetted on 23 March 1917. He was killed in action during his battalion's attack on the small hillock at the northern end of Vimy Ridge, known as 'The Pimple.' He also held a Bachelor of Science degree in Agriculture.

Lieutenant Reginald Perry CATTELL MC, 46th Battalion, Canadian Infantry, was killed in action on 6 May 1917. Although the battalion's war diary is very detailed, it makes no mention of Lieutenant CATTELL's death on 6 May. It does, however, refer to him on 8 May, but only in a summary of casualties for that tour of duty and merely notes that he was killed. His MC was awarded for conspicuous gallantry and devotion to duty in organizing and leading a successful raid on enemy trenches during which his party managed to destroy a mine shaft and inflict many casualties. His citation refers to other occasions when he had carried out fine work, but does not go into specific detail. The award was gazetted on 9 March 1917. (Plot V.J.2)

Private Robert Lauchlan GREENS, 85th Battalion, Canadian Infantry, was killed in action on 10 April 1917, aged 17 (Plot VII.J.6). He and his father, Lance Corporal John Greens, served in the same battalion. His father was killed in action the day before him on the opening day of the Battle of Arras and is now commemorated on the Vimy Memorial. Robert would probably have known of his father's death, or at least known that he was missing in action.

Private Donald NEALE, 46th Battalion, Canadian Infantry, was killed in action on 20 June 1917 (Plot VIII.D.14). His brother, George Neale, had been killed in action a few months earlier on 13 April whilst serving with the same battalion. George, who was 25 years old when he died, also happens to be buried in this cemetery near to his younger brother. (Plot VIII.A.5)

Lieutenant Cyril George HUGGINS, 102nd Battalion, Canadian Infantry, was badly wounded by a rifle grenade and died on 14 May 1917, despite being taken to the dressing station for treatment. Ten other men from the battalion were wounded that day. He was clearly held in very high regard, as the battalion war diary notes his death as a 'very heavy loss'. (Plot IX.B.7)

Lieutenant James Stuart RODGERSON, 102nd Battalion, Canadian Infantry, was killed in action on 13 May 1917 when the section of front line trench he and his men were holding came under very heavy fire from high explosive shells. Fifteen other ranks were also wounded during the bombardment. (Plot IX.B.8)

Lieutenant Caspar de Freitaz WEST, 102nd Battalion, Canadian Infantry, was mortally wounded on 12 May 1917. The war diary notes that shelling was heavy and that the bombardment included gas shells. Lieutenant WEST was wounded in the head by a shell fragment and died two hours later. (Plot IX.B.9)

Captain Lewis Emerson CLARK, Canadian Army Medical Corps, was killed in action on 8 June 1917. He had previously been mentioned in despatches and was killed serving with No. 2 Field Ambulance, though he had previously served with the 34th and 87th Battalions. He was born in Kansas, but lived in Canada. The war diary for the 2nd Field Ambulance makes no mention of his death. (Plot IX.C.17)

Lieutenant George LOWRIE, 102nd Battalion, Canadian Infantry, was killed in action on 8 June 1917 during local operations aimed at securing an area known as The Triangle. It was the site of a strongpoint that included a concrete machine-gun post set in the embankment of a railway and the whole position was well pro-tected by strong wire. This defensive system had been attacked the previous day, but had resisted all attempts to capture it. Although it was captured by LOWRIE and his men on 8 June and handed over to the 5th Leicestershire Regiment, The Triangle was lost the following morning during the early hours when the enemy launched a counter-attack. These operations were carried out at a time when German attention was firmly focused on the Battle of Messines, which began on 7 June well north of this location on the Belgian side of the border. Although timed to catch the enemy off guard, the Germans defending The Triangle proved to be very capable and very determined fighters. (Plot IX.C.19)

Lieutenant John Ernest NORWOOD, 102nd Battalion, Canadian Infantry, was also killed on 8 June 1917 during the same attack in which Lieutenant LOWRIE fell. He was 41 years old and had previously served in the South African campaign. (Plot IX.C.18)

There are three more majors buried here who died during the summer months while holding the new line that had been won during the previous few months of hard fighting.

Major William Robert GREEN, 'A' Company, 44th Battalion, Canadian Infantry, was killed in action on 3 June 1917, aged 27 (Plot VIII.C.14). Before the war he practised as a barrister. The operation in which he was killed was carried out near La Coulotte and resulted in little material gain, though the intelligence gathered proved useful. It concluded that the enemy's front trench was in good condition, that the majority of his dug-outs were also in good shape and that his front line contained plenty of accommodation, which was a good indication of the size of the garrison. However, casualties were high relative to the results obtained from the raid; two officers were killed, as were twenty-seven other ranks; seven officers were wounded, one of whom subsequently died, as were 138 other ranks, and a further two officers and seventy-five other ranks were also missing in action. The officer who died of wounds, Lieutenant Tully Wallace Anderson, is buried at Barlin Communal Cemetery Extension, several miles west of Lens. A few of the battalion's casualties from that attack are buried here.

Major Horace Greeley BAKER, 46th Battalion, Canadian Infantry, was killed in action on 20 August 1917, aged 29, during a period of trench duty near Liévin. The lines of both sides ran through ruined buildings and a great deal of patrolling took place during which various posts were alternately occupied and then vacated. Much effort went into locating these shifting posts and patrolling was always hazardous. Small raids took place from time to time and locations believed to be held by the other side were frequently shelled. The war diary makes no specific reference to the manner of BAKER's death, but as an officer he would probably have visited the posts and may even have carried out personal reconnaissance of the enemy's positions. Sniping was a constant threat. (Plot IX.F.6)

Major Reginald William DAVIS, 75th Battalion, Canadian Infantry, died of wounds on 2 July 1917, aged 30. The battalion war diary notes that he was wounded on 27 June in Zouave Valley, but it does not elaborate further. (Plot X.D.19)

There are a number of interesting graves and quite a few gallantry awards among those Canadians who fell between June 1917 and the end of the year.

Private Alexander BIGMAN is buried here under his anglicised name, but his original name was Alexander BIG MAN, another of the Native Americans who fought with the Canadian Expeditionary Force. He was also known as Alexander MISTEYENEW at home in Canada where he was a bookkeeper. He was killed in action on 6 February 1917 while serving with the 46th Battalion, Canadian Infantry. (Plot V.B.10)

Private Joseph CROW, 46th Battalion, Canadian Infantry, came from the Cote Reserve and was also a Canadian Native American soldier. He was killed in action by a shell on 22 March 1917. He was one of two men killed that day whilst attached to the 10th Field Company, Canadian Engineers, near Carency, probably as part of a working party. The other man killed was Private Arnold Douglas HARVEY and both men are now buried next to each other (Plot VII.F.1 and 2).

Private John Patrick STARINSKY, 54th Battalion, Canadian Infantry, was killed in action on 6 September 1917, aged 17 (Plot XI.A.2). At the other end of the age spectrum, Private Arthur Herbert CHARMAN, 47th Battalion, Canadian Infantry, was killed in action on 2 June 1917, aged 50 (Plot X.B.10). The following day, Private Alfred Henry BENNETT, was also killed in action. He served in the same battalion as CHARMAN, and was also 50 years old when he died (Plot VIII.C.7).

Private Charles SHAFFER, 44th Battalion, Canadian Infantry, was killed in action on 2 June 1917, aged 35. He was an American citizen, who like a number of his countrymen, went over the border to Canada in order to enlist. He was reported to be the first man from Williamson County, Illinois, to lose his life in the Great War. (Plot VIII.C.18)

Captain Percival MOLSON MC, Princess Patricia's Canadian Light Infantry, was killed in action on 5 July 1917. He was the son of Thomas Molson of Montreal and was a member of the well-known Molson family, which was involved in banking and the brewing industry. He was a very good athlete and had studied at McGill University in Montreal. He was out walking with a fellow officer, Lieutenant Donald McLean, when a shell exploded, killing him instantly. His death is described in the memoir: *Ghosts Have Warm Hands* by Will Bird, who did not actually witness the incident, but clearly heard the trench mortar bomb as it exploded on the cobblestones. Lieutenant McLean had his leg blown off in the explosion, but was still conscious, and was found holding the stump in an attempt to reduce the bleeding when Bird emerged from a nearby cellar. MOLSON was wounded near Sanctuary Wood on 2 June 1916. His MC was gazetted on 4 June 1917 and was awarded in the King's Birthday Honours List. (Plot VIII.E.1)

Private Colin Campbell MACDONALD, 87th Battalion, Canadian Infantry, was killed in action on 29 July 1917, aged 20. He was the son of Lieutenant Colonel Ronald St. John Macdonald, Canadian Army Medical Corps, attached to the 9th Stationary Hospital. This medical unit was formed in March 1916 and was based at Saint Omer between December 1917 and April 1918. After that, it moved to Étaples where it remained until September 1918. Its final location was at Camiers between September 1918 and the end of May 1919 and it was eventually disbanded in 1920. (Plot IX.E.5)

Captain James Watt LOWE MC, 46th Battalion, Canadian Infantry, was killed in action on 21 August 1917. His MC was awarded for gallantry in action after displaying great courage and determination as he led his men in an attack. He later consolidated the new position under the most trying conditions. The award was gazetted on 9 January 1917. (IX.F.7)

Company Sergeant Major George William DURRAN DCM MM, 4th Battalion, Canadian Infantry, was killed in action on 17 December 1917. His DCM was awarded after he went out from an advanced post and cut away the wire in front of an advanced post belonging to the enemy. Although it was becoming daylight and he was under heavy sniper fire, he carried out this task with great courage until the whole of the wire had been dragged back to our post and added to its defences. Both awards were announced several months after his death. His DCM was gazetted on 17 April 1918, and his MM a month earlier on 13 March 1918. (Plot XIII.A.9)

Though predominantly Canadian in character, the cemetery also contains sixty-six British casualties from 1917, some of whom are worthy of note.

Captain the Honourable Lawrence Ughtred KAY-SHUTTLEWORTH, 'D' Battery, 11 Brigade, Royal Field Artillery, was killed in action on 30 March 1917 (Plot VII.G.12). He was the eldest son of 1st Baron Shuttleworth. His brother, Captain the Honourable Edward James Kay-Shuttleworth, died on 10 July 1917, aged 27, while serving on the staff of 218 Infantry Brigade, to which he was attached from the 7th Rifle Brigade. This brigade belonged to the 73rd Division, which was one of three that were created in 1916 for Home Defence and training purposes. It was disbanded in April 1918. He was the youngest son and was educated at Eton, and then at Balliol College, Oxford, where he gained a Bachelor of Arts degree. He is buried in the United Kingdom at Barbon (St. Bartholomew's) Churchyard in Westmorland.

Buried there with him in the Shuttleworth family plot is Major Coleridge Eustace Hills, the son of Gilbert Hills KC, and the Honourable Mrs Nina Louisa Hills. Major Hills was another Old Etonian and former Exhibitioner at King's College, Cambridge. He was the grandson of the 1st Baron Shuttleworth. He fell while serving in the Second World War with the Royal Army Service Corps. Also buried there is Lieutenant Edward Derek Walter Leaf, DSC and Bar, Royal Naval Volunteer Reserve, who died on 15 February 1944, aged 25. He was the son of Lieutenant Charles Symonds Leaf, Royal Marines, who was a Gold Medal winner in sailing at the 1936 Olympic Games in Berlin.

During the Second World War the Shuttleworth family continued to serve its country and two of Captain Lawrence's sons fell. Flying Officer Richard Ughtred Paul Kay-Shuttleworth, 145 Squadron, Royal Air Force Volunteer Reserve, was killed in action on 8 August 1940. He held the title as 2nd Baron Shuttleworth of Gawthorpe for only eight months and is now commemorated on the Runnymede Memorial. He was succeeded by Lawrence's other son, Captain Ronald Orlando Lawrence Kay-Shuttleworth, 3rd Baron, who was killed in action on 17 November 1942, aged 25, serving with the 138th Field Regiment, Royal Artillery. He is buried at Tabarka Ras Rajel War Cemetery in Tunisia.

Company Serjeant Major Thomas CLEAVER, 14th Royal Warwickshire Regiment, died of wounds on 9 May 1917, aged 42. The CWGC register notes that he was awarded the Long Service and Good Conduct Medal. (Plot VIII.B.10)

Second Lieutenant Robert CAMERON, 16 Squadron, Royal Flying Corps, died of wounds on 4 June 1917 (Plot VIII.C.5). He is one of three men of the Royal Flying Corps buried here. CAMERON's observer, Second Lieutenant Sidney Herbert Inglis, died from his injures the following day and is buried at Barlin Communal Cemetery Extension.

Lieutenant the Honourable Charles Willoughby Murray MOLESWORTH, 1st Duke of Cornwall's Light Infantry, died of wounds on 15 April 1917, aged 19. He was badly wounded while carrying out a reconnaissance in no man's land to inspect the enemy's wire and positions. He was the son of the 9th Viscount Molesworth. Robert Molesworth, father of the 1st Viscount, was a supporter of Oliver Cromwell during his campaigns in Ireland. His son, the 1st Viscount, another Robert Molesworth, also championed the Protestant cause in Ireland as a supporter of William of Orange. He went on to become William III's ambassador in Denmark and a member of the Privy Council in Dublin. (Plot IX.A.13)

Private Harold George CARTER, 73rd Battalion, Canadian Infantry, was executed on 20 April 1917, aged 21. He was already under a suspended sentence of ten years imprisonment when he went missing for a second time. He received no second chance at his subsequent trial on 5 April. (Plot X.A.7)

Second Lieutenant Cecil McKenzie PAYNE, 16 Squadron, Royal Flying Corps, was killed in action on 21 September 1917 (Plot XI.A.19). PAYNE's observer that day, Second Lieutenant N.E. Wallace, was injured, but survived. PAYNE was a Canadian pilot and it is somehow fitting that he should be buried here with so many of his fellow countrymen. He never served with the Canadian Expeditionary Force, which is why he is shown in the CWGC records as serving in the Royal Flying Corps. Canadian airmen who had previously served with the Expeditionary Force are always shown in the CWGC records as serving in their former capacity.

Second Lieutenant William Patrick GARNETT, 60 Squadron, Royal Flying Corps, was killed in action flying a Nieuport 17 single-seater aircraft on 30 March 1917, aged 22. The Royal Flying Corps communiqué for that day contains very little information regarding aerial activity on the Western Front. However, the day after his death, 60 Squadron was in action and very busy near Arras where it scored a number of victories. (Plot XI.D.19)

1918

Canadian burials here from the final year of the war are relatively few, just thirty-three. However, there are individuals among them who may be of interest.

Lieutenant Colonel Heber Havelock MOSHIER, 11th Field Ambulance, Canadian Army Medical Corps, was killed in action on 29 August 1918

(Plot XII.C.1). He had been with the unit since spring 1916 and had served with it on the Somme. He was also in the field during fighting at Vimy Ridge, Lens and at Passchendaele, and in April 1918 he was mentioned in despatches. His death occurred near Wancourt whilst going forward to reconnoitre a suitable position for an advanced dressing station. At the outbreak of war he was Professor of Physiology at the University of Alberta. He and a number of students from the Faculty of Medicine in Alberta volunteered to serve in the Canadian Army Medical Corps and were posted to 11th Field Ambulance. The unit then went to France in March 1916. The first of the student volunteers from the University of Alberta to die in action was Staff Sergeant John Ralph HAMMOND, who was killed on 26 June 1917 by a shell while leading a group of men up the line to the front. He is also buried here at Villers Station Cemetery (Plot X.D.12).

Private Edward FAIRBURN, 18th Battalion, Canadian Infantry, was executed by firing squad on 2 March 1918. He was a company runner; on 16 April 1917 he went missing and remained at large until the end of January the following year. He was tried ten days later while his battalion was out of the line at Camblain l'Abbé, found guilty, and executed three weeks later. (Plot XI.B.21)

Captain Hugh Stowell PEDLEY MC, 85th Battalion, Canadian Infantry, attached 12th Canadian Light Trench Mortar Battery, was killed in action near Lens on 31 January 1918, aged 30. His MC was gazetted on 28 December 1917 and was awarded as part of the New Year's Honours List. He was the cousin of Lieutenant James H. Pedley MC, who served with the 4th Battalion, Canadian Infantry, and who went on to publish a memoir of the war, *Only This*. (Plot XI.B.21)

Captain Edwin SINTON MC, Royal Field Artillery, was a cinema manager in Belfast before the war. He had also fought in the South African campaign, and had even served in East Africa with the Camel Corps. Prior to his commission in the Royal Field Artillery he served as a trooper in the North Irish Horse where his previous military experience was soon recognized and led to his promotion to serjeant. He was killed in action on 21 August 1918, aged 35. His MC was gazetted on 16 September 1918 and was awarded for conspicuous gallantry and devotion to duty whilst under very heavy shelling, setting a fine example of cheerfulness and disregard of danger, and providing great assistance in evacuating railway stock. The citation states that he then continued to maintain traffic until the enemy's advance had reached a point where further work became impossible. (Plot XI.C.19)

Captain John Onion SLAGHT MC, 38th Battalion, Canadian Infantry, was killed in action on 16 March 1918, aged 31. His MC was won for his untiring work in maintaining the ammunition supply and evacuating the wounded. The citation continues by stating that, after carrying out a reconnaissance of the front line, he brought up his company in support of the battalion to which he was attached under difficult conditions and heavy shell fire. The citation concludes that the fine example he set to those under his command did much to maintain morale under the most difficult of conditions. (Plot XII.B.1)

Private Stephen McDermott FOWLES, 44th Battalion, Canadian Infantry, was executed by firing squad on 19 June 1918. He was already under a suspended sentence of death when he deserted for the third time in just over two years of military service. He was shot near Villers-au-Bois. (Plot XIII.B.1)

The forty-eight British casualties from 1918 are mainly from July and belonged to battalions of the 20th (Light) Division, particularly the 12th King's Regiment (Liverpool), the 7th Duke of Cornwall's Light Infantry and the 2nd Rifle Brigade. The majority are NCOs or privates, or equivalent ranks. There is, however, a group of six officers from the 3rd Rifle Brigade buried together, all of whom were killed in action or were mortally wounded on 22 May 1918 when a bomb was dropped from a German aircraft.

One of them is Second Lieutenant Edmund Nicholas PRIDEAUX-BRUNE, 3rd Rifle Brigade, attached 13th Battalion, who was 19 years old when he died. His father, Colonel Charles Robert Prideaux-Brune, also served with the Rifle Brigade and his mother, Cecilia Knatchbull-Hugessen, was the daughter of 1st Lord Brabourne. Edmund was the youngest of three sons and was born in Welwyn, Hertfordshire. He and his family subsequently moved to Prideaux Place, near Padstow in Cornwall, which had been the ancestral seat since the late 16th century. He had been Page of Honour to the Earl of Liverpool at the Coronation of King George V and the family was socially well-connected. He was also a promising musician and several of his own compositions were published. He was gazetted in the Rifle Brigade in September 1917 and had been in France for barely a month when he was killed. (Plot XII.B.16)

His eldest brother, Captain Denys Edward Prideaux-Brune, DSO and Bar, was wounded in March 1918 while organizing and carrying out a fighting retreat with the Rifle Brigade. The bar to his DSO was awarded in recognition of his conduct during that testing period. He was taken prisoner, but survived the war.

The middle brother, Fulke Knatchbull Prideaux-Brune, 6th (Inniskilling) Dragoons, was also wounded and taken prisoner in March 1918 near Abbécourt. Although he was repatriated in October 1918, he died in 1939 from complications connected to his wounds, one of which was a head wound caused by a shell fragment. He suffered paralysis from the waist downwards, though he did eventually recover some power over his bodily functions. Injuries to his arms left him with tremors and he suffered badly from conjunctivitis in his left eye for the rest of his life. The Knatchbull-Hugessen side of the family was associated with the Grenadier Guards and two of its members fell during the war.

The other officers buried with Second Lieutenant PIDEAUX-BRUNE are Lieutenant Basil Howard BAKER, aged 21; Lieutenant Alfred Herbert Bathurst MARSHALL, aged 22; Lieutenant Leonard BELL, aged 26; Second Lieutenant Reginald MINTY, aged 37, and Second Lieutenant Alexander Harold Percival LEITCH, aged 24. (Plot XII.B.14 to 19)

Private Frank BATEMAN, 1/4th York and Lancaster Regiment, had served on the Western Front since the middle of June 1915. He was wounded in 1916, but returned to the front once he had recovered and was posted to the 1/5th Battalion. The following year he went missing and received a custodial sentence at his trial, but that sentence was suspended. He was then returned to England suffering from what was believed to have been a self-inflicted wound. Once back at the front, this time with his old battalion, the 1/4th Battalion, he again went absent. He was tried and sentenced to fifteen years imprisonment, which was again suspended. In July 1918 he deserted for a third time, and not surprisingly, on this occasion he was sentenced to death. The sentence was carried out on 10 September 1918. He was 28 years old when he died. (Plot XII.C.4)

Reference has already been made to three of the twenty-one holders of the MM. The remaining eighteen are as follows:

Gunner Thomas George STYLES MM, Royal Field Artillery, killed in action on 17 November 1916. (Plot III.B.8)

Sergeant Paul Angus MACGILLIVRAY MM, 4th Canadian Division Signal Company, Canadian Signal Corps, killed in action on 4 February 1917. Around that time, he and his comrades were engaged laying new cable from Carency to the front line. On 1 February the war diary notes that ninety miles of cable had already been buried 7 feet deep. There is no indication of how Sergeant MAC-GILLIVRAY died, though the most likely cause was shelling. However, the diary records that another man, Corporal George Alfred Keen, was badly wounded the same day and died the following day from his injuries. Keen is buried at Lapugnoy Military Cemetery. (Plot V.B.8)

Corporal Richard RAINFORD MM, 38th Battalion, Canadian Infantry, killed in action on 9 April 1917. (Plot V.F.4)

Private Edwin OLSON MM, 46th Battalion, Canadian Infantry, killed in action on 6 May 1917. (Plot V.J.5)

Lance Corporal Thomas Percy WOODWARD MM, 'B' Company, 72nd Battalion, Canadian Infantry, killed in action on 3 March 1917, aged 22. (Plot VI.E.18)

Sergeant James Errol KNOX MM, 78th Battalion, Canadian Infantry, died on 1 March 1917, aged 27, probably as a result of wounds. His battalion was out of the line that day and its war diary notes that the men spent part their time bathing at Gouy-Servins. However, it had recently been involved in two brief raids near Kennedy Crater during the last week of February. The first raid, which took place on 19 February, had incurred twenty-four casualties after a fierce encounter with a party of the enemy in a sap. Nine of the twenty-four were killed, including Sergeant Lloyd. Lloyd had hurled a mobile explosive charge into a mine shaft and, unknown to him and the others, the shaft contained a quantity of high explosives. The explosion that followed not only killed Lloyd, but also created a new crater, which was subsequently known as 'Winnipeg Crater'.

The war diary recalls how a few days later, on 23 February, the battalion launched a repeat assault on the same location, which had two aims; firstly, to avenge the deaths from the previous raid, and secondly, to try to recover the dead from that raid. The renewed attack lasted just ten minutes and was deemed successful; casualties came to just eight men, all of whom received only slight wounds. The Germans did retaliate by putting down an artillery bombardment the same day, which caused some further casualties. It is not recorded how KNOX received his wounds, but he eventually died while undergoing treatment for them near Villers-au-Bois. (Plot VII.D.19)

Lance Sergeant Hervé Joseph CHENIER MM, 73rd Battalion, Canadian Infantry, killed in action on 28 March 1917. (Plot VII.G.22)

Corporal John Robert DUNCAN MM, 73rd Battalion, Canadian Infantry, killed in action on 28 March 1917. (Plot VII.G.27)

Lieutenant Percy Roach SAWTELL MM and Bar, 'D' Company, 50th Battalion, Canadian Infantry, killed in action on 21 June 1917, aged 27. His MM was gazetted on 19 February 1917. By the time his commission was announced in the *London Gazette* on 28 June 1917 he was dead, although it had taken effect from 7 May. The bar to his MM was gazetted posthumously on 9 July that year. He was born in Somerset, but later moved to Canada, settling in the Calgary area where he was involved working with horses. He enlisted on New Year's Eve 1914. His entire military service was spent with the 50th Battalion. (Plot VIII.D.9)

Corporal Reginald Heber RIBTON MM, 18th Battalion, Canadian Infantry, killed in action on 9 July 1917. He had enlisted back in October 1914 and had been in France since September 1915. (Plot VIII.E.4)

Private Michael SLATTERY MM, 87th Battalion, Canadian Infantry; killed in action on 14 August 1917, aged 20. His brother, Lieutenant Edward Slattery DCM MM and Bar, was killed in action on 30 August 1918 and is buried in Valley Cemetery, Vis-en-Artois. (Plot VIII.F.1)

Private Maurice Camden JORDAN MM, 46th Battalion, Canadian Infantry, killed in action on 21 August 1917. (Plot VIII.F.15)

Private John Ambrose MOGRIDGE MM, 50th Battalion, Canadian Infantry, killed in action on 3 June 1917. (Plot IX.C.2)

Private William Kinnear LESLIE MM, 102nd Battalion, Canadian Infantry, killed in action on 5 June 1917. (IX.C.3)

Sergeant Albert HILLARD MM, 75th Battalion, Canadian Infantry, killed in action on 14 June 1917. (Plot X.C.12)

Private Robert BROWN MM, 13th Battalion, Canadian Infantry, killed in action on 26 December 1917. (Plot XI.B.2)

Corporal Harry HOLMES MM, 78th Battalion, Canadian Infantry, killed in action on 30 March 1918, aged 36. (Plot XII.B.7)

Rifleman John TRACY MM, 2nd Battalion, Rifle Brigade, died of wounds on 1 August 1918. (Plot XIII.B.14)

Finally, the CWGC register shows just one casualty from 1919: Private Thomas Henry LAKE, 72nd Battalion, Canadian Infantry, who died on 1 March 1919, aged 20 (Plot VI.D.9). However, this is almost certainly a typographical error. His Canadian army record indicates that he died on 1 March 1917, almost certainly in the abortive raid that took place that day at the northern end of Vimy Ridge. There are, in fact, no 1919 casualties buried in this cemetery.

Chapter Six

The Man Who Made it on Broadway –
Tragedy on a Windy Night –
A Classic Overcoat

Duisans British Cemetery, Étrun

The cemetery is easy to find and lies just off the main Arras–Saint-Pol road, the D.939. It is clearly visible about 250 yards to the west of the main road in open fields. It will be obvious where to turn off, but the roundabout at the junction of the D.939 and the D.56 is the most appropriate point. After making the turn, just keep bearing right, and the cemetery is about 600 yards further on. This road is actually the D.339 rather than the D.56. The cemetery is roughly half way between the villages of Étrun and Agnez-les-Duisans and both locations were used for billeting and other purposes throughout the war.

This is a large cemetery and contains just over 3,200 identified casualties, though the initial impression suggests far fewer. From March 1916 this area was used extensively by our troops when out of the line, but in February 1917, in preparation for the Battle of Arras, the 8th Casualty Clearing Station set up adjacent to the current cemetery. It was followed in July that year by the 41st Casualty Clearing Station, then by a succession of others through to 1920. Canadian Casualty Clearing Stations No. 1 and No. 4 were also located here during the autumn of 1918. The cemetery is set out in a triangular form and broadens immediately beyond the arched entrance. It was designed by Sir Reginald Blomfield. The stonework around the entrance still bears the damage from the brief fighting that took place in this area in May 1940, when British and French troops tried to delay the German advance.

Given the size of the cemetery, there are relatively few gallantry awards beyond the eighty-two holders of the MM who are buried here. There are just six holders of the DSO, sixteen with the MC, and three with the DCM. There is also one man who held the MSM. Three of the men with the MM also won a bar to their original medal. I have not listed the MM holders on account of the sheer number. There are also eighty-eight German graves here from the Great War.

After passing through the archway at the entrance to the cemetery, a walk along Plot III will soon reveal how the chronological sequence of burials seems to run in alternate rows. Row D contains burials from 23, 24 and 25 April 1917; Row E contains burials dated 10, 11, 12 April; dates in Row F cover 25, 26 and 27 April; Row G 10, 11, 12 and 13 April 1917, and so it continues. This pattern can also be seen in the adjacent Plot IV.

Plot V, Rows A and B contain casualties from the 12th (Eastern) Division who died of wounds here between July and September 1917 when it was occupying the front line trenches and posts opposite Infantry Hill, east of Monchy-le-Preux. The Battle of Arras was over and the main fighting had moved north to Ypres, but the fighting here was still some of the most savage and relentless on the Western Front.

Captain Arthur Haldane STEEDMAN, 10th Cameronians, died of wounds on 30 March 1917 whilst commanding 'B' Company. He was badly wounded in the back by shell fragments from own artillery barrage whilst taking part in an attack on an enemy position on 24 March 1917 and died six days later. He was married and lived in Regent's Park Road, London. (Plot I.D.2)

Air Mechanic 2nd Class, Alfred Maurice KING, 9 Squadron, Royal Flying Corps, attached 47 Brigade, Royal Field Artillery, is one of several men here who died on active service from illness rather than enemy action. He died of pneumonia on 22 November 1917. (Plot I.G.4)

Bombardier Oliver Cromwell DUBOIS DCM, D Battery, 15 Brigade, Royal Field Artillery, had also been previously mentioned in despatches. He died of wounds on 9 April 1917, aged 28. His award was gazetted on 16 November 1915 while he was serving with the 460th (Howitzer) Battery, Royal Field Artillery. It was awarded for conspicuous gallantry and resource on 6 August 1915 at Cape Helles during the Gallipoli campaign after he had spent four hours repairing telephone wires under exceptionally heavy shell fire, carrying out his work efficiently and effectively. Previously, on 28 April, when sent to the French firing line with a message, he had collected a wounded Frenchman on his return and then carried him to the nearest dressing station, all of which was performed under heavy rifle fire. The citation concludes that throughout the campaign he had distinguished himself for his bravery under fire and his devotion to duty. (Plot I.N.5)

Second Lieutenant William Gardner BENZIE, 8th Cameronians, attached 10th Battalion, is shown in the CWGC records as dying on 9 April 1917, aged 33. *Officers Died in the Great War* indicates that he died of wounds the following day. He was certainly wounded with his battalion on the 9th near Feuchy during the advance by the 15th (Scottish) Division. Canadian army records indicate that he had previously served with the Transvaal Horse Artillery, presumably in the South African War, and that he had also served with a draft company of the 47th Battalion, Canadian Infantry, followed by a spell with the 72nd Battalion (Seaforth Highlanders of Canada). He enlisted in Canada in March 1915, but at some point decided to join what would have been one of his local regiments, the Cameronians. His family came from Glasgow. (Plot II.H.3)

Second Lieutenant Herbert Hamilton HAIG-SMELLIE, 7th Norfolk Regiment, died of wounds on 26 April 1917, aged 39. The battalion had returned to the line the previous day and a number of casualties were sustained, mainly as a result of sniper and machine-gun fire rather than shelling. The battalion was in trenches just north of Monchy-le-Preux when he died. (Plot II.M.9)

Company Quartermaster Serjeant Albert BECKINGHAM MM, 'B' Company, 7th Rifle Brigade, was killed in action on 16 April 1917, aged 37. He had also been mentioned in despatches and was a time-expired veteran of the British Army who re-enlisted on the outbreak of war. He is one of several veterans buried here, some of whom served during the South African campaign. (Plot III.B.7)

Second Lieutenant William Francis PADDOCK, 4th Battalion, Royal Fusiliers, was wounded in action on the opening day of the Battle of Arras, 9 April 1917, aged 22, and died the same day (Plot III.C.2). The family inscription on his headstone reads: '*Until the barrage lifts*'. He had served in the trenches prior to returning home to England where he underwent officer training. Once he had received his commission he returned to the front in January 1917. His battalion was making good progress around The Harp on the opening day of the Battle of Arras, but then two German machine guns began to cause casualties, holding up the advance. As he was organizing his platoon to deal with them he was shot by a sniper and wounded. He was evacuated from the battlefield but died the same day. His grandfather had served in the Royal Navy during the Crimean War.

Captain John Hugh MATHESON MC, 6th Gordon Highlanders, died of wounds on 24 April 1917. His MC was gazetted on 12 January 1917. It was awarded for conspicuous gallantry, leading his men with great courage and deter-mination and capturing an enemy officer and thirty-four other prisoners whilst clearing enemy trenches. Although the location is not referred to in the citation, it is obvious on reading the various entries in the *Gazette* that the events occurred on 13 November 1916 at Beaumont Hamel. (Plot III.D.26)

Second Lieutenant Charles Arthur Boileau ELLIOTT, 1st Somerset Light Infantry, died of wounds on 12 April 1917, aged 24. He had served with the 1/4th Norfolk Regiment at Gallipoli in 1915 and also in Egypt in 1916. (Plot III.E.32)

Lieutenant Colonel CARTWRIGHT DSO, 1st Royal Marine Light Infantry, died of wounds on 30 April 1917. His DSO was awarded for conspicuous gal-lantry in action between 13 and 15 November 1916 during the Battle of the Ancre, which marked the final phase of fighting on the Somme that year. When the attack was held up by heavy machine-gun and rifle fire, he went forward and re-organized the mixed parties of men from different units, pushing the attack forward to its objective under his personal supervision. The operations on 29 April 1917, during which Lieutenant Colonel Cartwright was mortally wounded, resulted in the capture of enemy positions around Gavrelle Windmill. During the advance his battalion was held up by German wire and came under heavy enfilade fire from a strongpoint on the railway embankment. The 7th Royal Fusiliers had been held up by the same enemy position a week earlier on 23 April when units of the 63rd (Royal Naval) Division managed to secure a line through Gavrelle village. The 1st Royal Marine Light Infantry not only lost its commanding officer in the attack on the 29th, it also suffered around 500 casualties, including six other officers. The 2nd Royal Marine Light Infantry, which also attacked that day, sustained some 600 casualties, of which ten officers and over 200 other ranks were killed in action or died of wounds. (Plot III.H.53)

Second Lieutenant John Howard WESTLAKE, 12 Squadron, Royal Flying Corps, died from injuries on 7 May 1917, aged 19, whilst acting as observer in a BE2d aircraft. His injuries occurred on 29 April, a week before his death. His pilot that day, Second Lieutenant Cyril John Pile, was also killed when their machine crashed and is now buried at Feuchy Chapel British Cemetery. Like WESTLAKE, he was 19 years old when he died. They were shot down in aerial combat by Lothar von Richthofen who went on to score a total of forty victories. Although Lother survived the war, he died in a flying accident in 1922. Pile's brother, Sir Frederick Alfred Pile, 2nd Baronet, served throughout the Great War from 1914 and went on to command Britain's anti-aircraft defences during the Second World War. Their father was Sir Thomas Devereux Pile, 1st Baronet, a former Lord Mayor of Dublin. (Plot III.K.57)

Captain John Eustace FIENNES, 2nd Gordon Highlanders, was born in August 1895, the only son of the Honourable Sir Eustace Fiennes, 1st Baronet and MP for Banbury in Oxfordshire. His mother was the Honourable Lady Fiennes OBE. His father, who had served as Governor of the Seychelles, and then as Governor of the Leeward Islands in the British West Indies, also served as Parliamentary Private Secretary to Sir Winston Churchill during his time as First Lord of the Admiralty between 1912 and 1914. John was educated at Winchester School and Eton. In 1914 he attended the Royal Military College, Sandhurst, and went to France the same year. He was promoted to captain in 1915 and was twice wounded in action. Whilst recuperating in 1916 he was offered a staff course at Cambridge, but chose instead to return to his regiment at the front. He died on 18 June 1917 from wounds received the previous day during an attack on Infantry Hill; his death occurred just short of his 22nd birthday. On a more contemporary note, his nephew is the soldier and explorer, Sir Ranulph Fiennes. (Plot III.L.16)

Private Ellis AUSTIN, 12th York & Lancaster Regiment, died of wounds on 20 June 1917 after he was hit by shell fragments whilst carrying up rations with a group of others. He had already had a very lucky escape back in 1916 when a shell struck the parapet where he was sheltering and ended up at his feet at the bottom of the trench. Fortunately it failed to detonate. (Plot III.L.32)

Second Lieutenant Patrick Walworth GRAY, 155 Brigade, Royal Field Artillery, was wounded near Monchy-le-Preux as a result of shell fire and died on 9 May 1917. He was a student at University College, London, where he was also a member of the OTC. He was the son of Sir Albert Grey KCB KC and Lady

Gray, a Bencher of the Inner Temple and Fellow of the Royal Geographical Society. (Plot III.M.11)

Major Martin Alan ANDERSON MC, 211th Field Company, Royal Engineers, died of wounds on 9 May 1917, aged 29. His MC was gazetted on 1 January 1917 in the New Year's Honours List whilst serving as a captain. (Plot III.M.15)

Second Lieutenant Ronald Hulbert CREERY MC, 121st Siege Battery, Royal Garrison Artillery, died of wounds on 23 April 1917, aged 20. His MC was gazetted on 20 July 1917 and was awarded while carrying out duties as forward observation officer during an attack in which he went forward with the infantry and sent back valuable information that enabled several enemy batteries to be engaged by his own and other batteries. (Plot IV.A.8)

Some years ago I took the family of Private John COCHRANE to the Arras battlefields. He was wounded during the morning of 23 April 1917 when his battalion, the 7th Black Watch, made a gallant effort to reach Greenland Hill. The battalion's assembly trenches ran beside the present day cemetery at Brown's Copse. Machine-gun fire from Greenland Hill, the Chemical Works and Roeux was intense. The fact that he was brought this far back from the battlefield tends to suggest that he was either hit whilst in the trench, getting out of it, or very close in front of it. Had he been wounded closer to Greenland Hill, he would never have made it back to casualty clearing facilities that day. The machine-gun fire was so heavy and the ground so open that his rescue would have been impossible. Under those circumstances, the best he could have hoped for was a nearby shell hole where he would have had to remain until after dark. It is interesting to note that the battalion war diary makes no reference to any attempts to bring the wounded in from the open ground in front of Greenland Hill during the hours of daylight.

Private COCHRANE would have been taken to a nearby Advanced Dressing Station, at which point he was clearly still alive. After being made as comfortable as possible, he then made the bumpy ride several miles to casualty clearing facilities at Duisans where, sadly, he died later that day. The British Army had done all that it could to save him. The battalion's casualty list for that day, where he is recorded as wounded, is included in full in the war diary. Had he not been rescued and evacuated from the battlefield that morning, he would probably have been buried in Brown's Copse Cemetery or commemorated on the Arras Memorial.

He arrived in France during the winter of 1916/1917 and spent his first few months in trenches on the old Somme battlefield near Courcelette. His war was a relatively short one. He was born in Kirkintilloch in Scotland, the son of a grocer; in 1914 his sister, Margaret, married Tom Johnstone. By that time Johnstone was a well-established journalist who, in 1906 at the age of 25, had set up the *Forward* newspaper based in Glasgow. The paper was a forum for Socialist debate and ran for the next fifty years or so. He was considered a gifted writer and editor and in

1922 he entered Parliament as one of the Clydeside Group of MPs. He was author of the *History of the Working Classes in Scotland* and went on to serve as Secretary of State for Scotland under Churchill during the Second World War. (Plot IV.A.12)

Captain John Eugene CROMBIE, 4th Gordon Highlanders, died of wounds on 23 April 1917, aged 20. His father, the late John William Crombie, had served as Liberal MP for Kinkardineshire, though the family address is shown in the CWGC register as Onslow Square, South Kensington. The Crombie family had made its fortune in Scotland as woollen manufacturers and was responsible for producing the famous 'Crombie' overcoat. John attended Winchester School and was destined for Christ Church College, Oxford, when the war broke out, inter-rupting his studies. He joined the 4th Gordon Highlanders in September 1914 and went to France in January 1915. He was wounded on 23 April that year and invalided back home where he spent a lengthy time recuperating, undergoing several operations before being passed fit for active service. He eventually re-joined his battalion in November 1916. He was badly wounded on 23 April 1917 during his battalion's attack near Roeux and the Chemical Works. He also wrote poetry and had several poems published, a number of which were written while he was in France. His father also had a keen interest in poetry. (Plot IV.A.22)

Second Lieutenant Robert MILLER MC, 3rd Cameronians, attached 10th Bat-talion, who came from Edinburgh, died of wounds on 25 April 1917, aged 19. His MC was gazetted on 20 July 1917 and was awarded for conspicuous gallantry and devotion to duty, leading his men with great skill and courage under shell fire. Whilst doing so, he continually sent back valuable reports and captured four field howitzers and several prisoners. (Plot IV.E.22)

Lance Corporal Alexander McLELLAN, 9th Gordon Highlanders, died of wounds on 25 April 1917 following action two days earlier just south of the Arras–Cambrai road (Plot IV.E.25). He was one of three sons who fell during the Great War. His brother, Private David McLellan, 2nd Gordon Highlanders, was killed in action at Loos on 25 September 1915 and is commemorated on the Loos Memorial. His other brother, Serjeant Rowat McLellan, was killed in action serving with the 2nd Seaforth Highlanders on 12 June 1918 and was awarded the MM. Rowat is buried at Saint-Venant-Robecq Road British Cemetery.

Private William Samuel FAIRBRASS, 7th Field Ambulance, Royal Army Medical Corps, died of wounds on 25 April 1917, aged 30 (Plot IV.E.35). He was one of six brothers who served during the Great War, three of whom were killed. Company Serjeant Major Joseph Sydney Fairbrass, 2nd South Wales Borderers, was killed in action on 1 July 1916, aged 27, on the Somme. He is buried in 'Y' Ravine Cemetery. The other brother, Ordinary Seaman Walter Daniel Fairbrass, was much younger and died on 3 November 1918, aged 18, serving on HMS *Pembroke*, which was part of the barracks at Chatham. He is buried at Southend-on-Sea (Leigh-on-Sea) Cemetery. (Plot IV.E.35)

Lieutenant Harold Willows JACKSON, 10th East Yorkshire Regiment, originally enlisted as a private in the East Yorkshire Regiment, but was later commissioned and posted to the regiment's 4th Battalion. He died of wounds on 14 May 1917, aged just 20. (Plot IV.G.31)

Second Lieutenant James Barker BRADFORD MC, 'C' Company, 18th Durham Light Infantry, died of wounds on 14 May 1917, aged 27 (Plot IV.G.33). He was the first of the 'Bradford Brothers' to be killed during the war. He served as an able seaman in the Royal Naval Reserve for three years prior to the outbreak of war and in civilian life he had been a director of the Dinsdale Wire and Steel Works in Co. Durham. Like his sister, he was a decent musician, but was also a keen sportsman, and whilst serving as a trooper in the Northumberland Hussars he recruited several men for the unit.

It was his brother, Roland, who persuaded him in 1915 to take a commission, which he went on to do, subsequently becoming an officer in the 18th Durham Light Infantry. He married in the summer of 1916, but soon afterwards, on 1 August, he sustained gunshot wounds to the arm and right ankle and was invalided home for several months. He then returned to the front and was awarded the MC in April 1917 for conspicuous gallantry and devotion to duty near Hébuterne on the Somme, gallantly leading his men into the enemy's trench and capturing many prisoners and two machine guns. He personally killed three of the enemy and later succeeded in repelling a determined enemy counter-attack. He was wounded again on 10 May, this time receiving gunshot wounds to the left shoulder and left thigh. His injuries were serious and his condition began to deteriorate; he never recovered and died a few days later.

All four brothers served during the war. His eldest brother, Thomas Andrews Bradford DSO, was wounded at the Second Battle of Ypres and was also mentioned in despatches. He went on to become a staff captain, then a brigade major, before serving with the York & Lancaster Regiment.

George Nicholson Bradford, another of the brothers, won the VC for his courage and leadership on 23 April 1918 during the audacious raid on Zeebrugge where he was killed. He held the rank of lieutenant commander in the Royal Navy. Before the war he had shown extraordinary courage whilst serving on the destroyer, HMS *Doon*, after it collided with a Lowestoft trawler, the SS *Halcyon*. Several men were rescued, but it became apparent that a young boy was still on board and unconscious as the trawler began to sink. Bradford went back and rescued the boy just before it went under, an act every bit as brave as the one for which he was awarded his VC. He is buried at Blankenberge Town Cemetery, near Zeebrugge.

Roland Boys Bradford VC MC was killed in action on 30 November 1917 while commanding 186 Brigade, which formed part of the 62nd (West Riding) Division. A shell fragment, which had entered his back, caused a fatal wound and he died almost immediately. He had the distinction, on his promotion, of being the youngest brigadier general in the British Army. His MC and mention in despatches, both for operations and services in the field, came in 1915 whilst serving as a lieutenant with the 2nd Durham Light Infantry. His VC was gazetted on 25 November 1916 when he was a temporary lieutenant colonel commanding the 9th Durham Light Infantry. It was awarded for bravery and leadership in an attack that took place on the Somme during the fighting that autumn near Eaucourt L'Abbaye. At a critical time, and under heavy fire, he took command of another battalion, the 6th Durham Light Infantry, after its commanding officer was wounded. He then rallied the men of this battalion, as well as his own, lead-ing the attack, capturing and defending all the objectives, and securing the right flank of the brigade and divisional front. He is now buried at Hermies British Cemetery, just south of the Arras–Cambrai road.

Captain Claud Romako à Beckett TERRELL MC, 15 Brigade, Royal Horse Artillery, attached Royal Field Artillery, died of wounds on 10 June 1917, aged 33. His MC was gazetted on 20 July 1917 and was awarded for conspicuous gallantry in action as a second lieutenant. His guns were subjected to very severe shell fire and five of the six detachments were put out of action. However, with great skill and courage, he supported the infantry with his only undamaged guns whilst being still under heavy fire the whole time. (Plot IV.J.9)

Air Mechanic 2nd Class Albert James HOLT, 12 Squadron, Royal Flying Corps, died of wounds on 1 June 1917, aged 20. He was serving as a wireless operator and attached to 35th Heavy Battery, Royal Garrison Artillery, at the time of his death. (Plot IV.M.48)

Second Lieutenant Peter Cunningham ROSS, 11 Squadron, Royal Flying Corps, died of wounds on 26 June 1917 flying a Bristol F2B aircraft. He and his observer, Air Mechanic 2nd Class W. Woodward, were out on patrol with other members of their squadron when they encountered a group of ten enemy aircraft. During the ensuing fight, ROSS and Woodward engaged four of their opponents, destroying one and driving another down out of control. Unfortunately, ROSS was wounded during the fight, but managed to land his machine safely. In spite of medical attention he died later that day. (Plot IV.N.10)

Lieutenant Thomas Edgar WYLDE, 11 Squadron, Royal Flying Corps, formerly 4th Norfolk Regiment, and a native of Johannesburg, died of wounds on 27 June 1917, aged 28 (Plot IV.N.11). His younger brother, Private Paul Arthur Wylde, was killed in action on 11 April 1918 serving with the 51st Battalion, Machine Gun Corps. He has no known grave and is commemorated on the Loos Memorial.

Corporal Samuel Ferguson NISBET, 2nd King's Own Scottish Borderers, died of wounds on 2 July 1917 (Plot IV.N.40). He was one of three brothers who fell during the war. His brother, Lance Corporal James Nisbet, also served with the 2nd King's Own Scottish Borderers and was killed in action on 30 September 1918, aged 27; he is buried at Dadizeele New British Cemetery. In *Soldiers Died in the Great War* James is shown as serving with the 6th Battalion under the surname 'Nisbit'. The war memorial at Prestonpans, where the family lived, shows the name 'R.H. Nisbet' alongside the other two, but gives no further details. The CWGC records show no trace of him regardless of spelling.

Lieutenant Handley Ernest Maxwell PORTER, 13 Squadron, Royal Flying Corps, is shown serving with the 3rd (Reserve) Battalion, Canadian Infantry. He was killed in action on 18 July 1917, aged 23. He is one of thirty-six men from Powassan in Ontario who fell during the war, though little appears to be known about him or how he died. Before the war he worked as a bookkeeper. (Plot IV.O. 48)

Private Joseph Wilfred WICKS, 'D' Company, 6th Queen's (Royal West Surrey Regiment) died of wounds on 18 July 1917, aged 20 (Plot V.A.1). His father, the late Joseph Wicks, had served with the 24th Regiment of Foot in the Zulu War 1878–79 and also in the Great War with the 2/4th Queen's (Royal West Surrey Regiment). He died at home on 20 July 1921 and is buried at Oxted (St. Mary's) Churchyard, Surrey.

Lieutenant Francis Charles Erlin CLARKE, 5 Squadron, Royal Flying Corps, formerly 5th Worcestershire Regiment, died on 11 October 1917, aged 21, from wounds received in aerial combat. *Officers Died in the Great War* shows his date of death as the following day and *Airmen Died in the Great War* records that he was killed in action. Such inconsistencies are not uncommon, but the manner of his death is hardly relevant. He was probably close to death on landing and his wounds proved to be fatal; and there the matter rests. He was a pupil at King's School, Worcester. His observer that day, Lieutenant Philip MIGHELL, 5 Squadron, Royal Flying Corps, died of wounds the following day, 12 October 1917, aged 24. They are buried next to one another. (Plot V.C.6 and 7)

Lieutenant Colonel Frederick Vivian THOMPSON DSO, Royal Engineers, attached 9th Essex Regiment, died of wounds on 14 October 1917, aged 37. He had previously served in the South African War with the Royal Engineers. His DSO was gazetted on 3 June 1916 in the King's Birthday Honours List. He went overseas in 1914 serving as a major in a signalling company, followed by service as a brigade major at divisional staff level, then at army corps level. He was eventually given command of a battalion, the 9th Essex Regiment, and during his military career he was mentioned in despatches on three occasions. His father, the late Major General Charles Thompson, served in the Indian Army. (Plot V.C.16)

Second Lieutenant Thomas Pate WHITE, 7th Cameronians, attached 10th Battalion, died in somewhat unusual circumstances. His death illustrates perfectly one of the hazards faced by officers who had to visit isolated posts and sentries at night, often in total darkness. He was tragically shot by one of his own sentries and died of wounds on 17 October 1917. He was new to the battalion and had set off the previous night unaccompanied to inspect some posts in no man's land. He was not familiar with the ground and it was a very windy night, which may have made verbal communication difficult. He may not have heard the sentry challenge him or the sentry may have been taken by surprise; whatever the reason, a shot rang out and WHITE was wounded from close range by one of his men. He was taken to the casualty clearing station at Duisans, but sadly died the next day. (Plot V.C.19)

Lieutenant Malcolm Bartlett BEATTIE, 5th Royal Berkshire Regiment, died of wounds on 16 October 1917, aged 21. He was a New Zealander who had originally come to England in order to study medicine. However, he decided to enlist, postponing his plans, and was subsequently commissioned in the Royal Berkshire Regiment. He was awarded the Order of the Crown of Belgium and the Belgian *Croix de Guerre* in connection with the rescue of another man, though I have yet to discover the circumstances of this incident. (Plot V.C.23)

Private Leonard HART, 6th Queen's Own (Royal West Kent Regiment), was killed in action on 18 October 1917. The CWGC register points out that he had been the organist and choirmaster at St. Mark's Church in North Audley Street, Mayfair, London, and was a Fellow of the Royal College of Organists and an Associate of the Royal Academy of Music. (Plot V.C.24)

Private Thomas Zenis BIRDSALL, 15th West Yorkshire Regiment (1st Leeds Pals), died of wounds on 23 October 1917, aged 26 (Plot V.C.37). His surname is shown as 'Bardsall' in *Soldiers Died in the Great War*. His brother, Private Ernest William Birdsall, 10th West Yorkshire Regiment, was killed in action on 12 October 1918 and is buried at Montay-Neuvilly Road Cemetery, Montay.

Lieutenant Colonel David MacLEOD DSO, 8th Gordon Highlanders, died of pneumonia on 19 December 1917, aged 47. He previously served in Egypt where he was involved in training the Egyptian Army. He served in the Dongola Expedition in 1896 and saw action at Firket. He was also present at the Battles of Atbara and Khartoum and was mentioned in despatches on 30 September 1898 in connection with these operations. He later served in the South African War. His DSO was gazetted on 4 November 1915 and was awarded for conspicuous gallantry and devotion to duty on 25 September 1915, the opening day of the Battle of Loos. He was wounded three times during the attack on the Hohenzollern Redoubt, but still led his company forward until he collapsed from exhaustion and the effect of his wounds. (Plot V.D.49)

Second Lieutenant Joseph Guillaume Henri Pierre HAMEL, a Canadian pilot from 5 Squadron, Royal Flying Corps, was killed in action on 10 January 1918 in company with Second Lieutenant Lawrence Castell Stanley TATHAM. Their RE8 aircraft was hit by a shell over Vimy Ridge whilst carrying out observation work. TATHAM, who had been a pupil at Harrow, had wanted to serve earlier in the war, but poor health had restricted him to working with the Red Cross in England and France. However, in June 1917 he was accepted for training with the Royal Flying Corps and became an observer later that year. The two are buried next to each other. (Plot V.E.21 and 22)

Second Lieutenant George Augustine CARTER, 13 Squadron, Royal Flying Corps, and his pilot, Second Lieutenant William Kenwick NUNNERLEY, were killed in action on 5 December 1917. NUNNERLEY was 19 years old when he died and CARTER was ten years his senior. They are now buried alongside each other. (Plot V.D.24 and 25)

Lieutenant Arthur Granville De YOUNG MC, 25th Battalion, Canadian Infantry, was killed in action on 12 January 1918, aged 27, whilst seconded to the Royal Flying Corps. His MC was gazetted on 16 November 1916 and was awarded for conspicuous gallantry in action during which he assumed command of his company and handled it with great courage and initiative. He was subsequently wounded twice during that operation, but still remained on duty and was instrumental in defeating an enemy counter-attack later that day. (Plot V.E.27)

Plot V, Row F consists entirely of burials from the last week of March 1918. This was potentially a critical period for the defence of Arras when the Germans made their main effort opposite the town and to the south of it on 28 March. It was known as Operation Mars and was a vain attempt by the German Seventeenth Army to break through beyond Arras on either side of the River Scarpe where the Third Army and the First Army fronts met. In reality, and notwithstanding some heavy fighting, it barely made a dent in the line and never stood a chance of achieving its aim. The 3rd Canadian Division lost a small parcel of ground near Arleux, the 56th (London) Division lost some ground between Oppy and Gavrelle to a depth of about a mile, and the 4th Division, the 15th (Scottish) Division and the 3rd Division all lost slightly more, but not much more. Some locations, such as Monchy-le-Preux were even given up voluntarily. Operation Mars did little to assist the flagging efforts of the German Second and Eighteenth Armies further south.

Gunners Herbert HANCOCK and David EVANS served with the Howitzer Brigade, Royal Marine Artillery, and died of wounds the same day, 26 March 1918. Casualties from this unit are not particularly common on the Western Front; there are just forty-nine buried in France and fifty-five in Belgium for the entire period of the war. There is another member of the unit buried here in Plot VIII, but he died in October 1918. (Plot V.F.9 and 10)

Lieutenant Gerald Annesley George GODLEY, 15th Division Train, Army Service Corps, was mortally wounded on 26 March 1918. He was the son of Major Harry Crewe Godley DSO. His father's DSO relates to his service in the South African War, when he was in charge of a post with two companies of the Northamptonshire Regiment at Enslin railway station in September 1899. He defended the post for nine hours against a force of around 900 Boers armed with two field guns. The Boers' intention was to destroy the line held by the post and capture its stores. His post was eventually relieved by Lord Methuen's forces and the Boers withdrew having failed to achieve their objective. He died in 1907 on the Isle of Wight after twenty-three years of distinguished service. His final position was that of Deputy Assistant Adjutant-General, Jersey. (Plot V.F.15)

Driver Andrew SCOTT, who also served with the 15th Division Train, Advanced Horse Transport, Army Service Corps, also died of wounds on 26 March 1918, aged 41. He very likely arrived at the casualty clearing station with Lieutenant GODLEY. (Plot V.F.14)

Lieutenant Percy Heath ANDREWS, 151st Field Company, Royal Engineers, died of wounds on 28 March 1918, aged 21. He was Prize Cadet at the Royal Military Academy, Woolwich, in 1915. *Officers Died in the Great War* shows him serving with 73rd Field Company when he died. (Plot V.F.49)

Lieutenant Gordon Francis COLLINGWOOD, 405th Siege Battery, Royal Garrison Artillery, died of wounds on 28 March 1918, aged 25. He had carried on the family tradition of serving with the Royal Artillery; his father, Clennell William Collingwood CMG DSO, served during the war, retiring as a major general, Royal Artillery, and Gordon's grandfather had also been an artilleryman. Several artillery casualties from 28 March lie alongside him. (Plot V.F.32)

Lance Corporal Edwin Alexander GRIGG, Military Mounted Police, Military Police Corps, attached 4th Division, died of wounds on 9 April 1918, aged 32. He is one of 451 men from this branch of the army who died or were killed during the Great War. The overwhelming majority were lance corporals. (Plot V.G.5)

Plot V.G.29 to 37 contains eight NCOs and privates from the 11th Argyll & Sutherland Highlanders, all of whom died or were killed on 20 April 1918. Second Lieutenant Archibald Campbell BROWN MC, 14th Argyll & Sutherland Highlanders, is the ninth grave in that sequence. He would have been attached to the 11th Battalion at the time of his death, not least because the 14th Battalion was further north around Merville. The CWGC register therefore refers to his former unit. Before the war he studied at Glasgow University where he gained a Master's degree in 1906. When war broke out he enlisted in the 17th Highland Light Infantry (Glasgow Commercials) and initially served overseas with that battalion. However, in April 1917 he was commissioned in the 14th Argyll and Sutherland Highlanders and served with that battalion in France from September until his attachment to the 11th Battalion some time later. Although records insist that he was killed in action, he almost certainly died of wounds. His MC was gazetted on 16 September 1918 and was awarded for conspicuous gallantry and devotion to duty while in command of a fighting patrol whose objective was to clear the enemy from a strongpoint in an advanced trench. When they reached the trench the party came under heavy machine-gun fire. He dashed forward, leading his men, and put three machine guns out of action, killing their teams and capturing a prisoner. Although wounded, he remained with his men throughout the operation. The actions referred to in the citation occurred near Feuchy. (Plot V.G.37)

Air Mechanic 2nd Class Charles Ernest WOODWARD, 10th Balloon Company, Royal Air Force, was accidentally killed on 29 April 1918, aged 40 (Plot V.G.39). According to *Airmen Died in the Great War* he is one of a total of 130 balloonists who died or were killed during the war. Only one other man from his unit died in action throughout the conflict and he happens to be buried here too, but his death occurred later and he is buried in the next row.

Corporal James REID, 6th Cameron Highlanders, was executed by firing squad on 11 May 1918, aged 26. He was a regular soldier who had served throughout the war. After going absent he was arrested, but whilst in custody he escaped, which was undoubtedly an aggravating factor at his trial. One can only suppose that mental fatigue had taken its toll on him after several years at the front. Had he not escaped, his length of service might just have saved him. (Plot V.G.46)

Captain John DAVIE MC, General List, was killed in action on 11 May 1917, aged 25, serving with the Royal Scots. His MC was gazetted on 2 January 1918 in the New Year's Honours List. (Plot V.G.49)

Major Harold Runciman TURNER MC and Bar, 297th Siege Battery, Royal Garrison Artillery, was killed in action on 19 May 1918, aged 27. His MC was gazetted on 22 June 1918, but unusually the bar to it was gazetted three weeks earlier on 3 June in the King's Birthday Honours List; clearly the award of the MC had already been determined, though it was yet to be published. His MC was awarded whilst serving as a temporary captain in command of a battery that was heavily shelled for a period of six hours, and intermittently throughout the day. Despite such difficulties, he succeeded in keeping his guns in action all day and never failed to engage any of the targets given to him. It was mainly thanks to his splendid example of courage and coolness that the whole battery acquitted itself magnificently. (Plot V.G.50)

Private 1st Class Robert Arthur PYE, 10th Balloon Company, Royal Air Force, was killed in action on 13 August 1918, aged 49. (Plot V.H.12)

Corporal W.A. WHITE, B Battery, 126 Brigade, Royal Field Artillery, was killed in action on 9 September 1918, aged 24. (Plot V.H.48) His brother, Herbert James White, also fell while serving as a private in No. 2 Company, 12th Royal Fusiliers. He was killed in action on 14 June 1917, aged 20. Unlike his brother, he has no known grave and is commemorated on the Menin Gate at Ypres. I could find no trace of Corporal W.A. WHITE in *Soldiers Died in the Great War*, hence the reference to him by his initials only.

Gunner Kenneth Norman McRAE MM, 9 Field Brigade, Canadian Field Artillery, was mortally wounded by a shell while operating with a forward section of his battery on 10 September 1918 near Écourt-Saint-Quentin, just west of the Canal du Nord. He was evacuated to No. 1 Canadian Casualty Clearing Station where he died. His MM was awarded posthumously. He interrupted his law studies in order to enlist at the end of November 1915 and was present on the Somme in 1916 and at Arras in 1917. He was wounded in August 1917 and spent a couple of months back in England where he received treatment for an abscess, but returned to the front in November. (Plot V.H.56)

Second Lieutenant Percy KING, 7th East Surrey Regiment, died of wounds on 5 August 1917, aged 28; he came from Chatham in Kent. In civilian life he had worked at Guy's Hospital and was a member of the Royal College of Surgeons. He also held a licence in Dental Surgery and had been a member of University of London OTC. (Plot VI.B.11)

Second Lieutenant Cecil Victor FAREY MC, 4th East Surrey Regiment, attached 7th Battalion, died of wounds on 11 August 1917, aged 20. His MC was gazetted on 27 September that year and the citation was published on 10 January 1918. It was awarded for conspicuous gallantry and devotion to duty during a raid in which he led his men into the enemy's trench system. Despite being severely wounded about half an hour into the operation, he remained with his men and only consented to return to the dressing station after he was wounded for a second time. Throughout the operation he set a fine example to his men. (Plot VI.B.45)

Major Edwin Baskerville HICKOX MC, 9th Essex Regiment, died of wounds on 15 August 1917, aged 28. His MC was gazetted on 28 August 1916 and was awarded for conspicuous gallantry in action as a temporary captain, leading his company with great coolness under heavy machine-gun fire. He went from one flank to the other, regardless of the danger to himself, in order to encourage his men. (Plot VI.B.53)

Lieutenant Francis Herbert THORNDIKE, 11 Squadron, Royal Flying Corps, who formerly served with the 2nd County of London Yeomanry and the Lincolnshire Yeomanry, died on 17 August 1917 from injuries received two days earlier in a Bristol F2B aircraft. Second Lieutenant H.M. Drake, who was flying with him, was fortunately uninjured. Although the CWGC register contains no biographical details regarding THORNDIKE, he was a pupil at King's School, Rochester, where he particularly enjoyed drama and music. His father, Arthur John Webster Thorndike, was a clergyman who went on to become a Canon of Rochester and was the father of Dame Sybil Thorndike, the celebrated actress; Francis was her younger brother. (Plot VI.C.5)

Serjeant Victor Frederick CLARKE DCM, 2/8thWorcestershire Regiment, died on 18 November 1917 from wounds received three days earlier whilst leading a raid against enemy trenches on Greenland Hill. This was not a large raid in terms of numbers and consisted of just three officers and fifty-four other ranks split into three sections. CLARKE led the right-hand party into the enemy's position opposite him and dealt with its garrison, capturing a machine gun. Some of the garrison had managed to take refuge in a deep dug-out there, but when they refused to surrender a large bomb was thrown down the steps, the explosion from which caused the entrance to collapse. CLARKE was obviously a very trusted and experienced NCO with good leadership skills, since the other two sections of the raiding party were commanded by officers, Lieutenant Butler in the centre and Second Lieutenant Fry, who was wounded, on the left. The DCM was posthumously awarded to CLARKE for his role in the raid, which speaks of him leading his party into the enemy's trench, attacking and killing two parties of the enemy, after which he got his men on to the enemy's parapet and drove a counter-attack back across the open. Though seriously wounded, he re-organized his party before handing it over. The award was gazetted on 28 March 1918. He died, aged 22, at nearby casualty clearing facilities. (Plot VI.D.40)

Captain Gilbert Aberdein HARVEY, Royal Army Medical Corps, attached 1st King's Own (Royal Lancaster Regiment), died on 25 November 1917. He is one of thirty-six Royal Army Medical Corps casualties buried in this cemetery. (Plot VI.D.57)

Occasionally there are reminders that common illness sometimes claimed soldiers' lives. Flight Serjeant Arthur Eric EVANS, 64 Squadron, Royal Flying Corps, became ill and was brought to casualty clearing facilities here, but died on 5 March 1918, aged 26, from what is thought to have been a brain abscess. (Plot VI.E.15)

Captain Frank Darley LIVINGSTONE DSO, 15th Divisional Train, Army Service Corps, died on 22 March 1918, aged 32. His DSO was gazetted on 1 January 1917. His father was a noted Anglican minister and Honorary Canon of Liverpool; his mother, the Honourable Millicent Julia Allanson-Winn, was the daughter of an Irish peer, Charles Allanson-Winn, 3rd Baron Headley. Frank's brother, Richard, became a distinguished classicist and academic who after the war served as Vice Chancellor of Queen's University, Belfast. (Plot VI.E.35)

Lieutenant Charles Harry BOVILL, 1st Coldstream Guards, died of wounds on 24 March 1918. The battalion was not in action that day, but as it was moving down to Mercatel from Arras, it came under shell fire. He was almost certainly wounded during that shelling and was brought here where he later died. BOVILL was an extremely accomplished lyricist and had written many songs for musicals performed on the London stage and on Broadway. He had worked with the writer and fellow lyricist, P.G. Wodehouse, at the London newspaper, *The Globe*, and for a short time the two men shared accommodation. They worked closely together as song writers and became very good friends. BOVILL also collaborated with Jerome Kern, one of the early twentieth century's most celebrated composers of theatre and popular music. Kern's most famous composition is probably *Ol' Man River*. BOVILL's father, Charles Edward Bovill, had served as a major with the Royal Inniskilling Fusiliers. (Plot VI.E.56)

Captain Edward Wilkes WAUD, 13th Canadian Infantry, died on 6 April 1918. Buried next to him are ten NCOs and privates, all from the same battalion, all of whom died on either 5 or 6 April. The battalion war diary shows that he was killed on 5 April along with nine other ranks when a large shell exploded outside Ronville Caves where the Battalion HQ was located. Twenty-one other ranks were injured in the blast. Clearly at least one of these latter men failed to survive. (Plot VI.F.44)

Lieutenant Colonel Thomas Pelham JOHNSON DSO, 15th Division Train, Army Service Corps, died on active service on 12 June 1918, aged 46. He was educated at Queen's College, Cambridge, and the Royal Military College, Sandhurst, where he passed out with honours in 1891. He also spent time travelling in Germany before going to India with the Bedfordshire Regiment where he took part in the Relief of Chitral. After that he transferred to the Army Service Corps and served in Uganda. It was while he was in Africa that he developed a keen interest in hunting big game. On the outbreak of war he went to France with the British Expeditionary Force and was mentioned in Sir John French's despatch in October 1914. He was again mentioned in despatches in 1916 and was awarded the DSO for services in the field in the New Year's Honours List on 1 January 1917. He spent most of the war in France where he was known for his great appetite for work. He appears to have died from natural causes. (Plot VI.G.22)

Second Lieutenant William Anderson WEST MC, 13th Royal Scots, died of wounds on 21 June 1918, aged 19. The inscription on the headstone reads: '*Faithful unto death*'. His MC was gazetted on 29 July 1918 and was awarded for conspicuous gallantry and devotion to duty during a heavy attack on 28 March 1918. The battalion was holding the line astride the Arras–Cambrai road, east of Orange Hill. Following a heavy bombardment, the German infantry began its advance and the battalion's position around Orange Hill came under great pressure. The Battalion HQ, which was located near the crossroads at Feuchy Chapel, had already lost communication with forward units; as the Germans began to emerge over the rise, all the HQ staff including Lieutenant Colonel Hannay had to take up rifles and open fire on the attackers. At the same time, men from various units of the division began falling back in some confusion, some of whom were commandeered by Hannay to help hold the position. Meanwhile, parties of Germans had also penetrated the line on the right flank of Hannay's group and began pressing forward in an effort to outflank it. WEST took a couple of men with him and began to bomb them back, fighting obstinately until the leader of the enemy party was killed and the remainder of the group dispersed. The citation to his MC notes that his coolness inspired those around him at a critical time, which, of course, was the day on which the main German assault took place around Arras.

WEST, who was just 19 years old, was also inspirational a few months later when his battalion carried out a brilliant raid on German positions north of Fampoux. The raid took place under cover of darkness, at 3am, and with the assistance of a demolition team from the Royal Engineers, the raiders completely wrecked the German posts and dug-outs within the targeted area. WEST was in charge of one of the raiding parties and, as usual, was in the thick of the action. There were very few casualties, but young WEST was one of those mortally wounded. He was quickly moved back to the Casualty Clearing Station at Duisans, but died soon afterwards from his wounds. Two other officers were wounded. The raid serves as a textbook example of the set-piece 'in and out' operation, and I often refer to it to illustrate the level of skill and confidence that existed within elements of the British Army during the summer of 1918. (Plot VI.G.29)

Corporal Charles Hurry EADIE, 13th Royal Scots, also died of wounds on 21 June 1918 (Plot VI.G.30). He was one of the 351 men and eighteen officers from the battalion who took part in the above raid. The battalion war diary contains the first casualty return for the raid and shows four other ranks killed, fifteen wounded and fifteen still missing up to 9.30am that morning. The regimental history subsequently corrected this to a total of six killed, twenty wounded and four missing in action. The CWGC records now show a total of nine who were killed or died of wounds on 21 June 1918, six of whom are commemorated on the Arras Memorial. One of the men, Lance Corporal Miller, is buried at Aubigny Communal Cemetery Extension.

Private Peter Shaw McLAGAN, 13th Royal Scots, was killed in action on 20 June 1918. He may have been killed in the hours before the raid when final preparations were under way, but the precise circumstances of his death are difficult to determine. (Plot VI.G.31)

Brigadier General Alfred Forbes LUMSDEN DSO, Royal Scots, was killed by a shell on 24 June 1918, aged 41, while commanding 46 Brigade, which was part of the 15th (Scottish) Division. As a captain, LUMSDEN was wounded in the trenches near Dickebusch in Belgium while serving with the 1st Royal Scots. In August 1916 he was again promoted, taking over the 2nd Battalion of the regiment while it was serving on the Somme. His DSO was gazetted on 4 June 1917 in the King's Birthday Honours List. According to CWGC records, he is one of 113 brigadier generals who died or were killed during the war. (Plot VI.G.33)

Private Joseph DODDS, 7/8th King's Own Scottish Borderers, was wounded on the night of 24/25 June 1918. He was one of a party that carried out a successful raid on German trenches, the main objective of which was the destruction of a large cave used to shelter its garrison. When it was time to withdraw, DODDS sounded the bugle to the tune of *Come to the Cookhouse Door*. Unfortunately, he was mortally wounded as the raiders were withdrawing and he died on 25 June from his injuries. (Plot VI.G.35)

Captain Charles Franklin GALBRAITH DFC, 5 Squadron, Royal Air Force, died on 16 September 1918 from wounds received the previous day, aged 26, while flying his RE8 aircraft. His DFC was gazetted on 4 November 1918 and was awarded for outstanding merit during recent operations, attacking enemy infantry and sending back information on the forward positions of our own infantry and cavalry units. The citation notes that he had also carried out flights in order to obtain urgently required photographs at low altitude. (Plot VI.H.12)

Sergeant Harold Lambert BUCK MM and Bar, 2nd Divisional Signalling Company, Canadian Engineers, was mortally wounded by shrapnel fragments while crossing open ground. He was taken to No. 1 Canadian Casualty Clearing Station where he later died from wounds to his chest and upper body. (Plot VI.H.26) The officer with him at the time, Lieutenant Robert William Ewart Christie, was killed instantly when he was struck in the face by a fragment of the same shell. He is buried on the battlefield at Sun Quarry Cemetery, Chérisy. Both men died on 21 September 1918.

Lieutenant George Frederick Jervaulx JARVIS MC, 5th Reserve Cavalry Regiment, attached 9th West Yorkshire Regiment, died of wounds on 28 September 1918, aged 34. His MC was gazetted on 2 January 1919 in the New Year's Honours List. (Plot VII.A.55)

Lieutenant Colonel Stanley Douglas GARDNER CMG MC, 7th Battalion, Canadian Infantry, attached 38th Battalion, died on 30 September 1918, aged 37, from wounds received two days earlier. The battalion had taken up positions in the Marquion Line, but the situation ahead was obscure. GARDNER was standing outside his HQ trying to observe forward operations when he was wounded by a shell burst. During his military service he was made a Chevalier of the *Légion d' Honneur*. His MC was gazetted on 14 January 1916 and his French decoration was announced on 28 February 1916. His CMG was published in the *London Gazette* dated 3 June 1918. He previously served with the Royal North-West Mounted Police. (Plot VII.A.85)

Captain Geoffrey Moore COWPER, Royal Army Medical Corps, died of wounds on 3 October 1918, aged 27. He was a former pupil at Darlington Grammar School and went on to Trinity College, Cambridge. After graduating in 1911, he studied medicine at St. Bartholomew's Teaching Hospital, London, and by 1914 he had become a Member of the Royal College of Surgeons and also a Licentiate of the Royal College of Physicians. He enlisted in 1914 and initially worked at a Base Hospital in England as an anaesthetist, though in February 1915 he went to France where he was posted to a hospital at Le Tréport. In 1917, after a brief spell attached to a battalion of the Duke of Wellington's Regiment, he was transferred to the 35th Field Ambulance where he was attached to the 5th Dorset Regiment as its medical officer. He was badly wounded when a shell scored a direct hit on the Regimental Aid Post where he was working and he died later that day. The Reverend Eric Oswald Read, Army Chaplan's Department, was also killed by the same shell and he is buried at Chapel Corner Cemetery, Sauchy-

Lestrée, which lies north-west of Cambrai and just east of the Canal du Nord. COWPER had previously been mentioned in despatches and is referred to in the war diary of the 5th Dorset Regiment as 'Captain Cooper'. The battalion was part of the 11th (Northern) Division. (Plot VII.B.11)

Lance Corporal Dalton Edgar FERRIS DCM, 4th Battalion, Canadian Infantry, won his award during a counter-attack at Upton Wood on 30 August 1918 during which he led his Lewis gun section with great gallantry and skill through thick undergrowth under heavy high explosive and machine gun fire. Taking up a favourable position, he inflicted heavy casualties on the advancing enemy. His able and determined leadership inspired his men with complete confidence. The award was gazetted on 16 January 1919. He was killed in action on 5 October 1918. (Plot VII.B.14)

Private Roger Victor RICHARD, 52nd Battalion, Canadian Infantry, died on 4 October 1918 after enlisting in January that year. He was a farm hand from St Amboise and though his surname offers no hint of his ancestry, he was one of the many Canadians of Native American descent who fought in the Great War. (Plot VII.B.19)

Second Lieutenant Murray HEARD, 209 Squadron, Royal Air Force, was killed in action on 11 October 1918, aged 20, flying a Sopwith Camel. He was the only fatality from his squadron that day. He was a Canadian pilot from St. Thomas in Ontario. (Plot VII.B.57)

Private Percy JOHNSON MM, 'C' Company, 10th Battalion, Canadian Infantry, was wounded during operations around Arleux and the Sensée Canal and died on 13 October 1918. He enlisted in 1914 and had served throughout the war. He originally came from Mareham-le-Fen in Lincolnshire where he is commemorated. Also commemorated on the memorial is Wilfred Henry Johnson, who was his brother. He died on 31 October 1922 and his name has clearly been added after the memorial was inscribed, though the exact circumstances of his death are not explained or referred to in the roll of honour. (Plot VII.B.86)

The cemetery is also notable for the large number of post-Armistice casualties buried here. There are some eighty-two burials relating to deaths that occurred between 11 November 1918 and 31 December 1920. No doubt many of these men died when the flu epidemic was rampant, but salvage work was an occupation not without its hazards and a number of deaths occurred as a result of accidents of various kinds.

Plot VII, Row C contains a number of men who died from various causes after the war. Many of them would have been attached to the Labour Corps.

Serjeant Walter Vere HEMINGWAY, 1st Garrison Battalion, Cheshire Regiment, died in a car accident on 19 October 1920, aged 33. He had previously served with the 6th South Lancashire Regiment, the local regiment to where he lived. He later transferred to the Cheshire Regiment and spent time during the war as part of the garrison on Gibraltar. However, he did not enjoy good health and as a former miner he suffered from recurrent respiratory problems. This may account for why he never served as a front line soldier. In May 1919 he joined the Labour Corps and went to France where it appears that his unit was involved in work with the Graves Registration and Enquiries. The car accident left him with severe head injuries from which he never recovered. (Plot VII.C.4)

Captain Sidney Harry WRIGHT, Labour Corps, died on 10 February 1919, aged 45. He had served on the *Hong Kong Telegraph* as a sub-editor. His headstone carries the inscription, '*A foreign field that is forever England*', a line taken from the poem, 'The Soldier', by Rupert Brooke. He was working with the 114th Company, Chinese Labour Corps when he died, apparently from natural causes (Plot VII.C.8). Next to him is Corporal Annibale BAGNOLESI, 5th Battalion, Tank Corps, who died of accidental injuries on 12 February 1919. The War Memorial Book of Remembrance relating to Bournemouth includes not only him, but also another man, Lance Corporal James Bagnolesi, who also died serving in the Tank Corps. *Soldiers Died in the Great War* makes no reference to either of these men. (Plot VII.C.9)

Second Lieutenant William Robertson REITH, 9th Battalion, Tank Corps, died on 17 February 1919, aged 27. He was hospitalized two days before his death from influenza, but had not been feeling well for several days before that. He had previously served with the Royal Sussex Regiment before transferring to the Tank Corps. He was one of four brothers who served. One of them was wounded serving with the Royal Engineers in 1918, but Douglas, who served as a Gunner with C Battery, 182 Brigade, Royal Field Artillery, was killed in action on 1 October 1916. He is buried on the Somme at the Guards' Cemetery, Lesboeufs. (Plot VII.C.14)

Quartermaster Serjeant G.D. UNTHANK, 12th Battalion, Tank Corps, died of pneumonia on 18 February 1919. (Plot VII.C.15)

Gunner Frederick NICHOLS, C Battery, 295 Brigade, Royal Field Artillery, died of accidental injuries on 24 June 1919, aged 40. By then he had transferred to the Labour Corps. The war memorial at Parham, Suffolk, where he lived shows his surname as 'Nicholls'. (Plot VII.C.34)

The Royal Defence Corps lost 1,240 men in the Great War, but only two are to be found in France. One of these is Serjeant G. WARWICK, who later transferred to the 225th Prisoner of War Company, which was part of the Labour Corps. He died on 7 November 1918 and is buried here at Duisans (Plot VII.C.48). The other man is Captain Horace Benjamin Goater who was killed in action on 10 August 1918 whilst attached to the 2/4th Royal Berkshire Regiment. He is buried at Merville Communal Cemetery Extension.

Private Thomas Greenfield CUTHBERT, 200th Company, Labour Corps, died on 17 January 1920, aged 52 (Plot VII.C.53). He is the oldest casualty here. The youngest soldiers buried here are aged 17 and there are several of them scattered amongst the various plots.

Lieutenant Robert Murray McCheyne GRAY MC, 46th Battalion, Canadian Infantry, died of wounds on 30 September 1918, aged 29. His MC was gazetted on 11 December 1919 and was awarded for conspicuous gallantry between 28 and 29th September 1918 during the fighting around Cambrai. The citation records that during the advance on the Canal du Nord he handled his assaulting company with great skill and ability. During that advance his unit encountered seven machine-gun nests, all of which were dealt with, mainly owing to his fearless leadership. (Plot VIII.A.2)

Corporal Harold George ARMITAGE MM, 28th Battalion, Canadian Infantry, died of wounds on 1 October 1918, aged 21. He enlisted in April 1916. One of his brothers, Clarence Valmore Armitage, had also enlisted, but was subsequently deemed to be medically unfit and was discharged from the service. Their younger brother, Flying Officer Irving Armitage, served with the Royal Canadian Air Force in the Second World War. He and the entire crew of their Halifax bomber were killed during a raid on Berlin. Their aircraft failed to return and their bodies have never been found. He and the rest of the crew are now commemorated on the Runnymede Memorial. (Plot VIII.A.39)

Lieutenant George Samuel DAY, 52 Squadron, Royal Air Force, and his observer, Second Lieutenant Frank Samuel OCCMORE DFC, were killed whilst flying on 1 October 1918. OCCOMORE's DFC was gazetted on 5 December 1918 and was awarded for his work on a number of occasions when he showed remarkable courage and determination while out on reconnaissance, each time returning with valuable and reliable information. One such occasion was on 31 August 1918 when he carried out a very successful contact patrol over the frontage of two divisions. He flew over the area twice at heights varying from 300 feet to just 150 feet, obtaining valuable information. During this flight his machine was subjected to heavy machine-gun fire and was hit in twenty places during an encounter with an enemy machine. (Plot VIII.A.60 and 61)

Corporal Rowland NELSON joined the Yorkshire Hussars Yeomanry in April 1915 and served in Egypt with the regiment from December 1915 until his transfer to the 9th West Yorkshire Regiment. He was a confectioner by trade and worked for J. Terry & Sons before the war. Apparently, he also had an unbroken attendance record for six years at school. This information, in the form of a newspaper cutting, had been slipped inside the cemetery register, presumably by relatives visiting his grave. Such small contributions help to breathe life back into the person, allowing us a glimpse of the man, not just the soldier or the headstone; in no way do they prejudice the details in the register in the way that crossings out, corrections and additions do. He was mortally wounded on 2 October 1918, aged 23. (Plot VIII.A.78)

Major Guy Robert HOWARD DSO, 18 Squadron, Royal Air Force, formerly Essex Regiment, died of wounds received on 23 October 1918 whilst on the ground. The circumstances of his death are somewhat unusual, in that he died from his injuries after he was hit by a round from a Very pistol during a squadron party. Howard's DSO was one of the earliest gazetted during the war when it was announced in the *London Gazette* on 9 November 1914. He had been part of the Special Reserve and went to France with the 2nd Battalion, Essex Regiment. He won his DSO for carrying out a patrol on 24 September, south of Vregny, during which he made a valuable reconnaissance through dense woodland to within 150 yards of the enemy's trenches. He came from Colchester in Essex, which is a well known garrison town. His father, W. Howard, held the rank of colonel. (Plot VIII.B.24)

Lieutenant Ernest Harold MASTERS, 45 Squadron, Royal Air Force, died on 24 December 1918, aged 19. Despite his youth, he had been awarded the French *Croix de Guerre* with Palm. He had served in France and Italy and was a British ace with eight victories to his credit, seven of which were recorded in Italy. Sadly, he was killed in a flying accident on Christmas Eve. (Plot VIII.B.60)

Private Mark LYDON, 5th Connaught Rangers, died on New Year's Eve, 1918, aged 39 (Plot VIII.B.62). Rifleman McDarra Lydon, 7th Royal Irish Rifles, was killed in action at Ypres with the 16th (Irish) Division on 16 August 1917, aged 20, and is now commemorated on the wall at Tyne Cot Cemetery. Both men came from Carna, Co. Galway, which is a small village on the west coast of Ireland. The CWGC register shows different parents for each of them, but there remains a good possibility that they were related to each other.

There are seven Germans buried in Plot VIII, Row D, all of whom died in 1919. Presumably, they were prisoners of war who were too ill or injured to be repatriated and who died in British care.

There are also several casualties in Plot VIII who died in 1920, including:

Lieutenant William Pearce EVANS MM, B Battery, 307 Brigade, Royal Field Artillery, died on 31 July 1920, aged 23. He had previously served with the 8th Signalling Company, Royal Engineers. (Plot VIII.C.1)

Corporal Albert Frederick BROWN, 116th Battery, Royal Field Artillery, died on 12 September 1920, aged 26. (Plot VIII.C.2)

Private A. HAWXWELL, 47th Royal Fusiliers, attached to the 11th Motor Ambulance Convoy, died on 13 October 1920. (Plot VIII.C.3)

Serjeant R. GRANT, 47th Royal Fusiliers, formerly 2nd Seaforth Highlanders, died on 15 November 1920, aged 35. He was possibly part of the Labour Corps at the time of his death, but he may equally have been serving with Private HAWXWELL. The 47th Battalion, Royal Fusiliers, had no existence before or during the war and was only formed as a Garrison Battalion on 14 May 1919. (Plot VIII.C.5)

Gunner WAZIRA, a Hindu soldier serving with the 14th Anti-Aircraft Transport, Royal Garrison Artillery (Indian Army), died on 20 November 1920. (Plot VIII.E.8)

As with all those who died in 1920, their regiments and units, as shown in the CWGC register, would bear little, if any, resemblance to the tasks on which they were then employed. Much the same can be said for those who died in 1919.

Louez Military Cemetery, Duisans

To avoid complications, the best route to this cemetery from Arras is via the D.939, the Arras–Saint-Pol road. Take the next right turn after the intersection with the Arras ring road, which is the D.60. Follow this road for about 500 yards and then turn right. The cemetery is situated at the end of the road. Although there are no French graves here today, the cemetery was begun by the French and then taken over by the British in spring 1916. There are two German graves, but all of the 204 British and Commonwealth graves are identified.

The cemetery consists mainly of burials from 1916. The 51st (Highland) Division established its HQ at Duisans on 12 March that year, the same day on which the death of two of its men occurred; Private John Cairns WILSON and Private William Samuel CARTER of the 9th Royal Scots. Private CARTER was 48 years old and the CWGC register notes that he had previously completed twenty-four years of service with the Royal Field Artillery. According to *Soldiers Died in the Great War* both men died from causes unconnected to wounds and neither is shown as being killed in action. (Plot II.A.1 and 2)

It would also appear that the only brigade within that division to use this cemetery was 154 Brigade. Only men of the 9th Royal Scots, the 7th Argyll and Sutherland Highlanders, the 4th Seaforth Highlanders and the 4th Gordon Highlanders make up the division's casualties here in 1916.

It is also very unusual to find two officers who commanded the same battalion buried in the same cemetery. Lieutenant Colonel Claude Henry CAMPBELL, DSO, 1st Cameron Highlanders, who was commanding the 4th Seaforth Highlanders at the time of his death, was killed by a sniper on 14 March 1916, aged 37, just a day after taking over the new line. His DSO was gazetted for services in the field on 29 June 1915 while serving as a captain attached to the 14th Battalion, London Regiment (London Scottish). (Plot I.A.1)

Lieutenant Colonel Algernon Bingham Anstruther STEWART DSO, 4th Seaforth Highlanders, was killed in action on 23 May 1916, aged 46, whilst inspecting trenches. He had only recently returned to France following his recovery from the effects of heavy concussion after a shell exploded close to him at Neuve Chapelle the previous year. He served in the South African campaign where he was mentioned in despatches and where he received his DSO for services in the field. His father, Charles Edward Stewart CB CMG CIE, also held the rank of colonel. (Plot I.C.1)

Another long-serving soldier was Serjeant Henry Albert Mitchel GRAINGER, 4th Gordon Highlanders, who was 40 years old when he died on 19 March 1916. He took part in the Samona Campaign in 1897 and the Tirah Campaign of 1897–98, both on the North-West Frontier in India, and served for sixteen years with the Royal Scots Fusiliers. (Plot I.A.6)

Lieutenant Charles Cameron DOUGLAS, 4th Cameron Highlanders, who is shown as having died on 25 May 1916, must have been serving with one of the battalions belonging to 154 Brigade at the time of his death. The 4th Cameron Highlanders was absorbed within the regiment's 1st Battalion as of 19 March 1916. His old battalion had been part of the 7th Division and took part in the Battles of Aubers Ridge, Festubert and Loos in 1915. (Plot I.C.4)

Colour Sergeant Robert DONALD, 4th Gordon Highlanders, was killed in action on 9 June 1916, aged 21. He was one of 'U' Company, which was made up of volunteers from Aberdeen University where he was an Arts and Divinity student with the intention of becoming a church minister. He had served with 'U' Company from 1913 and went over to France in February 1915. He was part of his company's sniping and intelligence section and was mortally wounded on Vimy Ridge whilst carrying out duties in connection with that role. (Plot I.D.5)

The 51st (Highland) Division had been on the Western Front since the start of May 1915, and so the move to the Arras sector was not its baptism of fire. That was not the case for the 60th (2nd/2nd London) Division, which was composed of men from second-line Territorial battalions of the London Regiment. The summer of 1916 was their first experience of life at the front and there are now sixty identified burials here from this division, including five men attached to the 181st Company, Machine Gun Corps. Again, all sixty casualties are from one brigade, 181 Brigade, and all date from July to October that year, after which the division moved to Salonika.

A third group of burials reinforces my belief that in 1916 this cemetery had been specifically allocated to a brigade area; 8 Brigade, 3rd Canadian Division, consisted of men from the 1st, 2nd, 4th and 5th Canadian Mounted Rifles. This brigade began using the cemetery in November 1916 and continued using it until February the following year. There are now forty-six men of the Canadian Mounted Rifles buried here out of a total of forty-nine Canadians.

Lance Corporal Gordon John McNAMARA DCM, 5th Canadian Mounted Rifles, was killed on 11 December 1916. His DCM was awarded for conspicuous gallantry. The citation states that he went out in broad daylight and, in full view of the enemy, brought in a wounded sergeant under machine-gun and rifle fire. (Plot I.H.12)

Company Sergeant-Major Edward Charles WOODROOF DCM, 4th Canadian Mounted Rifles, was killed just over a week later on 20 December. His DCM was awarded for conspicuous bravery and devotion to duty, volunteering to go out on two occasions as a scout during heavy bombardments. On both occasions he brought back much valuable information. The award was gazetted on 19 August 1916. (Plot III.C.2)

Private McIvor SINCLAIR, 1st Canadian Mounted Rifles, was killed on 8 November 1916 and was of Native American stock in spite of the apparent Scottish origins of his name. He came from the Fisher River Agency, Manitoba. (Plot II.G.11)

Private Walter Norrsey DANIELS, 1st Canadian Mounted Rifles, had resided on the St Peter Reserve, Manitoba, and was of Native American origin. He was killed in action on 3 December 1916. (Plot I.H.8)

The build up to the Battle of Arras made heavy demands on all the pioneer units attached to divisions, though in virtually every case their work was greatly supplemented by working parties from other battalions. A handful of men from the 8th Royal Scots are buried here. This battalion was the pioneer batalion attached to the 51st (Highland) Division. The men fell between 2 March and 6 March 1917, and although they are not buried in the same row, they happen to be buried in a kind of sequence. (Plot III.E.5, F.5 and G.5)

Another man who belonged to a pioneer unit was Private Peter GILES, 14th Northumberland Fusiliers, which was attached to the 21st Division. The division, like several others that had been engaged on the Somme, was moved to the Arras sector during the summer of 1916 in order to reorganize away from the stresses and strains of battle. For Private GILES, even this proved too much. He went absent and was gone for about a week. He was executed on 24 August 1916. (Plot II.F.6)

There is a curious entry in the CWGC register relating to Private Joseph READ, aged 47. The register shows his unit as the '6th Infantry, Devonshire Regiment'. Even if it is meant to be read as the '6th Battalion, Devonshire Regiment' it makes little sense, since the 6th Devonshire Regiment served in Mesopotamia and not France. The answer lies in the fact that some regiments formed their own labour companies, and the Devonshire Regiment had a number of these. Joseph READ died whilst serving with the 6th Labour Company, Devonshire Regiment. His widow's grave at Ryde Old Parish Cemetery also carries a dedication that indicates that his true age was 49. It may be that he was economical with the truth with regard to his age in order to be accepted for army service. The roll of honour for Ryde also indicates that he had served as a gunner in the Royal Field Artillery and also during the South African War. He is one of five men shown in *Soldiers Died in the Great War* from the Devonshire Regiment's 6th Infantry Labour Company who died of wounds, or were killed in action between 14 and 27 April 1917. (Plot III.A.6)

The cemetery appears not to have been used during the Battle of Arras, or indeed for the rest of that year. Only two burials were made in 1918, one being a sapper, killed on 28 March (Plot II.H.1), the other a gunner with the Royal Garrison Artillery who died just over a week later (Plot II.H.2).

Finally, there is just one holder of the MM buried here; Corporal Walter ALEX-ANDER, MM, 7th Gordon Highlanders, who was killed in action on 14 February 1917. (Plot III.D.5)

Chapter Seven

Some Whistlers – 'The Great Escape' – Avenging Captain Denham and the Daylight Raid

Aubigny Communal Cemetery Extension

Aubigny-en-Artois is a large village that lies just north of the D.939 on the main road between Arras and Saint-Pol. The cemetery sits between this road and the village and is visible from the main road. If arriving from the direction of Écoivres along the D.49 it is reached by bearing left where the Rue du General Barbot becomes the Rue d'Anneuse. At the roundabout the third exit runs along a lane with rising ground on either side. The cemetery lies about 250 yards further up on the left.

The CWGC register notes that the village lay behind the front held by the French Tenth Army and that the British then took over in March 1916. There are still 227 French graves here along with 2,771 British and Commonwealth burials and sixty-four Germans. Additionally, there are seven graves from the Second World War. The CWGC register shows an additional twelve names in respect of the number of identified casualties; this figure includes twelve men who fought under aliases and so they actually appear twice but are cross referenced. At first glance it appears that the register gives two sets of figures, but the maths do add up.

Aubigny-en-Artois was used extensively by a number of casualty clearing stations at various times between March 1916 and 1918. One feature of this cemetery is very unusual. On entering the military extension via the French civilian cemetery, Plots V and VI lie tucked away over on the far left hand side and left hand corner. All of the graves in these two plots are those of officers. This appears to have been set out deliberately, though some officers are buried elsewhere within the other plots. The CWGC register makes no reference to this arrangement, though it clearly came about when the cemetery was in use during the war. Many cemeteries have groups of officers buried together, but the configuration here is highly unusual.

The first burial in the cemetery appears to be Lance Corporal Alfred Arnold SIMPSON, 1/6th Sherwood Foresters, who died from wounds on 12 March 1916 (Plot I.A.1). This is also the case at Écoivres Military Cemetery where some of the first burials also come from the 46th (North Midland) Division. Casualties from the opening day of the Battle of Arras are to be found mainly in Plot II, Row A.

Corporal Wheeler Albert Edward RICE, 122nd Siege Battery, Royal Garrison Artillery, died of wounds on 10 April 1917, aged 38. The CWGC register notes that he served for twenty-four years in the Royal Garrison Artillery's Territorial Force (Brighton) and that he held the Territorial Efficiency Medal. (Plot I.A.7)

Serjeant G.G. MOORE DCM, 4th (Staffordshire) Battery, 1/3rd (North Midland) Brigade, Royal Field Artillery, was awarded his DCM for conspicuous gallantry and devotion to duty after the enemy had fired a mine. He was temporarily knocked out and injured by the explosion. However, once he had recovered, he assisted in rallying some of the men and laid down a rapid rate of fire until reinforcements arrived. The award was gazetted on 11 March 1916. He died of wounds here on 24 April 1916, aged 22. (Plot I.A.62)

Private Leslie Charles TANDY, 8th Argyll & Sutherland Highlanders, was killed in action on 28 April 1916, aged 19. His brother, Second Lieutenant Arthur Jesse Tandy, also served during the war, but with the West Yorkshire Regiment. He survived and returned home, but died on 28 June 1919. He is buried at Campbeltown (Kilkerran) Cemetery. (Plot I.B.6)

Lance Corporal Walter Herbert KILLICK, 1st Wiltshire Regiment, was killed in action on 25 May 1916, aged 23. His brother, Private Horace Alfred Killick, also served during the war. He died on 7 November 1917, aged 23, and previously served in the Wiltshire Regiment before transferring to the 2nd Oxfordshire & Buckinghamshire Light Infantry. He is buried at Shere (St James) Churchyard in Surrey. (Plot I.C.29)

Serjeant George Frederick Airlie JILBERT DCM, 2/14th Battalion, London Regiment (London Scottish), was killed in action on 15 October 1916, aged 24. His DCM was gazetted on 16 November 1916 and was awarded for conspicuous gallantry in action while leading a bombing party with great courage and determination. Later, though severely wounded, he continued to control his section and subsequently, when ordered to retire, helped a wounded comrade until exhaustion prevented him from doing so. (Plot I.E.51)

Private Francis HOWIE, 8th Black Watch, died of wounds on 11 March 1917, aged 28. He previously served as a second lieutenant with the 5th Connaught Rangers and the 12th Middlesex Regiment, but resigned his commission and rejoined as a private. He is one of nine officers shown in the *London Gazette* dated 9 April 1915 who relinquished their commission as of 10 April. (Plot I.H.1)

Private C. OFFICER, 1st South African Regiment, was killed in action on 6 April 1917, a few days prior to the opening of the Arras offensive. He was wounded during the fighting at Delville Wood the previous year. (Plot I.K.20)

Private Theodore Robert HOPKINSON, 2nd Battalion, Canadian Infantry, died here on 6 April 1917, aged 21. He joined the first Canadian contingent in 1914 and was in the line at the Second Battle of Ypres in 1915 where he was wounded and gassed. The battalion was out of the line at Camblain l'Abbé on the day he died. He may have been one of two men wounded in trenches near Maison Blanche on 2 April, although he could also have died of wounds incurred in one of two raids carried out by his unit on 5 April. The battalion war diary does not refer to any of these casualties by name. (Plot I.K.34)

Company Serjeant Major Jack NICHOLSON DCM, 10th Argyll & Sutherland Highlanders, died of wounds on 10 April 1917, aged 22. His DCM was gazetted on 26 July 1917 and was awarded for conspicuous gallantry and devotion to duty. The citation states that his cheerfulness was a fine example to all, as was his disregard of danger in the attack when leading his platoon. Although severely wounded, he refused all assistance. (Plot I.L.57)

Plot I, Rows M and N contain the bodies of four officers from the 11th Lancashire Fusiliers. Three were killed in action on 15 May 1916 and the fourth died of wounds the following day. They were involved in an attack that involved the detonation of several mines. Two of the mines were blown on the right-hand side of the area that was to be raided in order to protect the attackers from enfilade fire. The 9th Loyal North Lancashire Regiment was successful on the left, but the 11th Lancashire Fusiliers on the right were too close to one of the mines when it exploded killing and injuring a number of men, including the four officers.

    The officers are not buried consecutively. Second Lieutenant Edward Herbert JEWELL died of wounds on 16 May (Plot I.M.11); Second Lieutenant Arthur Keith McFARLAN was killed on 15 May, aged 19 (Plot I.M.26), as were Second Lieutenants William Frank BAKER (Plot I.N.12), and Reginald BARRETT (Plot I.N.15). There are now thirty-three officers and men of the 11th Lancashire Fusiliers buried in this cemetery, most of whom were killed or died of wounds on various dates throughout May 1916. The Loyal North Lancashire Regiment has rather more burials with fifty-five, again, mainly from May 1916, although the majority of them are from the 8th Battalion rather than the 9th Battalion. There are, however, some 9th Battalion men here too.

Private William SMITH, 1st Royal Irish Fusiliers, died of wounds on 12 April 1917. The circumstances of his death were probably the same as those of Serjeant MILLER who is buried further along the same row. The 1st Royal Irish Fusiliers and the 2nd Seaforth Highlanders were involved in an attack at midday on 11 April towards Roeux, the Chemical Works and the southern end of Greenland Hill. The day's events started badly when the men were about to move off from Fampoux to their assembly positions for the attack. Heavy shelling caused many casualties. When the men left their trenches and began to advance towards their objectives they were cut down by machine-gun and rifle fire. (Plot II.A.9)

Serjeant Alexander MILLER, 2nd Seaforth Highlanders, died on 12 April 1917 from wounds received the previous day. The likelihood is that MILLER was wounded shortly before his battalion's attack began, or fairly soon after he and his men had gone over the top. Had he been wounded closer to where Brown's Copse Cemetery now stands, it is very unlikely that he would have made it back to the relative safety of his own trenches and medical attention. The fact that he was recovered and was then evacuated to casualty clearing facilities at Aubigny, some distance from the battlefield, strongly suggests in favour of this argument. Many of those wounded in this attack would have died on the battlefield. The machine-gun fire was so intense and the ground so open that reaching them was simply out of the question, at least during daylight, and many of those who tried to make their own way back were either killed or forced to wait until after dark. (Plot II.A.46)

Serjeant Edwin SINGLE DCM, 126th Siege Battery, Royal Garrison Artillery, died of wounds on 22 April 1917, aged 26. His DCM was awarded for conspicuous gallantry and devotion to duty in attending to several of the wounded, even though he himself had been wounded. He then took charge of a fresh detachment and continued in action. The award was gazetted on 9 July 1917. (Plot II.B.47)

Company Serjeant Major John O'Brien DCM, 7th Royal Fusiliers, was killed in action on 23 April 1917. *Soldiers Died in the Great War* makes no mention of his DCM, though it was gazetted on 1 January 1918. He was acting regimental serjeant major with the 2/4th Battalion (City of London), London Regiment (Royal Fusiliers), when he won the award and the citation for it appeared on 17 April 1918. It was awarded for conspicuous gallantry and devotion to duty on many occasions in action. It goes on to state simply that his courage, energy, and cheerfulness under all circumstances added greatly to the efficiency of the battalion. (Plot II.B.72)

There are fifty South African burials here, the majority of whom are buried in Plots I and II, though the four officers are in Plots V and VI. They include Private L.G. FAIRBAIRN, 4th South African Regiment, who was among the last group of South Africans to be relieved in Delville Wood. He died of wounds on 12 April 1917. It is quite possible that he was wounded on the day he died, which was a disastrous day for the South African Brigade, but his battalion had also come under heavy machine-gun fire on 9 April suffering significant casualties. He is one of several Delville Wood veterans buried here. (Plot II.C.59)

Battery Serjeant Major Charles Frederick HUNTER DCM, D Battery, 50 Brigade, Royal Field Artillery, died of wounds on 24 April 1917, aged 41. His DCM was gazetted on 22 September 1916 and was awarded for conspicuous gallantry and presence of mind under trying circumstances. He succeeded in stopping a runaway team under heavy shell fire, and later extinguished a fire that had broken out in an ammunition pit single-handed. His courage and devotion to duty on that occasion undoubtedly saved many casualties. At the time of his death his unit was part of the 9th (Scottish) Division. (Plot II.D.12)

Private John Alexander FARISH, 1st South African Regiment, was a veteran of the fighting at Delville Wood in July 1916; in fact, he was wounded there on 16 July 1916. He died of wounds received in the failed attack on Roeux and the Chemical Works on 12 April 1917. The South African Brigade had come under such heavy shelling as it was assembling in Fampoux that it was unable to advance behind the supporting barrage put down by the field artillery. Once the barrage had moved well beyond the troops they were horribly exposed and suffered heavy casualties. (Plot II.E.16)

Corporal Francis William FILMER, 2nd South African Regiment, is another Delville Wood veteran who was wounded there in July 1916 serving as a private. Like Private FARISH, he was wounded in the attack on 12 April 1917 and died from his wounds a few days later on the 15th. (Plot II.E.37)

Private Harry WARD, 1st Royal Irish Fusiliers, formerly Bedfordshire Regiment, died of wounds on 18 April 1917, aged 39 (Plot II.E.79). His brother, Private Edward Ward, was killed in action on 5 November 1917, aged 36, serving with the 3/4th Queen's (Royal West Surrey Regiment).

Company Serjeant Major William BRANT DCM, 1st Royal Berkshire Regiment, died of wounds on 25 April 1917, aged 35. His DCM was gazetted on 11 May 1917 and was awarded for conspicuous gallantry and devotion to duty, having greatly assisted in reorganizing his company and consolidating a captured trench under very heavy hostile fire. He was also awarded the French *Croix de Guerre*, which was gazetted on 28 February 1916. (Plot II.G.30)

Private Charles Stanley SLADE, 4th South African Regiment, was another veteran of the fighting at Delville Wood. He was born at Potchefstroom, in Transvaal, and was killed in action on 11 May 1917, aged 40 (Plot II.H.71). He served for eight months in the Potchefstroom Commando before joining the South African Brigade. He was a merchant in civilian life and stood at over 6 feet tall. On 21 May 1916 he was burnt on his head and neck. Having recovered, he returned to duty and worked as a stretcher-bearer near Waterlot Farm where he came to notice for his continuous work collecting and evacuating wounded comrades. During the fighting at Delville Wood in July that year, he and his friend, Private James Royan, worked tirelessly, carrying the wounded through barrages and rescuing many of their wounded comrades under fire. Private Royan was killed in action on 19 July 1916 and has no known grave. He is now commemorated on the Thiepval Memorial.

The artillery relied heavily on its relationship with the airmen who carried out a multiplicity of tasks on its behalf. Two men who had a foot in both camps are buried close to each other in Plot III, Row B, and though they were from different squadrons, they were attached to the same artillery unit. Air Mechanic 1st Class Frederick Joseph NICHOLS, 2 Squadron, Royal Air Force, attached to 79th Siege Battery, Royal Garrison Artillery, was killed in action on 14 April

1918, aged 21 (Plot III.B.27). Air Mechanic 2nd Class Robert McCulloch BROWN, 5 Squadron, Royal Air Force, attached 79th Siege Battery, Royal Garrison Artillery, died of wounds on 15 April 1918, aged 22 (Plot III.B.33).

Serjeant Charles STORRIE DCM, 8th Seaforth Highlanders, died of wounds on 23 April 1917, aged 30 (Plot III.B.58). His DCM was gazetted on 12 March 1915 and the citation appeared on 6 April that year. It was awarded to him while he was serving as a private with the 1st Battalion on 20 December 1914 at Givenchy where he had shown conspicuous gallantry and resource as a telephone operator, remaining at his post at a critical time and until the last moment at which point he disconnected the wires and brought back his instruments.

Air Mechanic 1st Class, John Ernest BENTLEY, 64 Squadron, Royal Flying Corps, is shown as having been killed in action on 27 March 1918 in a German air raid over the village of Izel-les-Hameau. However, it is far more likely that he was wounded there and brought here to Aubigny where he died from his injuries. Had he been killed in the air raid itself, as claimed in *Airmen Died in the Great War*, he would almost certainly have been buried in the village cemetery at Izel-les-Hameau, or very near to that location. (Plot III. C.34)

Air Mechanic 1st Class Albert Michael SCHNEIDERS, aged 19, and Air Mechanic 2nd Class William George SANGER, 16 Squadron, Royal Flying Corps, were killed while flying on 26 March 1918. They are buried next to each other. (Plot III.C.37 and 38)

Private Albert Morley THOMAS, Royal Canadian Regiment, died of wounds on 28 March 1918, aged 49. The CWGC register notes that he fought in the Indian Frontier Wars at the end of the nineteenth century and also in the South African campaign. (Plot III.C.44)

Private Hallett Lemont NODWELL, 5th Canadian Mounted Rifles, was killed in action on 29 March 1918, aged 23. His brother, Aubrey Leroy Nodwell, also fell while serving with the 5th Canadian Mounted Rifles. He was killed in action at Mount Sorrel on 2 June 1916, aged 20, near Maple Copse when the Germans captured Hill 62. He has no known grave and is commemorated on the Menin Gate. (Plot III.D.6)

Private Walter Harding LEWIS, 'C' Company, 1st Battalion, Honourable Artillery Company, died on 26 May 1917, aged 25, from wounds received the previous day near Gavrelle. He had served overseas with the battalion since the start of July 1915 and was wounded on 30 September the same year near Zillebeke. When he returned to the front in January the following year he became part of a Lewis gun team. He was a pupil at Merchant Taylors' School before going on to King's College, London, where he graduated in 1911 with a Bachelor of Arts degree. (Plot III.G.19)

Gunner Alfred John JONES, C Battery, 52 Brigade, Royal Field Artillery, died of wounds on 5 September 1918, aged 24 (Plot IV.A.35). His parents came from Wednesbury in Staffordshire and he was the third son to be killed during the war, but the CWGC records offer no clues as to the identity of his brothers. The war memorial in Wednesbury shows sixteen men with the surname 'Jones' and the CWGC records connect eleven men of that surname with Wednesbury. One of the eleven, Lance Corporal Samuel Jones MM, 1st King's Own (Royal Lancaster Regiment), is shown as residing with his wife in the King's Hill district of Wednesbury where Alfred's parents lived. However, the link to Alfred is still unproven on that basis alone. Samuel died of wounds on 2 July 1916 and is buried at Doullens Communal Cemetery Extension No. 1.

Second Lieutenant Charles Norman GREENWOOD MC, A Battery, 70 Brigade, Royal Field Artillery, died of wounds on 5 September 1918, aged 25 (Plot IV.A.36). His MC was gazetted on 17 October 1918 and was awarded after the camouflage net of a gun caught fire, forcing its crew to withdraw. Setting an example by his own gallant behaviour, he rushed forward and secured the assistance of some of the men in removing the burning cover. His presence of mind undoubtedly saved the gun from being badly damaged, and quite possibly saved the lives of others.

Sergeant Jason G. SMART MM, 10th Battalion, Canadian Infantry, died of wounds on 4 September 1918, aged 22. He won his MM at Hill 70 on 16 August 1917 after setting up a block in an enemy communication trench, placing it as far forward as our barrage would permit. He then did all he could to keep it supplied with bombs, but in the face of repeated enemy attacks he was unable to maintain the supply. He even collected all the bombs he could from dead soldiers and was wounded whilst doing so. After the battle it was said that his determination and coolness in handling the post undoubtedly saved many casualties and were important reasons why the post in the chalk pit was able to be retained. The recommendation for the award concluded that he had behaved gallantly throughout. (Plot IV.A.54)

Captain Edgar PAUL MC and Bar DCM, 1st Somerset Light Infantry, died of wounds on 10 September 1918 while serving as the battalion's adjutant; all three of his awards were won while serving with the battalion. His MC was gazetted on 25 August 1915 and was won as a serjeant major. It was awarded for conspicuous gallantry and ability throughout the campaign to date. The citation notes that he had rendered very valuable service at all times, especially in the firing line, and particularly near Pilkem on 6 July 1915 where he had organized carrying and working parties, which he then supervised under heavy shell fire.

His DCM was gazetted the following year on 25 September 1916. It was awarded for conspicuous gallantry in action as regimental serjeant major after he had taken charge of a party of fifty men carrying Royal Engineer stores up to a captured part of the line. When held up by heavy machine-gun fire, he skilfully got his party through by means of a circuitous route. He then returned with valuable information regarding the situation there. The citation concludes that throughout the day he had continuously performed fine work.

The bar to his MC was gazetted on 5 February 1919 and was awarded for conspicuous gallantry and devotion to duty near Étaing on 2 September 1918. When the left of the attack was held up, he led a small party up a trench to tackle the machine guns that were causing the delay. When he got near them he left the trench in order to rush them, but was severely wounded. Regardless of his injuries, he then got a Lewis gun up to his position, which successfully dispersed the enemy. Throughout the operation his endurance and determination set a fine example to the men. At the time of writing this book, the CWGC register only shows the award of the MC. I have notified the Commission so that the record can be amended. (Plot IV.B.15)

Lieutenant Guy Arthur Jones ASHWIN, a pilot with L Flight, 1st Wing, Royal Air Force, was killed with Lieutenant Cyril Clive Glandfield RAVINE while flying on 16 September 1918. ASHWIN was 21 years old and RAVINE was just 18 years of age. They were killed in a flying accident and are now buried next to each other. The CWGC register notes that ASHWIN joined the 1st Battalion at the age of 17 and was wounded on two previous occasions. This refers to the 1st (City of London) Battalion, London Regiment (Royal Fusiliers). That day was one of heavy casualties for the Royal Air Force. (Plot IV.B.33 and 34)

Private Claude Patrick NUNNEY VC DCM MM, 38th Battalion, Canadian Infantry, died of wounds on 18 September 1918. His DCM, which was the first of his decorations to be gazetted, was awarded for conspicuous gallantry and devotion to duty while serving as a private. It was gazetted on 20 August 1917 and the citation states that, although wounded in two places and his section wiped out, he continued to advance, taking with him his gun and ammunition, and then while acting alone, stopped an attack by over 200 of the enemy. He continued on duty for three days showing exceptional fearlessness and doing magnificent work. His MM, gazetted on 19 September 1917, was won as a sergeant after he was promoted in the field.

His VC was gazetted on 17 December 1918 and was awarded for most conspicuous bravery on 1 and 2 September 1918 during operations against the Drocourt–Quéant Line. On 1 September his battalion was in the vicinity of Vis-en-Artois preparing for the advance the next day. During those preparations the Germans put down a heavy barrage and followed it up by launching a counterattack. At the time he was at his company's HQ, but on his own initiative he made his way through the barrage to the company's outpost lines, where he went from post to post encouraging the men by his own fearless example. The enemy was repulsed and a critical situation was saved. The following day, during the attack, his dash continually placed him ahead of his company and his fearless example was undoubtedly a key factor in helping to carry the company forward to its objectives. Throughout the operation he displayed the highest degree of valour until he was severely wounded.

NUNNEY is one of sixty-five holders of the MM buried here, but is the only one in this cemetery to hold the VC (Plot IV.B.39). His brother, Private Alfred Nunney, was killed in action a few weeks earlier on 10 August 1918 serving with the 44th Battalion, Canadian Infantry. He is buried in Plot I at Fouquescourt British Cemetery.

Two of the sixty-five holders of the MM were also awarded a bar. Sergeant George Edwin THOMPSON MM and Bar, 87th Battalion, Canadian Infantry, died of wounds on 4 September 1918 (Plot IV.E.54). Lance Corporal Alexander COOK MM and Bar, 72nd Battalion, Canadian Infantry, died of wounds on 16 April 1918. In civilian life COOK was a baker who emigrated to Canada from his native Scotland where his parents still lived. (Plot III.B.34)

Captain William LIDDLE, 9th Royal Scots, is shown in *Officers Died in the Great War* as having died of double pneumonia on 27 September 1918, aged 31. The battalion came out of trenches near Loos the day after his death. There was very little action there and at the time it was considered to be one of the quieter spots on the front where operations were confined to probing the enemy's defences and patrolling no man's land. An only son, he came from Edinburgh where he was a Writer to His Majesty's Signet, an ancient society of solicitors in Scotland with roots going back to the mid-fourteenth century. (Plot IV.B.58)

Lieutenant Charles Vincent TODMAN, 16 Squadron, Royal Air Force, formerly 10th Battalion, London Regiment (Hackney Rifles), was killed in aerial combat on 3 August 1918, aged 26, whilst observing for Lieutenant Percy Charles West, aged 19, in a RE8 machine. TODMAN was born in Carmarthenshire, but had been living in London where his parents also resided. The CWGC register notes that he held a Bachelor of Arts degree. (Plot IV.D.1 and 2)

Lieutenant Irvin Harrison DAWSON MC, 1 Brigade, Canadian Field Artillery, died of wounds on 1 September 1918, aged 30 (Plot IV. E.7). His MC was gazetted on 18 January 1918, but there appears to be no citation for it.

Air Mechanic 1st Class Leonard Arthur ELMES; Air Mechanic 2nd Class Ernest John FEAR; Private 1st Class Samuel Frederick HEIGHES; Air Mechanic 3rd Class George HINES; Private 2nd Class William HOWARD; Air Mechanic 1st Class George Robert PORTER; and Air Mechanic 1st Class C.W. RAYNER, all members of 5 Squadron, Royal Air Force, were killed on 1 August 1918 during an enemy air raid on Le Hameau. Another man killed in the same air raid was Lieutenant George Tait OLMSTEAD, 64 Squadron, Royal Air Force. The men are buried near to one another in Plot IV, Row F, between graves 41 and 54.

Major Audsley Ralph CARTER, Royal Garrison Artillery, was serving as liaison officer to 1st Wing, Royal Air Force, when he died of wounds on 28 August 1918, aged 24. Co-operation between the artillery and the air services had been a key feature throughout the war and it remained so in 1918. (Plot IV.G.1)

Major Reginald Vernon BLACKBURN DSO MC, 28th Battalion, Canadian Infantry, died of wounds at Aubigny on 29 August 1918, aged 33. He was badly wounded on 26 August whilst in charge of 'B' Company as it was forming up for the attack on the German positions around Wancourt. His MC was gazetted on 25 April 1918 and was awarded for conspicuous gallantry and devotion to duty while commanding a reserve company in an attack. On hearing that all the other company commanders had become casualties, he went forward and took command of the newly captured line where he organized the consolidation of the entire position. For the next thirty-six hours he moved about under heavy fire regardless of the danger, encouraging the men and assisting them. He also supervised the collection and removal of all the wounded, showing courage, setting a splendid example and inspiring all those around him. He was awarded his DSO for successfully leading his company in a raid under heavy fire during which he rushed a machine-gun post single-handed, killing two of its occupants and capturing the remaining three, together with their gun. The award was gazetted on 16 September 1918. He had also been mentioned in despatches. (Plot IV.G.4)

Second Lieutenant William David HOUSTON, 16 Squadron, Royal Air Force, was killed in action on 27 August 1918 whilst flying as an observer (Plot IV.B.59). His pilot that day, Second Lieutenant David Simpson REID, aged 19, also died with him in their RE8 aircraft. REID, however, is buried a few rows along from HOUSTON. (Plot IV.G.13)

Second Lieutenant George Wright GLOVER DSO, 6th Rifle Brigade, attached 1st Battalion, died of wounds on 1 September 1918, aged 33. His DSO was gazetted on 22 September 1916 and was awarded for conspicuous gallantry in action on 1 July 1916 south of Serre on the opening day of the Battle of the Somme. Though twice wounded in the advance, he continued to lead his men forward under heavy machine-gun and artillery fire and into the enemy's third line where he organized the defence of the position. Although his wounded left arm was useless, he continued to throw bombs until the supply ran out. Throughout the day he set a splendid example. He was also mentioned in despatches. He was mortally wounded in the attack on the Drocourt–Quéant Line during which the 4th Division was operating as part of the Canadian Corps. (Plot IV.G.40)

Sapper Lewis WILSON, 3rd Battalion, Canadian Engineers, was killed in action on 31 August 1918, aged 38. Despite his surname, he was a Native American of Iroquois descent from the Six Nations Reserve. (Plot IV.G.45)

Corporal Ernest THEODORE, Canadian Corps Military Police, died of wounds on 1 September 1918, aged 29 (Plot IV.G.46). He is one of only six men from this particular unit of the Canadian Expeditionary Force to be found in the cemeteries of France and Belgium from the Great War.

Corporal Henry PARTINGTON, 15th (Scottish) Division, Military Mounted Police, Military Police Corps, died of wounds on 27 April 1918. Just over a hundred members of the Military Police Corps who fell during the Great War are buried in France. Another forty-six are buried in cemeteries in Belgium. All of these casualties are NCOs with the exception of two men who are shown as still serving as privates. (Plot IV.K.47)

Private Arthur Alexander WILSON, 1/2nd (Highland) Field Ambulance, Royal Army Medical Corps, is buried here rather than at Écoivres Military Cemetery where twelve other men from the same unit are buried. They were killed in the same incident during the early hours of 27 May 1918 when a shell landed on the hut where they were sleeping. The incident happened at Mont-Saint-Éloi, not far from Écoivres. Those buried at Écoivres are almost certainly the ones who were killed outright, whereas he was brought here to Aubigny to be treated for his injuries and where he died later that day. Privates Duncan CAULFIELD and John THOMSON also died in the same tragic circumstances.

Private Angus McGLASHAN, 6th Black Watch, is buried with them, and although the CWGC register indicates that he died on 28 May, the regimental history claims that he died of wounds on 20 May 1918. This seems unlikely, especially as he is buried next to the other three who did die on the later date. It may well be that McGLASHAN was wounded on the 20th, but died just over a week later. There is no documentary evidence to indicate that he died in the same incident as the others, in fact that seems highly unlikely too. (Plot IV.K.48 to 51)

Lance Corporal Thomas MILLER, 13th Royal Scots, died here at Aubigny on 21 June 1918. He was one of fifteen men wounded that day during a well-executed raid on German front line trenches during the early hours. The trenches, including Newton Trench, which formed part of the German front line, were situated on the high, flat ground between Fampoux and Gavrelle, close to where Chili Trench Cemetery now sits. Of the 351 men and eighteen officers from the battalion who took part, only one officer and four other ranks were killed, though fifteen were reported as missing after the action. The raiders were accompanied by one officer and eighteen other men from the Royal Engineers who were successful in destroying dug-outs and other emplacements before the entire party withdrew. Two other men heavily involved in the raid, including the officer who was mortally wounded, are buried next to each other at Duisans British Cemetery. (Plot IV.L.39)

Serjeant Lionel Allan PRATT MSM, Royal Army Medical Corps, attached 1st Army Gas School, died of wounds on 23 June 1918. His injuries occurred whilst examining a shell. Whether this was part of a particular purpose or whether it was simply out of curiosity is difficult to determine. (Plot IV.L.44)

Lieutenant Gerald Howard SMITH MC, 6th South Staffordshire Regiment, was killed in action on 29 March 1916, aged 36. His MC was gazetted on 17 January

1916. SMITH, who was educated at Eton and Trinity College, Cambridge, was the eldest son of Judge Howard Smith. (Plot V.A.2)

Lieutenant William Henry FLETT MC, 6th Black Watch, joined the battalion from the 3rd Battalion in January 1915. He was awarded his MC for his gallantry and courage on 3 April 1916 after the Germans had exploded a mine in the section of trench held by FLETT. This was followed by a heavy bombardment after which the Germans carried out a raid. In the ensuing fight FLETT's ankle was smashed by a grenade and two subsequent enemy bombs wounded him in the thigh and knee. Despite his wounds, he continued to command his platoon and refused to leave the fight until the raiders had been beaten off. He eventually succumbed to his injuries and died a few weeks later on 19 April. (Plot V.A.5)

His brother, Lieutenant Arthur David Flett, who was killed in action on 9 April 1917 serving with the 16th Royal Scots, is buried at Bailleul Road East Cemetery, Saint-Laurent-Blangy. Another brother, Lieutenant John Edmund Flett, was killed in action with the 7th Royal Scots on 15 November 1915 during the Gallipoli campaign and was mentioned in despatches by General Sir Ian Hamilton for gallant and distinguished service in the field. He is buried at Pink Farm Cemetery, Helles.

All three boys had attended the Leys School, Cambridge, where they had all excelled at sports, especially football, cricket and lacrosse. William, like his brother Arthur, became a chartered accountant, but had gone to live and work in Vancouver. At the outbreak of war he had joined the 47th Battalion, Canadian Infantry, but later accepted a commission in the Black Watch. Another brother, Andrew Binny Flett, had played international rugby as a forward for Scotland between 1901 and 1902.

Second Lieutenant Ernest John AMOR, 23 Squadron, Royal Flying Corps, died on 17 May 1916, aged 19. *Casualties and Honours during The War of 1914–1917 – Royal Flying Corps – Military Wing* records that AMOR, who had previously served with 14th Middlesex Regiment, died on 15 May 1916 from wounds he received in action that day. The Royal Flying Corps Communiqué covering the period of his death makes no mention of his squadron being involved in any aerial activity on 15 of May, though it does mention unfavourable weather. Another source shows a different date for his death; *Airmen Died in the Great War* states that he was killed whilst flying on 12 May 1916. Fortunately such discrepancies are fairly rare, but they do occur. (Plot V.A.6)

Captain Herbert Ambrose COOPER, 11 Squadron, Royal Flying Corps, was killed in a flying accident on 21 June 1916. He was the first New Zealander to join the Royal Flying Corps. In 1915 he had flown as a observer with Second Lieutenant Gilbert Stuart Martin Insall, mainly operating over the Somme area flying a Vickers Gunbus. On 7 November that year Insall won the VC, though by this time COOPER was a pilot in his own right. However, on 26 November, COOPER was reunited with Insall on a photographic mission. Whilst over Bray, near the River Somme, they engaged an Albatros Scout flying above them, opening fire on the hostile machine from below. However, their opponent was believed to have fired back at them via a trap door in the floor of his machine, after which he flew off towards Péronne. COOPER and Insall were taken by surprise and, although curious, were unable to pursue the aircraft owing to engine trouble. Their squadron, which had arrived at the front in late July 1915 with its Vickers Gunbus Fighter Scouts, was the first all-fighter unit of the Royal Flying Corps to operate on the Western Front. (Plot V.A.11)

Captain Frank Edward GOODRICH MC, 60 Squadron, Royal Flying Corps, was killed in action on 12 September 1916, aged 27, a day described as one of low cloud. He was gazetted as a Second Lieutenant in the Royal Flying Corps in September 1915 and in December that year he became a pilot. His MC was gazetted in the King's Birthday Honours List on 3 June 1916. He was born in Boston, Massachusetts, but lived in Canada where he was a locomotive engineer. He enlisted at Valcartier, Quebec, in September 1914, joining the 15th Battalion, Canadian Infantry. He was wounded by a bullet and gassed on 23 April 1915 near Ypres and had to spend time in England recovering from his injuries. It was while he was there that he learned to fly at Hendon aerodrome. The recommendation for his MC notes that he had shown exceptional gallantry and skill as a pilot between December 1915 and March 1916, especially on 21 February, when he landed his machine safely despite the rudder and elevator controls being shot away. (Plot V.A.15)

Second Lieutenant Cecil Pelham TOWNEND, 1st (City of London) Battalion, London Regiment (Royal Fusiliers), and formerly the Honourable Artillery Company, was attached to the 2/21st Battalion, London Regiment (First Surrey Rifles), when he died of wounds on 24 September 1916. He is shown in the regimental history of the Honourable Artillery Company as also serving with the 4th (City of London) Battalion, London Regiment (Royal Fusiliers). He had joined the Honourable Artillery Company in June 1909 and went to the Western Front with its 1st Battalion on 18 September 1914. He was later wounded near Ypres on 14 November 1914 whilst digging trenches, a task that he and others had to carry out in full view of the enemy. One man was killed and eight others, including TOWNEND, were wounded. It was also the first time that the battalion experienced shell and machine-gun fire. He was invalided back to England the same month and spent some time recuperating there before returning to the front in March 1916. *Officers Died in the Great War* shows him serving with the 1st (City of London) Battalion, London Regiment (Royal Fusiliers). (Plot V.A.16)

Second Lieutenant Cyril Henry Marshall KING, 60 Squadron, Royal Flying Corps, was killed in action on 30 September 1916, aged 23. The youngest son of a clergyman, the Reverend E.G. King DD, from Northamptonshire, Cyril went on to Birmingham University where he studied Engineering. On the outbreak of war he enlisted in the one of the Universities and Public Schools battalions before gaining a commission in the Royal Garrison Artillery. He went to the front in 1915, but soon transferred to the Royal Flying Corps as an observer. In June 1916 he returned to England where he qualified as a pilot and returned to France in August that year, only to be killed the following month whilst flying a Nieuport 16 aircraft (Plot V.A.17). His brother, Second Lieutenant Edward Westcott King, died of wounds on 20 October 1918 serving with B Battery, 79 Brigade, Royal Field Artillery. He is buried at Awoingt British Cemetery, near Cambrai.

Second Lieutenant Frederick Paul KANE, 29 Squadron, Royal Flying Corps, a Canadian flyer, was killed in action on 1 November 1916 whilst flying a DH2 single-seater aircraft. This was not a day of heavy casualties for the Royal Flying Corps, which suffered only three fatalities, two of whom had been recorded initially as wounded in action. He was gazetted as a temporary second lieutenant in the Royal Flying Corps in June 1916. The question remains as to how much operational flying experience he had during the time leading up to his death. He is mentioned on 11 October 1916 in the Royal Flying Corps Communiqué covering that period. On that occasion he opened fire on a touring car, forcing it to stop and three people were seen to run away from the vehicle. (Plot V.A.20)

Second Lieutenant Harry Edward MARTIN, 60 Squadron, Royal Flying Corps, was killed in action on 16 November 1916, aged 22, when his squadron was heavily engaged with enemy aircraft over Gommecourt. Having already driven off an enemy formation, he and members of his unit were attacked from above by a second hostile formation. This second group was fought off successfully, but Second Lieutenant MARTIN was seen descending out of control pursued by one of the enemy machines. MARTIN qualified as a pilot at Hendon in June that year and was subsequently commissioned in the Royal Flying Corps on 1 August. He went to the front on 28 October where he lasted barely a fortnight. He was a keen athlete and motor cyclist. (Plot V.A.21)

Second Lieutenant Raymond HOPPER, 60 Squadron, Royal Flying Corps, General List, was killed in action while flying a Nieuport 16 single-seat fighter aircraft on 11 January 1917, aged 23. He was a pupil at Hull Grammar School and had spent six months serving with the one of the Public Schools battalions of the Royal Fusiliers before joining the Royal Flying Corps. He was the only Royal Flying Corps fatality that day, perhaps because the weather was bad and operational flying was therefore very difficult. (Plot V.A.22)

Second Lieutenant Alfred Harmer STEELE, 16 Squadron, Royal Flying Corps, was killed in action on 4 February 1917, aged 25, whilst flying with Second Lieutenant James William BOYD. Earlier that day they had driven down an enemy machine, causing it to crash on landing, even though it had descended under apparent control. However, they were soon to become victims themselves.

STEELE, who was educated at Wellington College, had served an apprenticeship at the naval dockyard at Rosyth before becoming an assistant engineer.

Owing to his position there he was unable to gain his release from work until July 1916. When he did so, he joined the Royal Flying Corps and served initially as a motorcycle dispatch rider before being recommended for a commission. He was gazetted in November 1916 and soon became an observer. He survived just a few months into the New Year before being killed. Second Lieutenant James William BOYD had previously served with the Canadian Infantry and in *Airmen Died in the Great War* he is shown serving with the 74th Battalion, although Canadian army records and the CWGC register show him originally serving with the Canadian Divisional Cyclist Company. The men share the same grave. (Plot V.A.25)

Second Lieutenant Noel Much Hodson VERNHAM, 16 Squadron, Royal Flying Corps, was also killed in action on 4 February 1917. His flying partner that day was Second Lieutenant Herbert Martin Massey MC, who was wounded when their BE2d was brought down in flames by the German ace, Werner Voss, over Givenchy. They were Voss's fifth victory. Massey's injuries required half of his leg to be amputated, but he continued flying with the Royal Air Force after the war. He was wounded again in 1936 in Palestine where he was awarded the DSO. He also flew during the Second World War and was shot down with his crew near the Dutch coast where they were captured. While detained in Stalag Luft III as a prisoner of war, he was the senior British officer, and as such sanctioned the prison break out that was to become the basis for the film, *The Great Escape*. In the film he was portrayed as the character, Group Captain Ramsey, played by actor, James Donald. Massey, who was also awarded the CBE, served continuously in the Royal Air Force from 1915 until 1950, reaching the rank of Air Commodore. (Plot V.A.27)

Second Lieutenant Charles John Morton HINTON, 4th South African Regiment, died of wounds on 15 February 1917. He served as a corporal with the South African Brigade at Delville Wood the previous summer. (Plot V.A.28)

Second Lieutenant Robert Lawrence Munro JACK, 16 Squadron, Royal Flying Corps, formerly Gordon Highlanders, was killed in action on 17 February 1917 (Plot V.A.32). He was an observer with pilot Lieutenant Harry Eric Bagot, who according to *Airmen Died in the Great War* was injured, but survived the crash. They were shot down over Écurie, near Vimy Ridge, by the German ace, Werner Voss, and were his ninth victory. Voss went on to score a total of forty-eight kills. JACK had originally enlisted as a private in the 1/5th Gordon Highlanders, and was commissioned on 18 December 1915. Lieutenant Bagot went on to become 7th Baron Bagot in 1961 when he succeeded his cousin, Caryl Ernest Bagot, who served with the Irish Guards as a lieutenant during the Great War.

Lieutenant Henry Fergus MACKAIN, 13 Squadron, Royal Flying Corps, was reported to have been killed in action on 27 February 1917 (Plot V.A.33). He was gazetted in March 1916, having initially enlisted in the Artists' Rifles in 1915. He was born in Paris where his parents continued to reside during the war. On the day that he died, MACKAIN was piloting his machine with Second Lieutenant John Albert Edward Robertson Daly as his observer. They were carrying out work near Arras on behalf of the artillery when they were surrounded by six German aircraft. Daly managed to drive off one of the machines, but then noticed that MACKAIN seemed to have lost control of their aircraft. With little left to lose, Daly climbed out of his seat, on to the wing, and into the pilot's seat. Whilst sitting on MACKAIN's lap, and with his left foot still resting on the wing, Daly regained control of the machine and successfully landed it in a field. MACKAIN was probably dead while the aircraft was still airborne. Remarkably, Daly was unhurt in the incident, but died on 8 July 1918 from injuries sustained a few days earlier on 3 July in a flying accident. He is now buried at Fienvillers British Cemetery. Daly, whose surname is often recorded as 'Daley', was awarded the DFC in July 1918 whilst flying with 24 Squadron, Royal Air Force.

Second Lieutenant William John LIDSEY, 16 Squadron, Royal Flying Corps, died on 22 March after being wounded in aerial combat the previous day. He had formerly served in the 1/4th Oxfordshire & Buckinghamshire Light Infantry, joining up on the outbreak of war and going to France with the battalion in 1915. He received his commission in February 1916 and was posted back to his old battalion in France in November that year following officer training. However, he subsequently transferred to the Royal Flying Corps. He was 21 years old when he died and was Manfred von Richthofen's twenty-ninth victory. His body was recovered from the wreckage of his aircraft, which he had managed to land behind our lines, but he was very badly injured in the head and in the leg and survived for only a few hours before dying here at Aubigny (V.A.38). His pilot, Flight Serjeant Sidney Herbert Quicke, also died when their aircraft came down, but he is buried at Bruay Communal Cemetery Extension, about sixteen miles north-west of Arras.

Captain Greville Oxley BRUNWIN-HALES, 13 Squadron, Royal Flying Corps, was killed in action on 24 March 1917, aged 27. His only brother, Second Lieutenant Henry-Tooke Brunwin-Hales, had already been killed in action at Loos on 13 October 1915 whilst serving with the 1/4th Lincolnshire Regiment, aged 22. He is now buried at Vermelles British Cemetery. Captain BRUNWIN-HALES, who had previously served with the 8th Essex Regiment, was educated at Winchester School and Jesus College, Cambridge. Before the war he was land agent to Lady Carnarvon. He was gazetted flight commander in December 1916. He was killed along with his observer that day, Lieutenant Ayton Richey LEGGO who had previously served with the Canadian Light Horse and the 58th Battalion, Canadian Infantry. He was gazetted in November 1915, subsequently transferring to the Royal Flying Corps a year later. He was 22 years old when he died. (Plot V.A.40 and 41)

Lieutenant Herbert Howell EVANS, 2nd Canadian Mounted Rifles, was on secondment to the Royal Flying Corps as an observer when he was killed in action on 5 April 1917 (Plot V.A.42). He was killed flying with Second Lieutenant Oswald Frederick Grevatte BALL from 13 Squadron, Royal Flying Corps, who died the same day, aged 22 (Plot V.A.43). They had been carrying out observations on a day of heavy cloud cover and were on their way back flying at low altitude when their BE2c was hit by a British shell. BALL, who initially joined the Royal Sussex Regiment on the outbreak of war, also served as a bombing instructor before transferring to the Royal Flying Corps. He was at the front for seven months before he was killed.

Second Lieutenant John Gershin GALBRAITH, 13 Squadron, Royal Air Force, was killed while flying his RE8 aircraft on 28 July 1918, aged 21. The Royal Air Force did have other casualties that day, but the numbers were not excessive and it was described as a day on which very few enemy aircraft were seen. Another soldier from Chatsworth, Ontario, with the same surname was killed in action on 26 October 1917, though I have been unable to establish whether Private Charles Wilmer Galbraith was related, although they were not brothers. (Plot V.B.1)

Major Sir Archibald Leonard LUCAS-TOOTH, B Battery, 2/1st Honourable Artillery Company, attached 126 Brigade, Royal Field Artillery, was the son of Sir Robert Lucas-Tooth, 1st Baronet, of Queen's Gate, Kensington, London, and Kameruka, New South Wales. He died of pneumonia on 12 July 1918, aged 34. A keen cricketer, he was a member of the MCC. (Plot V.B.4)

His two brothers were killed during the war: Captain Douglas Keith Lucas Lucas-Tooth DSO, 9th (Queen's Royal) Lancers, was killed in action on 14 September 1914; Captain Selwyn Lucas Lucas-Tooth, 3rd Lancashire Fusiliers, attached 2nd Battalion, was killed in action five weeks later on 20 October 1914. Douglas is buried in Moulins New Communal Cemetery on the Aisne and Selwyn is buried in Le Touquet Railway Crossing Cemetery just inside the Belgian border. Their father had brewing interests in Australia and was a keen philanthropist and supporter of the Empire. Among the other positions that he held, he was a member of the management committee of King Edward's Horse, and when war broke out in 1914 he donated £10,000 towards the setting up of Lady Dudley's Australian Volunteer Hospital which served on the Western Front. He also became the chairman of the hospital's London management committee.

Lieutenant Ian Moore MOLYNEAUX, 1/7th Royal Scots, died of wounds on 10 July 1918, aged 22. He was wounded the previous night whilst out patrolling and had been with the battalion for two and a half years. (Plot V.B.5) His family lived in Queen Street, Edinburgh, which was, and still is, quite a fashionable part of the city.

Lieutenant James Henry CARSON MC, 31st Battalion, Canadian Infantry, was killed in action on 1 July 1918. His MC was gazetted on 26 September 1918 and was awarded for his conspicuous gallantry during a raid in which he led his platoon with great dash, capturing six prisoners, a machine gun, and killing three of the enemy himself. Having gained the final objective, he was severely wounded. Throughout the operation he set a fine example of courage and leadership. The raid took place on 24/25th June. Despite several days of medical care and attention here at Aubigny, he died from complications connected to his injuries. (Plot V.B.7)

Second Lieutenant John David KING DCM, 242 Army Brigade, Royal Field Artillery, died on 30 June 1918 while attached to its signalling section. By pure coincidence, his DCM was gazetted on 30 June 1915, exactly three years to the day before his death. His DCM was won as an acting bombardier with 27 Brigade, Royal Field Artillery, and was awarded was for conspicuous gallantry and devotion to duty in training telephonists and maintaining telephone lines. The citation adds that for six months he had been constantly under fire whilst carrying out these duties. *Officers Died in the Great War* makes no reference to his dying of wounds, suggesting that he died of natural causes. (Plot V.B.8)

Second Lieutenant Joseph DRYBURGH, 7/8th King's Own Scottish Borderers, died on 26 June 1918 from wounds received during a raid on German trenches on the night of 24/25th. He was aged 24. The raid was covered by the usual box barrage and entry into the German position was aided by poor wiring. The raiders, in three parties, managed to secure prisoners, but eight captured by the right-hand party were killed by their own shells as the German guns responded by putting down a counter-barrage in front of the British line. The left-hand party also managed to bring back six prisoners for intelligence and identification purposes. Another key objective for the raiders was the destruction of a large cave, which the British knew about because it had been in British hands prior to the German Offensive in late March that year. The raid therefore included a demolition team from the Royal Engineers to destroy the cave and the centre section of the raiding party had the role of covering them while they fired their charges. Second Lieutenant DRYBURGH was seriously wounded during a brief fight that occurred before the raiders withdrew. He was brought back to medical facilities here at Aubigny where he died. (Plot V.B.9)

Captain Maxwell Stanfield Eaton ARCHIBALD MC, 18 Squadron, Royal Air Force, died on 12 May 1918, a day on which enemy activity along the entire front was described as negligible. He was 30 years old when he died and had previously served in the Royal Engineers. The CWGC register states that he had been mentioned in despatches and had been wounded on 23 April 1916. His MC was gazetted on 16 September 1918 and was awarded for his conspicuous gallantry and devotion to duty over a period of time during which he had taken part in fourteen successful bombing raids, twenty-five successful low-flying bombing and reconnaissance flights, and eleven successful photographic missions. On one of these occasions he was attacked by ten enemy scouts. He engaged them and drove one of them down completely out of control. He had also engaged enemy troops from low altitudes and the citation concludes that his good spirits, excellent work and total disregard of danger had been an example to all. His squadron had been a bomber squadron since June 1917. On 9 May he was out on a wireless/photographic operation when he was attacked by a formation of ten enemy machines. He became embroiled in a fight, but this time he was shot down, though he may have accounted for one of the enemy's machines, which was seen to fall out of control. (Plot V.B.18)

Captain Kenneth Travers STEPHEN MC, 2nd Trench Mortar Battery, Royal Field Artillery, died of wounds on 22 April 1918. He was a law student in Melbourne, Australia, before the war and had sailed to England in November 1915 where he enlisted in the Royal Field Artillery as a gunner. He was commissioned before going to France in June 1916. His MC was gazetted in the New Year's Honours List in January 1918. (Plot V.B.22)

Second Lieutenant Henry William ROBERTSON, 11th Argyll & Sutherland Highlanders, died of wounds on 21 April 1918, aged 30. Three weeks earlier the 15th (Scottish) Division was forced to give up ground as it fell back across Orange Hill towards Arras during the last few days of March, fighting splendidly as it did so. On the morning of 20 April 1918 he took part in a raid on the newly established German positions near Feuchy. Some posts were captured, but machine-gun fire prevented further progress that day. Second Lieutenant ROBERTSON was the only casualty from the early part of this operation. He was evacuated to Aubigny, but died the next day from his wounds. (Plot V.B.23)

Captain Andrew FRASER MC and Bar, 2nd Queen's Own Cameron Highlanders, died of wounds on 20 April 1918, aged 29. His MC was gazetted on 7 December 1915 and the bar to it on 29 July 1918. The bar was awarded for conspicuous gallantry and devotion to duty during a determined attack by the enemy. As the enemy barrage came down, he collected stragglers and led them with the rest of his company into shell holes. Throughout the fight he sent back valuable information, and when his company was finally outflanked and forced to withdraw, he was the last to leave, even carrying in a wounded man. Throughout the entire episode he acted with great coolness and resource. Curiously, *Officers Died in the Great War* only shows the MC next to his name and makes no reference to the award of any bar. The headstone also shows just the MC and not the bar. His bar is referred to in *Recipients of Bars to the Military Cross 1916–1920*, which gives the gazette date as 26 July 1918. (Plot V.B.24)

Major Alan Torrance POWELL DSO, 14th Battalion, Canadian Infantry, died of wounds on 19 April 1918, aged 31 (Plot V.B.25). He was mentioned in despatches and was a graduate of the Royal Military College, Kingston, in Canada. His DSO was awarded for services in the field and was gazetted in the New Year's Honours List on 1 January 1918. The battalion was out of the line at Aubrey when the German artillery shelled the camp at 4am. One of the high explosive shells hit a hut that was being used as the battalion's HQ. POWELL suffered a head wound and died later that day. Other officers, including the battalion's commanding officer, were wounded, and Major Arthur Plow MC, MM, the battalion's adjutant, was killed instantly. He is buried at Roclincourt Military Cemetery.

Second Lieutenant Henry Edward Otto Murray MURRAY-DIXON, 4th Seaforth Highlanders, was killed in action on 9 April 1917, aged 31. He died in agony from a stomach wound after part of his abdomen was blown away. He was leading his men forward on the left flank of the 51st (Highland) Division, next to the Canadian 1st Division, when he was critically injured. He was a good friend of Norman Collins, whose memoir, *Last Man Standing* makes fond mention of him. Collins describes him as a charming man, but points out that an inability to remember to lead off with the left foot when on parade made him an unlikely soldier and not a very efficient one. However, he was a very talented artist and some of his sketches were published in *The London Sporting and Dramatic Magazine*. Collins also mentions that he believed MURRAY-DIXON to be related to the Duchess of Sutherland, though he does not elaborate on this. Whether or not they were related, she too made a huge personal commitment to the war. She was awarded the Belgian *Croix de Guerre*, the Royal Red Cross, and the British Red Cross Medal in connection with her work with a field ambulance at Namur in 1914 and also for her later work with field hospitals on the Western Front. (Plot VI.A.7)

The brother of one of Collins's friends, Second Lieutenant Hugh Francis PITCAIRN, 47th (London) Division Supply Column, Mechanical Transport, Army Service Corps, is also buried in this cemetery. On 3 June 1917 PITCAIRN rode over to visit his brother, Arthur, whom he had not seen for eighteen months. After visiting him, he was riding back from Arras when he was involved in an accident on his motorcycle and subsequently died of his injuries. (Plot VI.G.15)

Captain John MACDONALD, 16th Royal Scots, died of wounds on 11 April 1917, aged 27. The battalion had pushed out from the positions gained on the opening day of battle and these movements took the form of contact patrols to locate the enemy. The patrols captured a few prisoners in an abandoned gun pit as they edged towards Gavrelle, as well as some artillery pieces that the Germans had left behind on the first day. Although there was little opposition from the enemy in the form of immediate counter-attacks, their artillery was active with harassing fire and Captain MACDONALD was badly wounded by shell fire.

Second Lieutenant Robert Cunningham BROWN, 9th Royal Scots, died of wounds on 11 April 1917, aged 24. This was a relatively uneventful day for the battalion. It was tasked with clearing remaining pockets of Germans from the Brown Line, but its patrols found that they had already vacated it, leaving behind many mangled dead as a result of our artillery fire. Although the regimental history is not specific as to the manner of BROWN's death, the Germans were found to be occupying the railway embankment north of Bailleul-Sir-Berthoult where they had snipers and some machine guns already deployed. There was also some enemy shelling on 11 April, partly in response to the 4th Division's attack further south around Fampoux. (Plot VI.A.9)

Second Lieutenant John Hogben HISLOP, 15th Royal Scots, died of wounds on 11 April 1917, aged 32. He originally joined the Scots Guards on 7 November 1914 and had served as a serjeant and acting regimental serjeant major with 2nd Battalion, Special Brigade, Royal Engineers. (Plot VI.B.3)

Second Lieutenant David Campbell MacEWEN, 'A' Company, 9th Royal Scots, died of wounds on 10 April 1917, aged 31. He went to France in August 1916 and took part in the fighting at Beaumont Hamel that November. He was badly wounded on the opening day of the Battle of Arras and was brought to the casualty clearing station here at Aubigny where he died. In civilian life he had been a Member of the Society of Writers to the Signet working in Edinburgh. (Plot VI.B.5)

Second Lieutenant William Montgomery LIVINGSTON, 6th Royal Irish Fusiliers, attached 1st Battalion, died on 15 April 1917, two days after being gassed. Along with seven other officers and 292 other ranks he was in reserve near the Brown Line. By this stage of the battle the advance had begun to slow down considerably and the Germans wasted no time in bringing their artillery into action against locations where it was known or suspected that British troops and artillery were likely to be found, including routes to and from the new front line; the Brown Line was one such locality. LIVINGSTON was one of ten casualties from his battalion to suffer from gas shells on the night of 13 April, and one of two who died as a result of its effects. (Plot VI.B.9)

Second Lieutenant C.C. McLEAN, 2nd South African Regiment, died at Aubigny on 13 April from wounds received the previous day when the South African Brigade made its unsuccessful attack on Roeux. He had been promoted within the South African ranks and had served as a private during the fighting at Delville Wood the previous summer. (Plot VI.B.10)

Captain Robert ROSS MC, 1/7th Gordon Highlanders, died of wounds on 18 April 1918. The CWGC records show that his parents lived at Banchory, which is where the 7th Gordon Highlanders was formed. With regard to his MC, I can find no reference to it in any of the *Gazettes*, nor is there any reference to it in his records held at the National Archives. (Plot VI.C.1)

Second Lieutenant Frederick Henry REYNELL, 35 Squadron, Royal Flying Corps, and General List, died in action on 23 April 1917, aged 25. He was flying that day with his observer, Captain Seymour BARNE MC. An old Etonian, BARNE initially joined the 20th Hussars and had been present with them during the Retreat from Mons. He had been wounded at the First Battle of Ypres and in 1915 served as a staff officer with 4 Cavalry Brigade. He had then volunteered to become an observer with the Royal Flying Corps. His MC was gazetted on 14 January 1916. He was the eldest son of Lieutenant Colonel St. John and Lady

Constance Barne of Sotterley and Dunwich in Suffolk, and was also the nephew of the Marquess of Hertford. Both men died after their aircraft was shot down and they are now buried next to each other. (Plot VI.C.11 and 12)

Seymour's brother, Major Miles Barne DSO, served with the Suffolk Yeomanry, but in 1913 he was gazetted in the Scots Guards, serving with the 1st Battalion. He had also served in the South African War. He was killed in action on 17 September 1917 and is now buried at Mendinghem Military Cemetery in Belgium. His DSO was gazetted on 1 January 1917 in the New Year's Honours List for distinguished service in the field.

Captain Leonard Lane TALBOT MC, 27 Brigade, Royal Field Artillery, died of wounds on 24 April 1917, aged 34. His MC was gazetted on 4 June 1917 in the King's Birthday Honours List. (Plot VI.C.13)

Lieutenant George Thomas BROWN MC, 27th Battalion, Canadian Infantry, died of wounds on 23 April 1917, aged 22. His MC was gazetted on 20 July 1917 and was awarded for conspicuous gallantry and devotion to duty in establishing communication within ten minutes of the objective having been gained, after which he personally repaired lines under heavy fire for some forty hours. The battalion's war diary makes no mention of his death or any other casualties on 23 April, but it does note that it was in reserve at Neuville-St. Vaast where it provided working parties. (Plot VI.D.2)

Lieutenant Colonel John WHITEMAN, 4th Middlesex Regiment, commanding Hawke Battalion, 63rd (Royal Naval) Division, died of wounds on 25 April 1917. He was one of several senior army officers who were posted to battalions of the Royal Naval Division after its losses at the Battle of the Ancre in November 1916. In 189 Brigade, Hawke, Drake, Hood and Nelson Battalions received new commanding officers, as did Anson Battalion in 188 Brigade. WHITEMAN, who was mentioned in despatches, was mortally wounded in the attack on Gavrelle on 23 April 1917. (Plot VI.D.5)

Captain Ralfe Allen Fuller WHISTLER, 2nd Highland Light Infantry, died of wounds on 28 April 1918, aged 21. He was educated at Worcester Cathedral Choir School and King's School, Canterbury, then at Sandhurst. After that he joined his father's regiment, the Highland Light Infantry, and was commissioned in March 1914. When war broke out he went to France with the battalion and was present at Mons and on the Aisne where he was wounded by shrapnel. He was wounded a second time in May 1915 at Festubert and was evacuated home in order to recuperate. On his return to action he was posted to the 1st Highland Light Infantry, which was fighting in Mesopotamia, and while he was there he was involved in operations to relieve the besieged town of Kut. It was here that he was also wounded again. Whilst recovering he contracted typhoid and was eventually invalided home again. Undeterred, he returned to the front in late March 1917, this time serving with his old unit, the 2nd Battalion. (Plot VI.D.7)

He was fatally injured on 28 April 1917 whilst carrying out the rescue of some men from a dug-out. The battalion was in the line near Arleux and the Battalion HQ was in a former German concrete gun pit which still contained live shells and cordite. It also contained two dug-outs that housed the battalion's orderlies and mess staff. When a German bombardment fell on the position, a shell scored a direct hit, igniting a box of Very lights, and another shell burst in the gun pit itself. The resulting fire caused the shells inside the pit to explode and the cordite to ignite. The members of the orderly room staff were able to escape, though one had to be rescued after he had been blown back down the dug-out steps by another shell. WHISTLER, who had arrived with a party of men, entered the dug-out where the mess staff were believed to be still trapped, but he was mortally wounded during the attempted rescue. When the fire was extinguished the bodies of the five mess staff were recovered. The battalion went into action later that day near Oppy against what had been part of the former German third line where it had seven officers and forty-three men killed and eight officers and 226 men wounded.

There are several men buried in this cemetery from the 2nd Battalion whose dates of death suggest they may have been wounded at the same time as WHISTLER, possibly in the same incident. However, they are fairly scattered throughout the cemetery; they include Private Charles Sidney KEMP (Plot II.G.46); Private William PATON (Plot II.J.21); Private Morton EUNSON (Plot II.J.33) and Private Henry TOAL (Plot II.J.57). The difficulty in determining how they died is complicated by the possibility that they may have died of wounds in the subsequent fighting that day. KEMP, who was 43 years old, would certainly have been older than many in the battalion, which tends to make me think that he may have been one of the orderly or mess room staff.

WHISTLER's immediate family came from Battle in Sussex. He was also related to the Edwardian novelist, Charles Watts Whistler, as well as Hugh Whistler, who went on to become a renowned ornithologist, and Sir Laurence Whistler who made his name as a poet and an engraver of glass.

General Lashmer Whistler GCB KBE DSO DL, who served with great distinction under Montgomery in the Second World War, and Major General Alwyne Michael Webster Whistler CB CBE were also members of the extended family, as was Rex Whistler, the painter, who was killed in action serving with the Guards Armoured Division near Caen. He is buried at Banneville-la-Campagne War Cemetery in Normandy. A more distant relative is reputed to be the artist, James McNeill Whistler, but if true, the links lie somewhere obscured in the far distance.

Lieutenant George Olaf Damien Ceadda JACKSON, 10th Battalion, Canadian Infantry, was killed in action on 28 April 1917, aged 33 (Plot VI.D.10). His brother, Lieutenant Hugo Antony Lancelot Ceadda Jackson, also served in the same battalion and fell in the same action as his brother. The tragic consequence of their death was that this line of the family became extinct. Hugo is buried not far from here in Écoivres Military Cemetery, Mont-Saint-Éloi.

Lieutenant Colonel Charles Frederick PRETOR-PINNEY DSO, 13th Rifle Brigade, died on 28 April 1917, aged 53, from wounds suffered a few days earlier. He was the eldest son of Colonel F.W. Pretor-Pinney and was educated at Eton and Cambridge. His original commission was in the Rifle Brigade, but he had already retired prior to the outbreak of the South African War. Nevertheless, he re-joined and served throughout that campaign, but once the war was over he again retired with the rank of major. In 1914 he rejoined the Rifle Brigade and was gazetted as a captain, though soon after he was reappointed as a major. In October 1914 he was given command of the regiment's 13th Battalion, and in July 1915 he went with it to the front. He was wounded a year later on 10 July 1916, but resumed command in early March 1917 when he took over from Lieutenant Colonel Savage-Armstrong DSO, who was killed at Arras, on 23 April 1917. (Plot VI.E.5)

Captain Stanley Hornsby KENT MC and Bar, 10th Battalion, Canadian Infantry, died of wounds at Aubigny on 29 April 1917. He had been seriously wounded the previous day whilst assembling his men for the attack on Arleux-en-Gohelle. His MC was gazetted on 16 March 1916 and was awarded for conspicuous gallantry in leading a wiring party that worked for six hours. He then led an attacking party through the gap. His party was heavily bombed and came under heavy rifle and machine-gun fire, but he and his men inflicted heavy loss on the enemy. He had also on two previous occasions led daring reconnaissance operations. The bar was gazetted on 20 July 1917 and was awarded for a similar exploit in which he led a successful raiding party into enemy lines capturing two prisoners and bringing back valuable information. Thanks to his untiring example and efforts, the raid was reckoned to have saved many lives. (Plot VI.E.4)

Lieutenant William Roberts LISTER MC, 1st Battalion, Canadian Infantry, died of wounds on 3 May 1917, aged 28. He initially enlisted in September 1914 with the 1st Canadian Division's signalling company. He was one of fifteen officers from his battalion who became casualties when it attacked trenches north of Fresnoy on 3 May, a figure that equates to approximately two thirds of the officer strength at the start of the day. His MC was gazetted on 30 July 1917 and was awarded for his conspicuous gallantry and devotion to duty after he had spent five hours in total darkness under very heavy fire ensuring that there was contact between the relieving unit and those on either flank. (Plot VI.E.12)

Second Lieutenant William Kennedy TROLLOPE, 13 Squadron, Royal Flying Corps, died of wounds on 3 May 1917, aged 21. He had also been wounded on 3 April, exactly a month before his death. He was returning from a flight when his aircraft was attacked by five German machines. His observer was killed outright, but despite being wounded in several places, Trollope managed to descend from 5,000 feet and land his machine in one piece. By then he was unconscious and German artillery started to lay down heavy fire on the location where he had landed just inside the British lines. He was pulled from his aircraft by a soldier who had left his trench to rescue him. The soldier was wounded in the process, but managed to get Trollope back to the comparative safety of the trenches. He was evacuated to Aubigny, but despite being operated on, he died from his wounds (Plot VI.E.13). His observer that day, Second Lieutenant Augustine Bonner, formerly Royal Warwickshire Regiment and South Staffordshire Regiment, is buried in Feuchy British Cemetery near to where their aircraft came down.

Lieutenant John DOBSON, 1st Royal Irish Fusiliers, died of wounds on 4 May 1917, the day after going into action against German positions around Greenland Hill as the 4th Division attempted to capture Roeux. A few of his men, with remnants of the Household Battalion, managed to reach their first objective about 500 yards east of the road that runs between Roeux and Gavrelle, but they were too few to make any difference to the day's outcome. He had only been with the battalion since mid-December the previous year. (Plot VI.E.14)

Lieutenant William John SHORTER, 46 Squadron, Royal Flying Corps, was killed whilst flying on 24 March 1918, aged, 20 (Plot VI.F.1). He formerly served with the 8th Essex Regiment and was flying a Camel at the time of his death. His squadron was involved in aerial combat that day, shooting down at least two enemy aircraft. It had also been heavily engaged with enemy machines the previous day during which he and Second Lieutenant Harry Noel Cornforth Robinson had driven one of their opponents down and out of control in a shared victory. Robinson is credited with one of the two victories the following day, but SHORTER is not mentioned in that day's communiqué. Robinson went on to earn the MC and the French *Croix de Guerre*.

Second Lieutenant Felix Charles BAILEY, 46 Squadron, Royal Flying Corps, died on 28 March 1918, aged 21, from injuries received the previous day whilst flying his Camel aircraft. His squadron had been in action on the 27th and had fought with enemy aircraft, claiming one victory. (Plot VI.F.2)

Lieutenant Frederick Horace THORP, Royal Flying Corps, formerly 24th Manchester Regiment, died on 31 March 1918, aged 24, from wounds sustained the previous day while observing for his pilot, Second Lieutenant F.H. Sharpe, who was wounded, but survived, when their RE8 crashed. THORP had begun working for the Home Office before the war. (Plot VI.F.4)

Lieutenant Vernon KING, 16 Squadron, Royal Air Force, aged 31, and his pilot, Captain Thomas Bright JONES, aged 26, were killed while flying a RE8 on 11 April 1918. KING had previously served with the Royal Marines. (Plot VI.F.8 and 9)

Lieutenant Robert Hutton BOYD, 5 Squadron, Royal Air Force, was killed in action with his pilot, Lieutenant Lewis MOGRIDGE, formerly King's Liverpool Regiment, when their RE8 machine came down on 12 April 1918. They were buried together. This was a busy day in the air for both sides, particularly around Hangard, but also north of the La Bassée Canal. (Plot VI.F.10 and 11)

Captain Cecil Francis Henry LITTLETON, 1st Cameron Highlanders, attached 5th Battalion, died of wounds on 6 May 1917, aged 26 (Plot VI.G.1). He was the son of Rear Admiral the Honourable Algernon Charles Littleton and Lady Margaret Littleton and was one of ten children. His maternal grandfather was Francis Jack Needham, Viscount Newry and Mourne. Cecil's brother, Richard, also fought in the Great War and served as a commander in the Royal Navy during the Second World War, though he was invalided out in 1940.

Second Lieutenant Thomas Johnston PARDY, 4th Argyll & Sutherland Highlanders, attached 10th Battalion, died of wounds on 7 May 1917. PARDY took part in what became known in the battalion as 'The Daylight Arras Raid', which took place on 6 January 1917. The raid involved three officers, nine NCOs and seventy-seven other ranks. However, before the day's events got under way, an accident occurred as a platoon sergeant was reading out orders for the raid in a cellar; a Mills bomb exploded, killing two men and wounding fourteen. However, the numbers were hastily made up from another platoon and the raid went ahead. It began at 3.08pm. and lasted just twenty minutes, after which the signal was given recalling the raiding party, which was described as sounding like French horns. Casualties from the raid were light; one man was killed and another was wounded, but he was carried in by Second Lieutenant Robertson. PARDY and another man, Private Burns, managed to reach the third parapet in the German lines during the raid where PARDY found time to light up a pipe, later claiming that they could have carried on all the way to Berlin!

PARDY was in command of 'C' Company when the battalion took part in renewed attacks on 3 May 1917. PARDY's group, together with men from 'D' Company under Second Lieutenant Law, managed to penetrate 600 yards into the German lines, but none of the units on either side had managed to keep pace with them; in fact, many that morning had become so mixed up in the darkness of the featureless landscape that they had returned to their original starting line. PARDY's men eventually met with enemy resistance and a stiff fight took place. Second Lieutenant Law died of wounds in German hands; but his uniform and revolver were subsequently returned to his family. He had been recommended for the MC, but it was never awarded. PARDY, who was seriously wounded, was recovered and taken from the battlefield to Aubigny where, despite medical attention, he died from his wounds. (Plot VI.G.4)

One of the architects of 'The Daylight Arras Raid' was Captain George Parsons Denham of 'A' Company. In civilian life he was a keen artist, but he was also described as a fine fighter. Denham also carried out a patrol on 4 April 1917 to find out the state of the enemy wire at a point known as the Parrot's Beak. He was eventually spotted, fired on, but managed to get back safely. On 9 April he was shot and seriously wounded by a German officer. Denham's men were so incensed that they not only bayoneted the German officer, but killed everyone with him in a pure act of vengeance; not an uncommon reaction in such circumstances. Denham made it as far as Étaples where he died on 14 April 1917, aged 37. He is buried in Étaples Military Cemetery.

Second Lieutenant Donald SIMPSON MC, 1/5th Seaforth Highlanders, died of wounds on 19 May 1917. His MC was gazetted on 30 July 1917 and was awarded for conspicuous gallantry and devotion to duty while in charge of a line of posts. He held his ground with his platoon against an enemy attack, and later in the day organized and led a counter-attack on the enemy, pressing it home with great vigour. He was severely wounded early that day, but remained in command until after dark when he was carried away by stretcher-bearers. His wounds were so severe that his leg had to be amputated. His personal example to his men was described as 'splendid'. (Plot VI.G.11)

Second Lieutenant Arthur Andrew CREASEY, 22 Squadron, Royal Flying Corps, formerly 1st Bedfordshire Regiment, was killed in action on 14 July 1917, aged 21, whilst flying as observer with Second Lieutenant Granado Walter FOREMAN, Royal Flying Corps (Special Reserve), who also died the same day, aged 23. The men are buried next to one another. FOREMAN was an Australian who worked as an engineer and surveying assistant for the Victoria State Railways. He obtained his commission in Australia and served with the Australian Imperial Force in Egypt before coming to the Western Front. He made the decision to apply for the Royal Flying Corps and was sent to England where he did his training. He gained his flying certificate in April 1917. In February 1917, while he was still serving with the Bedfordshire Regiment, CREASEY had played a key part in defeating an enemy raid. The battalion war diary points out that he and another named officer were the main reason why the raid failed, praising their alertness, personal courage and initiative. (Plot VI.H.3 and 4)

Lieutenant Robert Naylor TREADWELL MC, 22 Squadron, Royal Flying Corps, formerly 9th Essex Regiment, died on 9 September 1917 as a result of wounds received almost a month earlier on 11 August. He had won his MC as a second lieutenant for showing conspicuous gallantry and devotion to duty when severely wounded during aerial combat. Through sheer pluck and determination, and despite his injuries, he successfully brought his machine back to the aerodrome against a very strong wind, saving the machine and the life of his observer. When he landed he was so weak and exhausted that he had to be lifted from the aircraft. He took part in many successful patrols and bombing raids before this, and on every occasion he showed great courage, dash and devotion to duty. His award was gazetted on 9 January 1918. (Plot VI.H.8)

Lieutenant Edward Horace PEMBER, 5 Squadron, Royal Flying Corps, died on 30 September 1917, aged 19 (Plot VI.H.10). He previously served in the Royal Field Artillery and the CWGC register notes that he won a Mathematics Exhibition to Balliol College, Oxford, having previously been a pupil at Harrow. His father, Francis Pember, was Warden of All Souls College, Oxford, and also a noted barrister who went on to become Vice Chancellor of Oxford University.

PEMBER's mother was the Honourable Margaret Bowen-Pember, daughter of Baron Davey QC, Judge and Liberal politician. His observer that day, Air Mechanic 2nd Class Arthur MORLEY, was killed in action with him, but he is buried elsewhere in this cemetery (Plot III.F.15).

Lieutenant Augustus Orlando BALAAM, 16 Squadron, Royal Flying Corps, formerly 4th Suffolk Regiment, was killed in action on 24 October 1917, aged 25. The surname appears to be particularly common to areas of East Anglia and a glance through the CWGC records suggests that other members of his family may also have fallen in the Great War. His observer, Second Lieutenant Donald St. Patrick PRINCE-SMITH, formerly Royal Dublin Fusiliers, died the same day. Their aircraft was an RE8. (Plot VI.H.12 and 13)

Lieutenant Eric Cuthbert John ELLIOTT, 27 Squadron, Royal Flying Corps, was killed while flying on 22 November 1917. His pilot that day, Lieutenant H. Townsend, was wounded and appears to have survived the war. Their aircraft was a DH4. (Plot VI.H.14)

Captain Cyril Walter Carleton WASEY MC, Chevalier of the *Légion d' Honneur*, 16 Squadron, Royal Flying Corps, formerly Royal Warwickshire Regiment, was killed in action on 28 October 1917. He was awarded the French decoration in connection with the 1914 Retreat when his battalion co-operated with French units on its flank as it withdrew. His MC was gazetted on 1 January 1917 and he was mentioned in despatches in 1915. He was wounded on two occasions during his service. His pilot, Lieutenant Edward Hugh KEIR, formerly 3rd King's Own (Royal Lancaster Regiment), was also killed that day, aged 20, and is buried in the next grave. The men were involved in an encounter with a German aircraft. WASEY was killed by a bullet from his opponent and lost control of their aircraft, leaving KEIR little time to prepare for the inevitable. (Plot VI.J.1 and 2)

Second Lieutenant Leslie Lashbrook MEDLEN, 16 Squadron, Royal Flying Corps, was killed in action on 22 December 1917, aged 21. He had previously worked at the Royal Ordnance Factory in Woolwich and joined the Royal Flying Corps in June 1917. His two brothers also served during the Great War and survived, one in the Royal Flying Corps, the other in the Royal Garrison Artillery. His pilot, Second Lieutenant Frederick Ernest NEILY, a Canadian, was also killed with him that day in their RE8 aircraft. NEILY came from Nova Scotia and had previously served with the Canadian Expeditionary Force in the 18th Field Ambulance, Canadian Army Medical Corps. Their aircraft was shot down in an aerial combat during which MEDLEN was mortally wounded in the head. (Plot VI.J.3 and 4)

Lieutenant Edric Hurdman READ, 16 Squadron, Royal Flying Corps, was killed in action on 26 December 1917, aged 20. He came from Ontario, Canada. His observer that day, Second Lieutenant H.R. Donovan, was wounded. The previous few days had seen heavy mist set in and on Christmas Day and Boxing Day flying conditions became worse owing to snow resulting in very little flying activity. (Plot VI.J.5)

Second Lieutenant Robert SHERWOOD, 5 Squadron, Royal Flying Corps, and his observer, Lieutenant Terence Evelyn KENNARD, formerly Royal Field Artillery, were killed in action on 26 February 1918 when their RE8 came down. KENNARD's father, Colonel Henry Gerard Hegan Kennard, 5th Dragoon Guards, served as commander of the Dublin Garrison between 1915 and 1918. (Plot VI.J.6 and 7)

Second Lieutenant Ronald William St. George CARTWRIGHT, 16 Squadron, Royal Flying Corps, was killed in action on 26 February 1918 as observer to Lieutenant W.G. Duthie, who was wounded flying their RE8 aircraft. CART-WRIGHT's brother, Second Lieutenant Eric Percival St. George Cartwright, was killed in action near Martinpuich on 13 August 1916 whilst serving with Machine Gun Corps, to which he was attached from the 4th Leinster Regiment. He was 19 years old and is buried on the Somme at Bécourt Military Cemetery, Bécordel-Bécourt. There is a slight discrepancy over his actual date of death, which *Officers Died in the Great War* shows as 12 August, as does the memorial in the church where the boys lived in Herefordshire. (Plot VI.J.8)

Second Lieutenant Henry James Trevor WILKES, 16 Squadron, Royal Flying Corps, was killed while flying on 28 February 1918, aged 25. *Airmen Died in the Great War* shows him serving with 27 Squadron. His observer, Serjeant H.R. Eden, was injured, but survived. The Royal Flying Corps Communiqué covering that day notes that there was very little enemy activity and that very few combats took place. (Plot VI.J.9)

Second Lieutenant Douglas Alfred Stephen STEVENS, 16 Squadron, Royal Flying Corps, was killed in action on 9 March 1918, aged 18, along with his pilot, South African, Second Lieutenant Reuben Harold YELL, aged 21, in their RE8. (Plot VI.J.10 and 11)

Lieutenant Osborne George TANCOCK MC, 5 Squadron, Royal Flying Corps, formerly Royal Field Artillery, was killed while flying on 17 March 1918, aged 20. His pilot, Second Lieutenant George Cooper YOUNG who was a year older, also died with him. TANCOCK's father was Colonel Osborne Kendall Tancock CMG, late Royal Artillery. (Plot VI.J.12 and 13)

Air Mechanic 2nd Class Ernest Jesse BRACEY, 10th Kite Balloon Section, Royal Air Force, died on 8 July 1918, presumably from natural causes, aged 44. *Airmen Died in the Great War* makes no reference to any wounds or injuries, though it will often comment on the cause of death, particularly when it occurs through illness. (Plot IV.J.49)

Lieutenant William Gordon BROWN, 19 Squadron, Royal Air Force and General List, died on 7 May 1918, aged 21, when his aircraft, a Sopwith Dolphin, crashed during a practice flight, suggesting some kind of mechanical failure with the controls rather than the engine. When the aircraft pitched, the pilot appeared unable to control it. In the hands of a skilled and experienced pilot a machine with engine trouble could still be landed, provided that the control mechanisms were still functional. (Plot V.B.20)

Écoivres Military Cemetery, Mont-Saint-Éloi

The Arras-Bethune road, the D.937, meets the D.49 at Neuville-Saint-Vaast. Take the D.49 and head west towards Mont-Saint-Éloi, whose ruined abbey can be seen dominating the landscape. After a couple of miles the D.49 crosses the D.341, the Arras-Houdain road. Continue over the junction and the road passes through a stretch of dense woodland for about 200 yards before emerging into the open again. A couple of hundred yards further on, turn left, and the cemetery sits on the right-hand side.

Given the size of the cemetery there are comparatively few gallantry awards amongst the NCOs and privates buried here. There are just twenty-three holders of the MM, eighteen of whom are Canadian, and three of them are lieutenants. Two are buried close to each other in the same row (Plot VI.D.7 and 9) whilst the other is in a different plot (Plot V.J.5). Although there are twenty officers with the MC, there are just two holders of the DSO.

There are also a large number of French graves, the majority dating from 1915 when the French controlled the area around Arras, and a few German graves also still remain. The British and Commonwealth graves are largely buried in chronological order. Casualties would often be transported back using the French tramway that ran between here and the trenches close to the front line. Inevitably, some died en route to the casualty clearing stations that were dotted around this area, but divisions were also able to send bodies back here for burial rather than inter them close to the front line, and often did just that. Only thirteen of the 1,728 burials are unidentified.

Lieutenant Glyn Cuthbert ROBERTSON, who died on 16 March 1916, aged 22, was a member of the University of London's OTC. He was killed at Neuville-Saint-Vaast by a sniper whilst inspecting trenches that had been taken over from the French the previous day. He was serving with the 1/2nd (North Midland) Field Company, Royal Engineers, and his grave is one of the earliest in this cemetery (Plot I.D.1). In fact, the earliest burial is not in Plot I, but in Plot VIII. Private Andrew Craigie WALLACE, 7th Black Watch, died on 14 March 1916, aged 20 (Plot VIII.A.24). He is one of a number of men from the 51st (Highland) Division buried in this row.

Second Lieutenant Arthur Gorman MITCHELL, 5th Royal Irish Rifles, attached 2nd Battalion, is one of forty men from that regiment buried here (Plot I.K.18). All, apart from one of them, are buried in Plot I between Rows F and O. Second Lieutenant MITCHELL attended Queen's University, Belfast, where he was a member of its OTC. He was gazetted in the 5th Battalion in May

1915 and joined the 2nd Battalion overseas in April the following year. He was killed by a sniper whilst accompanying two platoons to reinforce a crater. He was just 19 years old when he died. His father was Lieutenant Colonel Arthur Brownlow Mitchell, Royal Army Medical Corps, who served as an Ulster Unionist MP for Queen's University, Belfast, in the 1930s.

Second Lieutenant Edward Frederick SHEFFIELD, 7th Kite Balloon Section, Royal Flying Corps, died from injuries sustained during a parachute descent from a balloon on 17 May 1916. He was 28 years old. (Plot I.M.4)

Captain Wilfrid Max LANGDON, 10th Cheshire Regiment, was killed in action on 21 May 1916, aged 27. He was educated at Rugby School and New College, Oxford, after which he worked as a barrister at the Inner Temple. When the Germans attacked trenches held by the 47th (London) Division on 21 May 1916, driving back the line, LANGDON and his men formed a defensive flank at the southern end of the area, but their position was overrun and he was killed in the ensuing fight. His battalion was part of the 25th Division. (Plot II.B.6)

Private Bernard CHAMPNESS, 2/13th Battalion, London Regiment (Kensingtons), was killed in action near Neuville-Saint-Vaast on 27 July 1916, aged 27 (Plot II.B.20). He was a Law Society scholar and went on to become a solicitor in 1913. He would have been an ideal candidate for a commission, and indeed was nominated for a commission in September the following year after joining the Artists' Rifles as a private on 10 November 1914. Although the commission was offered to him, he chose to transfer to the Kensingtons as a private owing to 'urgency', though the note in the CWGC register does not elaborate on the nature of that urgency. For a number of men the pressing need was to see action as soon as possible and this was possibly so in his case, though by November 1914 it would have been clear to just about everyone that the war was not likely to be over by Christmas.

Lance Corporal James HOLLAND, 10th Cheshire Regiment, was executed on 30 May 1916 (Plot II.E.17). His rank no doubt contributed to the verdict at his trial. He had been in charge of four other men in an advanced post at the end of a sap close to the enemy's trenches. When two Germans entered the trench system, HOLLAND and three of the men with him made their way back to company HQ where HOLLAND falsely declared that the post had been overrun. Meanwhile, the two Germans disappeared and an enquiry clearly showed that HOLLAND had left his post. This in itself was a military offence, but he was also tried and found guilty of cowardice. His family were originally told that he had been killed by shell fire.

Captain John Christopher Craven BARNES, 8th Border Regiment, was killed in action on 29 May 1916. He was the son of Henry John Barnes, who died on 27 June 1919 and who had served as a lieutenant colonel in the Royal Army Medical Corps during the South African campaign. (Plot II.E.19)

Seven casualties whose story is obviously intertwined can be found in Plot III, Row B. The first of the three graves has three names on the headstone: Private Edward William Murray THOMPSON, Private Ernest Charles SMITH and Private George William MAYHEW, who all served with the 2/13th Battalion, London Regiment (Kensingtons). The next headstone is that of Private James Robert SMITH of the same battalion, and the third grave also has three names: Private George ROGERS, 2/13th Battalion, London Regiment, and two Royal Engineers, Sappers John COLLINS and Sidney James HOLBORN. All seven died of wounds on the same day, 2 July 1916. Next to them are Captain Donald FRASER, Royal Engineers, who died on 1 July 1916, and Sapper James MALCOLM, who presumably, like the other seven, died of wounds or injuries the following day (Plot III.B.1 and 2).

The London men were members of a carrying party when they were killed by a shell on 1 July and were originally buried near the transport lines at Bray. They were the battalion's first casualties since its arrival in France. The Royal Engineer casualties suggest that the party was carrying material for use by the sappers. (Plot III.B.3 to 5)

Two young officers from the 2/20th Battalion, London Regiment (Blackheath and Woolwich), were killed as a result of fighting on the night of 26 July 1916 after the Germans had blown a mine under an existing crater, known as Duffield Crater, near Neuville-Saint-Vaast. Two other mines that had been prepared by the 172nd Tunnelling Company were also fired at around the same time. In all three instances, the British won the race to secure the lips of the newly formed craters closest to their own lines. Second Lieutenant Thomas GARDNER, aged 21, and Second Lieutenant Geoffrey Theodore HELLICAR, aged 19, were consolidating their hold on 'Tidza Crater' when they became involved in a brief fight with a party of Germans trying to oust them. Both officers were mortally wounded in that action and are now buried close to each other (Plot III.B.18 and 24). There are, however, conflicting dates of death for both men. *Officers Died in the Great War* shows GARDNER as having been killed in action on 22 July 1916 and HELLICAR on the 27th. This date of death for GARDNER is clearly incorrect and the CWGC record, which shows it as 28 July, makes far more sense, indicating that GARDNER died from his wounds two days later after both men had been brought back to Écoivres. HELLICAR's death is shown in the CWGC register as 26 July and fits closely with the narrative account. Their battalion was a second line Territorial battalion belonging to the 60th (2/2nd London) Division.

Lance Corporal ALSOP, 6th Inniskilling Dragoons, died of wounds on 14 August 1916 whilst out with one of the many working parties that were continuously supplied from units billeted behind the lines. Cavalry units were often used in this manner and any Royal Engineer unit would have been pleased to have fit, athletic cavalrymen billeted nearby who were available to assist them in their work. (Plot III.D.20)

Second Lieutenant Basil Armitage CARVER, 6th Inniskilling Dragoons, Lance Corporal Arthur Henry ROBINSON and Privates Percy TAYLOR, Bertram KING and Charles CLEMENTS were all killed on the same day as a result of an incident in a mine shaft on the morning of 21 August 1916. All are now buried adjacent to each other (Plot III.E.9 to 13). Throughout the month of August the three cavalry regiments that made up the Mhow Brigade, 1st Indian Cavalry Division, had been providing large working parties of 300 men, accompanied by their own officers, to assist the work of the Royal Engineers in the Neuville-Saint-Vaast sector. Half of the party was relieved every five days by the remaining third of the regiment on a rotational basis.

The war diary (WO95/404) gives a detailed account of the tragedy and the lessons that were drawn from it. It concludes that the Germans had fired a mine next to the location where 175 Tunnelling Company had placed their own charges. After waiting for any fumes to clear, the engineers went back into the mine shaft to examine for any damage, but were overcome by gas poisoning in a sap tunnel. It would appear that the German explosion had probably released gas trapped underground from previous mining activity. The diary also records the gallantry shown by Second Lieutenant CARVER and his men, who went to try to rescue the sappers. Two of the men, Serjeant W. Fletcher and Private W. Wood, both from Carver's regiment, were hospitalised suffering from the effects of the gas, but went on to make a good recovery.

Next to CARVER and his men is Sapper Edwin COOK, 175 Tunnelling Company, Royal Engineers. The CWGC register shows his grave reference as Plot III.E.3, but the correct reference is Plot III.E.14. The inscription on his headstone reads: *'Here is one of the best and bravest lads slain by the enemy's hands'.* His date of death is shown as 21 August 1916 and he is one of the unlucky sappers involved in this mining tragedy. The cemetery register also shows that he came from a mining background in Newark, Nottinghamshire. A few headstones away are the remaining three sappers who lost their lives with him. Sapper Thomas Hope WALNE, aged 26, and Lance Corporal Philip SCOTHERN, aged 34, were the first sappers to go down into the shaft, followed by Sapper William MILLER and another colleague. MILLER was the first to collapse. Another man, Sapper Keeling, climbed down the shaft and tried to rescue MILLER, but had to abandon his attempt; he survived the incident. Today WALNE, SCOTHERN and MILLER are buried next to each other (Plot III.E.19 to 21), not far from CARVER and his men. The post-incident report makes interesting reading, including future advice and guidance regarding the availability and use of breathing apparatus.

Private John Norbury SIDEBOTHAM, 17th Battalion, Army Cyclist Corps, also died on 21 August 1916, aged 22. My initial thoughts were that he may have been involved in the above incident, but he was actually struck by a sniper's bullet that passed through some sandbags, mortally wounding him in the head. He was attended to by his comrades, but died soon afterwards and was buried the same afternoon by men from his unit. (Plot III.E.15)

The headstone of Private Helgard Marthinus DU PREEZ, 4th South African Regiment, killed in action on 28 August 1916, aged 21, is very unusual in that the inscription is entirely in Afrikaans. Although the CWGC record shows his rank as private, the headstone shows it as 'Burg'. This appears to be a very clear and deliberate expression of Afrikaans culture, probably at the behest of his family. His headstone is not unique in this respect, but it is rare, and I have only ever come across one other example on the Western Front where the inscription is entirely in Afrikaans. The headstone of Private Pieter Van Heerden Botes, 1st South African Regiment, is similarly inscribed. He was just 17 years old when he was killed in action and is buried at Naves Communal Cemetery Extension. The word 'Burg' is a shortened version of 'Burgher' and the CWGC records show exactly 100 men of that rank killed during the Great War. All of them fell during the campaign in German South-West Africa and are buried in CWGC cemeteries in South Africa and Namibia. (Plot III.F.6)

Another cavalryman buried here is Private William Edward WESSON, 1/1st Yorkshire Hussars Yeomanry. He died of wounds on 18 September 1916 (Plot III.G.3). *Soldiers Died in the Great War* shows him as 'Weston'. Another man from the same regiment, Private John TAYLOR of 'A' Squadron, is shown as being killed in action the same day (Plot III.G.5). Private Montague Vivian BRAYSHAW, who is buried nearby, was killed in action on 5 October that year and also served with the Yorkshire Hussars (Plot III.G.17). The CWGC records show just eighteen men from this Territorial regiment buried on the Western Front. It had originally been divided up when it went overseas, but was reformed in May 1916. In late summer 1917 it retrained as an infantry unit, and later that year it was merged with the 9th Battalion, West Yorkshire Regiment, which then became known as the 9th (Yorkshire Hussars Yeomanry) Battalion. The regiment's second battalion was never deployed overseas.

Another second line Territorial officer buried here from the 60th (2/2nd London) Division is Second Lieutenant Ernest HICKS from the 2/18th Battalion, London Regiment. (London Irish) He was killed on the night of 9 October 1916, not long before the division left France for Salonika. The men that took part in the raid that night were unfortunate in so far as the cloud cover broke, and in the ensuing moonlight the raiding party was soon spotted by the Germans opposite them who even appeared to have been expecting the attack. Despite this, the London Irish managed to get into the enemy's trench where they bombed a dug-out, killing a number of the garrison as they did so. The party returned without obtaining any prisoners and suffered quite heavily. Although HICKS was the only officer killed, three other officers were wounded, thirty-one other ranks were also killed or wounded and a further five were reported as missing. Ironically, the 2/17th Battalion, London Regiment (Stepney and Poplar), carried out a raid that same night with a party of three officers and fifty men. They were able to bomb dug-outs and kill several of the occupants without incurring a single casualty. (Plot III.G.21)

Sapper William Cleaver BUTCHER, 5th Field Company, Canadian Engineers, was killed in action on 21 March 1917, aged 28. The CWGC register shows that his father, Elias George Butcher, served overseas with the 1st Pioneer Battalion, as did two of his brothers. One of the brothers, Private Edward Clive Butcher, served with the 7th Battalion, Canadian Infantry, but I have found no clues as to the identity of the other brother. (Plot III.K.8)

Another outstanding memoir of the Great War is one of the books written by William Richard Bird MM, *Ghosts Have Warm Hands*. Among the many individuals mentioned in the book is Lieutenant Kenneth Archibald CAMPBELL, 42nd Battalion, Canadian Infantry. The officer, whom Bird describes as naïve and inexperienced, was inspecting a post located in Vernon Crater on Vimy Ridge. When CAMPBELL asked how far away the German trenches were he was told that they were 60 yards away, and almost immediately a trench periscope was shot away. Then, to everyone's surprise, he insisted on taking a look over the parapet. Bird grabbed his coat to try and stop him, but he was too late and Lieutenant CAMPBELL was shot through the head. It was not possible to move the body until after dark, but Bird covered his face with a clean sandbag. CAMPBELL's death occurred on 23 January 1917 (Plot IV.B.19). He was one of six brothers who served, two of whom fell. Lieutenant Colin Gernon Palmer Campbell MC, 94 Brigade, Royal Field Artillery, was killed on 10 October 1917 and is buried at Godewaersvelde British Cemetery in France, near the Belgian border.

Private William Alexander FULTON, 42nd Battalion, Canadian Infantry, died in tragic circumstances. One of his comrades accidentally discharged a loaded rifle as he was handling it, mortally wounding FULTON who died from his injuries on 4 February 1917, aged 46. (Plot IV.C.13)

Private Egerton FERNLEY, 42nd Battalion, Canadian Infantry, was killed in action on 8 February 1917 when a German mortar shell, referred to as a 'dart', struck the parapet next to him. He was taken to the nearest aid post where his clothes were removed, but not a mark could be found on his body. One of the men who had been about 10 yards away in the same trench was William Richard Bird MM. Bird returned to the spot where the 'dart' had burst. He knew that FERNLEY's rifle had been propped against the wall of the trench and noticed that the top of his bayonet had snapped off. Bird had seen FERNLEY beating his arms across his chest trying to keep warm and concluded that the end of the bayonet must have been blown off and had probably lodged in his heart, entering via the armpit when his arms were outstretched. The wound had not bled. The account is just one of many recalled by Bird in his superb memoir. (Plot IV.C.27)

Private William James NASH, 26th Battalion, Canadian Infantry, was a battalion sniper whose luck ran out on 4 March 1917. He had already killed two Germans that day, but was himself killed by an enemy sniper. His story is illustrative of this deadly and very clinical aspect of warfare that was part of everyday life for soldiers at the front. The battalion history shows his death occurring the following day, and it may be that he was wounded on the 4th and evacuated to medical facilities close to Écoivres where he died the next day. Occasionally the date of burial is mistaken for the date of death; small inconsistencies such as this occasionally occur, though they rarely create confusion. (Plot IV.E.14)

Major Gregory Vincent NELSON, 18th Battalion, Canadian Infantry, was killed in action on 5 March 1917. He was killed by a shell as his battalion was being relieved and his funeral took place here at Écoivres two days later while the battalion was out of the line and billeted near Mont-Saint-Eloi. (Plot IV.E.29)

Lieutenant Charles Kenneth WHITTAKER MC and Bar, 10 Brigade, Canadian Field Artillery, was killed in action by German shell fire on 25 April 1917. His MC was gazetted on 4 June 1917 as part of the King's Birthday Honours List. The bar to it was gazetted on 20 August 1917 and was awarded for conspicuous gallantry and devotion to duty while moving his guns up to a forward position, a task that was accomplished over roads that were almost impassable and which were in full view of the enemy and under heavy shell fire. The guns subsequently proved to be of the greatest assistance to the infantry as it advanced. At the time of researching this book, neither the CWGC register, nor *Officers of the Canadian Expeditionary Force Who Died Overseas*, refers to the second award. The latter publication also shows his date of death as 26 April. I have notified the Commission so that the entry in the register can be amended. (Plot VI.G.14)

Easily lost amongst the many Canadian headstones in this cemetery is a group of six men from the 1/6th Argyll & Sutherland Highlanders killed in action on 26 March 1917 or who died of wounds the following day. The men are buried in Plot IV Row H. Corporal Ronald McLUGASH, who came from the tiny hamlet of Kilchoman on Islay, is shown as having died of wounds. The others are Lance Corporal Alexander THOMPSON and Privates William McAULAY, Robert KNOX, Thomas RODGER and George Frederick GREEN. (Plot IV.H.10 to 15) THOMPSON's brother, Duncan, was killed with the 6th King's Own Scottish Borderers on 19 July 1916 near Longueval on the Somme and is now commemorated on the memorial at Thiepval.

Serjeant Thomas BERRY DCM, 47th Trench Mortar Battery, was killed in action on 27 March 1917, aged 27. His DCM was gazetted on 25 November 1916 and was awarded for conspicuous gallantry in action. He had fought using his trench mortar throughout operations with great courage and skill. On one occasion a bomb fired by him landed just 20 yards from the gun, but failed to burst. Realising the potential danger to those nearby, he went out and removed the fuse, thereby almost certainly saving many lives. (Plot IV.J.2)

Privates Henry CROSSLEY and Walter CROSSLEY were brothers who served in the same battalion, the 27th Battalion, Canadian Infantry. They were killed within two days of each other just prior to the opening of the Battle of Arras. Henry died of his wounds on 29 March, aged 21, and Walter died on 31 March 1917, aged 25. They are now buried side by side. (Plot IV.K.13 and 12)

Another pair of brothers buried here are Privates David and Charles METEER. David died from his wounds on 1 April 1917 whilst serving with the 2nd Battalion, Canadian Infantry (Plot V.A.1), whilst Charles, who served in the same battalion, died two weeks later on 15 April (Plot VI.E.28).

Captain Eric Reginald DENNIS MC, 2nd Battalion, Canadian Infantry, was killed in action on 5 April 1917. His MC was awarded for conspicuous gallantry in action. Whilst under intense fire, he rescued some men who had been buried showing great courage and determination. Later on, he set a splendid example to his men under very trying conditions. The award was gazetted on 27 November 1916. He was the son of the Honourable William and Agnes Dennis. The CWGC record shows that he served with the 2nd Battalion from 2 July 1916 until his death. Although the war diary makes no specific reference to casualties, the battalion did carry out two raids that day; one at 4am and another at 3pm in which it encountered opposition in the enemy's support line. Captain Dennis's father was a member of the Canadian Senate and also an editor and publisher who owned the *Halifax Herald* and *Evening Mail*. (Plot V.B.6)

Captain Daniel Gordon CAMPBELL, 16th Battalion, Canadian Infantry, was killed in action on 9 April 1917, aged 29 (Plot V.D.9). He had been an accomplished athlete and Scottish high jump champion, affectionately known as 'Dodo'. He is known to have been killed during the early stages of the attack at Vimy Ridge. Another brother, Lieutenant Hugh Campbell, was killed in action at Gallipoli serving as a temporary captain with the 11th Manchester Regiment. He is buried at Green Hill Cemetery, dying of wounds on 22 August 1915.

Captain Victor Gordon TUPPER MC, the commanding officer of No. 3 Company, 16th Battalion, Canadian Infantry, was killed in action on 9 April 1917, aged 21. He was the grandson of Charles Tupper, the former Prime Minister of Canada, and the son of the Honourable Sir Charles Hibbert Tupper KCMG. His MC was gazetted on 16 November 1916 and was awarded for conspicuous gallantry in action after he had kept up signal communications under very heavy fire. Later, he had personally supervised the repair of wires that had been severed, displaying the same courage and determination as on previous occasions when he had also done fine work. (Plot V.D.10)

Major John Lant YOUNGS MC, 1st Battalion, Canadian Infantry, was killed in action on 9 April 1917, aged 21. He won his MC for conspicuous gallantry in action, leading his men with great courage and determination, and later on, attacking single-handed an enemy machine gun, capturing the gun and its crew.

The award was gazetted on 27 November 1916. His father, John Lant Youngs, also won the MC in 1916. His award, gazetted on 22 August 1916, was awarded for conspicuous gallantry. Though sick in hospital, he had insisted on joining his battalion when he heard that it was going into action. During those operations he led his company with great dash and skill under heavy shell fire. It was largely due to his efforts that the supply of grenades never failed. Unlike his son, he survived the war and attained the rank of colonel. (Plot V.D.11)

Lieutenant Lawrence Francis Cartney BOLE MC, Royal Canadian Regiment, was killed in action on 9 April 1917. His MC was gazetted on 28 September 1916 and was awarded for conspicuous gallantry following a raid during which he worked with two other officers for forty-five minutes under heavy fire clearing the casualties. The citation concludes that throughout the raid, and afterwards, he did fine work. Canadian records often show his third name as 'Gartner'. (Plot V.E.6)

Major James Arnold DELANCEY MC, 25th Battalion, Canadian Infantry, was killed in action on 9 April 1917 while leading his men at Vimy Ridge. He was shot through the head as he and his men were in the German second line trenches. His MC was gazetted on 1 January 1917 in the New Year's Honours List. He was a civil engineer by profession and had enlisted in May 1915. (Plot V.E.11)

Lieutenant John DICKINSON MC, 72 Brigade, Royal Field Artillery, was killed in action on 8 April 1917, though *Officers Died in the Great War* shows the date of death as 9 April. His MC was gazetted on 4 June 1917 in the King's Birthday Honours List. (Plot V.F.24)

Major Alfred Syer TRIMMER MC and Bar, 10th Battalion, Canadian Infantry, was killed in action on 28 April 1917. His MC was awarded for conspicuous gallantry after he had led a party of bombers through the enemy's wire inflicting heavy casualties. Although wounded, he remained behind until all his men had left the opposing trenches. The award was gazetted on 16 March 1916. Neither the CWGC records, nor *Officers of the Canadian Expeditionary Force who Died Overseas* show the award of the bar, the citation for which was gazetted on 12 September 1916. It was awarded for coolness, bravery and great devotion to duty whilst under heavy fire for two days. With the assistance of two other men from his platoon, he carried out the special duties assigned to him in a most heroic manner, though it does not mention what those duties were. The war diary, however, does mention him and two fellow officers in connection with events at Mount Sorrel between 2 and 4 June 1916, during which all three of them were described as showing great calm and coolness while exposed to constant danger. This is almost certainly the action to which the latter citation refers. (Plot V.H.2)

Lieutenant Hugo Antony Launcelot Ceadda JACKSON, 10th Canadian Infantry, was one of two brothers killed in the war. Both fought with the same battalion and they died on the same day, 28 April 1917, during the same action. The CWGC register points out the stark and chilling reality of their deaths, stating that as a result of this twist of fate '*this branch of the family becomes extinct*'. His brother, Lieutenant George Olaf Damien Ceadda Jackson, who died from his wounds, is buried not too far away in Plot VI at Aubigny Communal Cemetery Extension. Their late father was a church minister at Holy Trinity Church, Bampton in Oxfordshire. Hugo is buried here at Écoivres, possibly having died some hours before his brother. (Plot V.H.3)

Major Kenneth Leon Taylor CAMPBELL MC, 5th Battalion, Canadian Infantry, was killed in action on 28 April 1917. His MC was gazetted on 25 January 1916 and cites two specific actions. It was awarded for conspicuous gallantry, firstly on 15 December 1915 during an attack on an advanced German barricade on the Messines Road; secondly, for great gallantry in an attack on German trenches at Hill 63 on 16 November 1915. An account of the operation on 15 December can be found in *Cameos of the Western Front – A Walk Round Plugstreet Wood* by Tony Spagnoly and Ted Smith. (Plot V.H.19)

Major Angus George GILLMAN MC, 52nd Battery, Royal Field Artillery, was killed in action on 29 April 1917. The *London Gazette* dated 8 January 1915 sets out the institution of the Military Cross, though the award was officially created on 28 December 1914. Captain A.G. GILLMAN is shown receiving his MC in that same publication, which makes him one of the first recipients of the award. (Plot V.H.21)

Another notable grave is that of Driver Albert MORRISON, 9 Brigade, Canadian Field Artillery. He was killed in action on 5 July 1917, aged 22. His father, John, died as a passenger on the *Lusitania* when it was sunk on 7 May 1915 off the coast of Ireland by a German submarine. Almost 1,200 lives were lost in the disaster, which provoked world-wide condemnation. (Plot V.K.11)

Captain William Sowerby CLARK MC, 10th East Yorkshire Regiment, was recorded as having been killed in action on 10 July 1917, though his death did not occur as a result of enemy action. His MC was gazetted on 23 October 1916 and was awarded for leading a patrol across no man's land, entering an enemy trench and capturing three prisoners. He was slightly wounded during the operation. His death occurred as a result of an accident during bombing practice on 10 July 1917. He was 23 years old. (Plot V.K.17)

Lieutenant Colonel Michael Frederic Beauchamp DENNIS DSO and Bar, 7/8th King's Own Scottish Borderers, was killed on 19 May 1918 whilst visiting trenches with his runner, Corporal Adamson. Adamson, partially protected by the trench, partly by his commanding officer, received only minor wounds, but Lieutenant Colonel DENNIS took the full force of a shell when it exploded close to him. Ironically, the morning had been fairly quiet. However, his body was unable to be safely moved until midnight and his funeral took place at 12 noon the following day here at Écoivres.

As soon as he received the news that war had broken out, he sailed from South Africa to England with his wife and his uncle, Gordon Stewart Drummond Forbes, where both men joined the 7th King's Own Scottish Borderers. Forbes died of wounds from a random shell on 21 July 1915 during his first tour of duty in the trenches and is buried in Fouquières Churchyard Extension. 'Fred' DENNIS continued to serve with the battalion and won his first DSO as a captain at Hill 70 on 25 September 1915, the opening day of the Battle of Loos. He was wounded in the assembly trenches immediately before the attack, but after having his wound bandaged, he advanced with his company, encouraging his men until he was wounded for a second time. He had to be carried back to a dressing station to have his new wound attended to, after which he walked out and rejoined his company, again encouraging and spurring his men on until wounded for a third time.

He was wounded again in late June 1916, this time by shell splinters, though only slightly. After that he was promoted to major, followed by his appointment as commanding officer of the 7/8th Battalion. The bar to his DSO was awarded in 1917, details of which were published in the *London Gazette* on 9 January 1918. The citation notes that after he had been wounded in the back by shrapnel, he refused to leave the battlefield and continued to lead his men with the utmost gallantry and disregard of danger. With similar gallantry, he rallied his men after they had been driven back by a counter-attack, and by his splendid example the battalion succeeded in holding the line.

There is an excellent and detailed account of his funeral in the unit's history: *A Border Battalion*. It describes the cortege leaving Agnez-les-Duisans to the sound of 'Flowers of the Forest', which was again played as it arrived at Écoivres cemetery. All six pall-bearers, officers from his battalion, are named in the account, which points out that very few NCOs and men were able to attend, though many had wanted to, owing to the fact that the battalion was still in trenches holding the line. However, his charger, Blackbird, did attend the funeral and was led to the cemetery by Private McQuade. Major General Reed VC, commanding the 15th (Scottish) Division, was the most senior officer in attendance. Lieutenant Colonel DENNIS was lowered to his grave as the pipes played 'The Death of the Chief', after which the 'Last Post' was sounded. His battalion arranged for a stone cross to be erected on the site of the grave, but the Imperial War Graves Commission objected and the stone cross was replaced by a simple wooden one.

It was not just his long association with the 7/8th King's Own Scottish Borderers that made him a popular figure with his battalion. He often participated in sports days when out of the line and he once flew over a training ground where his battalion was being put through its paces, setting off a number of Very lights to the amusement of officers and men below. In March 1918 he returned to

France from leave in England in order to take charge of his battalion as the German offensive was looming.

He had also served in the South African War where he was seriously wounded in the lower leg by a bullet at Klips Drift. The limb became gangrenous and he was lucky to escape without it being amputated. The wound gave him continuous problems throughout the rest of his life, but he never let it deflect him from what he believed to be his duty, which was to serve his country and his men. During my research for this book I had the privilege to examine a number of original documents and photographs charting his life, thanks to his granddaughter to whom I am extremely grateful. (Plot V.L.1)

Private Malcolm RICHMOND, 6th Gordon Highlanders, was executed on 26 May 1918, aged 22. He was shot for desertion. He made a number of escapes from custody, firstly from Étaples in October 1917. He was re-arrested in Boulogne after being at large for a month. He then showed remarkable determination, or desperation, by escaping yet again in December while he was awaiting trial. He remained at large for another month, hiding out in Boulogne, but within a couple of weeks of his arrest, he managed to escape for the third and final time. He claimed at his trial that he was suffering from mental illness that ran in his family. The verdict dismissed his defence and he was shot by firing squad. (Plot V.L.8)

Close to the Cross of Sacrifice in Plot V, Row L, are twelve graves of men attached to the 2nd (Lowland) Field Ambulance, Royal Army Medical Corps, all of whom were killed on 27 May 1918 (Plot V.L.9 to 20). Their unit had recently been at Aux Rietz, near La Targette, where there was a main dressing station, but more importantly, there were deep dug-outs there that gave very good protection against shelling. However, on 25 May 1918 the unit moved to Mont Saint-Éloi, further back from the front line, where a new main dressing station was under construction and huts had been provided as billets. Unfortunately, at around 4am on the morning of 27 May, the Germans began shelling Mont Saint-Eloi and one of the first shells scored a direct hit on the far end of one of the wooden huts causing carnage. Ten men were killed outright and five others died of wounds soon afterwards. A further six were severely wounded and ten others, probably from the other end of the hut, were only slightly wounded. Intermittent shelling continued but thankfully resulted in no further loss of life or damage.

The war diary for the unit that month gives an interesting insight into the trying conditions under which its personnel were working, which included a shortage of basic supplies and seeming indifference from those in higher authority. Exasperation reaches near farcical levels when the unit's tailor is poached by a divisional concert troupe.

One of the men, Private David Rees EVANS (Plot V.L.15), had already lost a brother. Sapper Richard William Evans died at home on 1 February 1916 while serving with the Royal Engineers. He is buried at Llanelli (Box) Cemetery.

A couple of days before the tragic incident described above, Private William Turner ATKINSON, 1/1st (Highland) Mobile Veterinary Corps, died, aged 19. Throughout the war, horse transport made huge demands on supply and veterinary services up and down the front, and from time to time casualties did occur among veterinary staff, particularly from shelling, though some died from natural causes too. (Plot V.L.5)

The headstone of Gunner Sidney HOPKINS has a personal inscription written in his native Welsh. He was serving with B Battery, 56 Brigade, Royal Field Artillery, when he was killed in action on 23 May 1918, aged 27. (Plot V.L.7)

Another interesting collection of graves can be found in Plot VI.B.10 to 21. All twelve men are from No. 2 Company, Special Brigade, Royal Engineers, and all of them were killed on 6 April 1917, three days before the opening of the Battle of Arras. The group consists of one sergeant, two corporals and the rest are either sappers or pioneers. One of the men, Sergeant Reuben MITCHELL, had been awarded the MM.

Private John SINCLAIR, 43rd Battalion, Canadian Infantry, died of wounds on 5 April 1917, aged 27. He came from the Fisher River Agency and, despite his surname, he was another Canadian soldier of Native American origin. (Plot VI.B.27)

Private Eugene PERRY, 22nd Battalion, Canadian Infantry, was executed on 11 April 1917, aged 21. While undergoing a sentence of Field Punishment No. 1 imposed for a short period of absence from duty, he again went missing for just over six hours. This second offence, trivial as it may seem, was the one that cost him his life. His battalion was in action on 9 April at Vimy Ridge, but a small group of them were assembled two days later to form the firing party for his execution. (Plot VI.C.7)

Second Lieutenant Walter Josiah PEARSE MC, Z Battery, 5 Brigade, Royal Horse Artillery, was killed in action on 9 April 1917. His MC was gazetted on 4 June 1917 in the King's Birthday Honours List. (Plot VI.C.13)

Lieutenant Frederick Amblec HEATHER MC MM, 2nd Canadian Mounted Rifles, was killed in action on 9 April 1917. His MC was awarded for conspicuous gallantry in action when carrying out a daring reconnaissance prior to a raid. He then led the raid himself, showing great courage and determination, personally rescuing several wounded men during the operation. The award was gazetted on 12 January 1917. His MM, gazetted on 15 August 1916, was won whilst he was serving as a sergeant in the same regiment. He is one of twenty-three men buried here with the MM. (Plot VI.D.7)

Captain James Brown BRISCO MC, 172 Tunnelling Company, Royal Engineers, was killed in action on 9 April 1917, aged 39. His MC was gazetted on 10 December 1915 and was won while serving as a second lieutenant with the same unit. The award was the result of an action which he carried out with Second Lieutenant Arthur Hibbert during a mining operation south-east of Ypres when one of our galleries uncovered a German gallery. Both officers entered the enemy's workings to investigate the situation, BRISCO going left and Hibbert going right. After 80 yards, BRISCO came across a party of Germans who were still working. With his revolver, he shot the one nearest to him, whereupon the rest of the party returned fire, forcing him to retire back down the gallery. There, he rejoined Hibbert, who had already made the decision to blow in the enemy gallery. BRISCO then held the party of Germans at bay while Hibbert fetched sandbags and explosives. Together they placed and detonated the explosive charges, successfully disrupting German operations at that location.

On the opening day of the Battle of Arras, BRISCO was in charge of one of two parties of engineers that had rushed forward with the infantry in order to reach German tunnels beneath Vimy Ridge. BRISCO and his group followed the 1st Canadian Mounted Rifles and reached the Prinz Arnulf Tunnel where he and his men were involved in a fire-fight near the entrance. He was mortally wounded en route to make a report to Brigade HQ, but his men were successful in clearing the tunnel of demolition charges. The other party under Captain Cooper made safe the larger Voller Tunnel. (Plot VI.E.1)

Another Canadian grave of note is that of Private Stanley Tom STOKES, 1st Battalion, Canadian Infantry, who was killed in action, aged 16, on 9 April 1917 down towards the southern end of Vimy Ridge (Plot VI.E.3). His father, Private Horace Stokes, was killed later in the year on 19 September, aged 40, whilst also serving with the 1st Battalion, Canadian Infantry. He is now buried at Aix-Noulette Communal Cemetery.

According to the CWGC register, Private Murdo CROMARTY was the ward of a Caroline Grieves of Norway House, Manitoba. In spite of his very Scottish-sounding name, Murdo was actually of Native American descent and Norway House was one of several agencies responsible for the administration of Native American reserves in Canada. He enlisted on 5 May 1916 in the 203rd Battalion, but he served overseas with the 107th Battalion, Canadian Infantry, and was killed on 20 April 1917. (Plot VI.F.25)

Company Sergeant Major William FITZGERALD DCM, 42nd Battalion, Canadian Infantry, was killed in action on 26 April 1917. His DCM was awarded for conspicuous gallantry and devotion to duty over a period of time rather than for a particular act of gallantry. The citation records that he had rendered invaluable assistance to his company commander during operations and that he was untiring in his work, which he carried out with total disregard for personal danger. The award was gazetted on 16 August 1917. (Plot VI.G.13)

Second Lieutenant John Denis Circuit OLIVER MC, 123rd Battery, 28 Brigade, Royal Field Artillery, was killed in action on 27 April 1917, aged 19. His MC was gazetted on 1 January 1917 in the New Year's Honours List. (Plot VI.G.18)

Major Charles Edward COOPER MC, 3rd Battalion, Canadian Infantry, was killed in action on 28 April 1917 when his battalion was involved in an attack around Farbus Wood. The war diary does not elaborate on the manner of his death, but states that he was buried the next day at Écoivres. With the exception of one officer per company and the battalion adjutant, all of his fellow officers attended his funeral along with all the men of 'B' Company. (Plot VI.G.19)

Major William Beverley CROWTHER MC, 3rd Battalion, Canadian Infantry, was killed in action near Fresnoy on 3 May 1917 (Plot VI.H.11). His MC was gazetted on 30 July 1917 and was awarded for conspicuous gallantry and devotion to duty as a captain, leading his company with great courage and ability. Throughout operations he worked with great determination, and although wounded earlier in the day, he remained with his men under very heavy fire. The actions referred to in the citation occurred at Vimy Ridge. His brother, Second Lieutenant Stanley Lorne Crowther, was killed in action on 20 September 1917 whilst serving with 29 Squadron, Royal Flying Corps. He is buried at Passchendaele New British Cemetery.

Major Richard BOLSTER MC, 124th Battery, 28 Brigade, Royal Field Artillery, was killed in action on 5 June 1917. He had already been mentioned in despatches in connection with transport duties during the Dardanelles Campaign and his MC was gazetted on 1 January 1917 in the New Year's Honours List. His father served as Inspector General in the Royal Navy, while his own son, Pilot Officer Richard Vary Campbell Bolster, was killed in action over Germany with 10 Squadron, Royal Air Force, on 28 June 1941 and is buried in Hamburg Cemetery, Germany. (Plot VI.J.12)

Lieutenant John HAMPSHIRE DCM, 3 Brigade, Canadian Field Artillery, was killed in action on 12 July 1917 (Plot VI.K.8). For whatever reason, and according to the CWGC register, he appears to have served under the alias of HAMSHERE, though if this were the case, one wonders why he would have chosen a variant that is almost phonetically identical. My feeling is that the spelling of his surname is just a clerical error at the time of enlistment, and one which was only corrected when his parents, Edwin and Jane Hampshire, were informed of his death. His DCM was gazetted on 17 January 1916. The citation appeared on 14 March, but is very brief. It simply records that during important operations he had performed his duties with bravery and resource and had shown great devotion to duty on all occasions.

Private Dimitro SINIZKI, 52nd Battalion, Canadian Infantry, was executed on 9 October 1917, aged 22. He was born in Kiev, Russia. On the night of 24/25 August 1917 his battalion was on its way to the trenches when Dimitro sat down and refused to move. He had also refused to move off with his comrades earlier that evening, even refusing to put on his equipment, and was being escorted forward with the rest of the men when he decided to make his protest. These acts of defiance, committed in front of the rest of the men, were deemed to warrant the ultimate penalty. (Plot VI.K.19)

Lieutenant Arthur DURMAN MC, 24th Battalion, Canadian Infantry, was killed in action on 15 October 1917. His MC was gazetted on 11 March 1918. It was awarded for conspicuous gallantry and devotion to duty when in command of a trench mortar section during an attack in which he led his section to the final objective, having played a significant part in driving the enemy from it. He then took command of another trench mortar section, in addition to his own, and when a strong enemy counter-attack materialised and succeeded in entering the newly captured trench, he took charge of the situation, as all the infantry officers by then had become casualties. The enemy was driven back, and as they retired across the open, he opened heavy fire on them using all the available trench mortars, inflicting many casualties. Throughout the entire operation he showed great courage, determination and ability. He was killed in an enemy bombardment of his battalion's trenches in the Méricourt sector, near Lens. (Plot VI.K.23)

Lieutenant Colonel Alexander Thomas THOMSON DSO MC, 10th Canadian Infantry, attached 4th Battalion, was killed in action on 19 November 1917, aged 29. His DSO citation dates to 25 November 1916 when he was a temporary major. It was awarded for conspicuous gallantry in action handling his battalion under very trying circumstances with the greatest of courage and ability. The citation concludes that he had done very fine work on previous occasions. His MC was gazetted on 22 August 1916 and was awarded for conspicuous gallantry during operations in which he had set a fine example to his men and had shown the greatest coolness when consolidating a newly won position under heavy shell fire. Though twice wounded, he refused to be sent back. (Plot VI.K.27)

Second Lieutenant William Harold HOLDERNESS, 6th Sherwood Foresters, was killed in action on 17 April 1916, aged 34. He is one of several men buried here who had previously served in other campaigns. In his case he had served in the South African campaign, after which he served for two years in the South African Constabulary. (Plot I.A.19)

Driver Arthur Truscott HARTLEY, 5 Brigade, Canadian Field Artillery, was killed in action on 24 March 1917, aged 38, and had previously served with Paget's Horse in the South African campaign. (Plot IV.G.10)

Bombardier William Henry COVINGTON also served with the Canadian Field Artillery, but was with 8 Brigade. He was older than the others and was 45 years old at the time of his death on 8 May 1917. He served at the Relief of Chitral in India in 1895. (Plot VI.H.23)

Maroeuil British Cemetery

The first time that I visited this cemetery I had some difficulty finding it and even the two locals that I spoke with were rather vague when it came to directions. It lies behind a very low fold in the ground on the north-west side of the village. The point to aim for is the junction of the Rue du Stade and the Chemin de Bray. It is best to park here because the cemetery is located along a rough track, which can be found by walking a short distance of 50 yards back from the junction. The cemetery is about 200 yards along the path. Its position on the reverse slope meant that it could not be observed directly by the enemy, though this offered very little protection or comfort from shelling. The village was used extensively for billeting and a tramway that ran between here and the front line was able to bring bodies back for burial. Despite my difficulty locating it, I found this a very rewarding cemetery to visit.

In 1914, in the belief that the war would be a long drawn-out affair, Kitchener set about creating his citizen New Army rather than expanding the existing Territorial Army. Although he had little time for part-time soldiering, the Territorials did prove themselves equal to the challenge of serving overseas, and those units that fought on the Western Front, and often elsewhere, did so largely with distinction. Maroeuil British Cemetery is interesting because it contains quite a number of 'part-time' soldiers from first and second line Territorial units.

The Arras sector was, of course, entirely new to the British Army in March 1916, and at times it was used as something of a 'nursery' where units new to the Western Front could be introduced to the realities of trench warfare under instruction from more experienced troops. The area between Armentières and Ploegsteert was also used for the same purpose. The only 'real' school was the trenches and this cemetery reflects something of that education quite well. Surprisingly, it is mainly a 1916 cemetery in terms of its character where 369 of the 564 identified burials relate to that year. This compares with 118 from 1917 and seventy-six from 1918.

The 60th (2nd/2nd London) Division was comprised entirely of second line London Territorial units. These second-line battalions had no existence prior to the outbreak of war and only came into existence on 31 August 1914 when they were authorised by the War Office. The 60th (2/2nd London) Division arrived in France in late June 1916 and was sent to the XVII Corps sector just north of Arras. Here it was met by the 51st (Highland) Division, which was a first line Territorial division with a growing reputation for reliability. In 1915 this division had already instructed other New Army Divisions in the art of life in the trenches, namely the 18th (Eastern) Division, parts of the 22nd Division during its very brief time in France, and also the 32nd Division, and it was here in early 1916 that it did the same for the men of the 60th (2/2nd London) Division. The CWGC register notes that nearly half of the graves here are from the 51st (Highland) Division.

The Londoners arrived at Maroeuil on the night of 26 June 1916 in a show of remarkable naivety by carrying hurricane lamps to light their way. The reflections on the walls of the ruined buildings were easily spotted by the Germans and a salvo of shells soon fell on the village, fortunately wounding just two of the newcomers. It was a sharp wake-up call to the realities of warfare that also failed to impress their Highland neighbours. Although the village of Maroeuil was well within shelling range and had been knocked about a bit, the surrounding country-side was ablaze with poppies and made quite an attractive billet. About a week later, the Londoners took over the front line for the very first time, just north of Roclincourt, opposite Neuville-Saint-Vaast. The 2/15th Battalion, London Regiment (Prince of Wales's Own Civil Service Rifles), and the 2/14th Battalion, London Regiment (London Scottish), occupied the right sub-sector, whilst the 2/13th Battalion, London Regiment (Kensingtons), and the 2/16th Battalion, London Regiment (Queen's Westminster Rifles), took the left.

One of the graves here is that of Private John Ford SMALL, 2/15th Battalion, London Regiment (Prince of Wales's Own Civil Service Rifles). He was one of twenty men who volunteered to take part in the battalion's first offensive action, which was a raid on German trenches. It was led by two officers, Lieutenant Peatfield, who was to go on to win a bar to his MC, and Second Lieutenant Thompson. The plans for the raid were rehearsed out of the line and on 10 September 1916 the group made its way to Paris Redoubt, which lay within the battalion's right sub-sector. A round from a German trench mortar caused the raiding party's first casualty as it was making its preparations; Private Austin George Rule was mortally wounded and died at Aubigny where he is now buried in Plot I, Row E, of the Communal Cemetery Extension.

The next night the raid went ahead and the Londoners brought back intelligence, but several of the party, including the two officers, were wounded. When the roll call was taken, it became apparent that one of the party, Private John Ford SMALL, was missing. In spite of his injuries, Second Lieutenant Thompson volunteered to go out again with another man, Private A. Small, the brother of the missing man. With the enemy on full alert, they re-traced their route across no man's land. Private Small found his brother, who was still alive, but badly wounded. He and Thompson were able to bring him back to our lines, but sadly his wounds were so serious that he died soon afterwards. (Plot III.F.5)

Thompson received the DSO for his leadership that night, not only in connection with the raid in which he personally shot two of enemy, despite being wounded early on in the fight, but also for returning and carrying out the rescue, refusing to have his own wounds dressed until he had returned with the wounded man. Private A. Small, despite the tragic loss of his brother, was awarded the MM and survived the war.

Lieutenant Charles Stanley HIPWELL MC, 2/16th Battalion, London Regiment (Queen's Westminster Rifles), was killed in action on 15 October 1916, though *Officers Died in the Great War* shows his death occurring the previous day (Plot III.H.13). His MC was awarded for his leadership during a successful raid on 23 September 1916 that resulted in the capture of several prisoners. As the raid was under way, he came across a fire bay full of Germans and silenced them with his revolver. He then stood guard on the parapet while his men made their way back through the enemy's wire and only withdrew once the last man had returned safely. He also went out again under continuous fire in order to search for a wounded man. The success of the raid was attributed to his determination and resourceful leadership. He is commemorated on the war memorial at Olney in Buckinghamshire where another man with the same surname, Second Lieutenant Harry Reginald Hipwell, is also remembered. Although the CWGC records show no personal details for him, it seems likely that he was related to Charles. Harry is buried at Brown's Copse Cemetery and was killed in action on 23 April 1917 whilst serving with the 4th Seaforth Highlanders.

There are significant numbers of men from the Gordon Highlanders and Seaforth Highlanders buried here; in the former case, nearly all are from the 5th, 6th and 7th Battalions; in the latter, almost all are from the 4th, 5th and 6th Battalions. All of these units were part of the 51st (Highland) Division and the combined total from these two regiments comes to 120, or just under a quarter of the total identified burials within the cemetery.

Company Serjeant Major Charles NEILSON, 1/5th Gordon Highlanders, was killed in action on 1 June 1916, aged 26. In civilian life he had been a teacher (Plot I.F.6). His brother, Corporal Rolland Millar Neilson MSM, also served with the 5th Gordon Highlanders and had been mentioned in despatches. He was killed on 13 April 1918, but his body was never recovered and he is now commemorated on the Ploegsteert Memorial. His other brother, Serjeant James Hadden Neilson, also died on active service with the 10th Cameron Highlanders after contracting malaria in Salonika. He is buried at Kirechkoi-Hortakoi Military Cemetery in Greece. The youngest brother, William, who was only 14 years old when the Great War ended, went on to serve in the Second World War, but was killed on 12 June 1940, aged 36, serving with the 5th Gordon Highlanders. He is buried at Manneville-les-Plains Churchyard in France.

Captain George Andrew Christie MOIR, 5th Gordon Highlanders, was killed in action on 7 April 1917. In civilian life he was an architect. He was born in Methlick where the memorial plaque in the local church, which commemorates men of the parish who died in the Great War, was paid for by money that he left in his will. The war diary for 7 April 1917 shows that a hut used by officers of the battalion was hit by a German shell resulting in eight casualties, one of whom was Captain MOIR. (Plot IV.D.5)

Buried close to Captain MOIR are two fellow officers from his battalion: Second Lieutenant William Bruce ANDERSON MC (Plot IV.D.7), and Second Lieutenant Herbert John HALL (Plot IV.D.8). Both men were killed by the same shell that killed MOIR and *Officers Died in the Great War* incorrectly shows ANDERSON's death occurring on 7 March 1917. His MC was gazetted on 12 January 1917 and was awarded for conspicuous gallantry near Beaumont Hamel on 13 November 1916 where he assumed command of his company and led it with great courage and determination capturing 170 prisoners. HALL had been with the 5th Battalion before the war, but re-enlisted once war had broken out. He then served at home as quartermaster serjeant before gaining his commission in September 1916 and going to France in January 1917. He was educated at Peterhead Academy and spent several years in estate management before returning to work on the family farm where he lived until the outbreak of war. Another officer, Second Lieutenant George MacFarquhar McLEOD, 7th Gordon Highlanders, was almost certainly killed with MOIR, ANDERSON and HALL. Although the CWGC register shows McLEOD serving with the 7th Battalion, he was actually with the 5th Battalion at the time of his death. (Plot IV.D.6)

Private William Ethelbert HEYMER, 6th Seaforth Highlanders, was killed in action on 28 April 1916, aged 23 (Plot II.C.13). His younger brother, Serjeant Gilbert Heymer, was killed in action serving in the same battalion almost a year later on 21 April 1917. He is buried in Saint-Nicolas British Cemetery in Plot I, Row G.

Lieutenant Colonel William MacCallum MACFARLANE DSO, 15th Highland Light Infantry, attached 5th Seaforth Highlanders, was killed in action on 19 February 1917, aged 42. His DSO was awarded for conspicuous gallantry. Shortly after his company had been relieved, the Germans made a strong bombing attack, driving back the relieving troops. Realising this, MACFARLANE led his men back to their original position, repelling the enemy with a counter-attack. The citation makes particular reference to his coolness and courage during this fine action. The award was gazetted on 26 September 1916. (Plot III.L.5)

Second Lieutenant Edwin Victor DOWNIE-LESLIE, 4th Seaforth Highlanders, was only 19 years old when he was killed in action on 9 April 1917. His father was a successful advocate from Aberdeen and Edwin was one of several children. The family lived comfortably, and before receiving his commission in the 4th Seaforth Highlanders, Edwin joined the Inns of Court Regiment. According to one account, he was killed instantly by a bullet wound to the head whilst leading a party of his men forward towards their second objective on the opening day of the Battle of Arras. Another version of events is that he and his men were met by a hail of bombs as they came over a small rise and that he was hit in the head by one of them, presumably as it burst. The battalion history notes that the German positions here could not be bombarded for fear that shells might hit Canadian troops who were believed to be nearby. It was not until 12 April that his burial took place at Maroeuil. One of his brothers, William, served in Mesopotamia, whilst another, Frank, served in the Indian Army from 1908 and was mentioned in despatches in 1919. After the death of her first husband, his sister, Mary, married Frank Cooper, heir to the well-known company renowned for making jams and marmalade. (Plot IV.D.9)

Next to him is fellow officer, Second Lieutenant Harold Sidney George FOX, 4th Seaforth Highlanders, who was also killed on 9 April 1917. The battalion's history offers no explanation as to how he died. (Plot IV.D.10)

Captain Gerald STEWART, 1/6th Seaforth Highlanders, who came from Olney, Buckinghamshire, was killed in action on 9 April 1917, aged 25 (Plot IV.D.12). He enlisted in the Bedfordshire Yeomanry in September 1914 and received his commission in March 1915. His commanding officer paid tribute to him by saying that whenever there was a dangerous situation he was always there to set a fine example to his men. His brother, Captain Weston Stewart, died in German hands on 27 March 1918, aged 24, whilst attached to the 1/6th Seaforth Highlanders, though his battalion was actually the 1/4th Battalion. He is buried at Beaulencourt British Cemetery, Ligny-Thilloy.

Buried next to Captain STEWART are three more officers from his battalion killed on the same day. Second Lieutenant Charles Alexander WEBSTER, 6th Seaforth Highlanders, was killed in action on 9 April 1917, as was Second Lieutenant Edwin Relfe Barrett MIDDLETON, 6th Seaforth Highlanders (Plot IV.D.13 and 14). MIDDLETON's date of death is wrongly shown in *Officers Died in the Great War* as 9 April 1918. The battalion casualty roll confirms 9 April 1917 as the correct date of death. MIDDLETON's brother, Private Robert Middleton, was also killed in action. He served with the 4th Gordon Highlanders and was killed at Ypres by shell fire on 1 June 1915. He has no known grave and is commemorated on the Menin Gate.

Second Lieutenant Henry Milner LAW, 6th Seaforth Highlanders, is the last of the trio and was killed in action on 9 April 1917, aged 25. (Plot IV.D.15) Next to him is Second Lieutenant Clifford MOORE, 5th Seaforth Highlanders, who was also killed in action on 9 April 1917 (Plot IV.D.16). After his battalion had lost the protective barrage it came under heavy machine-gun fire near the second objective, the Blue Line, causing many casualties.

The Argyll & Sutherland Highlanders also make up a good proportion of the cemetery with a total of sixty-seven burials. Many are from the 7th and 8th Battalions, which formed part of the 51st (Highland) Division, but there are also men from the 9th Battalion. This last battalion began life as part of the 51st (Highland) Division, but left early in 1915, becoming successively part of the 27th Division, then the 4th Division. It then amalgamated briefly with the 7th Battalion before resuming its own identity as part of VI Corps Troops. Its role, eventually, was to provide drafts to other battalions of the regiment. The men here would have served with either the 7th or the 8th Battalions, but are shown under their original designation.

Serjeant William John BOYD DCM, 1/6th Argyll & Sutherland Highlanders, was killed in action on 25 March 1916, aged 29. His DCM was gazetted on 21 June 1916 and was awarded for his consistent good work and for proving himself a good and fearless leader. *Soldiers Died in the Great War* makes no reference to his DCM. (Plot I.A.12)

Second Lieutenant Archibald MACNEILL, 1/6th Argyll & Sutherland Highlanders, originally enlisted as a private in the 1/9th Highland Light Infantry

(Glasgow Highlanders) on 5 September 1914 and was wounded the following year on 13 March 1915 at La Bassée. He was only 19 years old when he was killed in action on 26 March 1916. (Plot I.A.13)

Lieutenant William Munro BENNETT, 8th Argyll & Sutherland Highlanders, the son of Major Alexander John Munro Bennett, died of wounds on 18 June 1916. (Plot II.F.13)

Second Lieutenant Robert Campbell McIntyre SMITH, 8th Argyll & Sutherland Highlanders, was killed in action on 20 June 1916, aged 20. His name is one of seventy on the very fine war memorial at Inveraray, Argyllshire, commemorating those who fell in the Great War. (Plot II.G.13)

Of course, not everyone buried in CWGC cemeteries is a casualty of action or a violent death. Second Lieutenant Taylor COOK, 7th Argyll & Sutherland Highlanders, died of heart failure in the ordinary course of duty on 21 March 1917. (Plot III.M.16)

Another curious entry in the CWGC register is that relating to Private William Lowson ADAMSON. It shows his unit as the 21st Division Highland Cyclist Battalion. The entry should read, '51st (Highland) Divisional Cyclist Company'. He was killed in action on 1 May 1916, aged 18. The CWGC register tells us that his parents lived in Argentina and that he had volunteered in Buenos Aires, though he actually enlisted in Dundee. The roll of honour for the Buenos Aires Great Southern Railway shows that at the time of enlistment he was 17 years old. British railway engineering and expertise was much sought after throughout the world, but especially in South America. A surprising number of British casualties are commemorated on the rolls of honour of various railway companies that were based in South America. (Plot I.D.7)

Lieutenant Arthur John Gordon THOMAS, 6th Black Watch, was killed in action on 31 May 1916, aged 20. Regimental sources show that he had been engaged in a 'cat and mouse' duel with a German sniper who unfortunately came out on top that day. (Plot I. F.7)

Private James TORRANCE (Plot I.F.12) and Sergeant William TORRANCE (Plot II.G.1) were brothers who served in the same battalion, the 7th Black Watch. James, the younger of the two, was killed in action on 28 May 1916, a few weeks before William, who was killed on 22 June, aged 25. They are not buried together, though they are buried close to each other on either side of the path that divides Plot I from Plot II.

Private William PAXTON, 6th Seaforth Highlanders, was killed in action by a shell on 13 March when the battalion was in trenches near Roclincourt known as the Labyrinth. He died soon after being wounded, as did another man who is buried at Faubourg d' Amiens Cemetery in Arras. PAXTON was wounded on three occasions during 1915. (Plot II. A.13)

Captain Gerald Blunt LUCAS, 38th King George's Own Central Indian Horse, attached 13 Squadron, Royal Flying Corps, followed in his father's footsteps when he joined the Indian Cavalry after leaving Sandhurst in 1910. His father was Lieutenant Colonel Charles Arthur de Neufville Lucas. Gerald was a pupil at Haileybury College. Royal Flying Corps Communiqué No. 36, which covers 16 May 1916, shows that he was flying with a Lieutenant Wright when he was wounded in aerial combat and died later that evening. The register shows that he held the Durbar Medal, which was issued in 1911 as part of the celebrations in India to commemorate the Coronation of King George V. (Plot II.D.6)

Second Lieutenant Alfred Trevanion POWELL, 4th Cameron Highlanders, died of wounds on 22 July 1916, aged 24, while attached to the 2/14th Battalion, London Regiment (London Scottish). According to regimental sources, he was probably the victim of trench mortar fire. He had previously served in the Buckinghamshire Yeomanry.

For the London Scottish this was its very first tour of duty holding front line trenches away from the watchful eyes of its instructors, the 7th Gordon High-landers from the 51st (Highland) Division. The front line was linked to Maroeuil, some four miles away, via a communication trench, known as Territorial Trench. Time spent 'learning on the job' was often a trying and frequently dangerous experience for both instructors and pupils. Trenches and dug-outs were often more congested than usual, rations could easily get mixed up or go astray, and in cramped conditions, casualties could be higher than normal, especially from shelling and trench mortars. Not surprisingly, a period of trench instruction was often one involving a good deal of confusion and irritability.

POWELL'S parent unit, the 4th Cameron Highlanders, was a first line Terri-torial battalion that had briefly been part of the 51st (Highland) Division during January and February 1916. Prior to that, it had seen action at Neuve Chapelle with the 8th Division, and at Aubers Ridge, Festubert and Loos as part of the 7th Division. However, by March 1916 it had been absorbed into the 1st Cameron Highlanders owing to successive heavy losses. Second Lieutenant POWELL would have been able to offer much needed guidance and experience to the 2/14th Battalion as it began life in the trenches. (Plot III.B.5)

The CWGC register notes that there are twenty-five graves belonging to men from the Royal Engineers who died in connection with mining activity. One of those men is Lieutenant Stanley Gordon KILLINGBACK, 2/4th Sanitary Com-pany, Royal Engineers, who was killed in action on 11 August 1916, though *Officers Died in the Great War* shows his date of death as the previous day. He had been a member of the London University OTC. He was in charge of a working party consolidating a mine crater when he was shot in the chest by a sniper. (Plot III.D.1)

Second Lieutenant Sidney Leigh FAITHFULL, 256 Tunnelling Company, Royal Engineers, was killed in action on 15 August 1916, aged 40. He had previously served in the South African War and in the German South-West Africa campaign. *Officers Died in the Great War* shows him as having died on that date, but not as killed in action. His daughter, who was just six years old when he died, and who was born in South Africa, went on to become Baroness Lucy Faithfull OBE, a distinguished figure in the field of social work and a champion of child welfare. She died in 1996 having been created a life peer under Margaret Thatcher. (Plot III.D.6)

Second Lieutenant Charles St. Lo AUBER, 4 Brigade, Royal Field Artillery, was killed in action by a sniper's bullet on 29 October 1916, aged 21. He previously served with the Devon Yeomanry before obtaining his commission. The manner of his death suggests that he was possibly performing duty as a forward observation officer when he was killed. A memorial service was held for him at Holy Cross Church in Crediton where his family lived. The service, and the dedication of a memorial to his memory, was led by the Reverend Walter Montgomery Smith-Dorrien, brother of General Horace Lockwood Smith-Dorrien who commanded II Corps in 1914 and the British Second Army for the first few days of the Second Battle of Ypres in 1915. (Plot III.J.13)

Private Vincent Harold FAULKNER MM, 52th Battalion, Canadian Infantry, was killed in action on 16 December 1916 while the battalion was occupying trenches in the Thélus sector. The brief entry in the war diary for that day records his death in clinical fashion: '*Privates Douglas, Fisher, and Faulkner killed in action. Private M.J. Grassie wounded, shell shock, as a result of shell fire. Bodies taken out and sent to Maroeuil for burial*'. All three men are buried here together (Plot III.K.1 to 3). Another man from the battalion, Private Albert James DOUCE (Plot III.K.9), is shown as dying on 25 December 1916, though the war diary records him and another man as being killed in action on 26 December rather than Christmas Day. CWGC records show no other men from the battalion killed in action on either day.

Corporal Frederic Charles BURCHELL, 3rd Canadian Divisional Ammunition Column, was killed in action on 27 February 1916, aged 23, by a shell in a trench mortar pit. He managed to warn those around him, thereby saving their lives, but was too late to save his own. The CWGC register tells us that during his brief career he had been a civil engineer. (Plot III.K.10)

Private Benjamin SENKOSKI DCM, 52nd Canadian Infantry, was killed in action on 10 February 1917. His name is also found under the slightly different spelling of 'SANKOSKE', but the CWGC register and the *London Gazette* show the same army number under both spellings. He won his DCM as a runner, courageously carrying a message under very heavy fire. The award was gazetted on 1 January 1917 and the citation for it appeared six weeks later on 14 February. (Plot III.L.3)

Private John SMITH, 7th Black Watch, was killed on 17 March 1917, aged 19 (Plot III.M.5). The fact that he is buried here, but the three men killed with him that day are not, strikes me as puzzling. The battalion was about to leave billets near Bray to march to Maroeuil when a high velocity shell hit one of the billets killing four men and wounding five. Of the three men killed outright with Private SMITH, two are buried at Écoivres Military Cemetery and the other is buried at Aubigny Communal Cemetery Extension. Maroeuil, however, is in the opposite direction to both of these locations and about one mile south-east of Bray. One possible explanation is that the three men supposedly killed outright were, in fact, wounded and evacuated towards casualty clearing facilities where they died later that day. One of the men, initially recorded as wounded, died the following day at Aubigny and two more died from their wounds on 21 March.

Second Lieutenant Charles John ROBERTSON, 6th Black Watch, was killed in action on 22 March 1917. His father C.J. Robertson had served as quartermaster at Colchester barracks. (Plot III.M.14)

The second battalion commander buried here is Lieutenant Colonel Robert Cochrane MORRIS, 80th Group, Royal Garrison Artillery. He was the son of the Honourable Alexander Morris of Toronto, a prominent Canadian lawyer, judge, politician and businessman, and was one of eleven children. Robert had served in the British Army since 1890. The CWGC register notes that in 1915 he was responsible for training No. 17 Siege Battery, consisting of four 6-inch howitzers, which he then took out to Gallipoli. He died on 25 March 1917, aged 48 (Plot III.M.15).

On 1 April 1917 two brothers, Private Joseph WILSON (268272) and Thomas WILSON (268276), both serving with the 1/6th Black Watch, were killed in action and are now buried next to each other (Plot IV.B.9 and 10). Thomas, who was 24 years old, was three years older than Joseph. The battalion had just moved to Maroeuil when a shell hit a building that was being used as a billet. Twenty-one men were killed outright and a further twenty-eight were wounded. According to battalion records, the WILSON brothers were among those killed in the incident. Another battalion casualty that day was Private Robert Mackie SIMPSON (Plot IV.B.5), an Arts student from Aberdeen University who was also a victim of the same shell and who is now buried a few graves along from the WILSON brothers. Plot IV, Rows B and C, contain another fourteen men of the 6th Black Watch killed in the same incident, whilst several of those who subsequently died of wounds can be traced to Aubigny Communal Cemetery Extension where they are buried in Plot I, Rows J and K.

Sowar KALI RAM, 5th Indian Cavalry, was killed in action on 20 August 1916. (Plot IV.A.1)

Lance Serjeant James WISHART MM, 1/7th Black Watch, was killed in action on 31 March 1917. There is no reference to his MM in *Soldiers Died in the Great War*. (Plot IV.A.7)

Private George William ARCHER, 7th Black Watch, was killed in action on 1 April 1917 (Plot IV.C.13). His elder brother, Serjeant John Smith Archer, also served with the Black Watch and was killed in action with the 2nd Battalion at Sennaiyat in Mesopotamia on 22 April 1916. The action was part of a last-ditch attempt to relieve General Townshend at Kut. He is buried at Amara War Cemetery. Their late father also served with the 2nd Battalion.

Captain Edward James BLAIR MC, Royal Army Medical Corps, was killed in action on 11 April 1917, aged 32. His MC was gazetted on 12 January 1917 and was awarded for conspicuous gallantry and devotion to duty, tending and dressing the wounded under heavy fire for a continuous period of eighteen hours and setting a splendid example of courage and determination throughout. (Plot IV.E.1)

Just a short distance along the same row is a British officer who was decorated for gallantry before being commissioned. Second Lieutenant Cecil Andrews CLARKE MM, 1/7th Middlesex Regiment, who had also been twice mentioned in despatches, was killed in action on 24 April 1917, aged 26. *Officers Died in the Great War* makes no reference to his MM and records his date of death as 23 April. (Plot IV.E.6)

Serjeant Albert WILSON DCM, 18th Durham Light Infantry, died of wounds on 18 February 1918. His DCM, gazetted on 4 March 1918, was won while he was serving as a lance serjeant. It was awarded for conspicuous gallantry and devotion to duty during enemy attacks in which he used rifle grenades to great effect in order to repel the assaults. When his trench was eventually captured, he and his company commander, with eleven other men, retook it, driving out sixty-nine of the enemy. (Plot IV.F.9)

Second Lieutenant Lawrence Norris GASKELL, 5 Squadron, Royal Flying Corps and General List, died on 1 March 1918, aged 19, from wounds received two days earlier on 27 February (Plot IV.G.9). The CWGC register tells us that he had attended St. Paul's School, Kensington, and was an Exhibitioner at Corpus Christi College, Oxford. His observer, Lieutenant L. McRitchie, was wounded, but survived.

Major Eric James TYSON DSO MC, 5 Squadron, Royal Flying Corps, and a former pupil of Westminster School, was killed in action on 12 March 1918, aged 24. His MC was gazetted on 23 October 1916 and was awarded for conspicuous gallantry and skill whilst engaged in bombing raids. On one occasion he descended to a height of 300 feet under very heavy fire of every description before dropping his bombs on a train and wrecking it. While doing so, he was attacked by several hostile aircraft, which he beat off with the help of Lieutenant John Reginald Philpott who was in another machine. Although he was wounded and his engine severely damaged, he and Lieutenant Philpott went on to attack a group of men who were trying to start up an enemy aircraft, causing them to scatter. When he returned to his base, his machine was found to be riddled by bullets. Philpott also received the MC for his part in the day's exploits and his award was gazetted on the same date as TYSON's. Philpott was eventually killed in action on 15 January 1918 in Mesopotamia, serving as a captain with 63 Squadron, Royal Flying Corps. He is buried in Baghdad (North Gate) War Cemetery.

TYSON's DSO was gazetted on 26 September 1917 and the citation for it appeared in the *London Gazette* dated 9 January 1918. It states that he had demonstrated conspicuous gallantry and devotion to duty on many occasions, including whilst carrying out photographic reconnaissance and artillery registration at extremely low altitudes with the utmost fearlessness. Though continually under fire while on these missions, he invariably did excellent work, obtaining very valuable information by his great skill and daring. A further measure of his skill emerged on 7 September 1916 when, in poor visibility, he navigated to his target by compass while on a bombing mission. He flew like that for seventy minutes before a gap appeared in the clouds just short of his target, which he then bombed causing damage to it. A week later, on 15 September, he was wounded whilst on a bombing mission over Bapaume at low altitude. (Plot IV.G.16)

In the north-east corner of the cemetery is a solitary member of the 42nd Company, Chinese Labour Corps, Yu Tsen Ku, who died on 9 July 1917. In the case of men from the Chinese Labour Corps it is virtually impossible to discover how they died. The notable exceptions are those who were executed or those killed in incidents, such as bombing raids, though the latter are never referred to as individuals.

Maroeuil Communal Cemetery
From Maroeuil British Cemetery it is relatively easy to locate the communal cemetery. At the opposite end of the Rue du Stade, heading back into the village, there is a T-junction. This is the junction with the Rue de Fresnoy. Turn left and continue for about 200 yards. Here the road forks, but ignore the right fork and keep to the main road, which is still the Rue de Fresnoy. The cemetery lies about 200 yards further on. It contains the graves of nearly forty men who died or were killed in action in May 1940, though only thirty-two of them have been identified. The exact date of death in a number of cases is undetermined, though these men are shown as having died between certain dates.

All of the men fell between here and Saint-Éloi and all the identified casualties are from the 2nd Northamptonshire Regiment, including one officer, Second Lieutenant Herbert Evelyn OSWALD, whose date of death is shown as 23 May. His brother, Noel Alexander Oswald, died on 6 April 1942 at Aldershot whilst serving as an officer cadet in the Royal Engineers.

Mont-Saint-Éloi Communal Cemetery
Of the five CWGC burials here, one is unidentified. All are Royal Artillery casualties killed in action on 22 May 1940. The men, Bombardier Thomas Frederick

William DEARLOVE, Gunner Cyril Thomas HUGHES, Lance-Bombardier William Henry Nathaniel PIPER and Sergeant Donald Francis BUDD, were all members of 208th Battery, 52nd Anti-Tank Regiment, which formed part of the 5th Infantry Division. The elevated nature of the ground around Saint-Éloi made it an obvious location for the unit to occupy as German armoured units advanced over the old 1914–1918 battlefields to the east and to the north of Arras.

Unfortunately, the men of 208th Battery mistook some French tanks for those of the enemy as they approached its position near Berthonval Farm, less than a mile away in fields to the west just off the D.49. The French returned fire, killing the four members of the gun crew who are now buried here. Berthonval Farm is frequently mentioned in Canadian war diaries, particularly in 1917, when its buildings were used extensively as an HQ. The farm was also used as Byng's advanced Corps HQ for the attack on Vimy Ridge on 9 April. The area adjacent to the farm was one of several locations used by Canadian artillery units in the build up to the Battle of Arras in April 1917.

Bibliography

In addition to the works referred to below, I have made extensive use of battalion war diaries held at the National Archives, Kew, and elsewhere. Similarly, I have referred to numerous Rolls of Honour, mainly those relating to schools, colleges, and universities but also those held by professional and commercial bodies, as well as other organizations throughout Britain and various parts of the world. Another key source of reference was the collection of battalion war diaries that forms part of the Canadian Great War Project.

It will also become evident to the reader that I have consulted just about every divisional and regimental history relevant to this work, whether from my own collection, or through the British Library or the reference section of the Imperial War Museum, London. The works listed below do not include those specifically mentioned within the text. The following titles are merely the works to which frequent reference was made; it is by no means exhaustive.

Military Operations in France & Belgium 1914 (2 Volumes); 1915 (2 Volumes); 1916 (2 Volumes); 1917 (3 Volumes); 1918 (5 Volumes) (All Appendices and Maps). Brig. General Sir James E. Edmonds, CB, CMG. IWM & Battery Press, 1995.

Military Operations: Gallipoli (2 Volumes). Brig. General Aspinall-Oglander CB CMG DSO. IWM & Battery Press.

Military Operations: Italy 1915–1919. Brigadier General Sir James Edmonds CB CMG D. Litt and Major General H.R. Davies, CB. IWM & Battery Press.

Military Operations Macedonia (2 Volumes). Captain Cyril Falls. IWM & Battery Press.

Military Operations Mesopotamia (4 Volumes). Brigadier General F.J. Moberly CB CSI DSO. IWM & Battery Press.

Military Operations Egypt & Palestine (3 Volumes). Lieutenant General Sir George Macmunn KCB KCSI DSO & Captain Cyril Falls. IWM & Battery Press.

Military Operations Togoland and the Cameroons. Brigadier General F.J. Moberly CB CSI DSO. IWM & Battery Press.

Military Operations East Africa. Lieutenant Colonel Charles Hordern. IWM & Battery Press.

The Register of the Victoria Cross. Compiled by Nora Buzzell. This England Books, 1988.

VCs of the First World War: Arras & Messines 1917. Gerald Gliddon. Sutton, Stroud, 1998.

VCs of the First World War: The Spring Offensive 1918. Gerald Gliddon. Stroud History, 2013.

VCs of the First World War: The Final Days 1918. Gerald Gliddon. Sutton, Stroud, 2000.

The Distinguished Service Order 1886–1923, Parts I & II. Sir O'Moore Creagh VC GCB GCSI and E.M. Humphris. J.B. Hayward & Son, 1978.

Citations of the Distinguished Conduct Medal in the Great War 1914–1920, Section One; Section Two (Part One); Section Two (Part Two); Section Three; Section Four. Naval & Military Press, 2007.

Recipients of the Distinguished Conduct Medal 1914–1920. R.W. Walker. Military Medals, Birmingham, 1981.

Recipients of the Distinguished Conduct Medal 1855–1909. P.E. Abbott. J.B. Hayward & Son, 1975.

The Distinguished Conduct Medal to the Canadian Expeditionary Force 1914–1920. David K. Riddle and Donald G. Mitchell. Kirkby Marlton Press, 1991.

Recipients of Bars to the Military Cross 1916–1920: To which is added MCs to Warrant Officers 1915–1919. J.V. Webb, 1988.

The Distinguished Flying Cross and how it was won 1918–1995. Nick Carter. Savannah, London, 1998.

The Distinguished Flying Medal: A Record of Courage 1918–1982. I.T.Tavender. J.B. Hayward, 1990.

For Gallantry in the Performance of Military Duty: An Account of the Use of the Army Meritorious Service Medal to Recognize Non-Combatant Gallantry 1916–1928. J.D. Sainsbury. Samson Books, London, 1980.

Soldiers Died in the Great War 1914–1919: Parts 1 to 80. J.B. Hayward & Sons, 1989.

Officers Died in the Great War 1914–1919: Parts I & II (3rd Edition). HMSO. Samson Books Ltd, 1979.

The House of Commons Book of Remembrance 1914–1918. Edward Whitaker Moss Blundell. Elkin Mathews & Marrot, London, 1931.

Officers of the Canadian Expeditionary Force who died Overseas 1914–1919. N.M. Christie. Eugene G. Ursual, 1989 (Canada).

Airmen Died in the Great War 1914–1918: The Roll of Honour of the British and Commonwealth Air Services of the First World War. Chris Hobson. Hayward, 1995.

Royal Flying Corps (Military Wing) Casualties and Honours during the War of 1914–1917. Captain G.L. Campbell RFA and R.H. Blinkhorn. Picton Publishing, 1987.

British Regiments 1914–1918. Brigadier E.A. James OBE TD. Samson Books Ltd, London, 1978.

The Bond of Sacrifice Volumes I & II. Naval & Military Press Ltd, 1992.

De Ruvigny's Roll of Honour: A Biographical Record of Members of His Majesty's Naval and Military Forces Who Fell in the Great War 1914–1918. Marquis de Ruvigny – London Stamp Exchange, 1987.

British Battalions in France & Belgium 1914. Ray Westlake. Leo Cooper, London, 1997.

British Battalions on the Western Front: January to June 1915. Ray Westlake. Leo Cooper, London, 2001.

British Battalions on the Somme. Ray Westlake. Leo Cooper, London, 1994.

British Regiments at Gallipoli. Ray Westlake. Leo Cooper, London, 1996.

Above the Lines. Norman L.R. Franks, Frank W. Bailey and Russell Guest. Grub Street, London, 1993.

Above the War Fronts. Norman L.R. Franks, Russell Guest and Gregory Alegi. Grub Street, 1997.

Royal Flying Corps Communiqués 1915–1916. Edited by Christopher Cole. Tom Donovan, London, 1990.

Royal Flying Corps Communiqués 1917–1918. Edited by Chaz Bowyer. Grub Street, London, 1998.

Royal Air Force Communiqués 1918. Edited by Christopher Cole. Tom Donovan, London, 1990.

Under the Guns of the Red Baron. Norman Franks, Hal Giblin and Nigel Mccrery. Grub Street, London, 1995.

The Royal Flying Corps in France: From Mons to the Somme. Ralph Barker. Constable & Co. Ltd, London, 1994.

The Royal Flying Corps in France: From Bloody April 1917 to Final Victory. Ralph Barker. Constable & Co. Ltd, London, 1995.

The Underground War – Vimy Ridge to Arras. Phillip Robinson and Nigel Cave. Pen & Sword Military, Barnsley, 2011.

The Student Soldiers. John McConachie. Moravian Press, Elgin, 1995.

The Sword of the North: Highland Memories of the Great War. Dugald Macechern. R. Carruthers & Sons, Inverness, 1993.

A Medico's Luck in the Great War: Royal Army Medical Corps Work with the 51st (Highland) Division. David Rorie. Milne & Hutchinson, 1929.

Warriors of the King: Prairie Indians in World War I. Lloyd James Dempsey. Association of Canadian Archivists, 1999.

Native Soldiers – Foreign Battlefields. Janice Summerby. Veterans Affairs Canada, Communications Division, 1993.

With the Royal Army Medical Corps at the Front. Evelyn Charles Vivian, 1914.

A Stretcher Bearer's Diary: Three Years in France with the 21st Division. J.H. Newton. A.H. Stockwell, London, 1932.

A Lack of Offensive Spirit? – The 46th (North Midland) Division at Gommecourt, 1st July 1916. Alan MacDonald. Iona Books, 2008.

Orange, Green & Khaki: The Story of Irish Regiments in the Great War 1914–1918. Tom Johnstone. Gill & Macmillan & Co., Dublin, 1992.

'Come On, Highlanders': Glasgow Territorials in the Great War. Alec Weir. Sutton Publishing Limited, Stroud, 2005.

The Letters of Agar Adamson. Edited N.M. Christie. CEF Books (Canada), 1997.

In Good Company: The First World War Letters & Diaries of the Hon. William Fraser, Gordon Highlanders. Edited by David Fraser. Michael Russell (Publishing) Ltd, Salisbury, 1990.

Shot at Dawn. Julian Putkowski & Julian Sykes. Wharncliffe Publishing Ltd, Barnsley, 1989.

With Rifle & Pick. Janet Dixon and John Dixon. Cwm Publications, Cardiff, 1991.

Prelude to Victory. Brigadier General E.L. Spears CB CBE MC. Jonathan Cape, London, 1939.

Surrender Be Damned: A History of the 1/1st Battalion, The Monmouthshire Regiment, 1914–1918. Les Hughes & John Dixon. Cwm Press, Caerphilly, 1995.

Brigadier General R.B. Bradford VC MC and his Brothers. Privately Printed, Eden Fisher & Co. Ltd, London. Copy signed & dated 1928.

Campaign in South-West Africa 1914–1915. Brigadier General J.J. Collyer. Pretoria, Government Print, 1937.

University of London OTC: Roll of Honour 1914–1919. Military Education Committee, University of London, 1921.

Etonians Who Fought in the Great War 1914–1919. (No Author or Publisher Shown)

Record of Service of Solicitors & Articled Clerks in HM Forces 1914–1918. Spottiswoode, Ballantyne & Co. Ltd, 1920.

Tanks in the Great War. J.F.C. Fuller DSO. John Murray, London, 1920.

The New Zealand Division 1916–1919 – Colonel H. Stewart CMG DSO MC. Whitcombe & Tombs Ltd, 1921.

The South African Forces in France. John Buchan. IWM & Battery Press, 1992.

The A.I.F. in France Volumes III, IV, V, VI. C.E.W. Bean. University of Queensland Press, 1982–1983.

Tyneside Scottish: (20th, 21st, 22nd & 23rd (Service) Battalions, Northumberland Fusiliers). Graham Stewart and John Sheen. Leo Cooper, London, 1999.

Tyneside Irish: (24th, 25th, 26th & 27th (Service) Battalions, Northumberland Fusiliers). John Sheen. Pen & Sword, Barnsley, 1998.

The First Birmingham Battalion in the Great War 1914–1919: Being a History of the 14th (Service) Battalion of the Royal Warwickshire Regiment. J.E.B. Fairclough. Cornish Brothers Ltd, Birmingham, 1933.

Birmingham Pals: (The 14th, 15th & 16th (Service) Battalions, Royal Warwickshire Regiment). Terry Carter. Pen & Sword, Barnsley, 1997.

Liverpool Pals: (The 17th, 18th, 19th & 20th (Service) Battalions, King's Liverpool Regiment). Graham Maddocks. Leo Cooper, London, 1991.

Bradford Pals: (The 16th (Service) Battalion, West Yorkshire Regiment). Ralph N. Hudson. Bradford Libraries, 2000.

Leeds Pals: (The 15th (Service) Battalion, West Yorkshire Regiment). Laurie Milner. Pen & Sword Books, Barnsley, 1998.

Hull Pals: (The 10th, 11th 12th & 13th (Service) Battalions, East Yorkshire Regiment). David Bilton. Leo Cooper, Barnsley, 2002.

The Tigers: (The 6th, 7th, 8th & 9th (Service) Battalions, Leicestershire Regiment). Matthew Richardson. Leo Cooper, London, 2000.

Salford Pals: (The 15th, 16th, 19th & 20th (Service) Battalions, Lancashire Fusiliers). Michael Stedman. Leo Cooper, London, 1993.

Accrington Pals: 11th (Service) Battalion, East Lancashire Regiment. William Turner. Leo Cooper, London, 1998.

The Blast of War: A History of Nottingham's Bantams: The 15th (Service) Battalion, Sherwood Foresters, 1915–1919. Maurice Bacon and David E. Langley. Sherwood Press, Nottingham, 1986.

Kitchener's Pioneers: The 5th (Service) Battalion, Northamptonshire Regiment. Geoffrey Moore, 1978.

On the Somme: The Kitchener Battalions of the Royal Berkshire Regiment 1916. Colin Fox & Others. University of Reading, 1996.

Arras To Cambrai: The Kitchener Battalions of the Royal Berkshire Regiment 1917. Colin Fox & Others. University of Reading, 1997.

Their Duty Done: The Kitchener Battalions of the Royal Berkshire Regiment. Colin Fox & Others. University of Reading, 1998.

Manchester Pals: The 16th, 17th, 18th, 19th, 20th, 21st, 22nd & 23rd (Service) Battalions, Manchester Regiment). Michael Stedman. Leo Cooper, Barnsley, 2004.

Cotton Town Comrades: The Story of the Oldham Pals Battalion. K.W. Mitchinson and I. McInnes. Bayonet Publications, 1993.

Sheffield City Battalion: (The 12th York & Lancaster Regiment). Ralph Gibson and Paul Oldfield. Barnsley Chronicle, 1988.

Barnsley Pals: (The 13th & 14th York & Lancaster Regiment). Jon Cooksey. Leo Cooper, London, 1996.

Campaign Reminiscences: The 6th Seaforth Highlanders. R.T. Peel and Captain A.H. Macdonald. W.R. Walker, Elgin, 1923.

List of Officers and Other Ranks of the Rifle Brigade Awarded Decorations, or Mentioned in Despatches for Services during the Great War (Published as Appendix to Above Work). Lieutenant Colonel T.R. Eastwood and Major H.G. Parkyn. The Rifle Brigade Club.

List of Officers and Other Ranks of the Rifle Brigade Awarded Decorations, or Mentioned in Despatches for Services during the Great War (Published as Appendix to Above Work). Lieutenant Colonel T.R. Eastwood and Major H.G. Parkyn. The Rifle Brigade Club.

The Bomber Command Diaries 1939–1945. Martin Middlebrook and Chris Everitt. Viking, Harmondsworth, 1985.

The History of the Northamptonshire Regiment 1934–1948. Brigadier General W.J. Jervois. Printed for the Regimental History Committee, 1953.

Index of Cemeteries